COGNITIVE DEVELOPMENT IN DIGITAL CONTEXTS

COGNITIVE DEVELOPMENT IN DIGITAL CONTEXTS

Edited by

FRAN C. BLUMBERG

PATRICIA J. BROOKS

ELSEVIER

ACADEMIC PRESS

An imprint of Elsevier

Academic Press is an imprint of Elsevier
125 London Wall, London EC2Y 5AS, United Kingdom
525 B Street, Suite 1800, San Diego, CA 92101-4495, United States
50 Hampshire Street, 5th Floor, Cambridge, MA 02139, United States
The Boulevard, Langford Lane, Kidlington, Oxford OX5 1GB, United Kingdom

Notices
Knowledge and best practice in this field are constantly changing. As new research and
experience broaden our understanding, changes in research methods, professional practices,
or medical treatment may become necessary.

Practitioners and researchers must always rely on their own experience and knowledge in
evaluating and using any information, methods, compounds, or experiments described
herein. In using such information or methods they should be mindful of their own safety and
the safety of others, including parties for whom they have a professional responsibility.

To the fullest extent of the law, neither the Publisher nor the authors, contributors, or editors,
assume any liability for any injury and/or damage to persons or property as a matter of
products liability, negligence or otherwise, or from any use or operation of any methods,
products, instructions, or ideas contained in the material herein.

Library of Congress Cataloging-in-Publication Data
A catalog record for this book is available from the Library of Congress

British Library Cataloguing-in-Publication Data
A catalogue record for this book is available from the British Library

ISBN: 978-0-12-809481-5

For information on all Academic Press publications visit our
website at https://www.elsevier.com/books-and-journals

Working together
to grow libraries in
developing countries

www.elsevier.com • www.bookaid.org

Publisher: Nikki Levy
Acquisition Editor: Emily Ekle
Editorial Project Manager: Barbara Makinster
Production Project Manager: Priya Kumaraguruparan
Cover Designer: Matthew Limbert

Typeset by SPi Global, India

CONTENTS

CONTRIBUTORS

Fran C. Blumberg
Fordham University, New York, NY, United States

Jeremy N. Bailenson
Stanford University, Stanford, CA, United States

Jakki O. Bailey
Stanford University, Stanford, CA, United States

Samantha Bordoff
University at Albany, SUNY, Albany, NY, United States

Patricia J. Brooks
College of Staten Island, CUNY, Staten Island, NY; The Graduate Center, CUNY, New York, NY, United States

Sandra L. Calvert
Georgetown University, Washington, DC, United States

Stephanie Chin
Hunter College, CUNY, New York, NY, United States

Mary L. Courage
Memorial University, St. John's, NL, Canada

Rebecca A. Dore
University of Delaware, Newark, DE, United States

Alexander W. Fietzer
Hunter College, CUNY, New York, NY, United States

Shalom M. Fisch
MediaKidz Research & Consulting, Teaneck, NJ, United States

Roberta M. Golinkoff
University of Delaware, Newark, DE, United States

Thomas E. Gorman
University of Wisconsin, Madison, WI, United States

C. Shawn Green
University of Wisconsin, Madison, WI, United States

Leslie Haddon
London School of Economics and Political Science, London, United Kingdom

Kathy Hirsh-Pasek
Temple University, Philadelphia, PA; The Brookings Institution, Washington, DC, United States

Renee Hobbs
University of Rhode Island, Kingston, RI, United States

Helen Johnson
Coventry University, Coventry, United Kingdom

Amy B. Jordan
University of Pennsylvania, Philadelphia, PA, United States

H. Chad Lane
University of Illinois, Urbana-Champaign, IL, United States

Alexis R. Lauricella
Northwestern University, Evanston, IL, United States

Sonia Livingstone
London School of Economics and Political Science, London, United Kingdom

Carmina Marcial
Fordham University, New York, NY, United States

Tiffany A. Pempek
Hollins University, Roanoke, VA, United States

Kasey L. Powers
The Graduate Center, CUNY, New York, NY, United States

Michael B. Robb
Common Sense Media, San Francisco, CA, United States

Colleen E. Russo Johnson
Vanderbilt University, Nashville, TN, United States

Gabrielle A. Strouse
University of South Dakota, Vermillion, SD, United States

Georgene L. Troseth
Vanderbilt University, Nashville, TN, United States

Yalda T. Uhls
UCLA, Los Angeles, CA; Common Sense Media, San Francisco, CA, United States

Sarah E. Vaala
Joan Ganz Cooney Center at Sesame Workshop, New York, NY, United States

Clare Wood
Nottingham Trent University, Nottingham, United Kingdom

Zheng Yan
University at Albany, SUNY, Albany, NY, United States

Sherry Yi
University of Illinois, Urbana-Champaign, IL, United States

Jennifer M. Zosh
Pennsylvania State University, Brandywine, PA, United States

PREFACE

This text is designed to provide a survey of the impact of digital media on key aspects of children's and adolescents' cognitive development pertaining to attention, memory, language, and executive functioning. In addition to our focus on learning, we examine how children and adolescents evaluate the content presented to them via the diverse screens they encounter, and how they understand the affordances of different types of screen media— topics subsumed by the term *media literacy*. In highlighting how screen media impact cognitive development, the text addresses a topic often neglected amid societal concerns about pathological media use and vulnerability to media effects (notably aggression, cyber-bullying, and Internet addiction).

The intended audience includes educators, researchers, policy makers, and media designers dedicated to promoting children and adolescents' cognitive growth in the digital era. The volume is written to be an accessible introduction for undergraduate or graduate students and researchers interested in how technology use impacts cognitive development. Because we anticipate that most readers will be academics in the fields of psychology, human development, education, communications, and media studies, we adopt a tone and presentation of content consistent with that found in research articles. It is conceivable that the volume could serve as a text for a seminar on technology in human development or a course on the psychology of media. We expect that the interested public including educational media producers and curriculum designers, school administrators, legislators, and pediatricians also may find the volume of interest.

The text surveys the impact of digital media on key aspects of children and adolescents' cognitive development from both theoretical and practical vantage points. To that end the volume includes topics such as parent-child interactions around media; video games, texting, and virtual reality as contexts for learning; the development of effective educational media; children's and adolescents' critical thinking about media; social policy for increasing access to high-quality education media and the Internet; and parenting strategies for coping with the challenges of raising children in the digital age.

This volume is organized into four sections. The first section addresses young children's learning from screens such as those provided via television and tablets and factors that contribute to that learning such as parental scaffolding of child-screen interactions. The second section focuses more specifically on the cognitive skills that are enhanced via children's and adolescents' interactions with screens during game play, while texting, and when immersed in virtual reality. The third section highlights children's and adolescents' cognitive abilities as reflected through their media literacy. The final and concluding section presents policy and practical recommendations for children's and adolescents' media use.

The volume overall addresses topics of relevance to developmental psychology, education, youth and family studies, media studies, and communication science.

Our focus on cognitive development as impacted by interaction with electronic screens other than television clearly distinguishes our text from potential competitors. Our text focuses specifically on how various screen-based electronic media impact children's and adolescents' cognitive development. While a great deal of scholarship has examined how technology-mediated interactions (via social network sites and massive multiplayer video games, for example) impact youth development, including mental health, aggression and other behavioral problems, peer interactions and bullying, cognitive development via screen-based media has been a relatively neglected topic in the popular press as well as in more academically oriented texts concerned with media usage.

Media Use as a Context for Cognitive Development: What Is and Should Be Known?

Fran C. Blumberg*, Patricia J. Brooks†, Kasey L. Powers‡, Carmina Marcial*

*Fordham University, New York, NY, United States
†College of Staten Island, CUNY, Staten Island, NY; The Graduate Center, CUNY, New York, NY, United States
‡The Graduate Center, CUNY, New York, NY, United States

This text is designed to provide a survey of the impact of media use on key aspects of children's and adolescents' cognitive development pertaining to attention, memory, language, and executive functioning. In addition to our focus on learning, we examine how children and adolescents evaluate the content presented to them via the diverse screens they encounter, and how they understand the affordances of different types of screen media—topics subsumed by the term *media literacy* (Potter, 2004). Media literacy has long been examined in the fields of communications and media studies but is largely unexamined from a developmental psychology perspective, despite strong concerns about the vulnerability of young audiences to screen-based content (Blumberg, Williams, & Kelley, 2014; Hobbs, 2004; Livingstone & Haddon, 2012).

The collection of chapters in this volume was motivated by the paucity of work concerning children and adolescents with regard to linkages between media use and cognitive development, and increasing acknowledgment that screen time is not necessarily detrimental to child development. For example, until 2016, the American Academy of Pediatrics (AAP) recommended no screen time for children under 2 years of age. However, given the ubiquity of mobile devices and television in young children's lives, the AAP Council on Communications and Media released a new policy statement (Council on Communications and Media, 2016). In this report, the AAP reaffirmed its position that early learning occurs primarily during interactions with caregivers, thus endorsing what many researchers and practitioners have long known about the cognitive and socio-emotional benefits of parental co-viewing and mediation of children's screen viewing habits (see Chakroff & Nathanson, 2011; Nathanson, 2015; Warren, 2005). Accordingly, the nature of parental interactions with their children around media features prominently in chapters in this volume. As will be demonstrated, parental goals when interacting with their children include facilitating their learning of content presented via different media platforms, and promoting their understanding of the explicit and implicit messages communicated via this content, as in the case of the advertisements. Such goals dovetail with concerns of media literacy educators. As children take more ownership of their media use, their ideas about what is appropriate content and activity may differ from that of their parents (Vaterlaus, Beckert, Tulane, & Bird, 2014). The vast number of media and apps available can be difficult even for the savviest adults to sort through, especially in light of aggressive marketing of products as educational without provision of what most researchers would consider to be sufficient evidence of their efficacy (DeLoache et al., 2010; Richert, Robb, Fender, & Wartella, 2010). As children are now users of digital media often from infancy, the need for direct media literacy instruction to guide children and their parents is increasingly necessary.

The prevalence of screens in the lives of children and adolescents is reflected in large-scale national surveys such as those conducted by Common Sense Media, the Kaiser Family Foundation, and the Pew Research Center. For example, in a survey of 1463 parents of children ages 8 years and younger, Common Sense Media reported that, as of 2013, more than a third (38%) of infants and toddlers under 2 years of age had access to mobile devices (e.g., smartphones and iPads) and used them for media-related activities (e.g., watching television or videos, playing games or apps)—a significant increase from the rate of 10% reported in 2011 (Rideout, 2013). Not surprisingly, usage is even higher among older children, as 80% of 2-to-4-year-olds (up from 39% in 2011) and 83% of 5-to-8-year-olds (up from 52% in 2011) have been found to use mobile devices for entertainment or educational purposes (Rideout, 2013). The usage of mobile devices for media use by tweens (8-to-12-year-olds) and teens (13-to-18-year-olds) is also high, with 41% of tweens' and 46% of teens' screen time spent on mobile devices (Rideout, 2015). Further, findings from the Entertainment Software Association (2016) indicate that 63% of US households include at least one individual who plays video games for three or more hours per week. Within these households, 27% of players are younger than 18 years of age.

Given the proliferation of educational games and apps aimed at school-age children in today's marketplace, there is increasing attention being paid to design and formal features that promote learning (Brunick, Putnam, McGarry, Richards, & Calvert, 2016; Hirsh-Pasek et al., 2015; Lee, Plass, & Homer, 2006; U.S. Department of Education, Office of Educational Technology, 2013). Much of the interest in serious games, characterized as games designed to train, educate, and entertain (see Blumberg, Almonte, Anthony, & Hashimoto, 2013), has been driven by federal funding agents such as the National Science Foundation and the Institute of Education and Sciences, and private funders such as the Bill and Melinda Gates Foundation and the MacArthur Foundation. In fact, as recently reported in a market analysis posted on the independent news site Gamesandlearning[1] in Sep. 2016, investment in game-based learning firms was slated to increase 20% in 2016 over that of investments in 2015.

With prominent national surveys attesting to increasing rates of media use among adolescent and preadolescent youth (see Lenhart, 2015; Rideout, Foehr, & Roberts, 2010), research on media usage has tended to focus on the vulnerability of these media users. Specifically, these users are seen as potential victims of privacy violation, cyber-bullying, exposure to inappropriate content and advertisements, and Internet and/or video game addiction (Anderson et al., 2010; O'Keeffe & Clarke-Pearson, 2011; Przybylski, 2014). Collectively, these concerns have dominated research on youth media use, and overshadowed studies highlighting possible benefits of digital media as tools for fostering cognitive development, many of which have been examined within the context of video game play. Specifically, frequent game play has been shown to facilitate mental rotation and spatial visualization skills (De Lisi & Wolford, 2002; Feng, Spence, & Pratt, 2007), control of attention (Dye, Green, & Bavelier, 2009; Greenfield, DeWinstanley, Kilpatrick, & Kaye, 1994), inferential reasoning (Pillay, 2002), and executive functioning (Staiano & Calvert, 2011). The accumulation of work demonstrating these benefits has helped shift the rhetoric on the effects of digital game play from primarily negative in emphasis (e.g., Funk, Baldacci, Pasold, & Baumgardner, 2004; Gentile, 2009) to facilitative (Blumberg & Fisch, 2013; Granic, Lobel, & Engels, 2014). Notably, much of this body of research includes late adolescents and young adults as participants rather than children.

However, much of what we do know about the impact of media on cognitive development is based on 40+ years of research on children's television. This literature includes seminal studies of the impact of educational programs such as *Sesame Street* on school readiness of preschool children, especially with regard to development of language and numeracy skills (Anderson & Pempek, 2005; Bogatz & Ball, 1971; Fisch & Truglio, 2001). Concern with

---

[1] Gamesandlearning.org was initiated as a project of Joan Ganz Cooney Center funded through the Bill and Melinda Gates Foundation. This nonprofit news organization is designed to provide researchers and educators with independent news to inform research and game development for children and young adults.

the impact of media on the cognitive development of young children continues as media forms become more interactive (see Anderson & Kirkorian, 2015; Barr & Linebarger, 2017; Kirkorian, Choi, & Pempek, 2016; Schroeder & Kirkorian, 2016; Sheehan & Uttal, 2016) with far fewer studies examining the impact of media on children's behavior once they begin formal schooling. In fact, when children and adolescents are examined with regard to how media affects their behavior, the examined behavior is usually socio-emotional in nature. For example, researchers have examined the use of social media as promoting a positive sense of self (Valkenburg, Schouten, & Peter, 2005), facilitating new friendships among children aged 9–18 (Lenhart & Madden, 2007; Pempek, Yermolayeva, & Calvert, 2009), and strengthening relationships with current friends, particularly among older adolescents aged 15–17 (Madden, Cortesi, Gasser, Lenhart, & Duggan, 2012; Pempek et al., 2009). Surveys of findings within the literature on social media use also attest to its potential to help adolescents regulate their mood and emotion more generally (see Blumberg, Rice, & Dickmeis, 2016 for a review). Examination of these behaviors is likely seen as elucidating factors that contribute to psychological well-being in the digital age (see Cillessen & Bellmore, 2014; Pea et al., 2012). This examination has helped to quell long-standing fears that digital media use, as reflected in, for example, game play, texting, and social media posting, is most likely to result in impaired peer interactions and social isolation (see Kraut et al., 1998).

In the chapters that follow, the potential benefits associated with screen use among children and adolescents are examined from up-to-date theoretical and practical vantage points as organized in four sections. The first section of the volume addresses young children's learning from screens, such as those provided via television and tablets, and factors that contribute to learning, such as parental scaffolding of child–screen interactions. The second section focuses more specifically on the cognitive skills that are enhanced via children's and adolescents' interactions with digital media during game play, while texting, and when immersed in virtual reality. The third section highlights children's and adolescents' cognitive abilities as reflected through their media literacy. The final and concluding section presents policy and practical recommendations for children's and adolescents' media use. A brief overview of each of these sections follows.

YOUNG CHILDREN'S LEARNING FROM DIGITAL MEDIA

Courage opens this section with a detailed summary of research on young children's attention and learning in the context of digital media. Specifically, she describes factors that contribute to learning, such as parental scaffolding and support of their child's understanding of concepts, and interactive features of e-books that potentially interfere with parents reading to their children by competing for the child's attention. Troseth, Strouse, and Russo address issues surrounding very young children's apparent difficulties in learning from video-based educational media. They review studies on young children's early symbolic development in relation to video-based educational media, and highlight how active co-viewing with an adult can support young children's learning by directing the child's attention to important information depicted in the video, helping interpret what the child sees, and connecting the information to real life.

Pempek and Lauricella explore how parent-child social interaction influences the child's learning from screen-based media, and how screen-based media influence the quality of parent-child interaction in the context of foreground media (i.e., media content intended for children) and background media (i.e., media content intended for older children and adults). Dore and colleagues examine the impact of interactive electronic toys and digital media on young children's language development. This examination highlights the importance of social contingency and feedback in supporting infants' and toddlers' learning from digital media, for example, by contrasting the efficiency of word learning from live interaction on Skype versus noncontingent video.

Calvert concludes this section by discussing how children's attachments to media characters (referred to as parasocial relationships), such as *Dora the Explorer*, can support their learning of STEM (science, technology, engineering, mathematics) concepts embedded in educational programs. Using examples from *Dora*, Calvert describes how children can collaborate with their screen friends to solve various types of problems that require mathematical concepts and other academically relevant skills.

CHILDREN AND ADOLESCENTS' COGNITIVE SKILLS ARE ENHANCED VIA MEDIA

The second section of this volume explores the affordances of digital media for enhancing a broad range of cognitive skills, including visual attention, executive functioning, and literacy. The first two chapters in this section focus specifically on video games. Gorman and Green emphasize the differential impact of action video games (first- and third-person shooter games) relative to other types of video games in enhancing aspects of perceptual and cognitive processing, including contrast sensitivity, peripheral vision, object tracking, and control of attention among primarily adult study participants. The authors further highlight the need for game developers to combine the perceptually demanding elements of action video games with more age-appropriate content for children. Lane and Yi consider the profound impact of the game *Minecraft* in today's youth culture and its adoption by schools as a means of engaging youth in creative projects that may spark their interest in STEM fields. The authors consider the need for research to evaluate how specific implementations of *Minecraft* in school settings impact both student motivation and targeted cognitive skills.

Fietzer and Chin evaluate claims that interactions with digital technologies, primarily video games, impact executive functioning, including their control of attention, working memory, planning, and problem solving among typically developing individuals and those with special needs. Bailey and Bailenson review what is meant by immersive virtual reality (IVR) and how it might be used as a venue for informal education and remediation of skills. The authors also consider the ramifications of IVR for cognitive development.

Wood and Johnson consider texting in relation to the development of literacy skills (reading, spelling, and writing). Specifically, they review recent research suggesting that the use of *textspeak* (i.e., texting language that includes acronyms, initials, and emoticons, and other abbreviations) facilitates phonological development, which includes awareness of how speech sounds map onto written units (orthography). They conclude that texting allows children and adolescents to practice skills necessary to master the writing system, which benefits their literacy development.

In the final chapter of this section, Fisch advocates for increased collaboration between children's media producers and academics. Specifically, he proposes that applying theory that can be used to examine children's learning from media (e.g., Sweller's Cognitive Load Theory and Fisch's Capacity Model) to the production of educational media results in products that maximize learning.

MEDIA LITERACY AS A COGNITIVE SKILL

The third section of this volume examines media literacy as an important aspect of children's cognitive development as media consumers. Bordoff and Yan review their work examining the developmental trajectory of children's understanding of the technical and social complexity of the Internet, which has ramifications for how they engage with others online, how much personal information they disclose, and with whom they disclose this information. Hobbs discusses varying approaches to media literacy designed to empower youth to utilize, evaluate, and create digital media and also protect them from potential threats, such as cyber-bullying, sexting, or targeted advertising. She also outlines methods of developing students' critical thinking skills in evaluating the purpose, targeted audience, point of view, and construction of media messages; necessary skills given the current widespread concern about fake news.

Haddon and Livingstone shift the point of view from educators to youth by examining 9- to 16-year-olds' views about cyber threats and safety issues associated with Internet use. Using interview data, the authors identify a number of themes in youth discussions about their online activities, which suggest that they are more savvy about the social complexity of the Internet than studies utilizing other methods (see Bordoff & Yan, this volume).

POLICY AND PRACTICE RECOMMENDATIONS FOR FACILITATING LEARNING FROM MEDIA

The final section of this volume considers policy and practice implications for facilitating learning among child media users. Vaala and Jordan discuss challenges in providing up-to-date recommendations for children's media use in a rapidly evolving digital world. They discuss efforts by organizations such as *Common Sense Media* to help mitigate this challenge by providing reviews of apps and games that are intended to guide parent choice given the lack of industry-wide rating systems for mobile media. Uhls and Robb conclude the text and volume with consideration of how parents can support their children's decision making around media use. Given the ubiquity of mobile devices in today's households, the authors recommend that parents and children work together to develop a family media plan, with adults modeling the media habits they wish their children to follow.

REFERENCES

Anderson, D. R., & Kirkorian, H. L. (2015). Media and cognitive development. In L. S. Liben, U. Müller, & R. H. Lerner (Eds.), *Handbook of child psychology and developmental science: Cognitive processes: Vol. 2* (7th ed., pp. 949–994). Hoboken, NJ: John Wiley & Sons Inc.

Anderson, D. R., & Pempek, T. A. (2005). Television and very young children. *American Behavioral Scientist, 48*(5), 505–522.

Anderson, C. A., Shibuya, A., Ihori, N., Swing, E. L., Bushman, B. J., Sakamoto, A., … Saleem, M. (2010). Violent video game effects on aggression, empathy, and prosocial behavior in Eastern and Western countries: A meta-analytic review. *Psychological Bulletin, 136*(2), 151–173.

Barr, R., & Linebarger, D. N. (2017). *Media exposure during infancy and early childhood: The effects of the content and context on learning and development.* Cham, CH: Springer.

Blumberg, F. C., Almonte, D. E., Anthony, J. S., & Hashimoto, N. (2013). Serious games: What are they? What do they do? Why should we play them? In K. Dill (Ed.), *Oxford handbook of media psychology* (pp. 334–351). New York: Oxford University Press.

Blumberg, F. C., & Fisch, S. M. (2013). Introduction: Digital games as a context for cognitive development, learning, and developmental research. In F. C. Blumberg & S. M. Fisch (Eds.), *New directions for child and adolescent development: Vol. 139* (pp. 1–9). Wiley Periodicals, Inc., A Wiley Company.

Blumberg, F. C., Rice, J. L., & Dickmeis, D. (2016). Social media as a venue for emotion regulation among adolescents. In S. Y. Tettegah (Ed.), *Emotions, technology, and social media* (pp. 105–116). New York: Elsevier.

Blumberg, F. C., Williams, J. M., & Kelley, B. (2014). Linkages between media literacy and children and adolescents' susceptibility to advertising. In M. Blades, C. J. Oates, F. C. Blumberg, & B. Gunter (Eds.), *Children and advertising: New issues and new media* (pp. 158–177). Basingstoke, United Kingdom: Palgrave-MacMillan.

Bogatz, G. A., & Ball, S. (1971). *The second year of Sesame Street: A continuing evaluation: A report to the Children's Television Workshop: Vol. 1.* Princeton, NJ: Educational Testing Service.

Brunick, K. L., Putnam, M. M., McGarry, L. E., Richards, M. N., & Calvert, S. L. (2016). Children's future parasocial relationships with media characters: The age of intelligent characters. *Journal of Children and Media, 10,* 181–190.

Chakroff, J. L., & Nathanson, A. I. (2011). Parent and school interventions: Mediation and media literacy. In S. L. Calvert & B. J. Wilson (Eds.), *The handbook of children, media, and development* (pp. 552–576). Malden, MA: Wiley-Blackwell.

Cillessen, A. H. N., & Bellmore, A. D. (2014). Social skills and social competence in inter-actions with peers. In P. K. Smith & C. H. Hart (Eds.), *The Wiley Blackwell handbook of childhood social development* (2nd ed., pp. 393–412). Malden, MA: Wiley.

Council on Communications and Media (2016). Media and young minds. *Pediatrics, 138*(5), e20162591. http://dx.doi.org/10.1542/peds.2016-2591.

De Lisi, R., & Wolford, J. L. (2002). Improving children's mental rotation accuracy with computer game playing. *The Journal of Genetic Psychology, 163*(3), 272–282.

DeLoache, J. S., Chiong, C., Sherman, K., Islam, N., Vanderborght, M., Troseth, G. L., et al. (2010). Do babies learn from baby media? *Psychological Science, 21*(11), 1570–1574.

Dye, M. W., Green, C. S., & Bavelier, D. (2009). The development of attention skills in action video game players. *Neuropsychologia, 47*(8), 1780–1789.

Entertainment Software Association (2016). *2016 essential facts about the computer and video game industry.* Retrieved from http://essentialfacts.theesa.com/Essential-Facts-2016.pdf.

Feng, J., Spence, I., & Pratt, J. (2007). Playing an action video game reduces gender differ-ences in spatial cognition. *Psychological Science, 18*(10), 850–855.

Fisch, S. M., & Truglio, R. T. (Eds.), (2001). *"G" is for growing: Thirty years of research on chil-dren and Sesame Street.* In Mahwah, NJ: Lawrence Erlbaum Associates, Inc.

Funk, J. B., Baldacci, H. B., Pasold, T., & Baumgardner, J. (2004). Violence exposure in real-life, video games, television, movies, and the internet: Is there desensitization? *Journal of Adolescence, 27*(1), 23–39.

Gentile, D. (2009). Pathological video-game use among youth ages 8 to 18: A national study. *Psychological Science, 20*(5), 594–602.

Granic, I., Lobel, A., & Engels, R. C. (2014). The benefits of playing video games. *American Psychologist, 69*(1), 66–78.

Greenfield, P. M., DeWinstanley, P., Kilpatrick, H., & Kaye, D. (1994). Action video games and informal education: Effects on strategies for dividing visual attention. *Journal of Applied Developmental Psychology, 15*(1), 105–123.

Hirsh-Pasek, K., Zosh, J. M., Golinkoff, R. M., Gray, J. H., Robb, M. B., & Kaufman, J. (2015). Putting education in "educational" apps. Lessons from the science of learning. *Psychological Science in the Public Interest, 16*, 3–34.

Hobbs, R. (2004). A review of school-based initiatives in media literacy education. *American Behavioral Scientist, 48*(1), 42–59.

Kirkorian, H. L., Choi, K., & Pempek, T. A. (2016). Toddlers' word learning from contingent and noncontingent video on touch screens. *Child Development, 87*(2), 405–413.

Kraut, R., Patterson, M., Lundmark, V., Kiesler, S., Mukopadhyay, T., & Scherlis, W. (1998). Internet paradox: A social technology that reduces social involvement and psychological well-being? *American Psychologist, 53*, 1017–1031.

Lee, H., Plass, J. L., & Homer, B. D. (2006). Optimizing cognitive load for learning from computer-based science simulations. *Journal of Educational Psychology, 98*(4), 902–913.

Lenhart, A. (2015). *Teens, social media & technology overview 2015.* Pew Research Center. Retrieved from: http://www.pewinternet.org/2015/04/09/teens-social-media-technology-2015/.

Lenhart, A., & Madden, M. (2007). *Teens, privacy, and online social networks.* Retrieved from Pew Research Center website: http://www.pewinternet.org/files/old-media//Files/Reports/2007/PIP_Teens_Privacy_SNS_Report_Final.pdf.pdf.

Livingstone, S., & Haddon, L. (2012). Theoretical framework for children's Internet use. In S. Livingstone, L. Haddon, & A. Görzig (Eds.), *Children, risk and safety on the Internet: Research and policy challenges in comparative perspective* (pp. 1–14). Bristol, UK: Policy Press.

Madden, M., Cortesi, S., Gasser, U., Lenhart, A., & Duggan, M. (2012). *Parents, teens, and online privacy.* Retrieved from Pew Research Center http://www.pewinternet.org/2012/11/20/parents-teens-and-online-privacy/.

Nathanson, A. I. (2015). Media and the family: Reflections and future directions. *Journal of Children and Media, 15*, 133–139.

O'Keeffe, G. S., & Clarke-Pearson, K. (2011). The impact of social media on children, adolescents, and families. *Pediatrics, 127*(4), 800–804.

Pea, R., Nass, C., Meheula, L., Rance, M., Kumar, A., Bamford, H., et al. (2012). Media use, face-to-face communication, media multitasking, and social well-being among 8-to 12-year-old girls. *Developmental Psychology, 48*(2), 327–336.

Pempek, T. A., Yermolayeva, Y. A., & Calvert, S. L. (2009). College students' social networking experiences on Facebook. *Journal of Applied Developmental Psychology, 30*, 227–238. http://dx.doi.org/10.1016/j.appdev.2008.12.010.

Pillay, H. (2002). An investigation of cognitive processes engaged in by recreational computer game players: Implications for skills of the future. *Journal of Research on Technology in Education, 34*(3), 336–350.

Potter, J. (2004). *Theory of media literacy.* Thousand Oaks, CA: Sage.

Przybylski, A. K. (2014). Electronic gaming and psychosocial adjustment. *Pediatrics, 134*(3), e716–e722.

Richert, R. A., Robb, M. B., Fender, J. G., & Wartella, E. (2010). Word learning from baby videos. *Archives of Pediatrics & Adolescent Medicine, 164*(5), 432–437.

Rideout, V. (2013). *Zero to eight: Children's media use in America 2013.* San Francisco, CA: Common Sense Media. Retrieved from Common Sense Media website: http://www.commonsensemedia.org.

Rideout, V. (2015). *Measuring time spent with media: The common sense census of media use by US 8- to 18-year-olds.* Retrieved from Common Sense Media website: http://www.commonsensemedia.org.

Rideout, V., Foehr, U. G., & Roberts, D. F. (2010). *Generation M^2: Media in the lives of 8- to 18-year-olds.* Menlo Park, CA: Henry J. Kaiser Family Foundation.

Schroeder, E. L., & Kirkorian, H. L. (2016). When seeing is better than doing: Preschoolers' transfer of STEM skills using touchscreen games. *Frontiers in Psychology, 7*, 1377.

Sheehan, K. J., & Uttal, D. H. (2016). Children's learning from touch screens: A dual representation perspective. *Frontiers in Psychology, 7,* 1220.

Staiano, A. E., & Calvert, S. L. (2011). Exergames for physical education courses: Physical, social, and cognitive benefits. *Child Development Perspectives, 5*(2), 93–98.

U.S. Department of Education, Office of Educational Technology (2013). *Expanding evidence approaches for learning in a digital world.* Washington, DC: Author.

Valkenburg, P. M., Schouten, A. P., & Peter, J. (2005). Adolescents' identity experiments on the Internet. *New Media & Society, 7,* 383–402.

Vaterlaus, J. M., Beckert, T. E., Tulane, S., & Bird, C. V. (2014). "They always ask what I'm doing and who I'm talking to": Parental mediation of adolescent interactive technology use. *Marriage and Family Review, 50,* 691–713.

Warren, R. (2005). Parental mediation of children's television viewing in low-income families. *Journal of Communication, 55,* 847–863.

SECTION 1

Young Children's Learning From Digital Media

CHAPTER 1

Screen Media and the Youngest Viewers: Implications for Attention and Learning

Mary L. Courage
Memorial University, St. John's, NL, Canada

Children under 2 years of age currently have unprecedented access to electronic media. A series of reports from large-scale surveys of parents indicate that from about 3 months of age most infants have been exposed to some television or video and that by age 2 years about 90% are regular viewers and spend about 1–2 h a day watching (Barr, Danziger, Hilliard, Andolina, & Ruskis, 2010; Linebarger & Vaala, 2010; Rideout & Hamel, 2006; Radesky, Silverstein, Zuckerman, & Christakis, 2014; Schmidt, Rich, Rifas-Shiman, Oken, & Taveras, 2009; Valkenburg et al., 2007; Zimmerman, Christakis, & Meltzoff, 2007b). More recent reports from *Common Sense Media* indicate that children under 2 years currently watch slightly less traditional TV and DVD material (about 56 min per day) but are beginning to spend more time viewing with other mobile devices (Rideout, 2013). Although parents report that most of the viewing is of child-appropriate material, infants and toddlers are also exposed to an additional 5.5 h daily of "background" TV that is not intended for them specifically but is usually viewed by older children and adults (Lapierre, Piotrowski, & Linebarger, 2012).

This amount of screen media exposure has raised a number of concerns among parents, developmental scientists, and other professionals, prompting both scientific inquiry and a public debate about the positive and negative potential of these media to affect young children's cognitive and social development. Among the most serious concerns are that the excitement of television with its formal features and rapid pace of scene change might hinder children's developing attention processes (Christakis, Zimmerman, DiGiuseppe, & McCarthy, 2004), and that television and DVDs are passive media and a poor substitute for the more interactive and brain-enriching activities implicit in social exchanges, language, storybook reading, and play

Cognitive Development in Digital Contexts
http://dx.doi.org/10.1016/B978-0-12-809481-5.00001-8
3

that are interrupted or displaced by video viewing (Christakis et al., 2009). Collectively, these concerns prompted the *American Academy of Pediatrics* (AAP, 1999) to recommend that children under 2 years of age be discouraged from watching any screen media at all. Although a recent policy statement of the AAP (2011) reaffirmed its original recommendation, parents' ownership of baby media continues (Linebarger & Vaala, 2010; Mol, Neuman, & Strouse, 2014; Rideout, 2013).

On the opposite side of the debate are those who support age-appropriate screen media for infants and toddlers as an opportunity to foster learning and brain development, and many videos either explicitly or implicitly endorse this expectation in their promotional materials (Fenstermacher et al., 2010; Garrison & Christakis, 2005; Vaala & Lapierre, 2014). Although claims about the enrichment value of these media are largely unsubstantiated (Garrison & Christakis, 2005; Hirsh-Pasek et al., 2015; Linebarger & Vaala, 2010), 30% of parents surveyed indicated that learning and brain development were among their primary reasons for providing age-appropriate videos to their infants (Zimmerman, Christakis, & Meltzoff, 2007a; Zimmerman et al., 2007b). Advocates of videos for babies who look to science for guidance point to research showing the: (1) greater readiness for school among preschoolers who watched *Sesame Street* and other educational programs (Anderson, 1998; Mares & Han, 2013; Wright et al., 2001) and (2) positive association between viewing certain types of television content (e.g., *Blue's Clues; Dora the Explorer*) and better language development (Anderson & Hanson, 2010; Linebarger & Walker, 2005) and prosocial behavior (Friedrich & Stein, 1973). These findings, along with research that documents infants' and toddlers' remarkable ability to learn and remember (Oakes & Bauer, 2007; Bauer, 2007), make the idea of optimizing early learning using high-quality video material both plausible and appealing to parents.

Over the past decade, research has provided a great deal of information about the potential effects of television and video material on very young children's development, and many of these concerns about attention and learning are now fairly well understood. Predictably, the questions and answers have become more complex as the research focus has shifted from the amount of time children spent viewing video to a number of other variables that are arguably even more important. These include the child's age and cognitive maturity, the content of the program being viewed, and the social context in which viewing occurs (Anderson & Hanson, 2010; Barr, 2013; Linebarger & Vaala, 2010). This literature will be reviewed along with more recent work on the impact of newer interactive mobile technologies such as tablets, smartphones, and e-storybooks on attention and learning in the youngest viewers.

TELEVISION AND THE DEVELOPMENT OF ATTENTION

Although the construct of attention defies simple definition, there is agreement that it is not a unitary process but comprises several different "varieties of attention" (James, 1890) such as alerting, detection, orienting, selectivity, focusing, shifting, and resisting distraction. Although a number of models of attention have been proposed over the years (see Raz & Buhle, 2006), the Posner and Rothbart (2007) framework is particularly well suited to consider its development. In that view, attention is made up of three independent through interactive networks: alerting, orienting, and executive control, each with its own neural foundation and characteristic behavior. Convergent evidence from behavioral and neuroimaging research indicates that these networks are immature at birth and emerge slowly from endogenous neurobiological processes in interaction with typical sensory, cognitive, and caregiving environments (Posner, 2012; Rothbart & Posner, 2015). The alerting and orienting networks that guide the direction of attention and the selection of targets are the earliest to develop and mature rapidly over the first 6 months. The higher-order executive network provides the basis for the voluntary control of attention that is needed to adapt to the demands of particular situations. This network undergoes a protracted period of development into adolescence, with significant advances between 2 and 7 years of age, although precursor signs of self-regulation appear earlier in infancy (Colombo, 2001; Rothbart & Posner, 2015). The executive attention network is foundational to the emergence of executive functions, those higher-order cognitive processes (i.e., working memory, inhibition, attention flexibility) that underlie children's capacity for self-regulation, planning, problem solving, and monitoring (Diamond, 2013; Garon, Bryson, & Smith, 2008).

Television and Attention Deficits

Concerns about the impact of television on the development of the attention networks were first raised in the 1970s following the appearance of fast-paced children's television programming such as *Sesame Street* and a correlated increase in reported attention problems (e.g., distractibility, hyperactivity) in school (Geist & Gibson, 2000; Singer, 1980). Although this complex question was not resolved at the time (Acevedo-Polakovich, Lorch, & Milich, 2007; Anderson & Hanson, 2010), it received renewed interest in the infant and toddler literature a decade ago with the marketing of television and video programming that specifically targeted that age group. Christakis et al. (2004) analyzed parent-report data from two large-scale surveys and found a significant correlation between the amount of television children viewed at 1 and 3 years of age and subsequent attention problems that were consistent with attention deficit hyperactivity disorder (ADHD). However, their data did not establish a causal link between television viewing and later attention and their criteria for identifying a deficit was very broad. Subsequently, Zimmerman and Christakis (2007) reported that the correlation between the amount of television viewed by children younger than 3 years and later attention was significant only when the content of the programs was categorized as violent entertainment. When the program content was educational or nonviolent entertainment, the correlation was not significant. Moreover, the amount and type of television viewed by 4- to 5-year-olds were unrelated to later attention. The authors concluded that the first 3 years were a sensitive period for potential harm from viewing fast-paced (violent) television, although the absence of an effect among older children implied that the problem may be transitory.

Christakis and Zimmerman suggested that exposure to the unnaturally fast pace of sound and image change in video material during this sensitive period might alter synaptic connections in the neural networks underlying attention and shorten the infant's attention span. Further, they contended that fast pace repeatedly elicited the orienting response at the expense of sustained attention and information processing, compelling infants to stare fixedly at the screen. However, this contention is not consistent with research showing that from as early as 6 months of age, infants regulate their attention during periods of extended viewing. They sustain their attention across changes in the formal features (e.g., pace, sound) of the material and coincident heart-rate decelerations and resistance to distraction during extended looking indicate that they process the material at some level (Richards & Anderson, 2004). Moreover, like older children and adults, infants and toddlers frequently look away from video material as toys or other competing stimuli attract their attention (Barr, Zack, Garcia, & Muentener, 2008; Schmidt, Pempek, Kirkorian, Lund, & Anderson, 2008; Setliff & Courage, 2011).

The initial study by Christakis et al. (2004) was widely cited and attracted media attention. However, most of the reporting overlooked other studies that used more stringent measures to identify childhood attention problems and failed to support the Christakis et al. interpretation of the data (Miller et al., 2007; Obel et al., 2004; Stevens & Muslow, 2006). The media reports also overlooked alternative explanations for the correlation between television viewing and deficits in attention. These include the fact that children with ADHD may be encouraged to watch television at home because it provides parents a respite from the higher level of care that these children require. Moreover, there is evidence that significant deficits in attention (e.g., ADHD) are attributable largely to neurological and genetic factors and to a lesser extent to biohazard exposure, with social factors being of lesser importance (Barkley, 2006, 2011; Posner, Rothbart, & Sheesh, 2007; Rietveld, Hudziak, Bartels, & van Beijsterveldt, 2004). A reanalysis of the Christakis et al. (2004) data indicated that the relation existed only for the 10% of the sample that viewed more than 7 h of television per day. Also, when certain confounding variables (e.g., maternal education; family income) were controlled, the correlation between TV viewing and attention deficits was no longer significant, regardless of content (Foster & Watkins, 2010).

Television and Executive Functioning

Although there is no compelling evidence that infant and toddler video viewing causes clinically significant attention deficits, several recent reports indicated a relation between early viewing and poorer executive functioning in preschool children. Executive functions underlie children's capacity for self-regulation and emerge from the maturation of the orienting and executive attention networks that enable children to increasingly control the information that they process, focus their attention on the task at hand, and to ignore distractors. Executive functions show rapid growth across the preschool years and are critical for success in many aspects of cognitive and social development and for achievement in school. They are also characteristically poor in children diagnosed with ADHD and some contend that the condition is actually a deficit in executive functioning and self-regulation (Barkley, 2011; Diamond, 2013).

Several recent studies directly assessed the relation between television viewing and the development of executive functions in typically developing children. In these studies, executive functions were assessed with various standard behavioral measures of inhibition, working memory, and attention shifting and through parent rating scales. Barr, Lauricella, Zack, and Calvert (2010) reported that children who were exposed to more adult content television at age 1 year had poorer executive functions age 4 years. Consistent with this, Nathanson, Alade, Sharp, Rasmussen, and Christy (2014) reported that preschoolers with poorer executive functions had a cumulative history of watching more television from infancy and viewing more television with fast-paced cartoon content than did preschoolers with more mature executive functions. In another study, Lillard and Peterson (2011) measured the immediate effect of exposure to fast-paced cartoons on 4-year-olds' executive functions and found poorer performance compared to those who viewed an educational cartoon or spent time drawing with markers. However, the relation between executive functioning and television viewing is not straightforward, as a subsequently study showed that it was the combination of the fantastical content of the material with the fast pace (rather than the pace per se) that diminished executive functions (Lillard, Drell, Richey, Bogguszewski, & Smith, 2015). Similarly, Linebarger, Barr, Lapierre, and Piotrowski (2014) reported data from a parent survey in which viewing noneducational foreground television and exposure to background television predicted poorer executive functions in preschoolers, but that certain parenting practices and parent socioeconomic status moderated the relation. Finally, Radesky et al. (2014) reported that infants who had difficulties in self-regulation (fussiness, irritability, poor self-soothing, difficulty with state changes (such as sleep) at 9 months and also at 2 years watched more television than those who did not. This finding suggested that, as for children with diagnosed ADHD, parents of infants with poorer self-regulation may have provided television as a calming strategy for these more difficult children (also see Thompson, Adair, & Bentley, 2013). In any case, the relation between television viewing and poorer executive functioning in young children is not unidirectional and should be interpreted in the context of the child's temperament and family characteristics, the viewing conditions, and the type of content viewed.

Background Television and Attention

One consequence of young children's immature executive functioning is that they are highly distractible. Research has shown that distractibility decreases across infancy and early childhood, although several endogenous (e.g., attentional state, engagement with the object) and exogenous (e.g., target salience or novelty, continuous or intermittent presence) factors interact with age (Kannass, Colombo, & Wyss, 2010; Oakes, Kannass, & Shaddy, 2002; Ruff & Capozzoli, 2003). Given the number of external and internal events to which infants and toddlers are exposed, the ability to direct and sustain attention selectively to some stimuli (e.g., toys) while resisting distraction from others that compete for their attention (e.g., television) is critical for early learning. As about 40% of parents report having the television on most or all of the time in the home independent of anyone watching (Masur & Flynn, 2008; Roberts & Foehr, 2008; Rideout, 2013) concerns have been expressed that the omnipresence of television and other screen media in the home might distract infants and young children from play and other activities (Courage & Setliff, 2010).

Research has confirmed that background television can be a significant source of distraction to young children at play as its formal features are salient, often novel, and signal interesting content. Setliff and Courage (2011) reported that 6-, 12-, and 24-month-olds who were engaged in toy play spent less time attending to the toys when the television was on in the background compared to when it was off (also see Schmidt et al., 2008). Children shifted their gaze from the toys to the television about three times per minute, though 46% of the looks were less than 2-s duration and, likely too short for much information processing. Setliff and Courage (2011) also found that the duration of children's focused attention decreased while the television was on. In contrast, Ruff and colleagues (Ruff & Capozzoli, 2003) found a preservation of focused attention during infants' toy play in an intermittent distractor condition. They suggested that infants might have used lower level processes such as "peripheral narrowing" to restrict their attention the target of interest, to resist distraction and maintain focus on a central activity. As the background television in the Setliff and Courage study provided a continuous and varied source of distraction, it may have provided more stimulation than the infants could tune out (Kannass & Colombo, 2007).

Exactly how, what, or even if young children process information from background television is an important question. It may be that as with older children (Anderson & Lorch, 1983; Hawkins, Pingree, Bruce, & Tapper, 1997; Huston & Wright, 1983; Lorch, Anderson, & Levin, 1979; Lorch & Castle, 1997), infants, and toddlers engage in an active and deliberate viewing strategy of monitoring the television rather than simply being distracted by it. In fact, observations indicate that young children often do continue to engage in cognitive and social activities necessary for healthy development when the television is on. Schmitt, Woolf, and Anderson (2003) reported that 2-year-olds present in a room where mixed content television programming was available did engage in several activities at once and spent 41% of their time looking at the screen, 39% socializing, 34% in physically activity, and 32% playing with toys. Similarly, Barr et al. (2008) found that about 35% of 12- to 18-month-old infants engaged in some toy play in the presence of an infant-directed video that was provided to them as foreground television. However, whether young children adapt to distractors with intensified focused attention or by selective monitoring, or whether their attention and play are simply disrupted by television remains an empirical question that will likely vary with the child's age, task complexity, and motivation (Higgins & Turnure, 1984). Finally, it is important to note the evidence that once preschoolers are interrupted from play, they return to it with more superficial engagement (akin to the resumption lag in adults' task switching) than before the distraction (DiLalla & Watson, 1988; Monsell, 2003).

When background TV is available, parent-child interaction is also diminished. In one study, a negative correlation was found between exposure to background television and time spent reading or being read to in children aged 3–6 years (Vandewater et al., 2005). More recently, Kirkorian, Pempek, Murphy, Schmidt, and Anderson (2009) compared parent engagement with their 12- to 36-month-old children in a 60-min free play session during which background TV was on during half of the session. Parents interacted significantly less with their infants and toddlers and responded less quickly and less enthusiastically to the child's bids for attention when the television was on compared to when it was off. Parents also used briefer and simpler language with their child when the TV was on. A reanalysis of the language data for quantity (number of words and utterances) and quality (number of new words and length of utterances) showed that background TV reduced the number of words per minute, utterances per minute, and the number of new words spoken (Pempek, Kirkorian, & Anderson, 2014). These findings are consistent with Christakis et al. (2009) who, using the LENA speech identification software system, reported that television exposure in 2- to 48-month-olds was associated with a 7% decrease in exposure to adult speech for each hour of exposure to television, decreased child vocalization, and decreased conversational turn-taking. They suggested that when the television is on, parents talk less to their children which might contribute to the associations between poorer language development and viewing baby video material (Zimmerman et al., 2007a) and other poor quality or background television material noted in children under 2 years of age (Hudson, Fennell, & Hoftyzer, 2013; Tomopoulos et al., 2010). In contrast, a longitudinal survey of the time infants spent viewing television (foreground or background) from 6 months to 2 years of age showed that it was unrelated to their receptive language skill at age 3 years, even when potentially confounding variables (e.g., maternal education, SES) were controlled (Schmidt et al., 2009).

Collectively, the implications of these studies are significant, as the primary way that infants and toddlers learn language is through exposure to "live" speech and through verbal interactions with others (Kuhl, 2011; Parish-Morris, Golinkoff, & Hirsh-Pasek, 2013; Schneidman, Arroyo, Levine, & Goldin-Meadow, 2013; Weisleder & Fernald, 2013; Werker & Hensch, 2015). Extensive literature has documented strong positive effects of parent–child verbal interactions on child language development, self-regulation, school readiness, and later academic achievement (Hart & Risley, 1995; NICHD Early Child Care Research Network, 2005; Whitehurst & Lonigan, 1998). Verbal response to and expansion of child vocalizations as well as labeling are particularly important and commonly emerge in the context of shared conversations, storybook reading, and play. To the extent that time spent viewing video diminishes these interactions, young children may be at risk for poorer language and literacy outcomes.

In summary, the relation between attention problems in very young children and television viewing is complex and depends on the amount of television viewed, and on the aspect of attention that is considered, how it is assessed, the content viewed, and child characteristics. It appears unlikely that television viewing "causes" either clinically significant ADHD at one extreme or poorer self-regulation in an otherwise typically developing child at the other. Nor is it clear whether toddlers and preschoolers who show poorer executive functions and self-regulation in the early years eventually become children with more serious attention deficits at school age. Finally, given that even typically developing infants and toddlers are highly distractible, exposure to hours of background television is unlikely to facilitate their efforts to focus their attention on the serious business of play. Although it is not entirely clear what or how young children are processing as they play in the presence of television, such "multitasking" will likely result in some response cost, just as with older children and adults (Monsell, 2003; Rosen, 2010).

TELEVISION AND LEARNING

As infants and toddlers are proficient at encoding, storing, and retrieving information about their experiences (Hayne, 2009; Oakes & Bauer, 2007), the anticipation that they might learn from age-appropriate video is logical. Several of the earliest studies used imitation paradigms to examine this question, as very young children cannot be easily instructed or expected to provide adequate verbal responses (Barr & Hayne, 1999; Hayne, Herbert, & Simcock, 2003; McCall, Parke, & Kavanaugh, 1977; Meltzoff, 1988). Nonverbal responses (e.g., reaching, pointing, looking, head turns, foot kicks) are well developed in infants and toddlers and have provided invaluable insights into their learning and memory processes (Rovee-Collier, Hayne, & Colombo, 2001).

The Video Deficit

A common finding from imitation research was that infants and toddlers did not readily imitate action sequences viewed on video, although they imitated the same actions when viewed live. This "video deficit" (Anderson & Pempek, 2005) was not limited to actions but was also seen with object-retrieval, word-learning, and language-recognition tasks (Kirkorian et al., 2016; Krcmar, Grela, & Lin, 2007; Kuhl, Tsao, & Liu, 2003; Schmitt & Anderson, 2002; Troseth & Deloache, 1998; Troseth, Saylor, & Archer, 2006). Recently, it has been more accurately called a "transfer deficit" (Barr, 2010). Research has shown that this deficit originates from the well-documented specificity of infant learning whereby the characteristics of the encoding (e.g., video) and retrieval (e.g., real world) contexts must match exactly for learning to be evident and transferable (Barnat, Klein, & Meltzoff, 1996; Hayne, 2009; Rovee-Collier, 1999). Over the course of the second year, infants develop greater "representational flexibility" and only then can they tolerate mismatches between encoding and retrieval contexts and begin to generalize and transfer learned information to new objects and situations. However, the transfer deficit is usually not fully resolved until late in the third year (Barr, 2013; Hayne, 2009).

Research on the video deficit showed that for infants and toddlers, mismatches can arise from immaturities in a number of perceptual, cognitive, and social processes. These include the (1) difficulties they have in equating information obtained from the 2-D video format with the corresponding 3-D live source and vice versa (Barr, 2010; Barr, Muentener, Garcia, Fujimoto, & Chavez, 2007; Troseth & Deloache, 1998), (2) understanding of dual representation; that the video is a thing in its own right and also represents the same information in the real world (DeLoache et al., 2010; Troseth, 2010), and the (3) fact that their everyday experience with responsive, contingent others tells them that the noncontingent video source is neither real nor directed to them personally and therefore not a source of useful information (Stouse & Troseth, 2014; Troseth, 2010). Mitigation of these factors (e.g., by repetition of the material, experience with closed-circuit video, embedded verbal prompting cues) improved the performance (e.g., Barr et al., 2007, 2008) but eliminated the advantage of live learning only when the video model interacted contingently with the child and familiarized herself to the child before testing (Troseth et al., 2006). Finally, very young children have limited understanding of the medium and conventions of television itself, the form and function of its formal features, the size, movement, and trajectory of the objects and characters, the format (narrative or expository) of the content delivery, or the interactional quality (noncontingency). Following experience with television and with coincident advances in language, cognition, and social awareness, these limitations become resolved and learning and transfer from video begin to occur (Anderson & Hanson, 2010; Barr, 2010).

Although infants and toddlers do not readily imitate from television before their third year, other behaviors indicate that they are sensitive to its content and can acquire new information from it long before then. In various studies, for example, 12- to 18-month-olds played more with toys that they saw on television than they did with novel toys (McCall et al., 1977); 12-month-olds avoided a novel toy after watching a televised model that showed negative affect toward it (Mumme & Fernald, 2003); 18- but not 14-month-olds showed a visual preference for a novel toy after a televised model engaged infants in joint reference during familiarization with another toy (Cleveland & Striano, 2008); and 18-month-olds who viewed video information related to a forgotten sequence of toy-play events had their recollection of the sequence reinstated (Sheffield & Hudson, 2006). Infants who are only 5 months old can integrate auditory and visual information presented from a video source. For example, they prefer to look at video with coordinated than mismatched image with voice or sound (Hollenbeck & Slaby, 1979; Kuhl & Meltzoff, 1982). By 6 months, they can recognize a video image of their parents and associate them with a familiar label (e.g., mama and papa; Tincoff & Jusczyk, 1999). Although these examples indicate that infants can interpret social cues and can discriminate correspondences between a video image and what it depicts at some level, the precise nature of what they acquire and their understanding of the video events are unclear.

Co-viewing With Young Children

Research has shown that a key factor in mitigating the transfer deficit is the presence of an adult who co-views with the child. Infants are inherently social beings, and much of their cognitive development emerges in a social context. From birth they are increasingly sensitive and responsive to the social cues they get from others (Baldwin & Moses, 2001; Muir & Nadel, 1998; Walden & Ogan, 1988). Consistent with this, Barr et al. (2008) showed that toddlers who viewed infant-directed videos with their parents looked longer at the videos and were more responsive (e.g., vocalizing, pointing) to them when the parents provided scaffolding (e.g., descriptions, labeling, pointing) during viewing. Even with parents' verbal scaffolding controlled, infants between 18 and 21 months old were more likely to look toward a baby video (and to look longer at it) during free-play immediately following a parent's look toward the video than to do so spontaneously (Demers, Hanson, Kirkorian, Pempek, & Anderson, 2013). Such interactions that direct the child's attention to important content can potentially increase comprehension and learning (Barr et al., 2007).

The critical question was whether parent–child interactions could in fact promote learning from video material. There is abundant evidence that such interactions are fundamental to learning during storybook reading (Bus, Van IJzendoorn, & Pellegrini, 1995; Fletcher & Reese, 2005). Adults talk to children in more complex ways during storybook reading than they do in other contexts. They use a "dialogic" strategy (Whitehurst & Lonigan, 1998) in which they direct children's attention to the elements of the story, engage them in conversation, ask distancing questions, and provide repetitions, expansions, recasts, and explanations of the story content. These shared reading experiences are associated with better literacy outcomes, word learning, story comprehension, school readiness, and interest in independent reading in later childhood (Mol, Bus, & De Jong, 2009; Whitehurst & Lonigan, 1998).

The results of several studies showed clearly that parent–child interactions can also have a positive impact on learning from video, particularly for children who are older than about 2 years and have begun to overcome the video deficit. In one study, adult scaffolding and contingent responsiveness facilitated 3-year-olds' learning of novel object labels from video and was especially effective if the intervention included dialogic questioning (Strouse, O'Doherty, & Troseth, 2013). Similarly, when 30- to 42-month-olds were taught action verbs either by video alone or through a combination of video and live interaction with an adult about the video content, only the children older than 36 months learned verbs in the video alone condition (Roseberry, Hirsh-Pasek, Parrish-Morris, & Golinkoff, 2009). In another study, 2- to 3-year-olds viewed a picture of an object five times on a screen while hearing a voice-over label the object. Children were then shown the target object with three distractors and correctly pointed to the target object (Scofield, Williams, & Behrend, 2007). Subsequently, the authors showed that toddlers could also transfer their learning to the live 3-D version of the target among the live distractors (Allen & Scofield, 2010). Stouse and Troseth (2014) reported that 2-year-olds showed reliable transfer of a novel word learned from video to the real object, but only when the parent pointed out that the real object and the video image were "the same." They concluded that toddlers' frequent failure to learn from video stemmed from failing to understand the relevance of video to real life, a marker of the video deficit. Similarly, Roseberry, Hirsh-Pasek, and Golinkoff (2014) showed that 24- to 30-month-olds, who experienced a simulated video "chat" in which they were taught novel verbs, were successful only when the video partner interacted contingently with them. O'Doherty, Troseth, Shimpi, Goldenberg, and Akhtar (2011) also showed that 2.5-year-old onlookers could learn a novel word from viewing a shared interaction between two adults on video although they did not learn words from the adults in a passive labeling condition without engagement. Collectively, these experimental studies show that from the age of about 24–30 months, children are able to learn some new words from video and that this is most effective in the presence of an engaging, contingent, supportive adult, and the provision of social cues.

In contrast, there is little evidence that children younger than 2 years learn much language from video, even with parent-child interaction (e.g., Krcmar, 2010, 2011, 2014; Krcmar et al., 2007; Robb, Richert, & Wartella, 2009). Video viewing in these very young children is still dominated by the transfer deficit, and the minimal learning they do show is often more readily learned from a live source (Barr, 2010). Although from birth human infants are biologically predisposed to process speech and language and are remarkably facile in their acquisition of this complex system of rules in just a few short years, their success depends heavily on exposure to and interaction with other talking, engaging "live" humans (Kuhl, 2011; Parish-Morris et al., 2013; Werker & Hensch, 2015).

Language Learning From "Baby" Video

The findings on the transfer deficit did not bode well for infant and toddler learning from television and video. However, the evidence that the video deficit could be lessened by adding social relevancy and contingency from adults as well as by repetition of the material, motivated researchers to identify the conditions that might optimize such learning. Moreover, many of the seminal studies on the video or transfer deficit did not use actual commercially available television or video content. Instead, they used simple filmed action sequences of playful events that were designed to achieve good experimental control over the format and content of the material so it could be related causally to learning outcomes. In contrast, infants' home viewing includes selections from hundreds of infant-directed television and videos (e.g., *Baby Einstein*; *Sesame Beginnings*; *Brainy Baby*; *BabyFirst TV*) that were especially designed to be highly attractive and engaging to very young children. Many of these videos included explicit or implicit claims that young viewers could make advances in cognitive and social development from viewing. These persuasive but arguably misleading claims have made the baby video market a 100 million dollar industry that continues to show exponential growth (Fenstermacher et al., 2010; Vaala & Lapierre, 2014; Zimmerman et al., 2007b).

The public concern about the widespread use and educational expectations of these videos prompted researchers to evaluate their potential impact and effectiveness. Many of the studies examined word learning, a landmark achievement in this age range that has been targeted in many baby videos. The results of these studies have been mixed. Even the youngest children will attend to video material as its movement, color, and formal features (sound, music, zooms, cuts, rapid scene changes) are attractive to them. However, as their language and story comprehension skills are limited, they are unlikely to follow the narrative content, the story line, or the information or lesson to be learned. This was confirmed in several studies in which groups of infants between 6- and 24-months old were shown comprehensible infant videos (*Sesame Street*, *Teletubbies*) and versions that were made noncomprehensible through distortion of the segments, backward speech, or speech in a foreign language. Infants who were 6- and 12-months old attended equally to both videos, indicating that their attention was guided by the formal features of the videos rather than its content. In contrast, the 18- and 24-month-olds looked longer at the comprehensible than the non-comprehensible videos, once meaningful content became important (Pempek et al., 2010; Richards & Cronise, 2000). Similarly, Kirkorian, Anderson, and Keen (2012) used eye tracking to show that when 12- to 15-month-olds were shown a clip from Sesame Street, their gaze pattern was more scattered around the screen than that of older preschoolers. The gaze pattern of the older children more closely followed the action in the story, indicating their greater comprehension of the narrative.

DeLoache et al. (2010) assessed word learning from a commercially available baby video designed to teach language to groups of 12- to 18-months-olds who viewed a DVD 20 times at home over a month. Parents were asked either to sit silently with the child during co-viewing or to interact with the child as they normally would during viewing. None of the infants recognized the target words from the video any better than control babies who had never seen it. Babies who did learn new words were those whose parents had been asked to teach them to their infants in natural everyday contexts over the month. Moreover, parents who had positive attitudes about the value of baby DVDs thought their infants learned more than those who were negative or neutral, indicating that consumers continue to be misled by learning potential of DVDs for infants and toddlers. In another study with children under 2-years old, no word learning occurred after 6 weeks of repeated viewing of baby DVDs with highlighted target words, although after a parent scaffolding condition in which words were labeled, some learning did occur (Robb et al., 2009; Richert, Robb, Fender, & Wartella, 2010). A more recent study examined the effectiveness of a series of learning aids including video material, flash cards, and books that purported to teach infants to read (Neuman, Kaefer, Pinkham, & Strouse, 2014). The authors found that 9- to 18-month-olds whose parents followed the reading program for 7 months did not show evidence of precursor (e.g., latter name, print awareness) or conventional (vocabulary, comprehension) reading skills compared to control infants who did not participate in the reading program. Regardless, parents remained enthusiastic about their infants having learned from the baby media material. These poor language outcomes from baby videos that target language are perhaps not surprising given that content analyses of the language learning strategies used in the videos showed that they were poorly integrated into the material and reflected poor understanding of how infants and toddlers learn (Linebarger & Vaala, 2010; Vaala et al., 2010). In a notable exception to this, Dayanim and Namy (2015) showed that 15-month-olds learned ASL baby signs from commercial infant video viewed repeatedly for 3 weeks. Infants learned both with and without parents support, although there was a trend toward better learning in the support condition.

Collectively, these studies indicate that young children can learn from baby video under certain constrained conditions, but that they do not readily do so, especially before 2 years of age (DeLoache et al., 2010; Krcmar, 2011; Robb et al., 2009). Importantly, even when infants do learn new information there is a video deficit; attenuated learning relative to learning from live and interactive instruction (Barr & Hayne, 1999; Krcmar et al., 2007). When parents co-view video with their infants and toddlers, scaffold their attention, talk to them about the story using a dialogic approach, young children can learn language from video. However, it does not come easily and these conditions are unlikely to occur when children view commercially available video content at home. Moreover, it is not clear that learning from video provides a better alternative to learning through engaging young children directly. Although parent co-viewing can facilitate infant learning from video, the rate of co-viewing at home is only about 50% (Zimmerman et al., 2007b), so in reality infants and toddlers often view videos alone and without supportive parent interaction.

MOBILE TECHNOLOGIES, ATTENTION, AND LEARNING

Many of the questions that were asked and answered about the effects of television on young children's cognitive and social development in the past are being re-raised, this time regarding newer interactive "screens" such as tablets, smartphones, e-books, and gaming consoles. One reason for this resurgence is that because of their mobility and touch screen capability, these devices are far more invasive in children's daily lives than is television. A report from *Common Sense Media* in 2013 indicated that 0- to 8-year-olds' access to some type of "smart" mobile device increased by 50% over the previous 2 years and that the average amount of time spent using the device tripled in that time frame. Children under 2 years have less access to mobile technologies but 38% have at least used one, a rate significantly up from 10% usage 2 years earlier. Infants and toddlers are very drawn to these devices and seem to be able to tap and swipe a screen even before they have developed fine motor control (Cristia & Seidi, 2015). Indeed, the web is replete with images of infants and toddlers doing just that. A second reason for a renewed inquiry into the potential effects of mobile devices is that unlike television, they are interactive rather than passive media and easy to operate without assistance. As such they hold a significant potential to engage children's attention, respond contingently to them, and to support effective learning (e.g., Mayer, 2005; Troseth, Russo, & Strouse, 2016).

Although the *American Academy of Pediatrics* (AAP, 2011) recently acknowledged this new potential for older children, they continued to recommend that children under 2 years be discouraged from having any screen time. Christakis (2014), a member of the AAP committee that drafted the previous policies on children and the media, questioned this caution.

He argued that newer mobile devices were unlike television as they were reactive, interactive, and motivating and could be tailored to match the individual needs of the child. When judiciously used with carefully designed apps, they may well support learning, especially in conjunction with parent scaffolding and support. The research required to confirm or negate this possibility is ongoing, but Hirsh-Pasek et al. (2015) have proposed detailed guidelines based on what science has told us about learning that will help guide the development and use of educational apps that can optimize and support learning.

In advance of available empirical evidence, a vigorous debate recently emerged in the media when the *Sunday Times* (June 14, 2015) cited researchers at Birkbeck, University of London, as saying that "babies should be exposed to iPads from birth" and that "they learn faster with tablet computers than books". Although the citations were inaccurate and later retracted, the conversation has continued to grow. One side of the debate is the argument that tablets and other mobile devices are here to stay and that even very young children need to become familiar with them. Further, these devices are seen as providing opportunities for joint use and cooperation during learning activities and provide a greater level of cognitive activity compared to books and toys. This in turn could facilitate sensory, perceptual, motor, and cognitive development (Karmiloff-Smith, 2015). Others contend that providing toddlers with tablets is "unnecessary, inappropriate, and harmful" (House, 2015). The case made is that infants and toddlers learn best from engaging, interactive humans and that time spent with any media is that the time taken from these more natural daily exchanges and activities. Moreover, there is no evidence that the "greater level of cognitive activity" provided by media is necessary or helpful and that it may actually be harmful. To resolve some of these issues, Tim Smith and Annette Karmiloff-Smith at Birkbeck initiated the TABLET (Toddler Attentional Behaviors and Learning with Touchscreens) project (see APS Observations, July 2015), the goal of which is to document the role that touch screen devices seem to play in family life and the enthusiasm that children seem to show for them. Important issues to be addressed include whether young children use tablets in a passive or interactive way, whether they use them alone or engaging with others, and the appropriateness of the content and design of the apps that they use (see also Hirsh-Pasek et al., 2015).

Those who advocate the use of tablets and other devices with very young children suggest that a critical aspect of those devices that make them preferable to television as a support for learning is their characteristic interactivity. Although there is no evidence from studies with infants and toddlers to support or negate this, evidence from studies with preschoolers on the efficacy of e-storybooks compared to traditional paper books is instructive. These studies showed that language learning and story comprehension from e-books depend on many factors (e.g., number of "hotspots," whether they are consistent with the story or not, parent scaffolding, the child's executive functioning), but that even under optimal conditions they do not appear to be superior to traditional paper books (Takacs, Swart, & Bus, 2015). Notably, preschoolers' experience with e-book reading differs from traditional storybook reading (Lauricella, Barr, & Calvert, 2009; Parish-Morris et al., 2013). For example, they look more often to the adult during traditional reading as the "live" narrator appears to elicit social referencing in a way that the e-narrator does not. The wider implications of this are unclear, but referencing others through eye gaze is an important socially guided form of learning that very young children use in shared contexts to interpret others' behavior to infer expectations and to guide their own behavior accordingly (Walden & Ogan, 1988). In addition, although adults do engage with children during e-book reading, the interactions differ from those during paper book reading (Lauricella et al., 2009; Parish-Morris et al., 2013). Parents initiate more communication during paper book reading, while children initiate more talk during the e-book (Korat, 2010). Parents also talk more about the book format, the device, or the child's behavior during e-book reading but ask more questions and provided more evaluative comments during the paper book (Krcmar & Cingel, 2014; Parish-Morris et al., 2013). A potential implication of this "tech talk" during e-book reading is the corresponding reduction in the dialogic style of communication that has been so important to language and literacy outcomes more generally (Fletcher & Reese, 2005). Finally, co-reading can be at odds with e-books that contain interactive features, as both parents and children can become frustrated when the parent's attempts to read interferes with children's interactions with the book features (Chiong, Ree, Takeuchi, & Erickson, 2012). Although there are no comparable studies with infants and toddlers, evidence to date does not suggest that e-book use would confer any additional advantage to these younger users.

Although definitive data on all of these questions are pending, there seems to be an expectation that just as the judicious and careful use of interactive mobile devices and gaming platforms has been beneficial to the development of language, literacy, story comprehension, and visual perception in older children (Bavelier, Green, & Dye, 2010; Korat & Shamir, 2012;

Smeets & Bus, 2012), that similar benefits might accrue to younger infants and toddlers. However, the proponents should not overlook the strong evidence that infants and toddlers have a video deficit (even with touch screen technology; Barr, 2010) and they do not really understand the medium of video itself. The fact that infants and toddlers pay avid attention to screens and quickly learn to activate their features should not be interpreted as learning from the content of the app or video (see Pempek et al., 2010). Moreover, as their language, narrative comprehension, and executive functions are immature, the cognitive resources required to navigate the devices might serve to distract very young children and diminish learning. Although these issues can be ameliorated (e.g., with age-appropriate content, parent scaffolding, repetition, adding social cues), there is no compelling evidence that such learning from video is a better option to engaging young children directly. In fact, if these devices are used inappropriately, they might well impede developing attention and self-regulation processes and language acquisition, just as has been documented with television viewing.

REFERENCES

Acevedo-Polakovich, I. D., Lorch, E. P., & Milich, R. (2007). Comparing television use and reading in children with ADHD and non-referred children across two age groups. *Media Psychology, 9*, 447–472.

Allen, R., & Scofield, J. (2010). Word learning from videos: More evidence from 2-year-olds. *Infant and Child Development, 19*, 649–660.

Anderson, D. R. (1998). Educational television is not an oxymoron. *Annals of the Academy of Political and Social Science, 557*, 24–38.

American Academy of Pediatrics. (1999). Media education. *Pediatrics, 104*, 341–342.

Anderson, D. R., & Lorch, E. P. (1983). Looking at television: Active or reactive? In J. Bryant & D. R. Anderson (Eds.), *Children's understanding of TV: Research on attention and comprehension* (pp. 1–34). New York: Academic Press.

American Academy of Pediatrics. (2011). Media use by children under two years. *Pediatrics, 128*, 1–6.

Anderson, D. R., & Hanson, K. G. (2010). From blooming, buzzing confusion to media literacy: The early development of television viewing. *Developmental Review, 30*, 239–255.

Anderson, D. R., & Pempek, T. A. (2005). Television and very young children. *American Behavioral Scientist, 48*, 505–522.

Baldwin, D. A., & Moses, L. J. (2001). Links between social understanding and early word learning: Challenges to current accounts. *Social Development, 10*, 309–329.

Barkley, R. A. (2006). Etiologies. In R. A. Barkley (Ed.), *Attention-deficit hyperactivity disorder: A handbook of diagnosis and treatment* (3rd ed., pp. 219–247). New York: Guilford Press.

Barkley, R. (2011). *The important role of executive functioning and self-regulation in ADHD.* Retrieved from http://www.russellbarkley.org/factsheets/ADHD_EF_and_SR.pdf.

Barnat, S. B., Klein, P. J., & Meltzoff, A. N. (1996). Deferred imitation across changes in context and object: Memory and generalization in 14-month-old infants. *Infant Behavior and Development, 19*, 241–251.

Barr, R. (2010). Transfer of learning between 2D and 3D sources during infancy: Informing theory and practice. *Developmental Review, 30*, 128–154.

Barr, R. (2013). Memory constraints on infant learning from picture books, television, and touchscreens. *Child Development Perspectives, 7*, 205–210.

Barr, R., Danziger, C., Hilliard, M., Andolina, C., & Ruskis, J. (2010a). Amount, content, and context of infant media exposure: A parental questionnaire and diary analysis. *International Journal of Early Years Education, 18*, 107–122.

Barr, R., & Hayne, H. (1999). Developmental changes in imitation from television during infancy. *Child Development, 70*, 1067–1081.

Barr, R., Lauricella, A., Zack, E., & Calvert, S. L. (2010b). The relation between infant exposure to television and executive functioning, cognitive skills, and school readiness at age four. *Merrill Palmer Quarterly, 56*, 21–48.

Barr, R., Muentener, P., Garcia, A., Fujimoto, M., & Chavez, V. (2007). The effect of repetition on imitation from television during infancy. *Developmental Psychobiology, 49*, 196–207.

Barr, R., Zack, E., Garcia, A., & Muentener, P. (2008). Infants' attention and responsiveness to television increases with prior exposure and parental interaction. *Infancy, 13*(1), 30–56.

Bauer, P. J. (2007). *Remembering the times of our lives: Memory in infancy and beyond.* Hove, UK: The Psychology Press.

Bavelier, D., Green, S., & Dye, W. G. (2010). Children wired: For better or for worse. *Neuron, 67*, 692–701.

Bus, A. G., Van IJzendoorn, M. H., & Pellegrini, A. D. (1995). Joint book reading makes for success in learning to read: A meta-analysis on intergenerational transmission of literacy. *Review of Educational Research, 65*, 1–21.

Chiong, C., Ree, J., Takeuchi, L., & Erickson, I. (2012). *Comparing parent-child co-reading on print, basic, and enhanced e-book platforms.* The Joan Ganz Cooney Center.

Christakis, D. A. (2014). Interactive media use at younger than the age of 2 years. *Pediatrics, 168*, 399–400.

Christakis, D. A., Gilkerson, J., Richards, J. A., Zimmerman, F. J., Garrison, M. M., Xu, D., Gray, S., & Yapanel, U. (2009). Audible television and decreased adult words, infant vocalizations and conversational turns. *Archives of Pediatric and Adolescent Medicine, 163*, 554–558.

Christakis, D. A., Zimmerman, F. J., DiGiuseppe, D. L., & McCarthy, C. A. (2004). Early television exposure and subsequent attention problems in children. *Pediatrics, 113*, 708–713.

Cleveland, A., & Striano, T. (2008). Televised social interaction and object learning in 14- and 18-month-old infants. *Infant Behavior and Development, 31*, 326–331.

Colombo, J. (2001). The development of visual attention in infancy. *Annual Review of Psychology, 52*, 337–367.

Courage, M. L., & Setliff, A. E. (2010). When babies watch television: Attention-getting, attention-holding and the implications for learning from video material. *Developmental Review, 30*, 220–238.

Cristia, A., & Seidi, A. (2015). Parental reports on touch screen use in early childhood. *PLoS One, 10*, e0128338.

Dayanim, S., & Namy, L. L. (2015). Infants learn baby signs from video. *Child Development, 86*, 800–811.

DeLoache, J. S., Chiong, C., Sherman, K., Islam, N., Vanderborgt, M., Troseth, G., Strouse, G. A., & O'Doherty, K. (2010). Do babies learn from baby media? *Psychological Science, 21*, 1570–1574.

Demers, L. B., Hanson, K. G., Kirkorian, H. L., Pempek, T. A., & Anderson, D. R. (2013). Infant gaze following during parent-child coviewing of baby videos. *Child Development, 84*, 591–603.

Diamond, A. (2013). Executive functions. *Annual Review of Psychology, 64*, 135–168.

DiLalla, L. F., & Watson, M. (1988). Differentiation of fantasy and reality: Preschoolers' reactions to interruptions in their play. *Developmental Psychology, 24*, 286–291.

Fenstermacher, S. K., Barr, R., Salerno, K., Garcia, A., Shwery, C. E., Calvert, S., & Linebarger, D. L. (2010). *Infant and Child Development, 19*, 557–576.

Fletcher, K. L., & Reese, E. (2005). Picture book reading with young children: A conceptual framework. *Developmental Review, 25*, 64–103.

Foster, E. M., & Watkins, S. (2010). The value of reanalysis: Television viewing and attention problems. *Child Development, 81*, 368–375.

Friedrich, L. J., & Stein, A. (1973). Aggressive and prosocial television programs and the natural behavior of preschool children. *Monographs of the Society for Research in Child Development, 38*, 1–64.

Garon, N., Bryson, S. E., & Smith, I. M. (2008). Executive function in preschoolers: A review using an integrative framework. *Psychological Bulletin, 134*, 31–60.

Garrison, M. M., & Christakis, D. A. (2005). *A teacher in the living room? Educational media for babies, toddlers and preschoolers (Report).* The Henry J Kaiser Family Foundation: Children's Digital Media Centers.

Geist, E. A., & Gibson, M. (2000). The effect of network and public television programs on 4- and 5-year-olds' ability to attend to educational tasks. *Journal of Instructional Psychology, 27*, 250–261.

Hart, B., & Risley, T. R. (1995). *Meaningful differences in the everyday experience of young American children.* Baltimore, MD: Paul Brooks Publishing Company.

Hawkins, R., Pingree, S., Bruce, L., & Tapper, J. (1997). Strategy and style in attention to television. *Journal of Broadcasting and Electronic Media, 41*, 245–264.

Hayne, H. (2009). Memory development in toddlers. In M. L. Courage & N. Cowan (Eds.), *The development of memory in infancy and childhood* (pp. 43–68). Hove, UK: Psychology Press.

Hayne, H., Herbert, J., & Simcock, G. (2003). Imitation from television in 24- and 36-month-olds. *Developmental Science, 6*, 254–261.

Higgins, A. T., & Turnure, J. E. (1984). Distractibility and concentration of attention in children's development. *Child Development, 55*, 1798–1810.

Hirsh-Pasek, K., Zosh, J. M., Golinkoff, R. M., Gray, J. H., Robb, M. B., & Kaufman, J. (2015). Putting education in "educational" apps: Lessons from the science of learning. *Psychological Science in the Public Interest, 16*, 3–34.

Hollenbeck, A. R., & Slaby, R. G. (1979). Infant visual and vocal responses to television. *Child Development, 50*, 41–45.

House, R. (2015). Toddlers, TV and touchscreens. In *Nursery World.* 21 September issue.

Hudson, T. M., Fennell, C. T., & Hoftyzer, M. (2013). Quality not quantity of television is associated with bilingual toddlers' vocabulary scores. *Infant Behavior and Development, 36*, 245–254.

Huston, A. C., & Wright, J. C. (1983). Children's processing of television: The informative functions of formal features. In J. Bryant & D. R. Anderson (Eds.), *Children's understanding of television: Research on attention and comprehension* (pp. 35–68). New York: Academic Press.

James, W. (1890). *Principles of psychology.* New York, NY: Holt.

Kannass, K. N., & Colombo, J. (2007). The effects of continuous and intermittent distractors on cognitive performance and attention in preschoolers. *Journal of Cognition and Development, 8*, 63–77.

Kannass, K. N., Colombo, J., & Wyss, N. (2010). Now pay attention! The effects of instruction on children's attention. *Journal of Cognition and Development, 11*, 509–532.

Karmiloff-Smith, A. (2015). Toddlers, TV and touchscreens. In *Nursery World.* 21 September issue.

Kirkorian, H. L., Anderson, D. R., & Keen, R. (2012). Age differences in online processing of video: An eye movement study. *Child Development, 83*, 497–507.

Kirkorian, H. L., Lavigne, H. J., Hanson, K. G., Troseth, G. L., Demers, L. B., & Anderson, D. R. (2016). Video deficit in toddlers object retrieval: What eye movements reveal about online cognition. *Infancy, 21*, 37–64.

Kirkorian, H. L., Pempek, T. A., Murphy, L. A., Schmidt, M. E., & Anderson, D. R. (2009). The impact of background television on parent-child interaction. *Child Development, 80* (5), 1350–1359.

Korat, O. (2010). Reading electronic books as a support for vocabulary, story comprehension, and word reading in kindergarten and first grade. *Computers and Education, 55*, 24–31.

Korat, O., & Shamir, A. (2012). Direct and indirect teaching: Using e-books for supporting vocabulary, word reading, and story comprehension for young children. *Journal of Educational Computing Research, 46*, 135–152.

Krcmar, M. (2010). Assessing the research on media, cognitive development, and infants. *Journal of Children and Media, 4*, 119–134.

Krcmar, M. (2011). Word learning in very young children from infant-directed videos. *Journal of Communication, 61*, 780–794.

Krcmar, M. (2014). Can infants and toddlers learn words from repeat exposure to an infant-directed DVD? *Journal of Broadcasting and Electronic Media, 58*, 196–214.

Krcmar, M., & Cingel, D. P. (2014). Parent–child joint reading in traditional and electronic formats. *Media Psychology, 17*, 262–281.

Krcmar, M., Grela, B., & Lin, K. (2007). Can toddlers learn language from television? An experimental approach. *Media Psychology, 10*, 41–63.

Kuhl, P. K. (2011). Who's talking? *Science, 333*, 529–530.

Kuhl, P. K., & Meltzoff, A. N. (1982). The bimodal perception of speech in infancy. *Science, 218*, 1138–1141.

Kuhl, P. K., Tsao, F. M., & Liu, H. M. (2003). Foreign language experience in infancy: Effects of short-term exposure and social interaction on phonetic learning. *Proceedings of the National Academy of Sciences USA, 100*, 9096–9101.

Lapierre, M. A., Piotrowski, J. T., & Linebarger, D. L. (2012). Background television in the homes of US children. *Pediatrics, 130*, 1–8.

Lauricella, A. R., Barr, R., & Calvert, S. L. (2009). Emerging computer skills: Influences of young children's executive functioning abilities and parental scaffolding techniques in the US. *Journal of Children and Media, 3*, 217–233.

Lillard, A. S., Drell, M. B., Richey, E. M., Bogguszewski, K., & Smith, E. D. (2015). Further examination of the immediate impact of television on children's executive function. *Developmental Psychology, 51*, 792–805.

Lillard, A. S., & Peterson, J. (2011). The immediate impact of different types of television on young children's executive function. *Pediatrics, 128*, 644–649.

Linebarger, D. L., Barr, R., Lapierre, M. A., & Piotrowski, J. T. (2014). Association between parenting, media use, cumulative risk, and children's executive functioning. *Journal of Developmental and Behavioral Pediatrics, 35*, 367–377.

Linebarger, D. L., & Vaala, S. E. (2010). Screen media and language development in infants and toddlers: An ecological perspective. *Developmental Review, 30*, 176–202.

Linebarger, D. L., & Walker, D. (2005). Infants' and toddlers' television viewing and language outcomes. *American Behavioral Scientist, 48*, 624–645.

Lorch, E. P., Anderson, D. R., & Levin, S. R. (1979). The relationship of visual attention to children's comprehension of television. *Child Development, 50*, 722–727.

Lorch, E. P., & Castle, V. J. (1997). Preschool children's attention to television: Visual attention and probe response times. *Journal of Experimental Child Psychology, 66*, 111–127.

Mares, M. -L., & Han, Z. (2013). Effects of Sesame Street: A meta-analysis of children's learning in 15 countries. *Journal of Applied Developmental Psychology, 34*, 140–151.

Masur, E. F., & Flynn, V. (2008). Infant and mother-infant play and the presence of the television. *Journal of Applied Developmental Psychology, 29*(1), 76–83.

Mayer, R. E. (2005). Cognitive theory of multimedia learning. In R. E. Mayer (Ed.), *Cambridge handbook of multimedia learning* (pp. 31–48). New York: Cambridge University Press.

McCall, R. B., Parke, R. D., & Kavanaugh, R. D. (1977). Imitation of live and televised models by children one to three years of age. *Monographs of the Society for Research in Child Development, 42*, [5, serial no. 173].

Meltzoff, A. N. (1988). Imitation of televised models by infants. *Child Development, 64*, 80–89.

Miller, C. J., Marks, D. J., Miller, S. R., Berwid, O. G., Kera, E. C., Santra, A., & Halperin, J. M. (2007). Television viewing and risk for attention problems in preschool children. *Journal of Pediatric Psychology, 32*, 448–452.

Mol, S. E., Bus, A. G., & De Jong, M. T. (2009). Interactive book reading in early education: A tool to stimulate print knowledge as well as oral language. *Review of Educational Technology and Research, 79*, 979–1007.

Mol, S. E., Neuman, S. B., & Strouse, G. A. (2014). From ABCs to DVDs: Profiles of infants' home media environments in the first two tears of life. *Early Child Development and Care, 184*, 1250–1266.

Monsell, S. (2003). Task switching. *Trends in Cognitive Sciences, 7*, 134–140.

Muir, D., & Nadel, J. (1998). Infant social perception. In A. Slater (Ed.), *Perceptual development: Visual, auditory, and speech perception in infancy* (pp. 247–286). Hove, UK: Psychology Press.

Mumme, D. L., & Fernald, A. (2003). The infant as onlooker: Learning from emotional reactions observed I a television scenario. *Child Development, 74*, 221–237.

Nathanson, A. I., Alade, F., Sharp, M. L., Rasmussen, E. E., & Christy, K. (2014). The relation between television exposure and executive function among preschoolers. *Psychology, 50*, 1497–1506.

Network, N. I. C. H. D. E. C. C. (2005). Predicting individual differences in attention, memory, and planning in first graders from experiences at home, child care, and school. *Developmental Psychology, 41*, 99–114.

Neuman, S. b., Kaefer, T., Pinkham, A., & Strouse, G. A. (2014). Can babies learn to read? A randomized trial of baby media. *Journal of Educational Psychology, 106*, 815–830.

Oakes, L. M., & Bauer, P. J. (2007). *Short- and long-term memory in infancy and early childhood*. Oxford: New York.

Oakes, L. M., Kannass, K. N., & Shaddy, D. J. (2002). Developmental changes in endogenous control of attention: The role of target familiarity on infants' distraction latency. *Child Development, 73*(6), 1644–1655.

Obel, C., Henriksen, T. B., Dalsgaard, S., Linnet, K. M., Skjaaa, E., Thomsen, P. H., & Olsen, J. (2004). *Pediatrics, 144*(5), 1372–1373Does children's watching of television cause attention problems? Retesting the hypothesis in a Danish cohort.

O'Doherty, K., Troseth, G., Shimpi, P. M., Goldenberg, E., & Akhtar, N. (2011). Third-party social interaction and word learning from video. *Child Development, 82*, 902–915.

Parish-Morris, J., Golinkoff, R. M., & Hirsh-Pasek, K. (2013). From coo to code: A brief history of language development. In: In P. D. Zelazo (Ed.), *Vol. 1. The Oxford handbook of developmental psychology* (pp. 867–901). New York: Oxford University Press.

Pempek, T. A., Kirkorian, H. L., & Anderson, D. L. (2014). The effects of background television on the quantity and quality of child-directed speech by parents. *Journal of Children and Media, 8*, 211–222.

Pempek, T. A., Kirkorian, H. L., Richards, J. E., Anderson, D. R., Lund, A. F., & Stevens, M. (2010). Video comprehensibility and attention in very young children. *Developmental Psychology, 4*, 1283–1293.

Posner, M. (2012). *Attention in a social world.* Oxford: New York.

Posner, M. I., & Rothbart, M. K. (2007). *Educating the human brain.* Washington, DC: American Psychological Association.

Posner, M. I., Rothbart, M. K., & Sheesh, B. E. (2007). Attention genes. *Developmental Science, 10,* 24–29.

Radesky, J. S., Silverstein, M., Zuckerman, B., & Christakis, D. A. (2014). Infant self-regulation and early childhood media exposure. *Pediatrics, 133,* 1172–1178.

Raz, A., & Buhle, J. (2006). Typologies of attention networks. *Nature Reviews Neuroscience, 7,* 367–379.

Richards, J. E., & Anderson, D. R. (2004). Attentional inertia in children's extended looking at television. *Advances in Child Development and Behavior, 32,* 163–212.

Richards, J. E., & Cronise, K. (2000). Extended visual fixation in the early preschool years: Look duration, heart rate changes, and attentional inertia. *Child Development, 71*(3), 602–620.

Richert, R. A., Robb, M. B., Fender, J. E., & Wartella, E. (2010). Word learning from baby videos. *Archives of pediatric and adolescent medicine, 164,* 432–437.

Rideout, V. (2013). *Zero to eight: Children's media use in America 2013.* San Francisco, CA: Common Sense Media.

Rideout, V. J., & Hamel, V. (2006). *The media family: Electronic media in the lives of infants, toddlers, preschoolers, and their parents (Report).* Oakland, CA: The Henry J. Kaiser Family Foundation: Children's Digital Media Centers.

Rietveld, M. J. H., Hudziak, J. J., Bartels, M., & van Beijsterveldt, C. E. M. (2004). Heritability of attention problems in children: Longitudinal results from a study of twins aged 3 to 12. *Journal of Child Psychology and Psychiatry, 45,* 577–588.

Robb, M., Richert, R., & Wartella, E. (2009). Just a talking book? Word learning from watching baby videos. *British Journal of Developmental Psychology, 27,* 27–45.

Roberts, D. F., & Foehr, U. G. (2008). Trends in media use. *The Future of Children, 18,* 11–37.

Roseberry, S., Hirsh-Pasek, K., & Golinkoff, R. M. (2014). Skype me! Socially contingent interactions help toddlers learn language. *Child Development, 85,* 956–970.

Roseberry, S., Hirsh-Pasek, K., Parrish-Morris, J., & Golinkoff, R. M. (2009). Live action: Can young children learn verbs from video? *Child Development, 80,* 1360–1375.

Rosen, L. D. (2010). *Rewired: Understanding the i-genration and the way they learn.* New York: Palgrave Macmilllan.

Rothbart, M. K., & Posner, M. I. (2015). The developing brain in a multitasking world. *Developmental Review, 35,* .

Rovee-Collier, C. (1999). The development of infant memory. *Current Directions in Psychological Science, 8,* 80–85.

Rovee-Collier, C., Hayne, H., & Colombo, M. (2001). *The development of implicit and explicit memory.* Amsterdam: J. Benjamins.

Ruff, H. A., & Capozzoli, M. C. (2003). Development of attention and distractibility in the first 4 years of life. *Developmental Psychology, 39*(5), 877–890.

Schmidt, M., Pempek, T. A., Kirkorian, H. L., Lund, A. F., & Anderson, D. R. (2008). The effects of background television on the toy play behavior of very young children. *Child Development, 79*(4), 1137–1151.

Schmidt, M. E., Rich, M., Rifas-Shiman, S. L., Oken, E., & Taveras, E. M. (2009). Television viewing in infancy and child cognition at 3 years of age in a US cohort. *Pediatrics, 123,* 370–375.

Schmitt, K. L., & Anderson, D. R. (2002). Television and reality: Toddlers use of visual information from video to guide behavior. *Media Psychology, 4,* 51–76.

Schmitt, K. L., Woolf, K. D., & Anderson, D. R. (2003). Viewing the viewers: Viewing behaviors by children and adults during television programs and commercials. *Journal of Communication*, *53*(2), 265–281.

Schneidman, L. A., Arroyo, M. E., Levine, S. C., & Goldin-Meadow, S. (2013). What counts as effective input for word learning? *Journal of Child Language*, *40*, 672–686.

Scofield, J., Williams, A., & Behrend, D. A. (2007). Word learning in the absence of a speaker. *First Language*, *27*, 297–311.

Setliff, A. S., & Courage, M. L. (2011). Background television and infants' allocation of their attention during toy play. *Infancy*, *16*, 611–639.

Sheffield, E. G., & Hudson, J. A. (2006). You must remember this: Effect of video and photograph reminders on 18-month-olds event memory. *Journal of Cognition and Development*, *7*, 73–93.

Singer, J. I. (1980). The power and limitations of television: A cognitive affective analysis. In P. H. Tannenbaum & R. Ableles (Eds.), *The entertainment functions of television*. Hillsdale, NJ: Lawrence Erlbaum.

Smeets, D. J. H., & Bus, A. (2012). Interactive electronic storybooks for kindergarteners to promote vocabulary growth. *Journal of Experimental Child Psychology*, *112*, 36–55.

Stevens, T., & Muslow, M. (2006). There is no meaningful relation between television exposure and the symptoms of attention-deficit/hyperactivity disorder. *Pediatrics*, *117*, 665–672.

Stouse, G. A., & Troseth, G. L. (2014). Supporting toddlers' transfer of word learning from video. *Cognitive Development*, *30*, 47–64.

Strouse, G. A., O'Doherty, K., & Troseth, G. L. (2013). Effective co-viewing: Preschoolers' learning from a video after a dialogic questioning intervention. *Developmental Psychology*, *49*, 2368–2381.

Takacs, Z. K., Swart, E. K., & Bus, A. G. (2015). Benefits and pitfalls of multimedia and interactive features in technology-enhanced storybooks: A meta-analysis. *Review of Educational Research*, *20*, 1–42.

Thompson, A. L., Adair, L. S., & Bentley, M. E. (2013). Maternal characteristics and perceptions of temperament associated with infant TV exposure. *Pediatrics*, *131*.

Tincoff, R., & Jusczyk, P. W. (1999). Some beginning of word comprehension in 6-month-olds. *Psychological Science*, *10*, 172–175.

Tomopoulos, S., Dreyer, B. P., Berkule, S., Fierman, A. H., Brockmeyer, C., & Mendelsohn, A. L. (2010). Infant media exposure and toddler development. *Archives of Pediatric and Adolescent Medicine*, *164*, 1105–1111.

Troseth, G. L. (2010). Is it life or is it Memorex? Video as a representation of reality. *Developmental Review*, *30*, 155–175.

Troseth, G. L., & Deloache, J. S. (1998). The medium can obscure the message: Young children's understanding of video. *Child Development*, *69*, 950–965.

Troseth, G. L., Russo, C. E., & Strouse, G. A. (2016). What's next for research on young children's interactive media? *Journal of Children and Media*, *10*, 54–62.

Troseth, G. L., Saylor, M. M., & Archer, A. H. (2006). Young children's use of videos as a source of socially relevant information. *Child Development*, *77*, 786–799.

Vaala, S. E., & Lapierre, M. A. (2014). Marketing genius: The impact of educational claims and cues on parents' reactions to infant/toddler DVDs. *The Journal of Consumer Affairs*, *48* (2), 323–350.

Vaala, S. E., Linebarger, D. L., Fenstermacher, S. K., Tedone, A., Brey, E., Barr, R., Moses, A., Shwery, C. E., & Calvert, S. L. (2010). Content analysis of language-promoting teaching strategies used in infant-directed media. *Infant and Child Development*, *19*, 628–648.

Valkenburg, E. A., Rideout, V. J., Wartella, E. A., Huang, X., Lee, J. H., & Shim, M. (2007). Digital childhood: Electronic media and technology use among infants, toddlers, and preschoolers. *Pediatrics, 119*(5), 1006–1015.

Vandewater, E. A., Bickham, D. S., Lee, J. H., Cummings, H. E., Wartella, E. A., & Rideout, V. J. (2005). When the television is always on: Heavy television exposure and young children's development. *American Behavioral Scientist, 48*(5), 562–577.

Walden, T., & Ogan, Y. (1988). The development of social referencing. *Child Development, 59*, 1230–1240.

Weisleder, A., & Fernald, A. (2013). Talking to children matters: Early language experience strengthens processing and builds vocabulary. *Psychological Science, 24*, 2143–2152.

Werker, J. F., & Hensch, T. K. (2015). Critical periods in speech perception: New directions. *Annual Review of Psychology, 66*, 173–196.

Whitehurst, G. J., & Lonigan, C. J. (1998). Child development and emergent literacy. *Child Development, 69*, 848–872.

Wright, J. C., Huston, A. C., Murphy, K. C., St. Peters, M., Pinon, M., Scantlin, R., & Kotler, J. (2001). The relation of early television viewing to school readiness and vocabulary of children from low-income families: The early window project. *Child Development, 72*, 1347–1366.

Zimmerman, F. J., & Christakis, D. A. (2007). Associations between content types of early media exposure and subsequent attention problems. *Pediatrics, 120*, 986–992.

Zimmerman, F. J., Christakis, D. A., & Meltzoff, A. N. (2007a). Associations between media viewing and language development in children under age 2 years. *Journal of Pediatrics, 151*, 364–368.

Zimmerman, F. J., Christakis, D. A., & Meltzoff, A. N. (2007b). Television and DVD/video viewing by children 2 years and younger. *Archives of Pediatric and Adolescent Medicine, 161*, 437–479.

CHAPTER 2

Early Digital Literacy: Learning to Watch, Watching to Learn

Georgene L. Troseth*, Gabrielle A. Strouse†,
Colleen E. Russo Johnson*
*Vanderbilt University, Nashville, TN, United States
†University of South Dakota, Vermillion, SD, United States

Since the 1960s, educational researchers have argued that in the early stages of literacy, teachers should focus on teaching children *how* to read before expecting them to read for meaning (Snow, 2015). For example, according to Chall (1983), when children first begin to master aspects of this complex skill, "reading is not for learning;" children must develop awareness of the sounds that make up words and learn to decode written letters before they can read to learn. In current thinking, this is a gradual progression: as the component skills develop, children become better able to learn independently from text (Soden et al., 2015). Individual differences in reading ability, largely determined by stable genetic differences, are found in children's earliest mastery of components and in reading comprehension throughout formal schooling; differences in home literacy environment contribute to reading comprehension most strongly in the early stages (Soden et al., 2015). In this chapter, we show that coming to understand and learn from video—a form of *digital literacy*—is similar in several respects.

The idea that children need to *learn how to learn* from video may be surprising, because watching video seems so much like watching and learning from real events. Although digital literacy develops earlier than mastering written language, research indicates that very young children do not learn efficiently from video. We will examine research suggesting why this might be and the experiences that help children to learn from video. These studies reveal information about what has been termed "early symbolic development," the beginning of representational skills that both help toddlers use video and help children of school age master a wide range of symbolic media, including writing, numerals, diagrams, and maps (Troseth & DeLoache, 1998).

Cognitive Development in Digital Contexts
http://dx.doi.org/10.1016/B978-0-12-809481-5.00002-X

29

PERCEPTION OF VIDEO IMAGES

One component of digital literacy develops early in infancy: the ability to make sense of two-dimensional (2D) still and moving images and see their similarity to what they depict. For instance, after 5-month-olds habituate to the sight of a doll, they transfer their habituation to a picture of the doll (DeLoache, Strauss, & Maynard, 1979), showing that they recognize it as the same doll. Between 2 and 5 months, infants use a video image of their otherwise out-of-sight legs to direct their kicks at a noisy toy (Rochat & Morgan, 1995) and respond to video of an adult as they would to the actual adult, with smiles and increased movement (Bigelow, 1996; Hayes & Watson, 1981; Muir, Hains, Cao, & D'Entremont, 1996; Murray & Trevarthen, 1985). At 9 months, infants express similar emotions to videos of various entities (a person, an interesting toy, a spooky mask) as they do to the real things (Diener, Pierroutsakos, Troseth, & Roberts, 2008). By 1 year, the emotional responses that adults on video make to toys influence infants' willingness to engage with the real toys (Mumme & Fernald, 2003).

Besides making sense of pictorial images, infants also discriminate images from reality. Newborns both see the similarities between and differentiate pictures of objects from real objects (Slater, Rose, & Morison, 1984). By 4–6 months, infants smile more at a real person than at live video of the same (equally responsive) person (Hains & Muir, 1996), and 9-month-olds look longer at actual people, objects, and events than at videos of these entities (Diener et al., 2008). Thus, perception of the contents of video appears to be relatively automatic, but infants *do* attend to perceptual cues that differentiate images from reality.

An initial challenge for children's digital literacy is posed by the conflicting cues that make pictorial images both similar to and different from the three-dimensional (3D) world. Realistic video images and pictures retain much of the information in their real-world referents, including color, shadows, relative size, and (in the case of video) movement. At the same time, infants can perceive the flatness of images. Sensitivity to depth cues based on binocular disparity and motion parallax develops by 4 months (Held, Birch, & Gwiazda, 1980; Nawrot, Mayo, & Nawrot, 2009): babies detect that the image of a 3D object to their two eyes is slightly different, and changes as they move their head.

Children's natural exploratory behavior gradually helps them determine the affordances of 2D images. For instance, young infants often attempt to grasp at objects depicted in realistic pictures (DeLoache, Pierroutsakos,

Uttal, Rosengren, & Gottlieb, 1998) and video. When 9-month-olds were seated within reach of a video screen on which a series of toys appeared, each child manually investigated by rubbing and patting the pictured objects and attempting to pluck them off the screen (Pierroutsakos & Troseth, 2003). As shown in Fig. 1, infants were especially persistent with moving

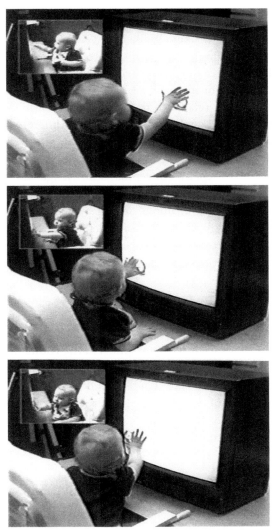

Fig. 1 A 9-month-old trying to grasp a moving object pictured on video.

toys, following them across the screen, and repeatedly trying to access them. Although 9-month-olds perceive information about the lack of depth in the images, they may not know the implications of these cues for their behavior, failing to realize that depictions do not afford the same set of responses as do the actual depicted objects.

LEARNING ABOUT PICTURES

Over the course of their second year, children "rapidly progress to treating pictures referentially" (Walker, Walker, & Ganea, 2013, p. 1321). Part of digital literacy is regarding images as related to, but distinct from, what they represent. Video images and pictures bring to mind stored knowledge about whatever is depicted. For instance, a picture of an apple will bring to mind conceptual information related to fruit, food, and possibly apple trees, but the affordances of a real apple and a picture are different. For those with mature "pictorial competence" (i.e., understanding of the picture-referent relation; Troseth, Pierroutsakos, & DeLoache, 2004), seeing a picture or a video automatically elicits conceptual knowledge about the contents and about the representational medium itself that blocks responding to the contents directly. For example, seeing a picture of an apple evokes knowledge of apples as food that can be held and eaten. But for those with mature pictorial competence, flatness cues that identify the apple as "*a picture of...*" elicit representational knowledge that blocks inappropriate responses such as trying to eat the picture.

In studies with both pictures (DeLoache et al., 1998) and video (Pierroutsakos & Troseth, 2003), 15-month-olds rarely tried to grasp at depicted objects, and 19-month-olds never did. Rather, the older infants pointed at the depictions, looking to adults in the room and attempting to talk about the images. By 15 months, infants realize that a verbal label used to describe a picture (e.g., "This is a whisk") refers to the depicted object, not just to the picture of the object (Allen Preissler & Carey, 2004; Ganea, Allen, Butler, Carey, & DeLoache, 2009). The realization that an image stands for and directs attention to something other than itself (DeLoache & Burns, 1994; Troseth et al., 2004) is a major development in digital literacy.

Young children's more mature stance toward pictures appears to stem from experience with adults' responses to them. Middle-class parents in western cultures spend substantial time reading and discussing picture books with their young children (Gelman, Coley, Rosengren, Hartman, & Pappas,

1998; Ninio & Bruner, 1978). This experience appears to promote children's representational understanding of pictures: US and Canadian children learn the novel names of pictured objects and generalize those labels to the real, depicted object at a younger age than children do in cultures without easy access to pictures (Callaghan et al., 2011; Walker et al., 2013). The ways that adults differentiate pictured objects during conversation support children's learning to treat them as representations. In one study, when parents and children in the US were given replica toys (animals, artifacts) and pictures of those toys one at a time, parents referred to pictured objects generically, as kinds of things ("Look, a dog"), whereas they referred to the replicas by name ("Hello, Spot"), treating them as imaginary conversational partners (Gelman, Chesnick, & Waxman, 2005). Of interest, the children (2.5- to 3-year-olds) also marked this distinction by how they referred to the toys and pictures. In this early aspect of digital literacy, social input plays an important role in helping children take a referential stance toward 2D images. Additionally, children's initial concepts may reflect the activities and parental behavior they have experienced with particular symbolic media. For instance, at an age when children recognize that a picture and its label (e.g., "This is a whisk") refer to the real, depicted entity (an experimental task very similar to the naming game that Western, middle-class parents and children play with picture books), children fail to use a picture in a novel way: as information about the location of a toy hidden during a "hide and seek" game (DeLoache & Burns, 1994).

Because children's inclination to treat a symbolic object referentially sometimes appears to be context bound, it is important to consider that children's concepts about pictures and about video may develop separately, based on different experiences with these media. For instance, most parents rarely if ever co-view video with their children in the same supportive way that they co-read picture books (Strouse, O'Doherty, & Troseth, 2013).

LEARNING TO USE INFORMATION FROM PEOPLE ON VIDEO

Starting in infancy, children perceive various matches and mismatches between video and reality. The very fact that video can (but does not always) depict ongoing events may challenge young children to work out the correct relation between a video and real life and affect their learning from the medium. At 2 months of age, babies respond the same to live and pretaped (delayed) video of their talking and smiling mothers (Marian, Neisser, & Rochat, 1996). Between 4 and 8 months, they become less responsive to noncontingent video (Bigelow, MacLean, & MacDonald, 1996; Hains & Muir, 1996). After watching people on pretaped video, infants of this age were less attentive and responsive to the same people on live video and in face-to-face interactions, compared to infants who saw the responsive partners first (Hains & Muir, 1996). Expectations of noncontingency apparently endured, affecting infants' responses to people on video as long as a week later (Bigelow & Birch, 2000).

In another study, missing social cues affected infants' learning of speech information from people on video. After interacting with a Mandarin speaker face-to-face during 12 sessions, infants (whose parents spoke English) could distinguish Mandarin sounds; however, infants who watched the same speaker on pretaped video for equivalent time showed no evidence of exposure to Mandarin (Kuhl, Tsao, & Liu, 2003). Although the speaker on video made apparent eye contact through the camera while she talked in Mandarin about picture books and toys, the 9-month-olds who watched were much less attentive than those who observed the real person facing them. The authors concluded that social cues in the direct interaction kept infants' attention and indicated what the speaker was talking about, which promoted infants' learning of speech information. The repeated sessions also gave infants ample time to form expectations about the nonresponsiveness of the on-screen person.

A large body of research examines young children's imitation of behavior that has been modeled on video. Typically, the target behavior is a simple series of actions to assemble a toy. To imitate, children must store a memory of the objects and event and then retrieve that memory when they later are given access to the real objects. In Barr and colleagues' research, the person demonstrating the series of three actions either was present in the children's living room, or appeared on the family television set. The youngest children that Barr, Muentener, and Garcia (2007) were able to test (6-month-olds) imitated just as much after watching the person on video or "face to face;" they required six repetitions of the demonstration to show significant imitation over a baseline control group, regardless of presentation mode. Infants from 12 to 30 months learned after just three repetitions from a modeler who was present (Barr, Dowden, & Hayne, 1996; Barr & Hayne, 1999; Hayne, Herbert, & Simcock, 2003). However, the same three repetitions of the person's actions on video elicited significantly less imitation (Barr, 2010; Barr & Hayne, 1999; Hayne et al., 2003; McCall et al., 1977). Across studies using this paradigm, 18-month-olds produced more target actions after watching them demonstrated on TV than a no-demonstration control group, but they imitated only half as many actions as infants who saw an in-person demonstration, and remembered these actions only half as long (Barr, 2013). Letting 24-month-old children see more repetitions of the target behaviors on video increased their imitation (Strouse & Troseth, 2008). Barr (2013) reasoned that repeated demonstrations allowed children to notice different aspects of the depicted event across repetitions, which strengthens the memory and enhances retrieval cues.

Several ideas have been proposed to explain why children imitate less from video. According to the *perceptual impoverishment* hypothesis (Barr, 2010), 2D images lack some perceptual features present in a 3D event (e.g., depth cues, matching size), whereby the child encodes a memory that is less rich and detailed and provides fewer retrieval cues—thus, a memory that is more difficult to access during the test than a memory of the actual event (Barr, 2013). However, it is difficult to use perceptual impoverishment to explain why the youngest viewers, but not the older infants, imitated equivalently from video and reality. Another explanation involves *context differences* between an event seen on a TV screen and reality. The idea is that young children encode details of an event's context (such as the frame around the TV screen) *with* the content, leading to a retrieval mismatch that hinders access to the memory in the testing situation (Barr, 2013). (A similar case was reflected by Butler and Rovee-Collier's (1989) infant participants failing to kick to get a mobile to move because the crib bumper present when they formed the memory had changed.) Barr's recent research with touchscreens reveals the difficulty of transferring a memory across contexts (Moser et al., 2015; Zack, Barr, Gerhardstein, Dickerson, & Meltzoff, 2009). Children saw an adult demonstrate pushing a button on a toy fire truck, or a virtual button on a 2D fire truck on a touchscreen, to make a siren sound. Children imitated the button push twice as often if they were given the object on which they saw the demonstration than they did when they had to transfer to the new item. Of interest, they did as poorly transferring from the real, 3D ("perceptually richer") toy to the touchscreen as they did from the "perceptually impoverished" touchscreen to the toy, suggesting that something other than diminished perceptual richness in the encoded memory blocked children's access to it. A mismatch between memories created in the different contexts may have compromised transfer in either direction.

More than *perceptual* details of the context (e.g., the frame of the TV) may contribute to a context mismatch between demonstration memory and testing situation—specifically, children's *concepts* about images on TV may impact whether they see the situations as different. Using Barr and Hayne's (1999) imitation task and replicas of their stimuli with 24-month-olds, we found an interesting contextual effect of children seeing the demonstration on their home TV (Strouse & Troseth, 2008). Children saw the demonstration at home or in the lab and were tested in the same context a day later. Children who saw the demonstration on their home TV produced only half as many target behaviors as children who watched the same video on an unfamiliar monitor in the lab; children who saw an in-person demonstration imitated at a high rate regardless of context. Seeing the video demonstration in their typical TV-viewing context seemed to impede children's access to the memory when they were presented with the real toy at home a day later. Presumably the video screen in both settings had a frame around it, which should have made it equally likely that children encoded context features. One possibility (discussed below) is that children's *concept* that events "on TV" are distinct from reality was heightened in the setting where they typically watched unrealistic video such as cartoons.

SOLVING A PROBLEM USING VIDEO

To imitate an adult's demonstration of toy assembly seen on video, children's memory of the event needs to be triggered when they are presented with the real, 3D components of the toy. However, to succeed, they do not need to know *where* they learned the information; in fact, contextual features about the source of the information may make the memory harder to access (Barr, 2013). In another frequently used task (Troseth & DeLoache, 1998), success may *require* a degree of awareness that video can provide information about current reality. Children are introduced to a toy (Snoopy) who, they are informed, likes to hide in a room. A researcher points out and labels each piece of furniture in the room. Next, she turns on a TV set, identifies a video camera connected to the TV, and demonstrates that children can see themselves, the researcher, their parent, Snoopy, and the furniture on the TV. She points out the correspondence between each real item of furniture and its image on the screen. Then she wheels the TV into an adjoining control room and spatially aligns it with the main room. The researcher tells the child that she will go hide Snoopy in his room, and "you can watch me on the TV." She leaves the control room, closes the door, appears on the screen, and deliberately hides Snoopy. An assistant with the child points out what is happening (making sure the child attends) without labeling the hiding place. The researcher returns to the control room, reminds the child that Snoopy is hiding "where you saw him on TV," and takes the child to the room to search.

Children who are 30 months of age usually succeed at this task; most find Snoopy using the information from video as he is hidden in four different places across trials (Troseth & DeLoache, 1998). To do so, they must update their mental representation of his current location on each trial using information from the video, rather than using outdated information from their direct experience (where they found Snoopy last time). What seems crucial for children of this age is getting the brief orientation to live video—seeing themselves, their parent, the toy, and the furniture on the TV "in real time." In a preliminary study in which children saw a stranger hide Snoopy in a pretaped video, they were unsuccessful (Troseth & DeLoache, 1998). Although the video of the hiding event showed them Snoopy's location in the familiar room, the children did not seem to realize that they had been given information relevant to the finding game.

For 24-month-olds, however, even the live video orientation was not sufficient. During the orientation phase, children appeared to see the similarity between the video image and what was depicted, identifying themselves and their parent, holding up the toy and commenting on its appearance on the screen, and identifying furniture items in the room when the researcher pointed to them on the TV. Nevertheless, once the TV was moved to the control room and the only way to know where Snoopy was hiding was to use information presented on screen, the children searched inconsistently (see Fig. 2). Quite frequently, children would find the toy on the first trial, showing some memory for an event seen on video. However, on subsequent trials, they would not update their knowledge of the toy's current location using information from the video. Rather, they would return to a location where they had previously found the toy and search there (Troseth & DeLoache, 1998).

One proposed explanation for 24-month-olds' poor performance was that memory limitations or difficulty inhibiting a previously successful response made the task challenging for this age group (Schmitt & Anderson, 2002; Suddendorf, 2003). Alternatively, the need to apply information from a symbolic medium (video) to reality was the challenge. To test this, we had 24-month-olds participate in the same search task, except they saw the hiding events directly through a window (the same size as the TV screen) between the rooms. All of the children found Snoopy on every trial. Rather than perseverating, they used what they saw through the window to update their mental representation of the toy's current location, and then used that

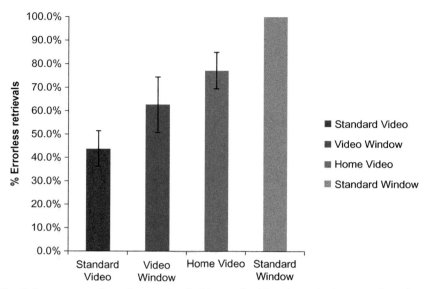

Fig. 2 Percentage of errorless retrievals 24-month-olds achieved when searching for a toy after seeing live video of hiding events (Standard Video); live video visible through a window, with the monitor hidden (Video Window); live video experience at home before the search task (Home Video); and a direct view through a window (Standard Window). Vertical lines depict standard errors of the means.

memory to search correctly (Troseth & DeLoache, 1998). Thus, searching across multiple trials was an age-appropriate task that did not strain children's memories or inhibitory capacity.

In follow-up studies, we gave 24-month-olds more support to see that the video represented the real event. In one study, the door between the control room and hiding room was left open on four trials, so children saw hiding events directly (through the doorway) and on the TV simultaneously (Troseth, 2003a). They were highly successful on these trials. Next there were four normal trials; the door was closed and children watched on video as the researcher hid the toy and were no more successful than the 24-month-olds were in the original study.

A "perceptual difference" explanation was proposed—searching in a 3D room based on a 2D video image of the hiding event was perceptually challenging (Schmidt, Crawley-Davis, & Anderson, 2007). To explore this hypothesis, Schmidt and colleagues invented two clever tasks. In one, rather than children *seeing* a researcher hiding a toy in a room, the researcher appeared on video and *verbally told* children where she had hidden the toy (also see Troseth, Saylor, & Archer, 2006). In the other task variation, the search space was a flat feltboard containing four distinctive flat shapes made of felt (e.g., a present, a cake) behind which a sticker could hide. Here, the 2D video image of a researcher's hand hiding a sticker behind a flat object on the feltboard was perceptually similar to the actual feltboard on which they searched. Despite the decreased need to map visually the toy's location across 2D-3D perceptual differences, children in both studies experienced great difficulty using information from video to find a hidden object.

CHILDREN'S CONCEPT OF VIDEO

Earlier we mentioned that babies developed enduring expectations about nonresponsive people on video (Bigelow & Birch, 2000; Hains & Muir, 1996) and that children had particular trouble imitating when they saw a demonstration on their home TV screen (Strouse & Troseth, 2008). Could toddlers' expectations about video—their concept about events appearing "on TV"—make using information from video a challenge?

One way to test this hypothesis was to convince children that they were watching directly through a window, when they were actually watching video—that is, interfere with children conceiving of the event as being "on TV." To do this, we ensured that the child never saw the television or video camera (Troseth & DeLoache, 1998). After they were introduced to Snoopy and the furniture, the researcher pointed out the window between the rooms and suggested that the child and parent go with her to the other room, and then "watch through the window" as she hid the toy. While the child was climbing up on a chair in the control room to "look through the window" (which was covered by a curtain), the assistant in the hiding room moved the video monitor into a place behind the window, so that only the screen appeared in the window once the curtain was opened. The illusion was quite compelling (see Fig. 3). After watching the hiding event, the child climbed down to go search; meanwhile, the sneaky assistant rolled the video equipment out of sight. Thus, when the child entered the room, no monitor was visible. A control group participated in the video condition where they saw the monitor (placed in front of the window curtain inside the control room, as usual) and knew they were watching on video.

Children in the two conditions were watching the identical 2D video image, yet when we told children in one condition that they were directly

Fig. 3 A 24-month-old watching through the Video Window.

watching the hiding event, and obscured the fact that they were watching on TV, significantly more children (9 of 16) succeeded on every trial (vs. 3 of 16 who saw the monitor). This result suggests that children's concept or expectations about video was interfering with their using the information.

Features that make video a versatile representational medium may actually contribute to young children's difficulty in using it for information. While looking so much like real events, video images relate to reality in a number of different ways. For instance, a realistic video can represent current reality (e.g., a video chat session with Grandma) or the past (instant replay is notoriously confusing for young children—Rice, Huston, & Wright, 1986). The sophistication of current CGI animation makes possible real-looking video of completely fictional entities (e.g., aliens or dragons). Cartoons and movies often involve events that contradict children's growing world knowledge: animals talk and wear clothes, and physical objects defy laws that babies recognize (e.g., that unsupported objects fall—Baillargeon, Needham, & Devos, 1992). Importantly, on television, people appear to be talking to the viewer, but they cannot respond if the viewer talks back (Troseth, 2010). It would not be surprising if very young children segregated events on video as *not-reality*, as events *"on TV,"* much as children are thought to mark pretend identities (e.g., banana = phone) as different from reality (banana = fruit) so as not to infect their real-world concepts (Harris & Kavanaugh, 1993; Leslie, 1987).

CONCEPTUAL DEVELOPMENT THROUGH NEW EXPERIENCE WITH VIDEO

If children's concepts about video develop from experience, we should be able to change their concepts by giving them different experience. In a study in the early 2000s, we gave 24-month-olds the most obvious evidence we could devise to show that video could represent current reality. We randomly assigned some parents to connect their video cameras to their televisions, and their children saw themselves "live" on the screen in several play sessions at home (Troseth, 2003b). We asked parents to do everything they could to help their children see the connection between video image and reality. Other children whose parents also had video equipment and willingness to participate were randomly assigned to a control group that did the play sessions but did not get live video experience. At the lab, all children received the typical brief orientation, during which they saw themselves and everything in the hiding room "live" on the TV. However, once the hiding game began, they could not see themselves on video. Now, they needed to realize that the image of the researcher hiding the toy on the TV showed them where to find it. That is, they needed to achieve what DeLoache (1987) calls *dual representation:* represent mentally both the 2D image that they saw on a TV screen, and the actual event happening behind the closed door to the room. On each subsequent trial, when they went to search for the toy, they needed to use the memory of what they saw on the screen, rather than a memory from direct experience (where they found the toy last time). The children who had received the special experience with live video were very successful at finding the toy, but a group without the live video experience was not (Troseth, 2003b).

This study also provided evidence that, although children's concepts of video and pictures may develop separately, some experiences build generalizable skills that are transferrable across symbolic media. The day after participating in the video search task, children returned to the lab and were asked to use a photo of the hiding place to find the hidden toy; that is, we asked them to transfer what they learned about using a video image from their at-home exposure and success in the video task to another symbolic medium. In a series of earlier studies, children of this age had failed to use pictures as clues in the search task (DeLoache & Burns, 1994). However, the children with live video experience were successful. The fact that the children transferred their insight across perceptual differences (from a moving image on a 20″ TV screen to small, static photos of furniture) suggested that they had gained some general understanding of how 2D images functioned as symbolic representations in this task, rather than just learning a procedure for how to respond to TV. Subsequently, in a correlational study based on parent questionnaire data, toddlers' real-world exposure to live video (defined as seeing themselves "live" on camcorder screens flipped to face them and/or on store security monitors) predicted their success in using video and pictures for information in search tasks at the lab (Troseth, Casey, Lawver, Walker, & Cole, 2007).

WHEN PEOPLE ON VIDEO RESPOND

Much has changed in the past decade regarding children's experience with digital media. For instance, children now can see themselves on live video on their parent's smartphone screen every time their parent takes a "selfie" family photo. Families are using video chat (Skype, FaceTime) with their young children on a regular basis, such as for regular visits with grandparents (McClure, Chentsova-Dutton, Barr, Holchwost, & Parrott, 2016; Tarasuik, Galligan, & Kaufman, 2011). Research indicates that if a person on video responds to them, children may be more likely to learn from the person, particularly if their parent views with them and supports their understanding. In the pre-Skype era, we used closed-circuit video to allow an on-screen researcher to talk to children (Troseth et al., 2006). The researcher conversed with the parent about the child's pet or birthday, then engaged the child in a game of "Simon Says," commenting when the child did/did not follow instructions. After singing a song with the parent and child, the researcher informed the child that there was a sticker under the child's chair, commenting on the sticker once the child (invariably) stuck it on his/her shirt. Thus, the researcher on the screen demonstrated that she could provide information that related to the child's ongoing experience. Following this 5-min contingent video interaction, children readily used verbal cues offered by the on-screen researcher to locate a hidden object, unlike in prior research in which no such interaction was offered (Schmidt et al., 2007). In more recent research, video chat experience has supported toddlers' use of video-presented information in a variety of contexts: copying a sequence of actions with a tool to open a box (Nielsen, Simcock, & Jenkins, 2008), learning verbs (Roseberry, Hirsh-Pasek, & Golinkoff, 2014), and recognizing, preferring, and learning from video chat partners (Myers, LeWitt, Gallo, & Maselli, 2016).

In the future, researchers must examine how being exposed to live video through regular video-chat visits may affect children's concepts of, and learning from, video. Tarasuik et al. (2011) have shown that young children are comforted by interacting with their parents via Skype during the separation phase of the "Strange Situation." It will be important to discover whether interacting with people by means of video chat leads to conceptual change, such that children seem to better understand video as a representation of reality at an earlier age. Another possibility is that children will respond to and learn from a person on video while the person interacts with them, but will not transfer this understanding across people or contexts. Recent work from our lab shows that while video chat increased 2.5-year-olds' engagement with an on-screen actress, the addition of scaffolding through parent participation was crucial for supporting learning (Strouse, Troseth, & Saylor, 2016). Thus, even when using live video, children may benefit when adults point out that video can function as a representational medium, similar to the way parents communicate the use of pictures as representations during picture book reading.

CONCEPTUAL DEVELOPMENT THROUGH ACTIVE CO-VIEWING

The way that adults co-view and talk about video with children may help children realize that the medium can be informative. We have suggested three possible mechanisms by which active co-viewing supports young children's learning from video (Strouse et al., 2013). First, when adults model attention to the screen, they guide children's attention. Demers, Hanson, Kirkorian, Pempek, and Anderson (2013) showed that when an infant's look to the screen follows their parent's look, the infant tends to look at the screen longer. The human tendency to follow gaze results in parent and child sharing attention to the video the same way they would jointly focus on a book or object in the environment. Because such triadic interactions are a frequent context for learning, young viewers may assume that what is on screen is informative.

In a recent study, we tested the role of parents' attention on children's learning (Strouse et al., 2016). An on-screen person led a game of "Simon Says," sang a song, and played other games (as in our earlier study), but this time, parents did not converse with the person. In one condition, the parent sat beside the child facing the TV and was asked to "play along" with the person (modeling participation), but not to instruct their child in any way. In the other condition, the parent was told we wanted to see what their child would learn on their own; the parent sat beside their child but faced away from the TV. After the games, the on-screen person labeled a novel object with a new word. Children whose parents modeled attention to the video participated more during the games and more often selected the correct object from the video as the referent of the new label. This study shows the power of the attention mechanism: parents merely "playing along" and sharing focus on the screen supported children's engagement and learning.

Active parental co-viewing may also provide cognitive support for learning, such as giving children a familiar context for encoding information from the screen (e.g., connecting it to real life), or practice retrieving, rehearsing, and applying what they have seen on screen through conversation and questioning. In a study that also used on-screen games followed by a demonstration of a new word, some 24-month-olds watched a pre-recorded demonstration without parental support (the parent was in the room but not actively participating), and the rest received a simple parent scaffold during the labeling event (Strouse & Troseth, 2014). Parents held up replicas of two on-screen objects and stated, "These are the same as the ones on TV," once before and once after the person on screen labeled one of the toys. Parents never repeated the novel word given in the video, so children had to learn it from the on-screen person. Parents simply but explicitly drew the connection between the video image of the toys and the actual toys. The simple act of aligning the real objects with their images on the screen may have helped children to encode the two mental representations of the objects together in memory (a representation of the 2D images and one of the 3D toys)—a cognitive support for learning. Even given this small amount of parental support, children scored better on a post-test of their word knowledge.

During active co-viewing, parents also may provide verbal and nonverbal social feedback to their children. In the prior study, for instance, parents provided a responsive scaffold: they placed the objects in the child's line of sight to draw their gaze and spoke directly to the child. This behavior not only provided factual information but also provided social information through responsive gaze, placement, and timing. Whereas attention direction and cognitive information may be provided by on-screen features such as sound effects, visual highlighting, or questioning by an on-screen character, social feedback is responsive and personal in nature and much more difficult to achieve without an in-person co-viewer.

Even children older than those discussed so far benefit from active parental co-viewing. In a study with commercial video storybooks (Strouse et al.,

2013), 3-year-olds were assigned to either a: (1) *dialogic questioning* condition, in which parents were trained to pause the videos and engage in high-quality questioning and conversations with their children about the videos; (2) *directed attention* condition, in which parents paused the videos and labeled things on screen but did not ask questions; (3) *dialogic actress* condition, in which an on-screen actress presented dialogic-style questions; or (4) *control* condition in which children watched "as usual" (typically without parents). Children in the different conditions therefore received different levels of help (or no help) through the various mechanisms of support. After watching the video stories for 4 weeks, children were tested on their story comprehension and learning of story vocabulary. Although all of the groups did learn some information from the video (even the "watch as usual" control group), children whose parents engaged in dialogic questioning while co-watching the videos (which incorporated attention-directing, cognitive, and social feedback supports) outscored the other groups. Children in the directed attention group did not score significantly better than the control group, showing the importance of asking questions and providing feedback (cognitive and social feedback mechanisms) to support 3-year-olds children's learning from video. The scores of children in the dialogic actress group were closer to those of the dialogic parent group, indicating that an on-screen person asking cognitively challenging questions may benefit learning—even without the attention or social feedback of an in-person partner.

The three mechanisms by which parental mediation operates (directing attention, supporting cognition, and social feedback) combine to help children *learn how to learn* from digital media: the adult directs children's attention to important information, helps children to interpret what they see, and supports children's transfer of information to their own lives. By talking about video and making connections to the real world, adults show that video can be attention-worthy and that the content of video can be meaningful and relevant to the current situation. Adult support may help override young children's tendency to dismiss video as unrelated to reality, acting as a cue that the situation of co-viewing is pedagogical and video content is worth learning.

DIGITAL LITERACY IN THE FUTURE

Recent developments in digital media may incorporate some of the benefits seen with active parental co-viewing, or lessen the perceptual and conceptual mismatches between video and reality, supporting children's learning from video. For instance, children who interacted more with the on-screen questioning characters in *Dora the Explorer* demonstrated increased comprehension of a TV episode (Calvert, Strong, Jacobs, & Conger, 2007). In newer touchscreen games, characters can respond to a child's touch or voice, adding an authentic bi-directional component to what was previously only an imitation of contingency (Troseth, Russo, & Strouse, 2016). Game applications (apps) can also adapt to a child's performance: when a child answers a question incorrectly, the app provides meaningful feedback based on the child's previous responses, partially simulating one of the mechanisms of parental support. Educational technology featuring interactive artificial intelligence has the potential to provide customized feedback. For example, older infants (18–21 months) learned more from an interactive stuffed animal that was personalized to them (e.g., knew the child's name and favorite things) than from a noncustomized stuffed animal (Calvert, Richards, & Kent, 2014).

Video that responds contingently to body movement (e.g., Wii, LeapTV) and virtual reality technology are blurring the perceptual distinction between video and reality. Televisions with 3D capabilities are becoming more common, and devices such as the Oculus Rift immerse users in a fully interactive 3D virtual environment. It remains to be determined how experience with these new kinds of media might change the course of development regarding digital literacy.

LEARNING TO LEARN FROM VIDEO

From early in development, children begin to learn to use the representational systems and symbolic media of their culture. Video is one of these symbolic media. As we have shown, adults cannot take for granted that young children detect and understand the representational role of video images. As DeLoache (1995) noted, "There are no fully transparent symbols." Instead, using symbols maturely requires developing an understanding of their nature and function. Learning to learn from video depends on children's perception of similarities, as well as differences, between video and reality.

Just as learning to read is supported by both experience with and direct instruction of the component skills of literacy such as phonics, vocabulary, and background contextual knowledge, digital literacy is supported through experience with and direct instruction of the component skills of representational competence. Highlighting the ways in which particular videos match current reality helps toddlers learn: this may include aligning the content of a video with the child's ongoing experience and using the social contingency possible in live video. Similar to the way children learn to take a referential stance to pictures during picture book reading with parents, social support promotes children's understanding of video as an informative representational medium. Adult co-viewing that includes three mechanisms of support (directing attention, supporting cognition, and social feedback) helps children to learn more from video than they do on their own. Such experiences and supports help children to develop representational skills they will use to learn from symbolic media throughout life.

REFERENCES

Allen Preissler, M., & Carey, S. (2004). Do both pictures and words function as symbols for18-and 24-month-old children? *Journal of Cognition and Development, 5*, 185–212. http://dx.doi.org/10.1207/s15327647jcd0502_2.

Baillargeon, R., Needham, A., & Devos, J. (1992). The development of young infants'intuitions about support. *Early Development and Parenting, 1*, 69–78. http://dx.doi.org/10.1002/edp.2430010203.

Barr, R. (2010). Transfer of learning between 2D and 3D sources during infancy: Informing theory and practice. *Developmental Review, 30*, 128–154. http://dx.doi.org/10.1016/j.dr.2010.03.001.

Barr, R. (2013). Memory constraints on infant learning from picture books, television, and touchscreens. *Child Development Perspectives, 7*, 205–210. http://dx.doi.org/10.1111/cdep.12041.

Barr, R., Dowden, A., & Hayne, H. (1996). Developmental changes in deferred imitation by 6- to 24-month-old infants. *Infant Behavior & Development, 19*, 159–170. http://dx.doi.org/10.1016/S0163-6383(96)90015-6.

Barr, R., & Hayne, H. (1999). Developmental changes in imitation from television during infancy. *Child Development, 70*, 1067–1081. http://dx.doi.org/10.1111/1467-8624.00079.

Barr, R., Muentener, P., & Garcia, A. (2007). Age-related changes in deferred imitation from television by 6-to 18-month-olds. *Developmental Science, 10*, 910–921. http://dx.doi.org/10.1111/j.1467-7687.2007.00641.x.

Bigelow, A. E. (1996). Infants' memory for contingently responding persons. *Infant Behavior & Development, 19*(Special ICIS Issue), 334. http://dx.doi.org/10.1016/S0163-6383(96)90388-4.

Bigelow, A. E., & Birch, S. A. J. (2000). The effects of contingency in previous interactions on infants' preference for social partners. *Infant Behavior & Development, 22*, 367–382. http://dx.doi.org/10.1016/S0163-6383(99)00016-8.

Bigelow, A. E., MacLean, B. K., & MacDonald, D. (1996). Infants' response to live and replay interactions with self and mother. *Merrill Palmer Quarterly, 42*, 596–611. www.jstor.org/stable/23087472.

Butler, J., & Rovee-Collier, C. (1989). Contextual gating of memory retrieval. *Developmental Psychobiology, 22*, 533–552. http://dx.doi.org/10.1002/dev.420220602.

Callaghan, T., Moll, H., Rakoczy, H., Warneken, F., Liszkowski, U., & Behne, T. (2011). Early social cognition in three contexts. *Monographs of the Society for Research in Child Development, 299*(76), 93–104.

Calvert, S. L., Richards, M. N., & Kent, C. C. (2014). Personalized interactive characters for toddlers' learning of seriation from a video presentation. *Journal of Applied Developmental Psychology, 35*, 148–155. http://dx.doi.org/10.1016/j.appdev.2014.03.004.

Calvert, S. L., Strong, B. L., Jacobs, E. L., & Conger, E. E. (2007). Interaction and participation for young Hispanic and Caucasian girls' and boys' learning of media content. *Media Psychology, 9*, 431–445. http://dx.doi.org/10.1080/15213260701291379.

Chall, J. S. (1983). *Learning to read: The great debate.* New York: McGraw-Hill.

DeLoache, J. S. (1987). Rapid change in the symbolic functioning of very young children. *Science, 238*, 1556–1557. http://www.jstor.org/stable/1700975.

DeLoache, J. S. (1995). Early understanding and use of symbols: The model model. *Current Directions in Psychological Science, 4*, 109–113. http://dx.doi.org/10.1111/1467-8721.ep10772408.

DeLoache, J. S., & Burns, N. M. (1994). Early understanding of the representational function of pictures. *Cognition, 52*(2), 83–110. http://dx.doi.org/10.1016/0010-0277(94)90063-9.

DeLoache, J. S., Pierroutsakos, S. L., Uttal, D. H., Rosengren, K. S., & Gottlieb, A. (1998). Grasping the nature of pictures. *Psychological Science, 9*, 205–210. http://dx.doi.org/10.1111/1467-9280.00039.

DeLoache, J. S., Strauss, M. S., & Maynard, J. (1979). Picture perception in infancy. *Infant Behavior & Development, 2*, 77–89. http://dx.doi.org/10.1016/S0163-6383(79)80010-7.

Demers, L. B., Hanson, K. G., Kirkorian, H. L., Pempek, T. A., & Anderson, D. R. (2013). Infant gaze following during parent-infant coviewing of baby videos. *Child Development, 84*, 591–603. http://dx.doi.org/10.1111/j.1467-8624.2012.01868.x.

Diener, M., Pierroutsakos, S. L., Troseth, G. L., & Roberts, A. (2008). Video versus reality: Infants' attention and affective responses to video and live presentations. *Media Psychology, 11*, 418–441. http://dx.doi.org/10.1080/15213260802103003.

Ganea, P. A., Allen, M. L., Butler, L., Carey, S., & DeLoache, J. S. (2009). Toddlers' referential understanding of pictures. *Journal of Experimental Child Psychology, 104*, 283–295. http://dx.doi.org/10.1016/j.jecp.2009.05.008.

Gelman, S. A., Chesnick, R. J., & Waxman, S. R. (2005). Mother-child conversations about pictures and objects: Referring to categories and individuals. *Child Development, 76*, 1129–1143. http://dx.doi.org/10.1111/j.1467-8624.2005.00876.x-i1.

Gelman, S. A., Coley, J. D., Rosengren, K. S., Hartman, E., & Pappas, A. (1998). Beyond labeling: The role of maternal input in the acquisition of richly structured categories. *Monographs of the Society for Research in Child Development, 63*(1) Serial No. 253. http://dx.doi.org/10.2307/1166211.

Hains, S. M. J., & Muir, D. W. (1996). Effects of stimulus contingency in infant-adult interactions. *Infant Behavior & Development, 19*, 49–61. http://dx.doi.org/10.1016/S0163-6383(96)90043-0.

Harris, P. L., & Kavanaugh, R. D. (1993). Young children's understanding of pretense. *Monographs of the Society for Research in Child Development, 58*(1) Series No. 231. http://dx.doi.org/10.2307/1166074.

Hayes, L. A., & Watson, J. S. (1981). Facial orientation of parents and elicited smiling by infants. *Infant Behavior & Development, 4*, 333–340. http://dx.doi.org/10.1016/S0163-6383(81)80035-5.

Hayne, H., Herbert, J., & Simcock, G. (2003). Imitation from television by 24-and 30-month-olds. *Developmental Science, 6*, 254–261. http://dx.doi.org/10.1111/1467-7687.00281.

Held, R., Birch, E., & Gwiazda, J. (1980). Stereoacuity of human infants. *Proceedings of the National Academy of Sciences of the United States of America, 77*, 5572–5574. http://dx.doi.org/10.1073/pnas.77.9.5572.

Kuhl, P. K., Tsao, F. -M., & Liu, H. -M. (2003). Foreign-language experience in infancy: Effects of short-term exposure and social interaction on phonetic learning. *Proceedings of the National Academy of Sciences of the United States of America, 100*(15), 9096–9101. http://dx.doi.org/10.1073/pnas.1532872100.

Leslie, A. M. (1987). Pretense and representations: The origins of "theory of mind" *Psychological Review, 94*, 412–426. http://dx.doi.org/10.1037/0033-295X.94.4.412.

Marian, V., Neisser, U., & Rochat, P. (1996). Can 2-month-old infants distinguish live from videotaped interactions with their mother. *Emory Cognition Project Report # 33*. Atlanta: Emory University.

McCall, R. B., Parke, R. D., Kavanaugh, R. D., Engstrom, R., Russell, J., & Wycoff, E. (1977). Imitation of live and televised models by children one to three years of age. *Monographs of the Society for Research in Child Development*, 1–94. http://dx.doi.org/10.2307/1165913.

McClure, E. R., Chentsova-Dutton, Y. E., Barr, R. F., Holchwost, S. J., & Parrott, W. G. (2016). "Facetime doesn't count": Video chat as an exception to media restrictions for infants and toddlers. *International Journal of Child-Computer Interaction*. http://dx.doi.org/10.1016/j.ijcci.2016.02.002.

Moser, A., Zimmerman, L., Dickerson, K., Grenell, A., Barr, R., & Gerhardstein, P. (2015). They can interact but can they learn? Toddlers' transfer from touchscreens and television. *Journal of Experimental Child Psychology, 137*, 137–155. http://dx.doi.org/10.1016/j.jecp.2015.04.002.

Muir, D., Hains, S. M. J., Cao, Y., & D'Entremont, B. (1996). Three-to six-month olds' sensitivity to adult intentionality: The role of adult contingency and eye direction in dyadic interactions. *Infant Behavior & Development, 19*, 200. http://dx.doi.org/10.1016/S0163-6383(96)90254-4.

Mumme, D. L., & Fernald, A. (2003). The infant as onlooker: Learning from emotional reactions observed in a television scenario. *Child Development, 74*(1), 221–237. http://dx.doi.org/10.1111/1467-8624.00532.

Murray, L., & Trevarthen, C. (1985). Emotional regulation of interactions between two-month-olds and their mothers. In T. Fields & N. Fox (Eds.), *Social perception in infants* (pp. 177–197). Norwood, NJ: Ablex.

Myers, L. J., LeWitt, R. B., Gallo, R. E., & Maselli, N. M. (2016). Baby FaceTime: Can toddlers learn from online video chat? *Developmental Science*. http://dx.doi.org/10.1111/desc.12430.

Nawrot, E., Mayo, S. L., & Nawrot, M. (2009). The development of depth perception from motion parallax in infancy. *Attention, Perception, & Psychophysics, 71*(1), 194–199. http://dx.doi.org/10.3758/APP.71.1.194.

Nielsen, M., Simcock, G., & Jenkins, L. (2008). The effect of social engagement on.24-month-olds' imitation from live and televised models. *Developmental Science, 11*(5), 722–731. http://dx.doi.org/10.1111/j.1467-7687.2008.00722.x.

Ninio, A., & Bruner, J. (1978). The achievement and antecedents of labelling. *Journal of Child Language, 5*, 1–15. http://dx.doi.org/10.1017/S0305000900001896.

Pierroutsakos, S. L., & Troseth, G. L. (2003). Video verite: Infants' manual investigation of objects on video. *Infant Behavior & Development, 26*(2), 183–199. http://dx.doi.org/10.1016/S0163-6383(03)00016-X.

Rice, M. L., Huston, A. C., & Wright, J. C. (1986). Replays as repetitions: Young children's interpretation of television forms. *Journal of Applied Developmental Psychology, 7*(1), 61–76. http://dx.doi.org/10.1016/0193-3973(86)90019-5.

Rochat, P., & Morgan, R. (1995). Spatial determinants in the perception of self-produced leg movements in 3- to 5-month-old infants. *Developmental Psychology, 31*(4), 626–636. http://dx.doi.org/10.1037/0012-1649.31.4.626.

Roseberry, S., Hirsh-Pasek, K., & Golinkoff, R. M. (2014). Skype me! Socially contingent interactions help toddlers learn language. *Child Development, 85,* 956–970. http://dx.doi.org/10.1111/cdev.12166.

Schmidt, M. E., Crawley-Davis, A. M., & Anderson, D. R. (2007). Two-year-olds' object retrieval based on television: Testing a perceptual account. *Media Psychology, 9*(2), 389–409. http://dx.doi.org/10.1207/S1532785XMEP0401_03.

Schmitt, K. L., & Anderson, D. R. (2002). Television and reality: Toddlers' use of visual information from video to guide behavior. *Media Psychology, 4*(1), 51–76. http://dx.doi.org/10.1207/S1532785XMEP0401_03.

Slater, A., Rose, D., & Morison, V. (1984). Newborn infants' perception of similarities and differences between two- and three dimensional stimuli. *British Journal of Developmental Psychology, 2*(4), 287–294. http://dx.doi.org/10.1111/j.2044-835X.1984.tb00936.x.

Snow, C. (2015). *50 years of research on reading.* In M. J. Feuer, A. I. Berman, & R. C. Atkinson (Eds.), *Past as prologue: The National Academy of Education at 50; Members reflect* (pp. 175–179). Washington, DC: National Academy of Education. http://www.naeducation.org/cs/groups/naedsite/documents/webpage/naed_169315.pdf#page=194.

Soden, B., Christopher, M. E., Hulslander, J., Olson, R. K., Cutting, L., Keenan, J. M., et al. (2015). Longitudinal stability in reading comprehension is largely heritable from grades 1 to 6. *PLoS ONE. 10*(1).e0113807. http://dx.doi.org/10.1371/journal.pone.0113807.

Strouse, G. A., & Troseth, G. L. (2008). "Don't try this at home": Toddlers' imitation of new skills from people on video. *Journal of Experimental Child Psychology, 101*(4), 262–280. http://dx.doi.org/10.1016/j.jecp.2008.05.010.

Strouse, G. A., & Troseth, G. L. (2014). Supporting toddlers' transfer of word learning from video. *Cognitive Development, 30,* 47–64. http://dx.doi.org/10.1016/j.cogdev.2014.01.002.

Strouse, G. A., O'Doherty, K., & Troseth, G. L. (2013). Effective coviewing: Preschoolers' learning from video after a dialogic questioning intervention. *Developmental Psychology, 49,* 2368–2382. http://dx.doi.org/10.1371/journal.pone.0113807.

Strouse, G.A., Troseth, G.L., O'Doherty, K., & Saylor, M.M. (2016). Co-viewing and contingency support toddlers' word learning from video. Manuscript submitted for publication.

Suddendorf, T. (2003). Early representational insight: Twenty-four-month-olds can use a photo to find an object in the world. *Child Development, 74,* 896–904. http://dx.doi.org/10.1111/1467-8624.00574.

Tarasuik, J. C., Galligan, R., & Kaufman, J. (2011). Almost being there: Video communication with young children. *PLoS ONE. 6*(2). e17129. http://dx.doi.org/10.1371/journal.pone.0017129.

Troseth, G. L. (2003a). Getting a clear picture: Young children's understanding of a televised image. *Developmental Science, 6*(3), 247–253. http://dx.doi.org/10.1111/1467-7687.00280.

Troseth, G. L. (2003b). TV guide: Two-year-old children learn to use video as a source of information. *Developmental Psychology, 39*(1), 140–150. http://dx.doi.org/10.1037/0012-1649.39.1.140.

Troseth, G. L. (2010). Is it life or is it Memorex? Video as a representation of reality. *Developmental Review, 30,* 155–175. http://dx.doi.org/10.1016/j.dr.2010.03.007.

Troseth, G. L., Casey, A. M., Lawver, K. A., Walker, J. M., & Cole, D. A. (2007). Naturalistic experience and the early use of symbolic artifacts. *Journal of Cognition and Development, 8*(3), 309–331. http://dx.doi.org/10.1080/15248370701446772.

Troseth, G. L., & DeLoache, J. S. (1998). The medium can obscure the message: Young children's understanding of video. *Child Development, 69,* 950–965. http://dx.doi.org/10.1111/j.1467-8624.1998.tb06153.x.

Troseth, G. L., Pierroutsakos, S. L., & DeLoache, J. S. (2004). From the innocent to the intelligent eye: The early development of pictorial competence. R. Kail (Ed.), *Vol. 32. Advances in child development and behavior* (pp. 1–35). Amsterdam: Elsevier. http://dx. doi.org/10.1016/s0065-2407(04)80003-x

Troseth, G. L., Russo, C. E., & Strouse, G. A. (2016). What's next for research on young children's interactive media? *Journal of Children and Media, 10*, 54–62. http://dx.doi.org/ 10.1080/17482798.2015.1123166.

Troseth, G. L., Saylor, M. M., & Archer, A. H. (2006). Young children's use of video as a source of socially relevant information. *Child Development, 77*(3), 786–799. http://dx. doi.org/10.1111/j.1467-8624.2006.00903.x.

Walker, C. M., Walker, L. B., & Ganea, P. A. (2013). The role of symbol-based experience in early learning and transfer from pictures: Evidence from Tanzania. *Developmental Psychology, 49*, 1315–1324. http://dx.doi.org/10.1037/a0029483.

Zack, E., Barr, R., Gerhardstein, P., Dickerson, K., & Meltzoff, A. N. (2009). Infant imitation from television using novel touch screen technology. *British Journal of Developmental Psychology, 27*, 13–26. http://dx.doi.org/10.1348/026151008X334700.

CHAPTER 3

The Effects of Parent-Child Interaction and Media Use on Cognitive Development in Infants, Toddlers, and Preschoolers

Tiffany A. Pempek*, Alexis R. Lauricella[†]
*Hollins University, Roanoke, VA, United States
[†]Northwestern University, Evanston, IL, United States

Decades of research have illustrated the importance of considering the content of media, such as games, apps, and television programs, when evaluating effects on children (e.g., Anderson, Huston, Schmitt, Linebarger, & Wright, 2001). More recently, researchers have also emphasized the context in which children's media use occurs (e.g., Barr & Linebarger, 2010). In general, one important contextual factor for early development is positive engagement with parents. A considerable body of research documents the importance of parent-child joint engagement in the first years of life for a variety of beneficial cognitive outcomes (e.g., Vygotsky, 1978) such as language development (e.g., Hart & Risley, 1995; Tamis-LeMonda, Bornstein, & Baumwell, 2001) and emotional development (e.g., Clark-Stewart, 1973). While the importance of parent-child engagement is well established in the child development literature, this chapter considers how the rapidly evolving media landscape in which young children are being raised may impact the relationship between parent-child interaction and media use. Greater media access may result in increased use by young children, either alone or jointly with parents. Greater access may also result in increases in parents' own media use, which may draw their attention away from their children. This chapter addresses both the role of parental engagement in children's media use and the influence of media on parent-child interaction. We focus primarily on early development in discussing the relationship between parent-child interaction and media use by infants, toddlers, and preschoolers.

Cognitive Development in Digital Contexts
http://dx.doi.org/10.1016/B978-0-12-809481-5.00003-1

PARENT-CHILD INTERACTION

Research has demonstrated the importance of positive parent–child interactions across the first few years of life for cognitive development as well as social and emotional growth (e.g., Carew, 1980; Clark-Stewart, 1973; Hart & Risley, 1995). Two specific cognitive activities influenced by engagement with parents are play and language skills. The classic theory of cognitive development proposed by Lev Vygotsky underscores how social interaction can facilitate the development for play, language, and other cognitive skills, such as attention and memory. While Vygotsky's theory focuses on social interaction with any individual more advanced than the child, his position is pertinent to the types of engagement that may occur between parents and children. Of particular relevance, Vygotsky discusses the zone of proximal development, or the distance between the child's current developmental level and the level of their potential development (Vygotsky, 1978). Vygotsky proposed that, within the zone of proximal development, interactions with others lead to internalization of cognitive processes first achieved in the social context (Vygotsky, 1978). The child will be able to utilize these cognitive skills on their own in new contexts once they are mastered through social interaction. Vygotsky's theory is reflected in modern research findings demonstrating that interactions with a parent can provide "scaffolding" to enhance the child's cognitive abilities (e.g., Dodici, Draper, & Peterson, 2003; Fiese, 1990; Slade, 1987).

In this way, parent-child interaction plays an important role in the development of early language and literacy skills. Hart and Risley's (1992, 1995) seminal longitudinal study of language exposure during the first 3 years of life found that greater amounts of parental language input correlated with better language outcomes in their children, such as larger vocabulary size and stronger cognitive abilities in general. Similarly, the amount of language used during the first 3 years, along with parental responsiveness and guidance, has been associated with positive literacy outcomes for low-income children entering kindergarten (Dodici et al., 2003). Beyond the amount of parental language input, the quality of social exchanges is also important for language acquisition. In particular, many studies have indicated that parental language input is most beneficial when it is contingent to the child's communicative bids, as demonstrated by positive effects of sensitive and responsive parenting behaviors and conversational turn-taking (e.g., Golinkoff, Can, Soderstrom, & Hirsh-Pasek, 2015; Hoff-Ginsberg, 1990; Masur, Flynn, & Eichorst, 2005; Tamis-LeMonda et al., 2001;

Zimmerman et al., 2009). Hart and Risley (1999) describe the combination of parental responsiveness, turn-taking, and talkativeness when engaging with their child in conversation as the "social dance" of American families. They argue that this dance between parent and child is crucial for children's successful language development.

A second area in which parent interaction can have a significant impact is young children's play. Play is a valuable activity that yields positive outcomes for cognitive, social, emotional, and physical development (for a review, see Ginsburg, 2007). Parents may enhance the positive effects of play by engaging with their child. In fact, parent-child interaction has been shown to increase both the quantity and quality of play in young children. For instance, both free-play and structured play sessions with the mother led to more advanced symbolic play compared to solitary play for children between 1 and 2 years of age (Fiese, 1990). Similarly, for preschoolers, maternal behaviors such as physical and verbal stimulation, involvement, and positive tone were associated with more mature play and better interactions with peers and caregivers (Alessandri, 1992). Active parental interaction (e.g., focusing on the child, showing interest, initiating, or extending play) has also been associated with longer play episodes and move advanced symbolic play (Slade, 1987). Thus, early cognitive development appears to be enhanced to the extent that parents enrich the play experience by actively engaging their children in these ways.

While some parental behaviors directed toward children appear to be beneficial for their early development, others lead to negative outcomes. For instance, behaviors by parents such as intrusiveness and questioning or instructing in a way that directs the child's attention have been associated with decreases in children's symbolic play (Fiese, 1990). Likewise, restricting children's behavior by terminating their activity or redirecting their attention to a new task has been associated with slower rates of cognitive and social development, which contrasts with supportive behaviors, such as maintaining children's focus on an activity, that are associated with faster rates of cognitive and social development (Landry, Smith, Miller-Loncar, & Swank, 1997).

Taken together, research and theory on early parent-child interaction point to many ways in which parental engagement can benefit cognitive growth. The social interaction between parents and children during the early years of development has a powerful influence on children's development of cognitive skills, such as language. Certain parental behaviors support children's development during play as well, which can be crucial for development since children spend much of their day in this activity. While there is opportunity for parent–child interaction to be supportive, parental behaviors such as interrupting or redirecting attention can be detrimental.

PARENT-CHILD INTERACTION & MEDIA USE

Given these findings for language and play, we would expect parental engagement with young children in the context of their exposure to media to influence similar developmental outcomes. However, before we review the relevant literature, it is important to note that, for children under 3 years of age, two distinct types of media exposure have been associated with dramatically different outcomes. As described by Anderson and Evans (2001), *foreground* exposure occurs when the child is actively attending to content designed for young children whereas *background* exposure occurs when the child is present while age-inappropriate media content is being consumed by an older user. In the latter case, exposure is incidental, and the child pays little active attention to the media content. This distinction is important because background media exposure has been shown to lead to negative effects for young children, whereas foreground media exposure can produce positive effects under certain conditions. For this reason, we divide our review of parent–child interaction in the context of young children's media usage on the basis of foreground versus background exposure.

Parent-Child Interaction and Foreground Media Exposure

Content produced for child audiences first became popular in the 1950s with the *Howdy Doody Show*, and continued to thrive with preschool programs such as *Sesame Street, Mister Roger's Neighborhood, Dora the Explorer,* and *Blue's Clues.* By the late 1990s, with the introduction of infant-directed programs such as the *Baby Einstein* video series, foreground media had become widely available to very young children (Anderson & Pempek, 2005). Not surprisingly, given the ubiquity of media content designed for young users, many families today provide their children with access to media from very early ages. A recent report from a nationally representative sample indicated total screen media use of approximately 2 h per day for children 0–8 years, with television accounting for about an hour of this time (Rideout, 2013). Nearly 60% of these children reportedly watched television every day, approximately equal to the number who read on their own or who were read to on a daily basis (Rideout, 2013).

Researchers have focused on two ways in which parent–child interaction and foreground media influence one another. First, parents may interact with their child such that they engage in media use together as a joint activity. Here, we refer to this physical and verbal interaction while jointly using media as "joint engagement." Second, foreground content designed for infants and parents to use together may facilitate parent–child interaction beyond the effects seen during media exposure by producing positive changes to parent–child interaction after the viewing session. Findings in both of these areas are reviewed here.

Joint Engagement With Foreground Media

Research on parent–child interaction and foreground media often considers joint engagement during media use. While researchers have considered joint engagement for children of all ages (e.g., Gentile, Reimer, Nathanson, Walsh, & Eisenmann, 2014; Nathanson, 2001, 2002, 2013; Valkenburg, Krcmar, Peeters, & Marseille, 1999; Valkenburg, Piotrowski, Hermanns, & Leeuw, 2013), we focus our review primarily on research including children of ages 5 years and under. We first consider frequency with which various forms of joint engagement with media occur and later address the impact these efforts have on learning and cognition.

Existing evidence suggests that the vast majority of young children experience media jointly with a parent at least some of the time. For example, in a questionnaire and diary study of infants 6–18 months of age, a parent was reported to be present 77% of the time infants were exposed to television in families with more than one child and 85% of time in families with no other children (Barr, Danziger, Hilliard, Andolina, & Ruskis, 2010). In a more recent analysis (Connell, Lauricella, & Wartella, 2015), approximately a third of parents with children 0–8 years reported jointly engaging with their child during media use "all or most of the time" for television (31%), computers (29%), and smartphones (29%), although fewer reported doing so for tablet use (21%). An additional 58% reported joint engagement "some of the time" for television, 42% for computers, 35% for smartphones, and 42% for tablets. Another study found that parents were more likely to engage with media with younger children (under age 6), noting a decrease in parent–child joint engagement with media for children of 6–8 years of age (Wartella, Rideout, Lauricella, & Connell, 2013).

Researchers assessing parent–child joint engagement with television sometimes draw a distinction between *mediation* and *co-viewing* (e.g., Valkenburg et al., 1999, 2013), with mediation referring to active intervention by the parent, such as limiting time or providing explanations, and *co-viewing* referring to watching alongside the child without necessarily intervening. In a study of parents with children of ages 1–18 years (Warren, Gerke, & Kelly, 2002), *restrictive mediation*, which was defined as a focus on media-use rules that limit the amount of time children are permitted to view or prohibit children from viewing specific content, was frequently reported (see also Valkenburg et al., 1999). Another commonly reported strategy was *instructive mediation* (i.e., active mediation), defined as explanations or discussions with children aimed at countering or endorsing a media message (Valkenburg et al., 1999; Warren et al., 2002).

Researchers have assessed the frequencies with which parents employ each of these techniques. In one study, parents of Dutch schoolchildren (ages 5–12 years) reported co-viewing most often, followed by instructive mediation and restrictive mediation (Valkenburg et al., 1999). Other studies have noted developmental differences in the types of mediation strategies used with children. For instance, restrictive and instructive forms of mediation were reported to be more common with children younger than 6 years of age, while co-viewing was more common with older children and adolescents (Warren, 2003; Warren et al., 2002). In a more recent study targeting infants and toddlers, the majority (75%) of parents of children 6–18 months of age reported placing restrictions on their infants' television viewing (Barr, Danziger et al., 2010). These included rules focused on limiting time use (57% of parents), allowing only nonviolent content (21%) or child-directed content (20%), or banning television use entirely (9%; Barr, Danziger et al., 2010). Importantly, a recent study of adolescent reports of parental mediation found that the style used by parents to implement restrictive and instructive (i.e., active) mediation was more important than frequency of use for determining its effect (Valkenburg et al., 2013), which suggests that researchers may need to consider how these techniques are employed by parents in their assessments of impact on the young child as well.

Other studies have assessed the parent and child verbal interactions during joint television viewing to identify ways in which parents engage their young children. In a longitudinal study that followed 16 young children (ages 6–30 months) for 6–8 months (Lemish & Rice, 1986), analyses of parent and child conversations during naturally occurring television viewing in the home indicated that both children and parents actively participated by labeling objects, asking questions, and discussing content. In another study, Stoneman and Brody (1982) asked mothers of preschoolers to record conversations at home with their children while viewing *Sesame Street* and again while viewing a situation of comedy. They observed that mothers adjusted how they engaged with their children during joint viewing depending on the program content. For instance, mothers spoke more often during *Sesame Street*, while also helping their children focus on the relevant educational content and assessing their understanding. In contrast, during the situation comedy, mothers were more likely to discuss characters' intentions and attributes.

In addition to documenting how often various types of parental engagement with media occur, researchers have also studied the effects of parental engagement on learning and other cognitive outcomes. A large body of research has demonstrated the effectiveness of educational programming for children from preschool age onward (Fisch, 2004). This research indicates that joint engagement with an adult is not a necessary condition for learning from television, at least for children of preschool age and beyond (Fisch, 2004). On the other hand, adult mediation may serve children by scaffolding their learning of educational content. For example, adults may individualize the child's viewing experience by drawing connections between television lessons and the child's own experiences, or they may provide elaboration that aids children in understanding information that might otherwise be too complex (Fisch, 2004). In light of Vygotsky's (1978) theory, if parents are able to engage their child within the zone of proximal development during joint media experiences, then cognitive development may be promoted by allowing the child to achieve more advanced understanding and learning than possible through independent media use.

Research focusing on preschool and kindergarten children has found that adult–child interaction during media use can positively influence a variety of learning outcomes. For instance, an early study by Salomon (1977) assessed co-viewing of *Sesame Street* by Israeli mothers of low socio-economic status (SES) kindergarteners and reported co-viewing to be associated with higher levels of program enjoyment as well as more time spent viewing, which in turn led to greater rates of learning. Reiser, Tessmer, and Phelps (1984) assessed several types of adult engagement to determine which were most effective in facilitating children's learning of letters and numbers. In this study, 3- and 4-year-olds watched a compilation of video segments focusing on numbers and letters. While some children co-viewed with an adult who did not intervene, others experienced intervention with the adult drawing the child's attention to relevant content, asking the child to label the letters and numbers, and providing feedback. Children who experienced adult intervention learned the target material better than those who did not receive the intervention. A follow-up study of 3- and 4-year-olds aimed to isolate these instructional components to assess their effectiveness (Reiser, Williamson, & Suzuki, 1988). In this study, questioning the child led to better performance regardless of whether feedback was provided. Directing the child's attention to relevant content without elaborating on the content, however, did not increase children's learning. Although Reiser and colleagues did not draw the distinction between mediation and co-viewing, the more effective methods used in their studies can be classified as mediation, whereas the less effective techniques can be classified as co-viewing.

In considering possible effects of parent engagement on media use in infants and toddlers, one must include the well-established finding that young children do not learn as well from traditional video as from equivalent experiences outside of the media context until approximately 30 months of age (see Anderson & Pempek, 2005; Barr, 2013 for a review). This finding is referred to as the *video deficit* (Anderson & Pempek, 2005) and, more recently, as the *transfer deficit* (Barr, 2013). Although we do not know of any research that has directly assessed the parent–child interaction as an approach for ameliorating the transfer deficit in infants and toddlers, a few studies have considered the means by which parent–child interaction during media use might be beneficial for early cognitive development. Parent engagement during television viewing has been shown to guide young children's attention and language. For example, research examining language use has shown that the types of behaviors employed by parents during television viewing with infants (e.g., asking questions, labeling objects) are similar to those seen during book reading with young children (Barr, Zack, Garcia, & Muentener, 2008; Lemish & Rice, 1986). In a study of parental co-viewing of infant-directed videos with 12- to 18-month-olds (Pempek, Demers, Hanson, Kirkorian, & Anderson, 2011), parents used program content as a means of stimulating engagement, for example by singing along with some videos and labeling objects with others. Another study found higher quality of parental speech during co-viewing (as compared to parent–child activities without media), resulting primarily from labeling of objects and actions on the screen (Lavigne, Hanson, & Anderson, 2015). Similarly, in a study assessing parents and their 12- to 25-month-old infants during viewing of an infant-directed DVD designed to teach language, parents with a "high teaching focus" (e.g., those more likely to present a variety of words and label and describe content on the screen) had infants who were more engaged with the video and who showed a greater quantity and quality of target word use than parents with a moderate or low teaching focus (Fender, Richert, Robb, & Wartella, 2010). Moreover, in a study of low-income families, mothers' verbal interactions with their 6-month-old infants during co-viewing of educational child-directed programming were predictive of their children's language skills at 14 months (Mendelsohn et al., 2010).

Parents rely on various styles and behaviors when interacting with their children, which have been related to varying effects. For example, parents use of a "high scaffold" style in which they employ verbal behaviors such as labeling, providing descriptions, and questioning that directs their toddlers' attention to the screen was associated with higher levels of child responsiveness to the content (Barr et al., 2008). Parents also influence their children in more subtle ways. For instance, toddlers tend to follow their parents gaze to a television screen and look longer at the screen if their parent initiated the look (Demers, Hanson, Kirkorian, Pempek, & Anderson, 2013). This finding complements other research with preschoolers who were found to follow their mother's lead by producing utterances that mirrored the content-specific language she used during joint television viewing (Stoneman & Brody, 1982).

While much of the existing research has focused on the positive effects of parent-child joint engagement with television, some negative results have also been noted, especially in relation to language exposure. Parent speech directed toward the child decreases in quantity during viewing of child-directed television as compared to during structured and unstructured parent-child activities without television (Lavigne et al., 2015; Nathanson & Rasmussen, 2011; Soderstrom & Wittebolle, 2013). Other positive parenting behaviors may also decrease during joint media engagement. For example, the overall quantity and quality of parent-infant engagement was lower during viewing of infant-directed videos than during free-play without television (Pempek et al., 2011). It appears that the presence of infant-directed videos displaced parent engagement with their young child, as the data demonstrate a negative relationship between parent-child interaction and looking at the television for both parents and children (Pempek et al., 2011). The long-term effect of these decreases in interaction has not yet been experimentally tested. Thus, negative effects found during viewing, in theory, could be offset by longer term benefits from parent mediation. Conversely, considerable time spent co-viewing television could be problematic to the extent that it displaces more beneficial parent-child engagement that may occur with the television off. More research is necessary to determine the short- and long-term effects of repeated joint media use at early ages.

In modern households, television is not the only platform that very young children are using. In a short period of time, access to mobile devices has increased rapidly for families with young children, with ownership of tablet computers, in particular, rising from 8% in 2011 to 40% in 2013 (Rideout, 2013). Given the potential for continuous access to mobile technology, the increased opportunities for young children to engage with media may affect the quality of their interactions with parents and other family members. Recently researchers have begun to examine how parents and children interact around newer media technologies, such as comparing the interactions of parents and preschoolers around digital versus traditional storybooks. The initial studies (Krcmar & Cingel, 2014; Lauricella, Barr, & Calvert, 2014) suggest that parents more often engage in manipulating the book when reading a digital book and may be more engaged overall when reading an electronic book compared to a traditional book. Lauricella et al. (2014) failed to find any differences in other facets of parent-child interaction or in child attention, verbalizations, or story comprehension as a function of storybook type. However, another study (Parish-Morris, Mahajan, Hirsh-Pasek, Golinkoff, & Collins, 2013) reported that parent-child dialogic reading (i.e., techniques such as questioning that encourage parent and child active participation in the reading process) and child story comprehension were negatively impacted when reading digital as compared to traditional storybooks. Clearly, more research is needed on this important topic, as parent-child book reading is one of the most critical contexts for promoting children's language development (Whitehurst et al., 1988).

The findings reviewed above suggest that, for the most part, parental engagement in the context of child-targeted media can be beneficial for children below 5 years of age. However, parents may engage less with their children when in the presence of media than in contexts without media. These findings point to the value of encouraging parents to engage actively in their children's media use and, at the same time, to ensure that their children also experience parent-child interaction without media. Despite advances in research on parent-child interaction during early media use, more research is warranted to determine the types of engagement strategies that are most beneficial for children's cognitive development. For instance, researchers might evaluate whether parent engagement during media use might be particularly influential before 30 months of age when children have diffi-culty in learning content from traditional, noninteractive video on their own.

The Effect of Foreground Media on Parent-Child Interaction

Media content specifically designed to educate parents may produce benefits for parent-child interaction that go beyond the immediate joint media expe-rience. While most of the research on parent-child interaction and media has focused on joint engagement during media use, as described above, a handful of studies have assessed the effects of infant-directed videos aimed at improv-ing long-term parent-child interaction. One study, in particular, compared interactions between parents and children 12–18 months of age after view-ing videos from one of two infant-directed video series that addressed parent-child interaction in distinct ways (Pempek et al., 2011). The *Baby Einstein* video series presents entertainment content for infants and uses ancillary materials such as DVD inserts to encourage parents to label on-screen objects for their child; the *Sesame Beginnings* video series presents entertainment content for infants and educational content for parents. In particular, the *Sesame Beginnings* videos model the types of behaviors found to enhance early development, such as reading to and engaging in play with the child. Parents in each video condition were asked to view videos from one of the two series at home for 2 weeks prior to two laboratory sessions, while those in the control group participated in laboratory sessions without having watched the videos at home. The quality of parent-child interaction during free-play in the laboratory was higher with more co-viewing of the videos at home, especially for families who watched *Sesame Beginnings* as opposed to *Baby Einstein*. Furthermore, parents who had experience with the *Sesame Beginnings* videos prior to visiting the laboratory showed more engagement with their children and higher quality engagement during free-play immediately after viewing the video together. Families who saw *Sesame Beginnings* for the first time in the laboratory also showed higher qual-ity parent-child interaction immediately after viewing than did those who had just watched *Baby Einstein*.

Another study utilized the *Sesame Beginnings* video series as part of an intervention aimed at enhancing the relationship between incarcerated teen males and their young children at 6–36 months of age (Barr et al., 2011). The training, which was performed either by facility staff or by volunteers, consisted of 10 sessions focusing on specific topics related to establishing a relationship, fostering communication, and social-emotional development.

Within the training sessions, clips from the *Sesame Beginnings* series were utilized to model desirable parent-child interactions. The intervention also included the development of a child-friendly space within the facility, with 10 father-child visits to allow participants to design and implement activities with their child based on content learned in the training. Results revealed an increase in the quality of parent-child interaction across sessions in several areas, including joint attention and turn-taking, with fathers' perceptions of the influence they had on their children's development also improving over time.

Of note, the *Sesame Beginnings* series targeted in these studies was designed to engage and teach parents while also entertaining children. This model may be useful because it allows parents to focus on the video while also engaging with their children. While successful parent training interventions have been developed in the past, limitations affecting their feasibility include cost, time involved in implementation, and poor attendance rates (Lim, Stormshak, & Dishion, 2005). The dissemination of information via video eliminates these problems, presenting an easy and cost-effective way to convey information to a wide audience (Barr et al., 2011; Pempek et al., 2011).

Parent-Child Interaction and Background Media Exposure

Background media refers to incidental exposure to (often age inappropriate) media by an infant or toddler. This may occur when an older family member is watching a television program and the young child is in the room. Compared to foreground exposure, far less research has addressed background media and parent-child interaction. Nevertheless, the studies that have been conducted generally point to negative effects.

Young children's exposure to background media is a common occurrence. In a large nationally representative survey, 36% of families with children 0–8 years of age reported that the television was on "all the time" or "most of the time" in their homes (Rideout, 2013). This rate was highest for lower income families (income less than $30,000), with 47% reporting that the television at home was on all or most of the time (Rideout, 2013). Given the relatively small amount of foreground exposure reported by parents in this same study (roughly 2 h per day), these data suggest that young children are exposed to a substantial amount of background television every day. Likewise, a study of infants between 4 and 19 months of age found that most mothers reported that their children were exposed to background television more than half of the time during solitary and dyadic play (Masur, Flynn, & Olson, 2015). This was particularly true for children from lower income households (Masur et al., 2015). It should be noted that these authors define background exposure as the television or video on for half the time or more during the child's play activities regardless of whether the content was primarily directed at children or adults. This deviates slightly from the definition by Anderson and Evans (2001), which assumes that background exposure is likely to be age-inappropriate content.

These findings indicating high rates of background media exposure are corroborated by a large nationally representative survey of parents with children 8 months to 8 years of age that was specifically aimed at assessing background television exposure (Lapierre, Piotrowski, & Linebarger, 2012). These researchers used a diary measure in which parents were asked to report all activities their child engaged in during the most recent typical day. For any activity that involved the child in the same location as the parent and did not involve television viewing as the primary activity, the parent was asked if the television was on in the background. Overall, children were exposed to nearly 4 h of background television each day. Exposure was higher for African American children, children under 24 months, and children of parents with less formal education. Additionally, having a television in the child's bedroom was associated with significantly higher levels of background exposure.

By definition, young children do not pay active attention to background media. However, media in the background does elicit some attention, albeit infrequently. One laboratory study of background television exposure by infants between 12 and 36 months found that looking at the television occurred just fewer than 5% of the time the television was on (Schmidt, Pempek, Kirkorian, Lund, & Anderson, 2008). While rate of looking averaged about one to two looks per minute of exposure, these looks were short in length, at roughly 3 s each on average (Schmidt et al., 2008).

In theory, background media exposure can have an effect either by influencing the child's behavior or by influencing the parent's behavior directed toward the child. Some research has found negative effects of background television on young children's behavior (e.g., Nathanson & Fries, 2014; Nathanson, Sharp, Aladé, Rasmussen, & Christy, 2013; Schmidt et al., 2008; Setliff & Courage, 2011). However, here we focus exclusively on evidence in which exposure to media influences the parent's behavior, particularly with regard to interactions with the child.

The presence of adult television in the background has been shown to influence the overall amount of parent-child interaction. In an experimental study, children of ages 12, 24, and 36 months engaged in an hour-long laboratory session with a parent (Kirkorian, Pempek, Murphy, Schmidt, & Anderson, 2009). The television was on for half of the session (playing a pre-recorded video chosen by the parent from a variety of popular programs) and was off for the other half of the session. Families were provided with an assortment of age-appropriate toys for the child as well as reading materials for the parent. Parents were asked to behave as they would in a similar situation at home. Detailed analysis of parent-child interaction across 10-s intervals indicated that parents interacted less with their children when the television was on and that the quality of these interactions was poorer than without television (Kirkorian et al., 2009). Thus, the use of television in the background interrupted the types of parent-child joint engagement which is demonstrated to be beneficial for children's development.

Several studies have identified negative effects of background television exposure on parental language input (i.e., child-directed speech). Evaluations of parent and child vocalizations in the home environment found a 7% decrease in discernible words heard by the child for each additional hour of television exposure for children 2–48 months of age (Christakis et al., 2009). In an experimental study, both the quantity and quality of parental language directed toward the child were lower during free-play in the presence of background television as compared to when the television was off (Pempek, Kirkorian, & Anderson, 2014). Two studies also point to negative effects of exposure on the child's language abilities, implying that lower quality language environments seen with background exposure may translate into diminished language development. Specifically, exposure to background television was associated with lower levels of cognitive and language development for infants (Tomopoulos et al., 2010) and lower levels of receptive language for preschoolers (Barr, Lauricella, Zack, & Calvert, 2010). However, because the latter two studies are correlational, it is impossible to determine whether background exposure or other related factors led to the decreases seen in language learning.

Research on background media exposure and parent-child interaction has primarily focused on television; however, other forms of digital media may have similar detrimental effects on parent-child interaction to the extent that they draw the parent's attention away from the child. In particular, portable electronic devices such as cell phones and tablet computers have the potential to interfere with parent-child interaction, with the little evidence that exists pointing toward detrimental effects on parental engagement. For instance, preliminary findings from an experiment manipulating maternal distraction indicated that toddlers' word learning was negatively affected when a cell phone call interrupted the learning experience (Reed, Hirsh-Pasek, & Golinkoff, 2012). Another study found that approximately 23% of low-income mothers spontaneously used their mobile devices during a structured parent-child task in which they were asked to try familiar and unfamiliar foods with their 6-year-old children (Radesky et al., 2015). This analysis revealed that active mobile device use was associated with reductions of both verbal and nonverbal interactions during the task. While children in the latter study were slightly older than the ages targeted in this review, the task utilized is similar to the types of parent-child activities that commonly occur with younger children.

Because of the ease of access to media content afforded by portable Internet-enabled devices, there is a growing possibility that parents will be distracted when engaging with their young children. Recent studies have documented the rapid adoption of cell phones and tablets by families of young children, with ownership of any type of mobile device (e.g., tablet, smartphone) rising from 52% to 75% between 2011 and 2013, respectively, in homes with children 0–8 years of age (Rideout, 2013). Recent assessment of low-income families with children between 6 months and 4 years of age found that 83% owned a tablet and 77% owned a smartphone (Kabali et al., 2015).

Collectively, these findings point to the possibility that background media may result in significant detrimental effects on parent-child interaction. Given the importance of active positive parental engagement for a variety of cognitive and social outcomes, this may be particularly problematic for children in households in which the television is on most or all of the time. However, more research is warranted to assess whether parent-child interaction is equally affected by background media exposure outside the laboratory setting and whether effects do, in fact, hold true for media beyond television. Likewise, longitudinal assessments are needed to determine whether negative influences have a long-term detrimental effect on important cognitive outcomes throughout early childhood and beyond.

CONCLUSIONS

The potential for active parent-child interaction to enhance cognitive development is well established (e.g., Carew, 1980; Clark-Stewart, 1973). There are also dramatic differences in the ways in which families interact and communicate with their young children (e.g., Hart & Risley, 1995;

Tamis-LeMonda et al., 2001). At a time when digital media technology has become a universal presence in the lives of young children and their parents, it is essential that we continue to investigate the complex relationship between media use and parent–child interaction.

The research reviewed here on parent–child interaction and media use illustrates the importance of both the content (e.g., foreground or background) and context (e.g., with a co-viewing parent or without) when considering media effects on cognitive development. Specifically, parent–child engagement with foreground media exposure, consisting of content designed for young children, may have both positive and negative effects on cognitive development. Studies have demonstrated that parents who actively engage with their child during media use help draw their children's attention to appropriate content (e.g., Reiser et al., 1988), increase enjoyment of the program (e.g., Salomon, 1977), and increase learning (e.g., Reiser et al., 1984; Salomon, 1977). However, other studies suggest that the quantity and quality of parent–child interaction and language spoken to the child are lower during co-viewing of television as compared to parent–child interaction in the absence of television (e.g., Lavigne et al., 2015; Nathanson & Rasmussen, 2011; Pempek et al., 2011). It is possible that these reductions may be detrimental, if extensive, because the types of parent behaviors affected are important for cognitive development. In contrast to the mixed results as a function of foreground media use, background media exposure, which by definition often includes content not designed for young children, has consistent negative effects on parent–child interaction, including decreases in child-directed speech (e.g., Christakis et al., 2009; Pempek et al., 2014) and in parent–child interaction overall (Kirkorian et al., 2009).

Despite advances in our understanding of parent–child interaction and media use by young children, additional research is warranted. Given the rapid increase in the number of media products being developed specifically for infants, toddlers, and preschoolers across all platforms, it is imperative that researchers continue to examine how such devices both support and hinder parent–child interaction. Specifically, the types of strategies employed by parents to engage their children with media as well as the effects that these strategies have on language and other cognitive outcomes should be considered further. Researchers should also investigate parent–child interaction throughout the developmental shift from toddlers' difficulty in learning from media (i.e., the transfer deficit) to preschoolers' relative ease in learning educational messages from well-designed content embedded in developmentally appropriate media. Longitudinal assessments of parent–child interactions surrounding media use during the first 5 years of life would capture this transition so that potential changes in effective parent strategies can be examined and implemented in intervention studies. Assessments of later cognitive abilities and academic achievement should also be conducted to consider the longer-term impact of parent–child interaction during media use. In addition, documentation of the incredible rate at which new digital technologies are being adopted by families across the socio-economic spectrum points to the importance of moving beyond consideration of television to investigation of parental engagement with all types of media used by infants, toddlers, and preschoolers today, from video games to apps on portable devices.

Along with the increased availability of content intended for young children, there is an endless stream of information directed toward adults, with new technologies providing increased opportunities to engage with media, from text messages to fitness trackers that ping or vibrate to solicit attention. While directed toward parents, these technologies have the potential to influence all members of the household, including young children. Detailed assessments of the home media environment are necessary to capture how these relatively new forms of background media impact young children's everyday lives. As with foreground exposure, longitudinal assessments of possible compounding effects of media use on parent–child interaction over time are needed in order to draw more detailed conclusions. Furthermore, the extent to which negative effects of parents' own media use applies beyond television is yet unclear. In theory, any activity that draws parental attention away from the child could cause effects similar to those seen for background television. Importantly, researchers must address the methodological challenges of assessing young children's background exposure to new technology, which may be as fleeting as the parent pulling out his or her cell phone to quickly respond to a new text message.

While much work remains to better understand the relationship between parent–child interaction and media use during early development, existing evidence points to several key issues that may prove useful in recommending guidelines to parents about early media exposure. With respect to foreground media, active joint engagement of parents with young children in the context of media use should be promoted and supported. For instance, parents may be provided with descriptions and examples of techniques that are useful (e.g., drawing the child's attention to relevant educational content) as well as instructions for implementation. Likewise, parents should be informed about the strong evidence indicating that children do not readily learn from traditional, noninteractive video until about 30 months of age (see Anderson & Pempek, 2005; Barr, 2013). Thus, if parents choose to allow their infants and toddlers to use media, they might be encouraged to engage with the child by using the media content as a way to stimulate their interactions with their young children, such as labeling objects on the screen or singing along. While active joint engagement during media use can lead to positive outcomes for children when compared to children using media on their own, initial studies point to decreases in the quality and quantity of parent–child interaction during media use as compared to activities without television. For this reason, parents should be told of the potentially detrimental effects of foreground media on parent–child interactions, particularly if this exposure is extensive and displaces a great deal of media-free parent–child interaction. Parent–child engagement without media should be encouraged.

With respect to recommendations for background media exposure, preliminary evidence of negative effects on child development should be emphasized. Interventions should aim to increase awareness among parents of their own media use habits and their potential effects on their ability to attend to and actively engage with their children. While it is impractical to ask parents to eliminate all background media exposure for young children, heightened awareness of potential negative effects may help parents to be more vigilant about minimizing this exposure whenever possible. For example, they might be encouraged to turn off the television when the young child is present and no one is actively watching.

Continuing research that incorporates assessments of long-term effects and new technologies will be necessary to increase our understanding of the complex relationship between the effects of parent–child interaction and media use on cognitive development in infants, toddlers, and preschoolers. With this knowledge, recommendations for parents can be refined. Given the vast research on the importance of parental engagement for positive development in many domains, including cognition, helping parents understand how their actions affect and are affected by media use may have lasting beneficial outcomes for development in infants, toddlers, and preschoolers.

REFERENCES

Alessandri, S. M. (1992). Mother-child interactional correlates of maltreated and nonmaltreated children's play behavior. *Development and Psychopathology*, 4, 257–270. http://dx.doi.org/10.1017/S0954579400000134.
Anderson, D. R., & Evans, M. K. (2001). Peril and potential of media for infants and toddlers. *Zero to Three: National Center for Infants, Toddlers, and Families*, 22, 10–16.

Anderson, D. R., Huston, A. C., Schmitt, K. L., Linebarger, D. L., & Wright, J. C. (2001). Early childhood television viewing and adolescent behavior: The recontact study. *Monographs of the Society for Research in Child Development, 68,* 1–147. http://dx.doi.org/10.1111/1540-5834.00120.

Anderson, D. R., & Pempek, T. A. (2005). Television and very young children. *American Behavioral Scientist January, 48,* 505–522. http://dx.doi.org/10.1177/0002764204271506.

Barr, R. (2013). Memory constraints on infant learning from picture books, television, and touchscreens. *Child Development Perspectives, 7,* 205–210. http://dx.doi.org/10.1111/cdep.12041.

Barr, R., Brito, N., Zocca, J., Reina, S., Rodriguez, J., & Shauffer, C. (2011). The baby Elmo program: Improving teen father-child interactions within juvenile justice facilities. *Children and Youth Services Review, 33,* 1555–1562. http://dx.doi.org/10.1016/j.childyouth.2011.03.020.

Barr, R., Danziger, C., Hilliard, M. E., Andolina, C., & Ruskis, J. (2010a). Amount, content and context of infant media exposure: A parental questionnaire and diary analysis. *International Journal of Early Years Education, 18,* 107–122. http://dx.doi.org/10.1080/09669760.2010.494431.

Barr, R., Lauricella, A., Zack, E., & Calvert, S. L. (2010b). Infant and early childhood exposure to adult-directed and child-directed television programming: Relations with cognitive skills at age four. *Merrill-Palmer Quarterly, 56,* 21–48. http://dx.doi.org/10.1353/mpq.0.0038.

Barr, R., & Linebarger, D. L. (2010). Special issue on the content and context of early media exposure. *Infant and Child Development, 19,* 553–556. http://dx.doi.org/10.1002/icd.716.

Barr, R., Zack, E., Garcia, A., & Muentener, P. (2008). Infants' attention and responsiveness to television increases with prior exposure and parental interaction. *Infancy, 13,* 30–56. http://dx.doi.org/10.1080/15250000701779378.

Carew, J. V. (1980). Experience and the development of intelligence in young children at home and in day care. *Monographs of the Society for Research in Child Development, 45* (6–7). Serial No. 187. http://dx.doi.org/10.2307/1166011.

Christakis, D. A., Gilkerson, J., Richards, J. A., Zimmerman, F. J., Garrison, M. M., Xu, D., & Yapanel, U. (2009). Audible television and decreased adult words, infant vocalizations, and conversational turns: A population-based study. *Archives of Pediatrics & Adolescent Medicine, 163,* 554–558. http://dx.doi.org/10.1001/archpediatrics.2009.61.

Clark-Stewart, K. A. (1973). Interactions between mothers and their young children: Characteristics and consequences. *Monographs of the Society for Research in Child Development, 38* (6-7). Serial No. 153. http://dx.doi.org/10.2307/1165928.

Connell, S. L., Lauricella, A. R., & Wartella, E. (2015). Parental co-use of media technology with their young children in the USA. *Journal of Children and Media, 9,* 5–21.

Demers, L. B., Hanson, K. G., Kirkorian, H. L., Pempek, T. A., & Anderson, D. R. (2013). Infant gaze following during parent-infant coviewing of baby videos. *Child Development, 84,* 591–603. http://dx.doi.org/10.1111/j.1467-8624.2012.01868.x.

Dodici, B. J., Draper, D. C., & Peterson, C. A. (2003). Early parent-child interactions and early literacy development. *Topics in Early Childhood Special Education, 23,* 124–136. http://dx.doi.org/10.1177/02711214030230030301.

Fender, J. G., Richert, R. A., Robb, M. B., & Wartella, E. (2010). Parent teaching focus and toddlers' learning from an infant DVD. *Infant and Child Development, 19,* 613–627. http://dx.doi.org/10.1002/icd.713.

Fiese, B. H. (1990). Playful relationships: A contextual analysis of mother-toddler interaction and symbolic play. *Child Development, 61,* 1648–1656. http://dx.doi.org/10.2307/1130772.

Fisch, S. M. (2004). *Children's learning from educational television: Sesame Street and beyond.* Mahwah, NJ: Lawrence Erlbaum.

Gentile, D. A., Reimer, R. A., Nathanson, A. I., Walsh, D. A., & Eisenmann, J. C. (2014). Protective effects of parental monitoring of children's media use: A prospective study. *JAMA Pediatrics*, *168*, 479–484. http://dx.doi.org/10.1001/jamapediatrics.2014.146.

Ginsburg, K. R. (2007). The importance of play in promoting healthy child development and maintaining strong parent-child bonds. *Pediatrics*, *119*, 182–191. http://dx.doi.org/10.1542/peds.2006-2697.

Golinkoff, R. M., Can, D. D., Soderstrom, M., & Hirsh-Pasek, K. (2015). (Baby) talk to me: The social context of infant-directed speech and its effects on early language acquisition. *Current Directions in Psychological Science*, *24*, 339–344. http://dx.doi.org/10.1177/0963721415595345.

Hart, B., & Risley, T. R. (1992). American parenting of language-learning children: Persisting differences in family-child interactions observed in natural home environments. *Developmental Psychology*, *28*, 1096–1105.

Hart, B., & Risley, T. R. (1995). *Meaningful differences in the everyday experience of young American children*. Baltimore: Paul H. Brookes Publishing Co.

Hart, B., & Risley, T. R. (1999). *The social world of children: Learning to talk*. Baltimore, MD: Paul H. Brookes Publishing Co.

Hoff-Ginsberg, E. (1990). Maternal speech and the child's development of syntax: A further look. *Journal of Child Language*, *17*, 85–99. http://dx.doi.org/10.1017/S0305000900013118.

Kabali, H. K., Irigoyen, M. M., Nunez-Davis, R., Budacki, J. G., Mohanty, S. H., Leister, K. P., et al. (2015). Exposure and use of mobile media devices by young children. *Pediatrics*. http://dx.doi.org/10.1542/peds.2015-2151.

Kirkorian, H. L., Pempek, T. A., Murphy, L. A., Schmidt, M. E., & Anderson, D. R. (2009). The impact of background television on parent-child interaction. *Child Development*, *80*, 1350–1359. http://dx.doi.org/10.1111/cdev.2009.80.issue-510.1111/j.1467-8624.2009.01337.x.

Krcmar, M., & Cingel, D. P. (2014). Parent–child joint reading in traditional and electronic formats. *Media Psychology*, *17*, 262–281. http://dx.doi.org/10.1080/15213269.2013.840243.

Landry, S. H., Smith, K. E., Miller-Loncar, C. L., & Swank, P. R. (1997). Predicting cognitive-language and social growth curves from early maternal behaviors in children and varying degrees of biological risk. *Developmental Psychology*, *33*, 1040–1053. http://dx.doi.org/10.1037/0012-1649.33.6.1040.

Lapierre, M. A., Piotrowski, J. T., & Linebarger, D. L. (2012). Background television in the homes of US children. *Pediatrics*, *130*, 1–8. http://dx.doi.org/10.1542/peds.2011-2581.

Lauricella, A. R., Barr, R., & Calvert, S. (2014). Parent-child interactions during traditional and computer storybook reading predict children's story comprehension. *International Journal of Child-Computer Interaction*. http://dx.doi.org/10.1016/j.ijcci.2014.07.001.

Lavigne, H. J., Hanson, H. G., & Anderson, D. R. (2015). The influence of television coviewing on parent language directed at toddlers. *Journal of Applied Developmental Psychology*, *36*, 1–10. http://dx.doi.org/10.1016/j.appdev.2014.11.004.

Lemish, D., & Rice, M. L. (1986). Television as a talking picture book: A prop for language acquisition. *Journal of Child Language*, *13*, 251–274. http://dx.doi.org/10.1017/S0305000900008047.

Lim, M., Stormshak, E. A., & Dishion, T. J. (2005). A one-session intervention for parents of young adolescents: Videotape modeling and motivational group discussion. *Journal of Emotional and Behavioral Disorders*, *13*, 194–199. http://dx.doi.org/10.1177/10634266050130040101.

Masur, E. F., Flynn, V., & Eichorst, D. L. (2005). Maternal responsive and directive behaviours and utterances as predictors of children's lexical development. *Journal of Child Language*, *32*, 63–91. http://dx.doi.org/10.1017/S0305000904006634.

Masur, E. F., Flynn, V., & Olson, J. (2015). The presence of background television during young children's play in American homes. *Journal of Children and Media, 9*, 349–367. http://dx.doi.org/10.1080/17482798.2015.1056818.

Mendelsohn, A. L., Brockmeyer, C. A., Dreyer, B. P., Fierman, A. H., Berkule-Silberman, S. B., & Tomopoulos, S. (2010). Do verbal interactions with infants during electronic media exposure mitigate adverse impacts on their language development as toddlers? *Infant and Child Development, 19*, 577–593. http://dx.doi.org/10.1002/icd.711.

Nathanson, A. I. (2001). Parent and child perspectives on the presence and meaning of parental television mediation. *Journal of Broadcasting & Electronic Media, 45*, 201–220. http://dx.doi.org/10.1207/s15506878jobem4502_1.

Nathanson, A. I. (2002). The unintended effects of parental mediation of television on adolescents. *Media Psychology, 4*, 207–230. http://dx.doi.org/10.1207/S1532785XMEP0403_01.

Nathanson, A. I. (2013). Media and the family context. In D. Lemish (Ed.), *The Routledge international handbook of children, adolescents, and media* (pp. 299–306). New York: Routledge.

Nathanson, A. I., & Fries, P. T. (2014). Television exposure, sleep time, and neuropsychological function among preschoolers. *Media Psychology, 17*, 237–261. http://dx.doi.org/10.1080/15213269.2014.915197.

Nathanson, A. I., & Rasmussen, E. E. (2011). TV viewing compared to book reading and toy playing reduces responsive maternal communication with toddlers and preschoolers. *Human Communication Research, 37*, 465–487. http://dx.doi.org/10.1111/j.1468-2958.2011.01413.x.

Nathanson, A. I., Sharp, M. L., Aladé, F., Rasmussen, E. E., & Christy, K. (2013). The relation between television exposure and theory of mind among preschoolers. *Journal of Communication, 63*, 1088–1108. http://dx.doi.org/10.1111/jcom.12062.

Parish-Morris, J., Mahajan, N., Hirsh-Pasek, K., Golinkoff, R. M., & Collins, M. F. (2013). Once upon a time: Parent–child dialogue and storybook reading in the electronic era. *Mind, Brain, and Education, 7*, 200–211. http://dx.doi.org/10.1111/mbe.12028.

Pempek, T. A., Demers, L. B., Hanson, K. G., Kirkorian, H. L., & Anderson, D. R. (2011). The impact of infant-directed videos on parent-child interaction. *Journal of Applied Developmental Psychology, 32*, 10–19. http://dx.doi.org/10.1016/j.appdev.2010.10.001.

Pempek, T. A., Kirkorian, H. L., & Anderson, D. R. (2014). The effects of background television on the quantity and quality of child-directed speech by parents. *Journal of Children and Media, 8*, 211–222. http://dx.doi.org/10.1080/17482798.2014.920715.

Radesky, J., Miller, A. L., Rosenblum, K. L., Appugliese, D., Kaciroti, N., & Lumeng, J. C. (2015). Maternal mobile device use during a structured parent-child interaction task. *Academic Pediatrics, 15*, 238–244. http://dx.doi.org/10.1016/j.acap.2014.10.001.

Reed, J., Hirsh-Pasek, K., & Golinkoff, R. M. (2012). In *iPhone, Blackberries, and Androids, oh my: The effects of interruption in parent-child word learning interactions. Poster presented at the international conference on infant studies, Minneapolis, MN*.

Reiser, R. A., Tessmer, M. A., & Phelps, P. C. (1984). Adult-child interaction in children's learning from *Sesame Street*. *Educational Communication & Technology Journal, 32*, 217–223. http://dx.doi.org/10.1007/BF02768893.

Reiser, R. A., Williamson, N., & Suzuki, K. (1988). Using *Sesame Street* to facilitate children's recognition of letters and numbers. *Educational Communication & Technology Journal, 36*, 15–21. http://dx.doi.org/10.1007/BF02770013.

Rideout, V. J. (2013). *Zero to eight: Children's media use in America 2013: A Common Sense Media research study*. Retrieved from http://www.commonsensemedia.org/research/zero-to-eight-childrens-media-use-in-america-2013.

Salomon, G. (1977). Effects of encouraging Israeli mothers to co-observe *Sesame Street* with their five-year-olds. *Child Development, 48*, 1146–1151. http://dx.doi.org/10.2307/1128378.

Schmidt, M. E., Pempek, T. A., Kirkorian, H. L., Lund, A. F., & Anderson, D. R. (2008). The effects of background television on the toy play behaviors of very young children. *Child Development, 79*, 1137–1151. http://dx.doi.org/10.1111/j.1467-8624.2008.01180.x.

Setliff, A. E., & Courage, M. L. (2011). Background television and infants' allocation of their attention during toy play. *Infancy, 16*, 611–639. http://dx.doi.org/10.1111/j.1532-7078.2011.00070.x.

Slade, A. (1987). A longitudinal study of maternal involvement and symbolic play during the toddler period. *Child Development, 58*, 367–375. http://dx.doi.org/10.2307/1130513.

Soderstrom, M., & Wittebolle, K. (2013). When do caregivers talk? The influences of activity and time of day on caregiver speech and child vocalizations in two childcare environments. *PLoS ONE. 8*(11)e80646. http://dx.doi.org/10.1371/journal.pone.0080646.

Stoneman, Z., & Brody, G. H. (1982). An in-home investigation of maternal teaching strategies during *Sesame Street* and a popular situation comedy. *Journal of Applied Developmental Psychology, 3*, 275–284. http://dx.doi.org/10.1016/0193-3973(82)90020-X.

Tamis-LeMonda, C. S., Bornstein, M. H., & Baumwell, L. (2001). Maternal responsiveness and children's achievement of language milestones. *Child Development, 72*, 748–767. http://dx.doi.org/10.1111/1467-8624.00313.

Tomopoulos, S., Dreyer, B. P., Berkule, S., Fierman, A. H., Brockmeyer, C., & Mendelsohn, A. L. (2010). Infant media exposure and toddler development. *Archives of Pediatrics & Adolescent Medicine, 164*, 1105–1111. http://dx.doi.org/10.1001/archpediatrics.2010.235.

Valkenburg, P. M., Krcmar, M., Peeters, A. L., & Marseille, N. M. (1999). Developing a scale to assess three styles of television mediation: "instructive mediation," "restrictive mediation," and "social coviewing". *Journal of Broadcasting & Electronic Media, 43*, 52–66. http://dx.doi.org/10.1080/08838159909364474.

Valkenburg, P. M., Piotrowski, J. T., Hermanns, J., & Leeuw, R. (2013). Developing and validating the perceived parental media mediation scale: A self-determination perspective. *Human Communication Research, 39*, 445–469. http://dx.doi.org/10.1111/hcre.12010.

Vygotsky, L. S. (1978). In M. Cole, V. John-Steiner, S. Scribner, & E. Souberman (Eds.), *Mind in society: The development of higher psychological processes*. Cambridge, MA: Harvard University press.

Warren, R. (2003). Parental mediation of preschool children's television viewing. *Journal of Broadcasting & Electronic Media, 47*, 394–417. http://dx.doi.org/10.1207/s15506878jobem4703_5.

Warren, R., Gerke, P., & Kelly, M. A. (2002). Is there enough time on the clock? Parental involvement and mediation of children's television viewing. *Journal of Broadcasting & Electronic Media, 46*, 87–111. http://dx.doi.org/10.1207/s15506878jobem4601_6.

Wartella, E., Rideout, V., Lauricella, A., & Connell, S. (2013). *Parenting in the age of digital technology: A national survey. Report of the Center on Media and Human Development*. School of Communication, Northwestern University.

Whitehurst, G. J., Falco, F. L., Lonigan, C. J., Fischel, J. E., DeBaryshe, B. D., Valdez-Menchaca, M. C., et al. (1988). Accelerating language development through picture book reading. *Developmental Psychology, 24*, 552–559.

Zimmerman, F. J., Gilkerson, J., Richards, J. A., Christakis, D. A., Xu, D., Gray, S., et al. (2009). Teaching by listening: The importance of adult–child conversations to language development. *Pediatrics, 124*, 342–349. http://dx.doi.org/10.1542/peds.2008-2267.

CHAPTER 4

Plugging Into Word Learning: The Role of Electronic Toys and Digital Media in Language Development

**Rebecca A. Dore*, Jennifer M. Zosh[†], Kathy Hirsh-Pasek[‡,§],
Roberta M. Golinkoff***
[*]University of Delaware, Newark, DE, United States
[†]Pennsylvania State University, Brandywine, PA, United States
[‡]Temple University, Philadelphia, PA, United States
[§]The Brookings Institution, Washington, DC, United States

In the late 1980s and early 1990s, the most technologically advanced toys might be a *Lite Brite* (a light box with colored pegs used to make an illuminated picture) and a 10-button play-a-sound storybook with a panel on the side. When you touched the pictures, various sound effects played. Favorite television shows had to be watched on a big (and we mean big) box in the living room at whatever time they were being aired. Today's reality offers a stark contrast. In 2016, children can play with a *Lite Brite* app on the iPad and read e-books with built-in games, interactive animations, and 3D visuals. Children now watch their favorite shows whenever they want to on DVRs and You-Tube and take these experiences to the car, to the restaurant, to the park, and even to the bathroom on mobile devices. The world of children's toys and media, along with the digital world more broadly, is changing at a rapid clip.

Although children's experiences in this media-saturated world may influence their development across a variety of domains (Wartella et al., 2016), in this chapter we focus on the role of electronic toys and digital media on language development. We outline six principles of language development derived from the Science of Learning (Harris, Golinkoff, & Hirsh-Pasek, 2011) and examine how these principles, in combination with recent research, can shed light on language learning in the age of interactive toys and media. These principles correspond to the section headings below.

Cognitive Development in Digital Contexts
http://dx.doi.org/10.1016/B978-0-12-809481-5.00004-3

CHILDREN LEARN WORDS FOR THINGS AND EVENTS THAT INTEREST THEM

Those of you who are parents will not be surprised by the idea that children learn words for things they are interested in as it is likely that your child's first words were about some of their favorite things, including yourself. Some of the most common early words for children in the US are "Daddy" and "Mommy," and "Hi" and "Bye," reflecting infants' early social interest in their parents and their comings and goings (Tardif et al., 2008). "Kitty," "dog," and "duck" are not far behind. Children learn these words early because they are focused on these topics and motivated to express these ideas.

In our new digital era, children's apparent interest in digital media may be good news, given its potential for supporting language learning. On average, children under the age of 8 spend almost 2 h a day using screen media and between 2011 and 2013, the average amount of time that children spent using mobile devices tripled (Common Sense Media, 2013). More recent data from an urban, low-income community show that these children have almost universal exposure to mobile devices (Kabali et al., 2015). Strikingly, these parents reported that over 90% of children under the age of 1 had already begun to use mobile devices daily and by the age of 4, 75% of children owned their own device (Kabali et al., 2015). Apps and mobile media may be especially appealing to children, perhaps because of their accessibility: most parents at least occasionally allow their child to use their smart mobile device and children often get passed their parents' or other family members' devices to use during travel or while waiting (Chiong & Shuler, 2010). Furthermore, most parents say that they have to make their child stop playing with the iPhone by taking it away rather than children getting bored or choosing another activity (Chiong & Shuler, 2010). The complete integration of mobile devices into our daily lives and those of our children can make it difficult to keep in mind that the use of mobile devices is a relatively new phenomenon—the first iPhone was introduced in 2007. Even the American Academy of Pediatrics may be struggling to keep up with this dizzying pace of change: In the fall of 2015, an announcement from the group signaled that their current media guideline discouraging any screen time for children under the age of 2 would soon be amended, because as they write, "our policies must evolve or become obsolete" (Brown, Shifrin, & Hill, 2015) and in the fall of 2016, the group released a new report that discourages screen time for children under 18 months, rather than age 2, and excludes video chat from this recommendation (AAP Council on Communications and Media, 2016).

The changing landscape of childhood extends beyond the screen and also includes electronic toys. Today's toys are not limited to the plastic cooking sets, cars, blocks, and games of our youth. Instead, they range from a Barbie with artificial intelligence that learns about your child's life and responds contingently to your child, to drones that your child can fly and use to watch video footage of your neighborhood, to electronic building block sets, to robot monkeys that follow children with their eyes, do tricks, and communicate; indeed, we appear to be in the midst of a digital revolution of toys (Hassinger-Das, Zosh, Hirsh-Pasek, & Golinkoff, 2017). While specific information is not available about electronic toys and media versus more traditional toys, related data suggest that electronic toys are quickly coming to dominate the marketplace. By way of example, among the top 20 best-selling items of 2015 in the "Kids' toys and gifts" category on Target's website, 14 were digital (Target.com, Retrieved February 16, 2016). These include a unicorn stuffed animal that "responds to voice and touch with more than 100 sound and motion combinations," an electronic pretend guitar targeted to children as young as 2, and a UNICEF Kid Power Band which is a kid-friendly version of the *FitBit* motion-tracker.

Given children's apparent interest in electronic toys and digital media, the language-learning principle that children learn words related to things that interest them suggests that digital devices could potentially be valuable sources of language learning—but they can only do so if they can use the other five principles, discussed next, to capitalize on this potential.

CHILDREN LEARN THE WORDS THAT THEY HEAR MOST

The second principle reflects the basic idea that children have to hear language to learn language. Although this may seem obvious, it has important implications. For example, children who hear more language should, in turn, learn more language. Indeed, research has shown that children's language skills at age 3 are strongly related to the amount that their parents talked to them in the previous 2 years (Hart & Risley, 1995). Even more important than the *quantity* of language is the *quality* of the language that young children hear: a recent study found that although the number of words children heard predicted language skills a year later, even more predictive was how much parents interacted with children by engaging in rituals (such as book reading), having fluid back and forth conversations, and adding gestures or words to enrich those conversations (Hirsh-Pasek, Adamson, et al., 2015). These findings show that to learn language, children must hear many words but also have high-quality interactions with adults who scaffold their developing language skills.

These effects are also apparent in more specific domains. Children who hear more spatial language from their parents later do better on tests of spatial cognition (Pruden, Levine, & Huttenlocher, 2011). Similarly, the more parents talk to their toddlers about number, the better children understand the meaning of number words—especially numbers above three—in preschool (Levine, Ratliff, Huttenlocher, & Cannon, 2012). Given the focus on the STEM field (Science, Technology, Engineering, and Math) in the education system and broader economy, it is increasingly important to consider how children's early experiences can impact their future success in these areas (Office of the Press Secretary, 2010).

Recent research has expanded on these ideas by assessing the effect of digital toys and screen media on the quantity and quality of language interactions between children and their parents. For example, in a recent study our lab group gave young children and their parents either a traditional shape sorter toy or an electronic shape sorter toy to play with and video recorded their interactions. The results showed that although parents said approximately the same number of words to their children regardless of which toy they were playing with, parents who were playing with the traditional toy used more varied language, and said more spatial words, compared to parents who were playing with the electronic toy (Zosh et al., 2015). When parents were playing with the electronic toy, they talked more about the non-shape-related functions of the toy, like telling children to push a particular button and less about spatial concepts when compared to parent-child dyads playing with the traditional toy. These findings suggest that traditional toys may promote more high-quality language, as well as more on-topic talk from parents compared to electronic toys. Given what we know about the link between these kinds of language quality indicators, including the importance of high-quality spatial language specifically, it seems that replacing traditional toys with their electronic counterparts may come at a cost to children's developing language skills by degrading the quality of parent-child interactions.

But this issue is not restricted to spatial toys and spatial language. Studies have found similar effects with other types of toys like books and animal figures, showing that mothers are less responsive and teach less when using electronic versions of these toys with their infants than when using traditional versions (Wooldridge & Shapka, 2012) and that parents focus less on relevant content and engage in fewer back-and-forth conversational turns with children when using electronic as compared to traditional toys (Sosa, 2015).

Furthermore, playing with toys is not the only victim of the electronic era. Traditional books are now in competition with digital e-books, which have expanded over the years from electronic console books like the child-friendly *LeapFrog* to apps that present storybooks on smartphones or tablets. As these technologies have emerged, research has followed to examine how parent-child interaction might be affected by reading an e-book as compared to a traditional book. For example, one study in our lab had preschoolers and their parents read either a traditional book or an e-book together. Compared to parents reading traditional books, parents reading e-books talked less about the story and used fewer distancing prompts relating the content of the book to aspects of children's lives outside the book (Parish-Morris, Mahajan, Hirsh-Pasek, Golinkoff, & Collins, 2013). All children learned superficial information from both e-books and traditional books, and 4- and 5-year-olds also answered more difficult questions from both types of books. But 3-year-olds who were read the e-book did worse than those who were read the traditional book on the more difficult tasks assessing their understanding of the deeper story structure and details, suggesting that the youngest children may need the type of parental support that is related to traditional book reading. Other research continues to find differences in how parents and children interact around traditional books and e-books, although some studies find similar levels of comprehension between the two types of media (Lauricella, Barr, & Calvert, 2014) and others suggest that e-books can have positive effects, such as more child-initiated discourse and greater responsiveness to maternal talk (Korat & Or, 2010). Clearly, more research is needed in this area to determine what features of e-books might best promote positive parent-child interaction and children's learning.

Another line of research shows that children do not have to be actively engaging with electronic or screen media for it to affect the potential for their language learning; even having a television on in the background while parents play with their children can affect the type of language input children receive. Researchers compared parent-child interaction while an adult-directed television program was on in the background to parent-child interaction without background television. The results showed that parents were less verbally interactive with their children and less responsive to their children's bids for attention when the television was on in the background (Kirkorian, Pempek, Murphy, Schmidt, & Anderson, 2009). Furthermore, when parents did interact with children in the presence of background television, those interactions were more likely to be passive rather than active. That is, they were more likely to, for example, take a toy offered by the child without speaking and less likely to have reciprocal exchanges, e.g., engaging in a conversation.

Overall, the research in this area suggests that electronic toys, e-books, and even background television and mobile device use can lead to lower quality parent–child interactions, which may have negative effects on children's later language development. However, electronic books, toys, and media are not necessarily always worse than their traditional counterparts. Furthermore, caregivers are not always present and available for high-quality interactions, and in those cases, the digital technology offers information not available from adult playmates. Thus, it is important for research to determine which features of digital technology may promote learning and which may detract from learning.

INTERACTIVE AND RESPONSIVE RATHER THAN PASSIVE CONTEXTS FAVOR VOCABULARY LEARNING

Studies from the Science of Learning suggest that children learn best in contexts that are active, not passive (Chi, 2009; Hirsh-Pasek, Zosh, et al., 2015). One key to promoting active learning is through joint attention, turn-taking, and contingent responses to children's communicative bids. Even very young children are sensitive to the back-and-forth nature of social interactions that promote active engagement. One study found that when parents were instructed to listen while their infant vocalized and then immediately vocalize in return, their infants produced more syllabic, or speech-like, vocalizations than those whose parents were instructed to vocalize at random times (Bloom, Russell, & Wassenberg, 1987; Goldstein, King, & West, 2003; Goldstein & Schwade, 2008). Given this early sensitivity, it is unsurprising that when adults take turns in interactions and share periods of joint attention with their children, they provide the scaffolding needed to help promote children's language learning (Bradley et al., 1989; Clarke-Stewart, 1973; Tomasello & Farrar, 1986).

The implications of this principle for children's language learning from digital media are profound: If children learn words better from interactions involving turn-taking and joint attention, traditional screen media does not seem like an optimal learning environment. Indeed, a large body of research has provided evidence for a "video deficit effect" in which children under 2.5 or 3 years of age cannot learn from a video as well as they learn from a live person (Anderson & Pempek, 2005). Similarly, research has tested infants' and toddlers' learning from commercially produced educational videos and found that they are ineffective in teaching new vocabulary (DeLoache et al., 2010; Richert, Robb, Fender, & Wartella, 2010).

Traditionally, the video technology available to young children often contained language samples that were not contingent. The "speaker" would follow a script and could not respond meaningfully or temporally to the language used by the child. At best, a "gap" might be inserted so that children could respond to a scripted question, as in *Blues Clues*. However, modern technology has progressed such that video chat software like Skype now allows live social interactions to take place through a screen. And indeed, when contingency is added back to video, it appears that this video deficit is eliminated. A study in our lab group presented toddlers with new words in one of three conditions: live interaction, socially contingent video over Skype, or non-contingent video over Skype (i.e., observed another child's Skype interaction with the trainer). Results indicated that children learned the words just as well from the contingent Skype chat as they did from the live interaction, whereas they did worse after seeing a non-contingent video (Roseberry, Hirsh-Pasek, & Golinkoff, 2014). These findings suggest that although traditional screen media is not as facilitative of language learning as interacting live, the problem is not the screen, but rather the lack of social interaction.

Another way that digital media may affect language learning is by influencing parents' responsiveness during interactions with their children. Survey data show that 32% of parents report sometimes or often using mobile devices themselves while playing with their children (Common Sense Media, 2013). Radesky and colleagues (2014) completed a recent naturalistic observation study of 55 families in a fast-food restaurant, and found that 40 of them (72%) used mobile devices during the meal, ranging from the devices being on the table, to the parents being completely absorbed with the device. The authors also analyzed the interactions between parents and children and noted, "we did find it striking that during caregiver absorption with devices, some children appeared to accept the lack of engagement and entertained themselves, whereas others showed increasing bids for attention that were often answered with negative parent responses" (p. 6). It is clear that these devices are as intrusive, if not more intrusive than background television and have the potential to change the nature of crucial parent–child interaction in negative ways.

Given the extent to which mobile devices are integrated into parents' daily lives, it is important to examine how these devices may be affecting their interactions with children and children's language development specifically. In a recent study from our lab group to address these issues, parents of

2-year-olds were asked to teach their children two novel words with one of the two teaching periods interrupted by a brief cell phone call. Children learned the word when the teaching was not interrupted, but did not learn the word when the session was interrupted by the phone call (Reed, Hirsh-Pasek, & Golinkoff, 2015). These results suggest that the disruption of parents' contingent responsiveness led to children's difficulty in learning. If this study reflects what is occurring in children's everyday lives, it seems that parents' use of mobile devices may have important negative consequences for interactions with their children, and subsequently for children's language learning.

Overall, the research on contingency and responsiveness in language learning suggests that children learn language best from partners who are responsive to them, whether that is in a live interaction or mediated through a screen; they do not learn as well from less responsive adults, such as prerecorded actors on video or adults who are distracted from interactions by mobile devices. It is important to note, however, that electronic media is quickly changing with apps and devices becoming increasingly responsive and contingent to children's taps, clicks, and vocalizations (even without a human on the other end). Given this rapidly changing profile of electronic devices and digital media, it will be crucial to investigate learning from more advanced digital media that harnesses the power of contingency in ways that more closely mimic human-to-human interaction.

CHILDREN LEARN WORDS BEST IN MEANINGFUL CONTEXTS

Adding meaning to facilitate memory is one of the oldest mnemonic tricks in the book. Think about how hard it is to remember a PIN number that the bank gives you compared to remembering the one you created. It is likely easier to remember the number you created because it had meaning for you (e.g., using your child's birthday, your anniversary, or your first address). Indeed, studies have shown that when adults are given a list of words to memorize in order, participants who are told to construct a story around the words remember the lists better later, presumably because the words acquire meaning (Bower & Clark, 1969). Language learning works in a similar way; children learn words better when they are put in a meaningful context, rather than being presented as random, disconnected facts to memorize.

Embedding new vocabulary in storybooks is effective in promoting word learning because a narrative can provide a meaningful context for new words. However, young children sometimes need additional support in translating the narrative's meaning to their real lives. Parents can support this kind of meaning-making by asking questions and providing the necessary scaffolding for children to understand a story and, in turn, learn new words. Research shows that having parents read with their children using these kinds of techniques, called dialogic reading, can help children learn the specific vocabulary words in a book and improve their performance on general measures of expressive language (Hargrave & Sénéchal, 2000; Whitehurst et al., 1988).

More recent research has shown that the same is true of children's learning from digital media. For example, when parents who watched a video with their child made connections between objects in the video and their real-life counterparts, children were more likely to demonstrate transfer of the new words from the video to reality (Strouse & Troseth, 2014). In another study, researchers trained parents to use dialogic questioning techniques during educational television viewing and found that children of these parents learned more vocabulary from a video than children whose parents did not receive the training (Strouse, O'Doherty, & Troseth, 2013). Another group of children saw a video that included an actress engaging in dialogic questioning; children also learned from this method but not as much as when their parent used the dialogic techniques.

These findings suggest that electronic media can use the principle of meaning-making to promote language learning. One way to do so is to provide meaningful information within the app itself. Imagine an app designed to teach shapes that present a traditional, equilateral, brightly colored shape on a colored background while children hear the word "triangle" and the image floats peacefully around the screen. Contrast that with another app that may begin by showing a child an image of an equilateral triangle, but then presents the child other examples of isosceles and obtuse triangles, with children asked to discover the "secret" of the triangle shape. Then, children are tasked with finding as many triangles of all shapes and sizes in real-world pictures of kitchens, playgrounds, and family rooms. In the former example, more basic, rote learning may occur but when we—either adults or a well-designed app—help them to find meaning as in the later example, deeper learning will likely occur. Indeed, in a completely non-electronic study of shape learning, our lab discovered that children learn best when adults scaffold children to discover new knowledge (as in the latter case) rather than by explicitly telling them or not providing any guidance at all (Fisher, Hirsh-Pasek, Newcombe, & Golinkoff, 2013). Lessons learned in nontraditional formats can and should be applied to digital learning across domains.[1]

More recently, companies have begun to produce toys that blend on-screen and off-screen experiences that help children to draw connections between content on the screen or in an app and what it happening in the real world. In Alien Assignment, an app produced by Fred Rogers, children are given a mission to help a newly landed alien (on the screen) make sense of the real world around them (off the screen). Children go on missions to take pictures of items that match certain qualities (e.g., is a certain shape or has a certain function) and parents provide feedback and presumably discuss the answers with the child. The Words app, by *Osmo*, presents children with an on-screen challenge, such as spelling a word or finding a missing letter, but the app allows children to play with real-life manipulable letter tiles that the tablet can recognize. The app then provides a contingent response to the actual 3D tiles in front of the child. As technology becomes more advanced, it will be important that developers, educators, and researchers promote activities that use language in a meaningful context—whether those activities happen on the screen, off the screen, or in a hybrid on-and-off-the-screen format.

Overall, this principle suggests that digital media may be useful in language development to the extent that it can be made meaningful and connected to children's lives. Parents and teachers are the best source of these connections but there may also be ways that we can adapt media content and/or promote high-quality interactions to help children make meaning from these sources.

CHILDREN NEED CLEAR INFORMATION ABOUT WORD MEANING

The old adage that children are like sponges likely rings true if you have ever heard a child repeat a word that they have only heard once or twice. Indeed, this kind of "fast mapping" is an important feature of early word learning (Carey & Bartlett, 1978). However, the construction of a deeper

---

[1] See Hirsh-Pasek, Zosh, et al. (2015) for an example of taking the lessons from the Science of Learning and applying them to the specific case of educational apps.

understanding of word meaning requires more explicit definitional information (Hadley, Dickinson, Hirsh-Pasek, Golinkoff, & Nesbitt, 2016). For example, one observational study found that although the proportion of sophisticated words mothers used with their children predicted later language outcomes, how often those words were embedded in helpful or instructive interactions was also related to later vocabulary (Weizman & Snow, 2001). This suggests that hearing more information about these sophisticated words helped children construct a more complete understanding of word meanings. Similarly, other research has found that including explanations of words in book reading increases children's learning substantially, especially for children with weaker language skills (Biemiller & Boothe, 2006; Penno, Wilkinson, & Moore, 2002).

In the domain of digital media, this principle relates to a series of findings in children's vocabulary learning from e-books. As discussed above, research is mixed as to the effectiveness of e-books overall in story comprehension and vocabulary. However, the findings in this literature do suggest an important dichotomy in the types of e-book features that are supportive of and detrimental to language learning (Bus, Takacs, & Kegel, 2015; Takacs, Swart, & Bus, 2015). Specifically, some multimedia features like animated pictures, music, and sound effects seem to be beneficial for word learning, likely because these features can point to a word's meaning or support definitional information in the text. For example, an animation of someone fanning a fire would likely lead to a more complete understanding of the meaning of the word "fanning" than a still image would because the back and forth motion would be visible in the animation, whereas motion is more difficult to depict in a still image. On the other hand, not all features that e-books afford are beneficial for word learning: interactive features like games and hotspots that can be touched to activate a sound or animation seem to disrupt word learning, likely because they are often not focused on central aspects of the text and distract children from more relevant information (Parish-Morris et al., 2013).

This principle highlights both the promise and the danger of modern technology in children's language learning. To the extent that creators and users of digital media capitalize on technology's increasing abilities to support children's learning by providing additional information about word meaning, these sources may provide an overall advantage for language development. As devices become more and more diagnostic and adaptive to each individual child, the potential for them to meet children where they are is unparalleled. Indeed, this approach is already beginning to revolutionize the college classroom through modern technologies like adaptive learning software (Oremus, 2015). This technology uses students' responses and can pinpoint exactly what issues are well understood by the student and which are not—and the software will individually tailor what comes next based on an individual student's performance. However, it is crucial for app and toy developers to keep in mind that more does not always equal better. When technological features are included in children's media for their own sake and are tangentially related to the to-be-learned information, digital media may prove ineffective compared to more traditional sources of vocabulary information.

VOCABULARY LEARNING AND GRAMMATICAL DEVELOPMENT ARE RECIPROCAL PROCESSES

In thinking about language development, we often jump straight to vocabulary, but it is important to not leave grammar and syntax out of the equation. Research shows that vocabulary and grammar develop together across childhood (Bates & Goodman, 2001; Gillette, Gleitman, Gleitman, & Lederer, 1999). In other words, children need to know some vocabulary to learn grammar and can use cues from grammar and syntax to support word learning. For example, studies have shown that by paying attention to the linguistic context of a new word, children can better induce that word's part of speech (Imai et al., 2008).

However, despite the importance of grammar in language development generally, the existing evidence suggests that digital media may encourage a focus on vocabulary without much consideration of grammar. A recent analysis from the Joan Cooney Center culled a list of top educational apps for children and examined the most common language and literacy skills the apps claimed to target. Grammar was not even in the top eight most common skills targeted by these apps; specifically, it was represented in less than 7% of the apps identified (Vaala, Ly, & Levine, 2015).

This principle suggests that grammar's important supporting role in children's language development should not be lost in the age of digital and screen media. Vocabulary learning is certainly vital and may be easier than grammar to present in electronic and interactive formats, but words taught in isolation will likely not be learned as effectively as words presented in richer linguistic contexts. Apps and other media sources that reflect the importance of grammar will likely best support language development in general.

CONCLUSIONS

We are in the midst of a digital revolution. But it is crucial to remember that electronic toys and digital media are neither savior nor Satan for children's language development. Rather, today's technology has opened up a wide range of new features and possibilities for children's play and media, and each of these affordances must be considered in the context of what research shows us about how children learn language. Certainly, the existing research has shown some ways that these digital media can have negative effects on children's ability to learn, but if used in a thoughtful and responsible way, these sources may be able to be used to have a positive impact on language development. Indeed, given the availability of these devices in homes varying in SES, and the low cost of apps, harnessing the power of the digital revolution presents a potential intervention that could bring high-quality experiences to millions of families.

Digital media can take us to new horizons in learning more generally. For example, a digital diagram with moving parts can help us understand the cause and effect in science and the ability to zoom-in on Google Earth allows us to see what life looks like across the world. In these cases, the digital format offers real advantages over the static book or even the moving color of television. Our challenge now is to identify how we can use digital media in new and innovative ways to promote learning. In the early years of the digital revolution, creators of children's digital media and electronic toys have spent too much time transferring our traditional options into digital formats—creating apps from books and adding sound effects and flashing lights to shape sorters. In the second wave of the revolution, we need to instead focus on optimizing the affordances of these novel platforms so that we can fully realize their potential. It is important for future research to continue to study how language learning occurs within the context of today's increasingly digital and connected world. Although we can make educated guesses about the utility or danger of new innovations, researchers will need to investigate how children's interactions with toys and media might change as technology blurs the lines between live and mediated interactions and between real and digital objects. Only by studying the effects of the changing world can we hope to shed light on how to use the substantial resources at our fingertips to best promote healthy development in language and beyond.

ACKNOWLEDGMENTS

This research was supported by Institute of Education Sciences Grant R305A150435 to KHP and RMG and Institute of Education Sciences Grant R305A110284 to KHP and RMG, as well as an IES postdoctoral training grant supporting fellow RAD.

REFERENCES

AAP Council on Communications and Media (2016). Media and young minds. *Pediatrics*, *138*(5), e2016591. http://dx.doi.org/10.1542/peds.2016-2591.

Anderson, D. R., & Pempek, T. A. (2005). Television and very young children. *The American Behavioral Scientist*, *48*, 505–522.

Bates, E., & Goodman, J. C. (2001). On the inseparability of grammar and the lexicon: Evidence from acquisition. In M. Tomasello & E. Bates (Eds.), *Language Development: The Essential Readings* (pp. 134–162). Malden: Blackwell Publishing.

Biemiller, A., & Boothe, C. (2006). An effective method for building meaning vocabulary in primary grades. *Journal of Educational Psychology*, *98*, 44–62.

Bloom, K., Russell, A., & Wassenberg, K. (1987). Turn taking affects the quality of infant vocalizations. *Journal of Child Language*, *14*, 211–227.

Bower, G. H., & Clark, M. C. (1969). Narrative stories as mediators for serial learning. *Psychonomic Science*, *14*, 181–182.

Bradley, R. H., Caldwell, B. M., Rock, S. L., Ramey, C. T., Barnard, K. E., Gray, C., et al. (1989). Home environment and cognitive development in the first 3 years: A collaborative study involving six sites and three ethnic groups in North America. *Developmental Psychology*, *25*, 217–235.

Brown, A., Shifrin, D. L., & Hill, D. L. (2015). Beyond 'turn it off': How to advise families on media use. *AAP News*, *36*(10), 54. http://dx.doi.org/10.1542/aapnews.20153610-54.

Bus, A. G., Takacs, Z. K., & Kegel, C. A. T. (2015). Affordances and limitations of electronic storybooks for young children's emergent literacy. *Developmental Review*, *35*, 79–97.

Carey, S., & Bartlett, E. (1978). Acquiring a single new word. *Papers and Reports on Child Language Development*, *15*, 17–29.

Chi, M. T. H. (2009). Active-constructive-interactive: A conceptual framework for differentiating learning activities. *Topics in Cognitive Science*, *1*, 73–105. http://dx.doi.org/10.1111/j.1756-8765.2008.01005.

Chiong, C., & Shuler, C. (2010). *Learning: Is there an app for that? Investigations of young children's usage and learning with mobile devices and apps*. New York: The Joan Ganz Cooney Center at Sesame Workshop.

Clarke-Stewart, K. A. (1973). Interactions between mothers and their young children: Characteristics and consequences. *Monographs of the Society for Research in Child Development*, *35* (6–7), 1–109.

Common Sense Media (2013). *Zero to eight: Children's media use in America*. Retrieved from the Common Sense Media website: http://www.commonsensemedia.org/research/zero-to-eight-childrens-media-use-in-america-2013.

DeLoache, J. S., Chiong, C., Sherman, K., Islam, N., Vanderborght, M., Troseth, G. L., et al. (2010). Do babies learn from baby media? *Psychological Science*, *21*(11), 1570–1574. http://dx.doi.org/10.1177/0956797610384145.

Fisher, K. R., Hirsh-Pasek, K., Newcombe, N., & Golinkoff, R. M. (2013). Taking shape: Supporting preschoolers' acquisition of geometric knowledge through guided play. *Child Development*, *84*, 1872–1878.

Gillette, J., Gleitman, H., Gleitman, L., & Lederer, A. (1999). Human simulations of vocabulary learning. *Cognition*, *73*, 135–176.

Goldstein, M. H., King, A. P., & West, M. J. (2003). Social interaction shapes babbling: Testing parallels between birdsong and speech. *Proceedings of the National Academy of Sciences*, *100*(13), 8030–8035.

Goldstein, M. H., & Schwade, J. A. (2008). Social feedback to infants' babbling facilitates rapid phonological learning. *Psychological Science*, *19*(5), 515–523.

Hadley, E. B., Dickinson, D. K., Hirsh-Pasek, K., Golinkoff, R. M., & Nesbitt, K. T. (2016). Examining the acquisition of vocabulary knowledge depth among preschool students. *Reading Research Quarterly*, *51*(2), 181–198. http://dx.doi.org/10.1002/rrq.130.

Hargrave, A. C., & Sénéchal, M. (2000). A book reading intervention with preschool children who have limited vocabularies: The benefits of regular reading and dialogic reading. *Early Childhood Research Quarterly*, *15*(1), 75–90. http://dx.doi.org/10.1016/S0885-2006(99)00038-1.

Harris, J., Golinkoff, R. M., & Hirsh-Pasek, K. (2011). Lessons from the crib for the classroom: How children really learn vocabulary. In S. B. Neuman & D. K. Dickinson (Eds.), *Handbook of early literacy research* (pp. 49–66). New York: Guilford Press.

Hart, B., & Risley, T. R. (1995). *Meaningful differences in the everyday experience of young American children*. Baltimore, MD: Paul H. Brookes.

Hassinger-Das, B., Zosh, J. M., Hirsh-Pasek, K., & Golinkoff, R. (2017). Toys. In K. Peppler (Ed.), *Sage encyclopedia of out-of-school learning* (pp. 781–783). Thousand Oaks, CA: Sage. http://dx.doi.org/10.4135/9781483385198.n297.

Hirsh-Pasek, K., Adamson, L. B., Bakeman, R., Owen, M. T., Golinkoff, R. M., Pace, A., et al. (2015). The contribution of early communication quality to low-income children's language success. *Psychological Science*, *26*(7), 1071–1083. http://dx.doi.org/10.1177/0956797615581493.

Hirsh-Pasek, K., Zosh, J. M., Golinkoff, R. M., Gray, J. H., Robb, M. B., & Kaufman, J. (2015). Putting Education in "Educational" Apps: Lessons From the Science of Learning. *Psychological Science in the Public Interest*, *16*(1), 3–34. http://dx.doi.org/10.1177/1529100615569721.

Imai, M., Li, L., Haryu, E., Okada, H., Hirsh-Pasek, K., Golinkoff, R. M., et al. (2008). Novel noun and verb learning in Chinese-, English-, and Japanese-speaking children. *Child Development*, *79*(4), 979–1000. http://dx.doi.org/10.1111/j.1467-8624.2008.01171.x.

Kabali, H. K., Irigoyen, M. M., Nunez-Davis, R., Budacki, J. G., Mohanty, S. H., Leister, K. P., et al. (2015). Exposure and use of mobile media devices by young children. *Pediatrics*, *136*(6), 1044–1050. http://dx.doi.org/10.1542/peds.2015-2151.

Kirkorian, H. L., Pempek, T. A., Murphy, L. A., Schmidt, M. E., & Anderson, D. R. (2009). The impact of background television on parent-child interaction. *Child Development*, *80*(5), 1350–1359. http://dx.doi.org/10.1111/j.1467-8624.2009.01337.x.

Korat, O., & Or, T. (2010). How new technology influences parent-child interaction: The case of e-book reading. *First Language*, *30*(2), 139–154. http://dx.doi.org/10.1177/0142723709359242.

Lauricella, A. R., Barr, R., & Calvert, S. L. (2014). Parent-child interactions during traditional and computer storybook reading for children's comprehension: Implications for electronic storybook design. *International Journal of Child-Computer Interaction*, *2*(1), 17–25. http://dx.doi.org/10.1016/j.ijcci.2014.07.001.

Levine, S. C., Ratliff, K. R., Huttenlocher, J., & Cannon, J. (2012). Early puzzle play: A predictor of preschoolers' spatial transformation skill. *Developmental Psychology*, *48*(2), 530–542. http://dx.doi.org/10.1037/a0025913.

Office of the Press Secretary (2010). *President Obama to announce major expansion of "Educate to Innovate" campaign to improve science, technology, enginnering an math (STEM) Education.* Retrieved from https://obamawhitehouse.archives.gov/the-press-office/2010/09/16/president-obama-announce-major-expansion-educate-innovate-campaign-impro.

Oremus, W. (2015). *No more pencils, no more books. In Slate Magazine.* Retrieved from http://www.slate.com/articles/technology/technology/2015/10/adaptive_learning_software_is_replacing_textbooks_and_upending_american.html.

Parish-Morris, J., Mahajan, N., Hirsh-Pasek, K., Golinkoff, R. M., & Collins, M. F. (2013). Once upon a time: Parent-child dialogue and storybook reading in the electronic era. *Mind, Brain, and Education, 7*(3), 200–211. http://dx.doi.org/10.1111/mbe.12028.

Penno, J. F., Wilkinson, I. A., & Moore, D. W. (2002). Vocabulary acquisition from teacher explanation and repeated listening to stories: Do they overcome the Matthew effect? *Journal of Educational Psychology, 94*(1), 23–33. http://dx.doi.org/10.1037/0022-0663.94.1.23.

Pruden, S. M., Levine, S. C., & Huttenlocher, J. (2011). Children's spatial thinking: Does talk about the spatial world matter? *Developmental Science, 14*(6), 1417–1430. http://dx.doi.org/10.1111/j.1467-7687.2011.01088.x.

Radesky, J. S., Kistin, C. J., Zuckerman, B., Nitzberg, K., Gross, J., & Kaplan-Sanoff, M., et al. (2014). Patterns of mobile device use by caregivers and children during meals in fast food restaurants. *Pediatrics, 133*(4), e843–e849. http://dx.doi.org/10.1542/peds.2013-3703.

Reed, J., Hirsh-Pasek, K., & Golinkoff, R. M. (2015). *Learning on hold: Cell phones sidetrack parent-child interactions.* Unpublished manuscript.

Richert, R. A., Robb, M. B., Fender, J. G., & Wartella, E. (2010). Word learning from baby videos. *Archives of Pediatrics & Adolescent Medicine, 164*(5), 432–437. http://dx.doi.org/10.1001/archpediatrics.2010.24.

Roseberry, S., Hirsh-Pasek, K., & Golinkoff, R. M. (2014). Skype me! Socially contingent interactions help toddlers learn language. *Child Development, 85*(3), 956–970. http://dx.doi.org/10.1111/cdev.12166.

Sosa, A. V. (2015). Association of the type of toy used during play with the quantity and quality of parent-infant communication. *JAMA Pediatrics, 170*(2), 132–137. http://dx.doi.org/10.1001/jamapediatrics.2015.3753.

Strouse, G. A., O'Doherty, K., & Troseth, G. L. (2013). Effective coviewing: Preschoolers' learning from video after a dialogic questioning intervention. *Developmental Psychology, 49*(12), 2368–2382. http://dx.doi.org/10.1037/a0032463.

Strouse, G. A., & Troseth, G. L. (2014). Supporting toddlers' transfer of word learning from video. *Cognitive Development, 30*(1), 47–64. http://dx.doi.org/10.1016/j.cogdev.2014.01.002.

Takacs, Z. K., Swart, E. K., & Bus, A. G. (2015). Benefits and pitfalls of multimedia and interactive features in technology-enhanced storybooks: A meta-analysis. *Review of Educational Research, 85*(4), 698–739. http://dx.doi.org/10.3102/0034654314566989.

Tardif, T., Fletcher, P., Liang, W., Zhang, Z., Kaciroti, N., & Marchman, V. A. (2008). Baby's first 10 words. *Developmental Psychology, 44*(4), 929–938. http://dx.doi.org/10.1037/0012-1649.44.4.929.

Tomasello, M., & Farrar, J. (1986). Joint attention and early language. *Child Development, 57*(6), 1454–1463.

Vaala, S., Ly, A., & Levine, M. H. (2015). *Getting a read on the app stores: A market scan and analysis of children's literacy apps.* Downloaded from: http://www.joanganzcooneycenter.org/publication/getting-a-read-on-the-app-stores-a-market-scan-and-analysis-of-childrens-literacy-apps/.

Wartella, E., Beaudoin-Ryan, L., Blackwell, C. K., Cingel, D. P., Hurwitz, L. B., & Lauricella, A. R. (2016). What kind of adults will our children become? The impact of growing up in a media-saturated world. *Journal of Children and Media, 10*(1), 13–20. http://dx.doi.org/10.1080/17482798.2015.1124796.

Weizman, Z. O., & Snow, C. E. (2001). Lexical input as related to children's vocabulary acquisition: Effects of sophisticated exposure and support for meaning. *Developmental Psychology, 37*(2), 265–279. http://dx.doi.org/10.1037/0012-1649.37.2.265.

Whitehurst, G. J., Falco, F. L., Lonigan, C. J., Fischel, J. E., DeBaryshe, B. D., Valdez-Menchaca, M. C., et al. (1988). Accelerating language development through picture book reading. *Developmental Psychology*, *24*(4), 552–559. http://dx.doi.org/10.1037/0012-1649.24.4.552.

Wooldridge, M. B., & Shapka, J. (2012). Playing with technology: Mother-toddler interaction scores lower during play with electronic toys. *Journal of Applied Developmental Psychology*, *33*(5), 211–218. http://dx.doi.org/10.1016/j.appdev.2012.05.005.

Zosh, J. M., Verdine, B. N., Filipowicz, A., Golinkoff, R. M., Hirsh-Pasek, K., & Newcombe, N. S. (2015). Talking shape: Parental language with electronic versus traditional shape sorters. *Mind, Brain, and Education*, *9*(3), 136–144. http://dx.doi.org/10.1111/mbe.12082.

CHAPTER 5

Parasocial Relationships With Media Characters: Imaginary Companions for Young Children's Social and Cognitive Development

Sandra L. Calvert
Georgetown University, Washington, DC, United States

Early childhood is a time when imagination develops (Singer & Singer, 2005), as do first friendships (Hartup, 1989). When these two processes meet in the information age, parasocial relationships, which are emotionally tinged one-way relationships with media personae, including media characters (Bond & Calvert, 2014a; Horton & Wohl, 1956), can emerge. Put another way, children's close relationships with media characters are in essence their imaginary friends, which are not real, but are treated by children as such (Gleason, 2013). This bending of reality can serve children's social and cognitive development (Richert, Robb, & Smith, 2011).

In this chapter, I explore early parasocial relationships that children develop with media characters in a world that increasingly blurs the line between what is real and what is pretend, particularly when interactive media provide contingent replies to children's behaviors (Brunick, Putnam, Richards, McGarry, & Calvert, 2016). Just as young children's real relationships with people provide a basis for social and cognitive advancements, so too can parasocial relationships provide a network of symbolic experiences that can be beneficial for their development (Calvert, 2015; Calvert & Richards, 2014).

WHAT ARE PARASOCIAL RELATIONSHIPS?

Early social skills unfold in close emotional relationships; they initially emerge in vertical relationships, such as from parent to child, and are later refined in horizontal relationships with peers (Hartup, 1989). It is in these

Cognitive Development in Digital Contexts
http://dx.doi.org/10.1016/B978-0-12-809481-5.00005-5

horizontal relationships that early friendships with peers first develop in about their third year of life (Hartup, 1989). These early friendships often involve play with someone who is located in physical proximity, and can be trusted to be available for support when needed (Furman & Rose, 2015).

Children do not limit their social relationships to real people. Pretend friends, for instance, are common among young children (Singer & Singer, 2005). Pretense provides a forum for learning about others—about their thoughts, feelings, likes, and dislikes (Singer & Singer, 2005). Children talk to and anthropomorphize their imaginary friends, including those who come from their media experiences (Calvert & Richards, 2014).

Why do young children often treat these imaginary characters as if they are real? Better yet, why wouldn't they? Media characters stand on two legs, whether they are a person, an animal, or an object (Calvert & Richards, 2014). They do what children do: they have birthday parties, jump in puddles, eat breakfast, and play with their friends (Calvert & Richards, 2014). By treating the characters "as if" they are real, children suspend reality, such as it is in early childhood, entering into an imaginary world where animals can talk, trains can smile to express their feelings, and robots can fly. This animistic approach to reality is both engaging, as well as potentially informative, to young children (Calvert & Richards, 2014). This approach is also found among adolescents who suspend reality and act "as if" the characters that they see in media are actually real (Giles & Maltby, 2004).

Many of the characters in children's programs talk to their young audiences using parasocial interaction techniques. For instance, characters often ask children to help them solve problems in simulated conversations, thereby prompting interactive exchanges with their audiences. A prototypical example is as follows: the character raises a query, pauses for a reply, and then acts as if they have heard what the child said (Lauricella, Gola, & Calvert, 2011). Indeed, many children do reply to the characters, acting as if the characters can hear what they are saying (Anderson et al., 2000; Calvert, Strong, Jacobs, & Conger, 2007; Calvert et al., 2016). These kinds of conversations are a facet of interactivity (Rafaeli, 1988), and they are linked to better story comprehension and problem solving skills (Calvert et al., 2007).

MEASURING EARLY PARASOCIAL RELATIONSHIPS AND PARASOCIAL INTERACTIONS

What exactly is a parasocial relationship for a young child? To answer this question, Bond and Calvert (2014a) began with the premise, as other scholars have (e.g., Wilson & Drogos, 2007), that favorite characters would be most likely to enjoy the status of an emotionally close relationship with children. Therefore, we had parents answer an online survey that initially asked them to identify who they thought their child's favorite media character was, followed by numerous questions about their child's favorite media character.

Using factor analysis of parent reports, we identified three distinct categories that comprised children's parasocial relationships: character personification (treating a character as if they were a person), attachment (feeling close to and using the character for contact comfort, e.g., holding a soft plush toy of their favorite character when upset), and social realism (e.g., believing the character was real or pretend) (see Fig. 1). Table 1 presents the questions that emerged in the factor analysis of the parent assessment of their children's parasocial relationships with a favorite media character (Bond & Calvert, 2014a).

In a subsequent study, we collected parent data about a character that their 24- and 32-month-old child knew, Elmo the Muppet from *Sesame Street*, even though he may not have been their child's favorite character (Richards & Calvert, 2015). Results indicated that the internal consistency (Cronbach's alpha) for the three parent subscales of children's parasocial relationship with Elmo was good to excellent for the character personification and attachment subscales in three related experiments, and they were acceptable or good for social realism in two of those three experiments. Thus, the parent measure of children's parasocial relationships yields consistent, reliable findings for two factors across studies whether it is a favorite and/or

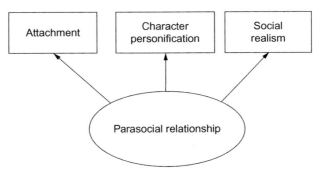

Fig. 1 Components of parasocial relationships. *(From Bond, B. J., & Calvert, S. L. (2014a). A model and measure of U.S. parents' perceptions of young children's parasocial relationships.* Journal of Children and Media, 8, *286–304. http://dx.doi.org/10. 1080/17482798.2014.890948.)*

Table 1 Parasocial relationship items: parent questions & factors assessing child's favorite character (Bond & Calvert, 2014a)

Character personification	[Child] thinks that [character] has thoughts and emotions
	[Child] gets sad when [character] gets sad or makes a mistake
	[Child] trusts [character]
	[Child] treats [character] as a friend
	[Child] believes that [character] has needs
	[Child] believes that [character] has wants
Social realism	[Child] knows that [character] is imaginary[a]
	When [character] acts out a behavior on screen (like dancing, singing, or playing a game), [child] believes that [character] is performing the behavior in real life
	[Child] believes that [character] is real
Attachment	[Character] makes [child] feel comfortable
	[Character] makes [child] feel safe
	The voice of [character] soothes [child]

Note: Each item is rated 1–5 on a 5-point Likert scale. The child's name and the favorite character are imputed into this online survey.
[a]The item is reverse coded.

a popular character. The exception was social realism, which was a bit weaker on internal consistency when a popular rather than the favorite child character was the focus.

Parent data from Bond and Calvert (2014a) were also used to create a path analysis to describe how parasocial relationships with media characters develop. As seen in Fig. 2, we discovered that parent encouragement, engagement with toy replicas that resembled the character, repeated exposure to the character across platforms, and parasocial interaction predicted parasocial relationships. Parent encouragement, toy play, and parasocial interaction were directly linked to the development of parasocial relationships. Indirect links occurred through parasocial interactions to parasocial relationship development for parent encouragement, toy play, and also repeated exposure to the character across media platforms. These results suggested that parasocial interactions with favorite media characters created a potential trajectory for the development of parasocial relationships, with toy play and parent encouragement also having their own independent links to these relationships.

Based on this initial study (Bond & Calvert, 2014a), we developed a child measure of parasocial relationships and sampled different parents and their children (Richards & Calvert, 2016a). We examined preschool-aged children's choices of favorite characters, compared them to what their parents said, and asked both the child and the parent samples the questions that had

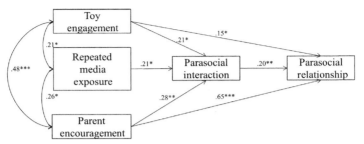

Fig. 2 Parasocial relationship development model. *(Adapted from Bond, B. J., & Calvert, S. L. (2014a). A model and measure of U.S. parents' perceptions of young children's parasocial relationships.* Journal of Children and Media, 8, 286–304. *http:// dx.doi.org/10.1080/17482798.2014.890948.)*

comprised children's parasocial relationships via parent report in the original Bond and Calvert (2014a) study. We simplified the children's questions, and also dropped questions that were too abstract for them to understand. We used a 5-point smiley face Likert scale to make response choices easier for children.

Using factor analysis, Richards and Calvert (2016a) found consistent but somewhat different clusters of features that defined parasocial relationships when compared to the original factor analysis by Bond and Calvert (2014a). Specifically, the factors that described children's parasocial relationships with their favorite characters, via the child smiley face scale, were attachment and friendship, human needs, and social realism. Similar factors—attachment and character personification, human needs, and social realism—were found in analyzing the data from the parents of those children via the parent survey. See Tables 2 and 3, respectively, for the questions and factors derived for the Child Parasocial Relationship and the Parent Parasocial Relationship measure in the Richards and Calvert (2016a) study.

The new human needs factor included questions about the character getting hungry, sleepy, or feeling sad when the character made a mistake. Interestingly, caring for a character's human needs also emerged in behavioral studies of parasocial relationships (see Calvert, Richards, & Kent, 2014; Gola, Richards, Lauricella, & Calvert, 2013), providing evidence of construct validity. These findings are consistent with kindergartners' beliefs that a mouse's mind continues to exist, in terms of being hungry or feeling sad, even after death (Bering & Bjorklund, 2004).

There were two main caveats for the findings of the Richards and Calvert (2016a) study. One was that only about 30% of parents agreed with their child about who the child's favorite character was. The other was that the parasocial relationship subscales on the parent parasocial relationship measure were internally consistent, but the child measure reached acceptable

Table 2 Parasocial relationship items: child questions & factors assessing child's favorite character (Richards & Calvert, 2016a)

Attachment & friendship	How safe does [character] make you feel when you are scared? Really safe, safe, kind of safe, a little bit safe, or not safe at all?
	Is [character] your best friend, your good friend, kind of a good friend, a little bit of a friend, or not your friend at all?
	Is [character] really cute, kind of cute, a little bit cute, or not cute at all?"
	Does [character] have a whole lot of feelings, a lot of feelings, kind of has feelings, a little bit of feelings, or no feelings at all?
Social realism	Is the character totally real, mostly real, kind of real, mostly pretend, or totally pretend?[a]
	Is [character] totally pretend, mostly pretend, kind of pretend, mostly real, or totally real?
Human-like needs	Does [character] get really hungry, hungry, kind of hungry, a little bit hungry, or not hungry at all?
	Does [character] get really sleepy, sleepy, kind of sleepy, a little bit sleepy, or not sleepy at all?
	How do you feel when [character] makes a mistake? Really sad, sad, kind of sad, a little bit sad, not sad at all

Note: Each item is rated 1–5 on a 5-point Likert smiley face scale. The child's favorite character is imputed into this oral survey.
[a]The item is reverse coded.

Table 3 Parasocial relationship items: parent questions & factors assessing child's favorite character (Richards & Calvert, 2016a)

Attachment & character personification	[Child] thinks that [character] has thoughts and emotions
	[Character] makes [child] feel safe
	[Child] trusts [character]
	The voice of [character] soothes the child
	[Character] makes child feel comfortable
Social realism	[Child] knows that [character] is imaginary[a]
	When [character] acts out a behavior on screen (like dancing, singing, or playing a game), [child] believes that [character] is performing the behavior in real life
	[Child] believes that [character] is real
Human-like needs	Child] believes that [character] has needs
	[Child] believes that [character] has wants

Note: Each item is rated 1–5 on a 5-point Likert scale. The child's name and the favorite character are imputed into this online survey.
[a]The item is reverse coded.

levels of internal consistency only for the attachment and friendship subscale. The fantasy/reality subscale may have been particularly difficult for the children, as the lines between what is pretend and what is real are often blurred for young children (Singer & Singer, 2005), but internal consistency improved on that measure for older children in the sample (Richards & Calvert, 2017). Complicating matters is the reality that children sometimes reported seeing embodied characters like Mickey Mouse and the Disney princesses walking around at theme parks like Disney Land (Richards & Calvert, 2016a). The internal consistency of the human needs subcategory of parasocial relationship via children's self-reports was not in the acceptable range either and did not improve for older children (Richards & Calvert, 2017), but that dimension had been found and validated through behavioral data in other empirical studies (Calvert et al., 2014; Gola et al., 2013).

One possible solution to the child parasocial relationship measurement problem is to merge the responses of the child and adult parasocial relationship scales, with the child's favorite character being imputed into the parent online survey. If the scores of parents and children are highly positively correlated, the internal consistency measures of the parent measure could be used to bolster the child measure. Another option is to use the parent measure alone, particularly when assessing the parasocial relationship with a character who is not necessarily the child's favorite, since it has demonstrated high internal consistency for items in subscales for three studies, including favorite characters and a popular, nonfavorite character (Bond & Calvert, 2014a; Richards & Calvert, 2015, 2016a). The problem with this approach is that parents often do not reply to the online survey, making it necessary to increase the sample size of children substantially to get enough parent responses. A third option is to focus primarily on the attachment and friendship child subscale, as it demonstrates sufficient internal consistency for use as a measure of parasocial relationships (Richards & Calvert, 2017). A final option is to use individual items from the measure. Trust is one such option as discussed below.

MEANINGFUL PARASOCIAL RELATIONSHIPS FOR EARLY STEM LEARNING

Trust is a facet of onscreen relationships that is linked to credibility decisions by young children. For instance, Corriveau and Harris (2009) showed

3- to 5-year-old children two onscreen teachers, one of whom the child knew and the other who was unknown to them. Next, they varied how accurate each teacher was in naming familiar objects to the children after which each teacher named novel objects. For the novel words, the younger 3-year-old children selected the familiar teacher as the most trustworthy to them, even if she had previously made mistakes in labeling the familiar objects. In essence, they forgave their teacher for her previous errors. By contrast, the older 4- and 5-year-old children chose the teacher who had previously named the familiar objects accurately when faced with the uncertainty of naming novel objects. Harris and Corriveau (2011) described children's decisions as evolutionary advantageous: that is, children trust those who are familiar to them at very young ages given the evolutionary advantage of attachment biases. This early attachment preference then shifts with age to finding the accurate person, regardless of personal closeness to them, as accuracy becomes more important for survival.

Building on this line of research, Richards and Calvert (2015) varied the familiarity and accuracy of a media character, in this case the popular US character Elmo versus DoDo, a popular character from Taiwan that was unknown to US children. Using an iPad interface, 32-month-old children interacted with a game in which they had to choose the character who labeled novel foods correctly after having experienced the two characters naming familiar foods correctly or incorrectly. Interestingly, 32-month-old children selected the accurate novel character over the inaccurate familiar, meaningful character for the novel food names if the unfamiliar character had previously labeled the familiar foods correctly. This effect occurred regardless of whether the child received feedback about their choices in the familiar food trials. Even 24-month-old toddlers selected the unfamiliar character for the novel food names when the familiar character had previously labeled familiar foods incorrectly. Put simply, their trust was reserved for the credible character. Our results differed from those of Corriveau and Harris (2009), we think, partly because they observed real people on video whereas our study used puppets with interactive apps that elicited responses from children (Richards & Calvert, 2015).

In a video study assessing early acquisition of math skills, Lauricella et al. (2011) compared 21-month-old toddlers' performances on a seriation task in which they nested cups after viewing the meaningful Elmo character versus the unknown DoDo character demonstrate the task. There was also a no exposure control group who were simply given the cups. In this instance, children who viewed Elmo perform the task onscreen subsequently outperformed those who viewed DoDo sequencing the items. Those who viewed Elmo demonstrate the task also performed significantly better on the seriation task than the control group; by contrast, those who viewed DoDo demonstrate the task did not perform significantly better than the control group (Lauricella et al., 2011).

We then decided to build parasocial relationships between toddlers and the unfamiliar DoDo character. In this study, Gola et al. (2013) had one group of toddlers play with DoDo toys in their homes from ages 18–21 months before viewing DoDo perform the seriation task onscreen. Another group viewed the onscreen DoDo character demonstration only at age 21 months without any prior toy play with DoDo. There was also a no exposure control group. The toddlers who had played with DoDo for 3 months and then viewed DoDo performing the seriation task at age 21 months performed significantly better on the sequencing task than the no exposure control group. By contrast, those who were exposed to DoDo only when he performed the onscreen seriation task did not perform significantly better than the control group. More importantly, the more that toddlers in the play experience condition nurtured DoDo by pretending to feed the character or put him down for a nap, the better they performed on the subsequent seriation task. Given that parasocial relationships are emotionally tinged relationships, we concluded that nurturing the character by taking care of its needs was a behavioral measure of parasocial relationships (Gola et al., 2013). These findings dovetail nicely with the results of the factor analyses of both parent and child report in which human needs (e.g., feeding the character and putting it to sleep) were a component of parasocial relationships (Richards & Calvert, 2016a).

In the final study in this series, Calvert et al. (2014) used interactive characters, the Leapfrog puppies Scout and Violet, to teach the seriation task. Scout, the boy character, had bright green markings, and Violet, the girl character, had soft lavender markings. Both had the same child-like voice. These characters were programmed so that they were or were not personalized to be like the 18-month-old child. In particular, the personalized character was programmed to know the toddler's name, gender, and share the same favorites, such as the child's preferred songs and foods. By contrast, the nonpersonalized character called the toddler by the generic name "Pal," was the opposite gender, and had different favorites from the child. Once again, we observed the toddler playing with the toys with a caregiver over a 3-month period. Then we had them view their character onscreen performing the seriation task. There was also a no exposure control group.

After viewing the character demonstrate the seriation task, the children who had been in the personalized condition performed significantly better on that task than those in the no exposure control condition. However, those in the nonpersonalized condition did not perform the seriation task significantly better than the control group. Toddlers who had personalized characters also increased in parasocial, nurturing behaviors over time during their play sessions, unlike those with nonpersonalized characters. The more that toddlers increased in nurturing, parasocial behaviors with the toys, the better they did on the seriation task; that outcome was only true, however, for those who had the personalized character (Calvert et al., 2014).

Taken together, these studies demonstrate that emotionally close relationships with toy replicas of media characters can result in better performance when children observe onscreen cognitive tasks demonstrated by those characters. Nurturing the character during play, be it a traditional puppet or an interactive toy, is the key for developing this close relationship at young ages. For interactive toys, the character assists subsequent transfer tasks when it is personalized to the child; that is, it is made to be "like" the child. This kind of homophily in real-life relationships as well as with these toy media characters is a component of friendships and reinforces the premise that children treat their imaginary friends just as they do their real-life friends (Bond & Calvert, 2014a). However, if those characters have been previously wrong, young children will select an unfamiliar character that labels novel objects over a familiar character's incorrect labels (Richards & Calvert, 2015). These findings indicate that parasocial relationships are beneficial for early cognitive outcomes, but only if the character is credible and worthy of their trust.

PARASOCIAL BREAKUPS

Just as is found in relationships with real people, children eventually break up with their favorite media characters. In early childhood, parasocial relationships last about 2.4 years (Brunick & Calvert, 2016).

The reasons that children break up with media characters are varied, but one is key. While children's media characters are often ageless, remaining much the same in terms of age and behaviors, the child is growing up with new social and cognitive needs emerging. According to the survey by Bond and Calvert (2014b), which used parent report, the main reasons for parasocial break up include outgrowing the character, growing tired of the character, or finding a new favorite. During the preschool years, peer pressure also emerges for children to give up the neotenous, baby-like favorite characters of early childhood in favor of those who look and act in more mature ways (Brunick & Calvert, 2016). Indeed, children often prefer older characters to younger ones (Calvert & Kotler, 2003).

One reason that babyish characters may be left behind involves an increasing preference for gender-stereotyped characters as children age. Compared to earlier parasocial relationships with favorite characters, new favorites tend to be more gender stereotyped in terms of masculine and feminine attributes (Bond & Calvert, 2014b; Brunick & Calvert, 2016). For instance, one boy switched his favorite character to the rough and tumble superhero male character Buzz Lightyear from his previous favorite, the more benign babyish looking Caillou. Similarly, a girl changed her favorite character to the more physically attractive Disney Tinkerbell character from her previous favorite, the inquisitive Sesame Street Muppet Abby Cadabby (Bond & Calvert, 2014b). The colors of favorite characters also become more gender stereotyped as children age. In particular, girls prefer their characters to be softer feminine lighter colors, whereas boys prefer their characters to be darker, masculine colors (Brunick & Calvert, 2016). These findings suggest that by the preschool years, favorite characters increasingly reflect children's growing understanding of what is traditionally gender appropriate for girls and boys, a pattern that is consistent with more general patterns of traditional gender stereotypes (Huston, 1983).

INTELLIGENT CHARACTERS

Observational media rely heavily on children's imagination to create pseudo interactions with characters. Newer media, by contrast, allow contingent replies to children's actions, potentially providing an avenue to channel their love of media characters into more advanced types of learning. Notably, animated intelligent characters do not fall prey to the "uncanny valley," in which more realistic animated characters look "creepy" (Mori, MacDorman, & Kageki, 2012), as was the case of the animated but too realistic-looking characters in the movie *The Polar Express* (Noë, 2012). This familiarity and attachment to animated characters makes them ideal as potential playmates and teachers in this emerging and interactive world of intelligent characters (Brunick et al., 2016).

Based on this idea, we created an intelligent character prototype using Dora from the children's program *Dora the Explorer* to teach an early math skill, the add-one-concept (Calvert et al., 2016). The add-one concept involves automatically understanding that adding one to a number advances the sum by one unit (e.g., 3 + 1 is 4) rather than counting one by one on one's fingers, as often occurs during early childhood (Baroody, 1987). The development of the add-one concept allows children to free up cognitive resources to compute higher order math skills (Baroody, Eiland, Purpura, & Reid, 2012).

In our game prototype, children solve 16 math problems to help Dora from the children's animated program *Dora the Explorer* count supplies that come down a grocery store conveyor belt for her cousin Diego's birthday party. There are four rounds increasing in the level of difficulty, as regulated by the speed and whether the math problems are presented in canonical or random order. If children miss a problem or fail to reply before the object disappears into a grocery bag at the end of the conveyor belt, the character Swiper the fox steals the bag. Two levels of scaffolding, which include having Dora's sidekick monkey Boots assist children, are built into the game if they have difficulty solving the addition problems.

The interface verbally engages children in *parasocial interaction techniques.* Specifically, Dora asks children questions, pauses for a reply, and responds contingently to children's answers via a second, hidden experimenter, the Wizard, who remotely controls the game from behind a screen, just as the Wizard from *The Wizard of Oz* did from behind his curtain. In our case, the Wizard of Oz paradigm allows an experimenter to deliver accurate, contingent responses to each child.

The parasocial interaction techniques include *small talk* to build repertoire (e.g., "Have you ever had a birthday party?") and *add-one math problems* (e.g., "What is 3 + 1?"; Calvert et al., 2016). Small talk allows children to avoid face threat (Cassell, 2016), as they become comfortable "talking" to a character, and do not have to respond only to an addition question that may be difficult for them to answer. Visual attention was recorded via a camera as children played the game beside an experimenter. We also assessed how emotionally close children felt to Dora via the attachment and friendship subscale of the child parasocial relationship measure (see Richards & Calvert, 2017).

Our initial results suggest that the prototype was engaging and effective. Overall, 90% of preschool-aged children completed the add-one game, with an average completion time of about 13 min. Children answered an average of 12.95 problems correctly on their first attempts, needing an average of 1.28 first level scaffolds and about one second level scaffold per game. Older children answered more problems correctly on the first try and more quickly than younger children. Children looked at the game about 88% of the time, looked at the first experimenter beside them about 5% of the time, and looked elsewhere about 7% of the time. The verbal parasocial interaction interface was effective, with children responding on average to 84% of small talk prompts and 94% of number prompts. Children who felt more emotionally close to Dora answered more small talk prompts, thereby providing a link between parasocial relationships and parasocial interactions (see Calvert et al., 2016). Our initial findings suggest that popular media characters demonstrate promise as intelligent characters who can contingently interact with children in academic settings, potentially providing pathways for the development of the fundamental mathematical skills necessary for future scholastic success.

In a follow-up study, we are currently comparing the Dora intelligent character prototype game with a no character control that only depicts the game in the grocery store setting. The no character control has an adult female voice present the same script that is used in the Dora game with the same grocery store check-out line background. In this study, we added questions to ask children if they thought that Dora could see them or hear them after they had interacted with the game. Thus far, their reply is overwhelmingly "yes" to Dora hearing them. One boy in the Dora condition elaborated by saying "because it kept answering me!" During actual game play, one girl also looked at the experimenter and excitedly commented, "She's talking to me!" The majority of children in the Dora condition also thought that she could see them, probably because she was physically present on the screen. Children in the no character condition also thought that they could be heard by the game, and interestingly, also believed that they could be seen when no character was present. Given that the contingency of replies in this game are built upon verbal spoken parasocial interaction techniques, the finding that children think that they can be heard suggests that the interface is believable to them. These findings are consistent with research demonstrating that contingency is a trigger for the belief of a human mind (Waytz, Klein, & Epley, 2013).

Both the Dora and the no character game versions get children to reply to questions through parasocial interaction techniques, thereby engaging them with an onscreen or an offscreen character who has a voice, and both versions result in accurate performance on add-one-concept problems. If the character serves to motivate children through parasocial relationships, as we think is the case, then faster response times on the transfer task should take place in the character than in the no character condition, which was in fact the case (Calvert et al., 2017).

Personalized intelligent character interfaces are also emerging to teach older minority children STEM skills. For instance, Cassell (2016) built an animated, intelligent virtual peer to teach science concepts through language that mapped into the child's dialect. The basic premise is that minority children, who tend to lag behind others in STEM skills, are disadvantaged in part because African American Vernacular English is not the same as the Standard American English that is typically used in school systems. Hence, there are minimal links between who the child is and what the learning setting demands. It is, if you will, like asking children to speak in a foreign language.

To address this issue, Cassell (2016) created an African American virtual character named Alex who spoke to third grade children in one of three ways: Standard American English only, African American Vernacular English only, or a mixture of African American Vernacular English and Standard American English (i.e., code switching). Alex's African American Vernacular English language patterns are based on 8- to 10-year-old African American children's verbal and nonverbal patterns. In the Standard American English condition, the character only interacts in Standard American English with the child. In the African American Vernacular English condition, the character speaks only in African American dialect. In the code switching condition, the character switches between African American Vernacular English and Standard American English. Specifically, repertoire building is done in African American Vernacular English in which the child chats about everyday events with the character. Then the character uses "school talk" of the sort that is typically used in classrooms to do the science problems. The character looks like a middle schooler who is racially ambiguous.

The study is conducted using *the Wizard of Oz* paradigm in which a hidden experimenter responds to the child from behind a screen. Results indicated that African American children presented stronger science arguments in the African American Vernacular English speaking condition than when the virtual peer exclusively spoke Standard American English (Cassell, 2016). In a longitudinal 6-week long follow-up study, students in the code switching condition discussed more science concepts than those who were exposed to the virtual peer who only spoke Standard American English. Student engagement increased, as indicated by the use of more pitch fluctuations, louder voices, and faster speaking patterns, by children in the code switching than in the Standard American English speaking condition. Finally, children themselves used more code switching in their subsequent conversations with teachers in a learning context, revealing transfer effects.

Overall, Cassell's (2016) argument is that social connectedness is facilitated by tasks that support who the child is than those that attempt to make a child fit in with a dominant culture. This sense of social connectedness, comprising trust, rapport, and perceptions of sameness, in turn, then improves student learning of science concepts. This link to trust is consistent with our work on close, emotional parasocial relationships as a key to learning math concepts from the media characters who are their trusted friends (Calvert et al., 2014; Gola et al., 2013).

THE CREATION OF ENGAGING MEDIA CHARACTERS IN EDUCATIONAL PRODUCTIONS

Certainly children use educational materials in formal school settings, but the key to success is getting them to engage in scientific concepts at home as well (Brunick et al., 2016). If children do not voluntarily spend time with educational content, then the opportunities to learn from media characters are limited. What kinds of qualities create engaging media characters? How do the production features that present and represent content influence children's engagement, learning, and cognitive skill development? These questions are addressed next.

The character. One mystery of creating educational content for children is making characters that engage them, that spark their curiosity, that make them want to watch them and/or interact with them. What are the optimal ways to design and present media characters? How should they look, and how should they act?

One dimension of interest is whether the characters are animated or live. In the United States, the majority of the characters and educational programs designed for children are animated (Calvert & Kotler, 2003). There are numerous reasons for this decision, many of which are financial. Live child actors have contracts with limits on how much time they can work. Further complications are that the characters grow up, and may tire of the program they are doing. By contrast, animated characters are properties. Their images are controlled by their creators. They can be bought and sold to market products. They can work morning, noon, and night. Animated characters easily traverse cultural boundaries as dubbing languages onto them for a native dialect is far easier than dubbing a different language onto a real person whose lips more closely match the words being said, and their voices can be made to sound child-like. Animated characters are, in essence, cost effective.

Puppets and Muppets are also a relatively cost effective way to develop characters, as they have adult puppeteers who have fewer limits than child actors do in terms of work schedules. Adult Muppeteers can also follow directions much easier than a young child actor. While some argue that children's media should return to the day of live characters (Kleeman, 2016), that day has passed into one in which the characters are human-like, but animated or puppets/Muppets. This approach dovetails nicely with the imaginary capabilities of their young viewers (Valkenburg & Calvert, 2012).

Animated characters have key features that make them who they are. They are embodied; they have an age and a gender; they have nonverbal behaviors and voices that are characteristic of who they are; and they have characteristic ways of acting, including personality attributes (Calvert & Richards, 2014). For very young children, neotenous features are appealing to them (Brunick & Calvert, 2016) as are child-like voices (Anderson & Kirkorian, 2015). These qualities parallel the kinds of properties that appeal to babies, such as the high-pitched voices used in infant directed speech (Fernald, 1985). The *Sesame Street* Muppet character Elmo is a perfect example of a popular character that appeals to very young children. He has a large round face and big eyes, a bright red furry body, and a high-pitched voice. His very persona is perceptually salient, filled with high contrast (his dark eyes on white irises with his bright red body), incongruity (his voice), and his prototypical 2-year-old child personality filled with surprise and wonder. Elmo is also everywhere—in children's television programs, in their games, as toys, on their clothes, and on the foods that they purchase at the supermarket (Richards & Calvert, 2017. All of these personal qualities coupled with ubiquitous access make him appealing to children, and it is difficult though not impossible to duplicate this formula.

As children grow older and move into the preschool years, their developmental needs shift. For instance, children develop their first real friends (Hartup, 1989). They prefer characters that continue to reflect who they are. Throughout the world, their identity, and hence their friends, increasingly involve their gender (Huston, 1983; Maccoby, 1999). Knowing that you a boy or a girl is a watershed moment in the life of a child. The world becomes black and white, or perhaps better said, blue and pink. Categories are constructed about what you should like (and not like), about what you should (and should not do), about who your friends should be. With development, real friends tend to be of the same gender as the child (Huston, 1983), as are the imaginary media friends of their lives (Richards & Calvert, 2016b). Rough and tumble play, which reflects the aggressive reality of young male culture, becomes the preferred mode of interaction for many boys, and playing with dolls is often enjoyed in the social world of girls (Huston, 1983). The imaginations of children flourish at this time in development (Singer & Singer, 2005), and how they express those fantasies reflects who they are.

By middle childhood, virtual characters are sometimes created based on prototypical children, as is the case of the virtual character, Alex (Cassell, 2016). Alex's body was made to appear neutral in terms of race and gender, reflecting perhaps, a perspective that emphasizes gender neutrality over a traditional gender-stereotyped worldview. Nevertheless, what Alex says and does is modeled after 8- to 10-year-old African American children, again making it clear that we have certain ways about us that fit our identity as we search for characters who are like us. Put another way, there is an element of truth, an element of authenticity, in who Alex is. He resonates with the ways that African American children talk to one another, and children like him. They talk to him, they laugh with him, and they learn from him. Unlike typical animation in children's television programs, Alex is not moving around the screen. Although movement about the speed of a walk is highly comprehensible for children (Calvert, Huston, Watkins, & Wright, 1982), it is more difficult to program than having a stationary character. The use of movement will come more often in the interactive technologies of our future as interfaces such as virtual reality become more common.

Beliefs in animism and anthropomorphism remain with us, even as our understanding of what is real and what is pretend becomes clearer (Waytz et al., 2013). We give virtual animals "human-like" personalities, such as Silas the virtual dog that gets thirsty and drinks (human-like needs; Richards & Calvert, 2016a), who likes to play ball (attachment and friendship; Richards & Calvert, 2016a), and who feels complex emotions like jealousy and sadness (character personification; Bond & Calvert, 2014a). Students who are exposed to artificial agents that display emotion and are responsive to children's emotions are more motivated and they learn more (Woolf et al., 2009), a finding that is consistent with our work on parasocial relationships (Calvert et al., 2014).

What of the robots that are increasingly part of children's lives? Interestingly, we treat them as if they are real, too. For instance, children who were ages 3–6 gave life-like qualities to robotic dogs more so than to traditional stuffed animals, expecting the robotic dog to respond contingently to them (Kahn, Friedman, Perez-Granados, & Freier, 2006). From ages 7 to 15, children think that robotic dogs can be their friends, providing social companionship (Melson et al., 2009). When a robot named Robovie told children from ages 9 to 16 that he was scared of the dark and did not want to be put in a closet, most children thought that it was not fair to put him there (Kahn et al., 2012). Similarly, adults who were shown a video of a robot who cried when he was tortured felt pity for the robot and anger towards his tormentor (Rosenthal-von der Putten, Kramer, Hoffmann, Sobieraj, & Eimler, 2013). Taken together, these findings suggest that animism continues to color our perceptions of nonliving entities, regardless of our age.

Faces, human-like movements, and contingent replies trigger perceptions of similarity by children and adults, increasing the likelihood that life-like qualities will be attributed to that entity (Waytz et al., 2013). Not surprisingly, we often make robots with a face that has eyes and ears, and bodies with arms and legs that move. Indeed, 3- and 4-year-old children's decisions about whether an object should have a name, which included a robot dog, depended on whether it had a face (Jipson & Gelman, 2007). When military robots are created with only the bottom half of a torso, attached to legs and feet that run through battlefields, they fall into the uncanny valley (Mori et al., 2012), potentially creating a sense of unease and creepiness because they lack a face. But a voice is human and can be personified without a body, as was done in the movie *Her*, in which a computer was but an intelligent voice, but became a voice that was conscious of herself and of her own unique identity.

The backstory is also essential in bringing a media character to life. Who are these characters? What are their relationships to others? What do they like to do? Are they like us? Can children play with them when they are young? What are their hopes and dreams? What are their challenges? Much of this information is transmitted in dialogue, but much is also communicated by how characters dress, speak, move, and relate to others. Their eyes are windows into making them look alive, and considerable time is spent getting animated characters' eyes to look right, down to their very blinks.

Finally, engaging characters must meet the developmental needs of the children that use them to become and to remain a part of their lives. For very young children, their needs involve succorance and attachments to those who can care for them when they need assistance. As they grow older, they seek playmates who entertain them and can be trusted.

Production features. The way that programs are presented to children also influences their engagement with the character and the program content. Production features of children's preschool television programs targeted at boys include rapid action, rapid pacing, loud music, and frequent sound effects to convey the content—features that reflect a traditionally bold masculine image (Huston et al., 1981). By contrast, the production features of girls' programs have dreamy dissolves, more dialogue, and soft music, conveying a stereotypical feminine world in which girls often live (Huston et al., 1981). Certainly there are exceptions to these rules of thumb, but they are exceptions to the highly gendered worlds of children, which is reflected, in part, by their own choice of favorite characters that are the same gender as the child viewer (Bond & Calvert, 2014b; Brunick & Calvert, 2016; Richards & Calvert, 2016a).

Educational techniques include reflective production features such as moderate levels of action at about the speed of a walk, long slow zooms that provide focus, and singing (Huston et al., 1981). When characters move at about the speed of a walk, they often provide dual visual and verbal modes to represent content that is particularly beneficial to young children (Calvert et al., 1982). Singing elicits an automatic rehearsal option for children as songs replay in our heads (Calvert & Tart, 1993), although recall is often more of a superficial verbatim memory of content rather than a deeper understanding of the material (Calvert, 2001). Moving in a way that represents the meaning of song lyrics, such as making downward motions of your hands to represent "washing the spider out" in the song the *Itsy Bitsy Spider*, however, can improve the memorability of the meaning of those lyrics (Calvert & Goodman, 1999). Characters also have a theme song that represents them and their program which provides an introduction, thematic integration at key points throughout the story, and which draws the action to a conclusion. The theme song of Dora the Explorer is one such example, and we used it to introduce our intelligent character math game (Calvert et al., 2016).

Visual production features such as long slow zooms supplant the cognitive skill of going from a part to a whole whereas a cut activates that cognitive skill; in the latter instance, the viewer has to perform that representational skill without a production feature to provide a scaffold to guide them (Salomon, 1972). Similarly, dissolves provide a slow way of transiting between major shifts in time and place whereas cuts, once again, activate cognitive skills and require viewers to fill in that gap (Calvert, 1988). Reflective features are ideal for younger audiences who need more scaffolds to aid their learning; by middle childhood, there is a shift to presentations that require more mental effort as they challenge the child to think (Salomon, 1972).

When playing video games, the player creates their own character (Calvert & Valkenburg, 2013). That character can be a visual icon that the player manipulates onscreen with some kind of joystick or player movement, with the player generally taking some role in creating an identity for their character (e.g., name, costume, physical attributes). Another option is for the player to be literally embedded within the point of view of the character, which is called a first-person perspective (O'Keefe & Zehnder, 2004). In both instances, the player has control over what their character does, which provides opportunities for the player to develop various cognitive skills.

Video game use, particularly with games that involve the production feature of action, has been linked to the cultivation of attentional skills, visual spatial skills, and iconic representational skills (Subrahmanyam & Greenfield, 2006). The development of these kinds of cognitive skills is a requirement of multitasking and provides a foundation for the development of STEM professions such as engineering.

In the attentional domain, college students who were expert video game players were better than novices at dividing their attention when objects were presented on a screen. Thus, these skills can be developed by playing action video games, and the attentional skills that were developed through video game play transfer to other contexts (Green & Bavalier, 2003; Greenfield, deWinstanley, Kilpatrick, & Kaye, 1994).

Spatial skills include mental rotation of objects, judging speeds and distances, and visualizing two-dimensional depictions in three-dimensional spaces (Subrahmanyam & Greenfield, 2006). Training visual spatial skills via a computer game improved 10- to 11-year-old children's skills at visualizing paths of objects in a game (Subrahmanyam & Greenfield, 1994); adolescents' and college students' mental rotation and visualization skills have also been linked to video game use (Greenfield, Brannon, & Lohr, 1994; Okagaki & Frensch, 1994).

Because most video games involve visual action, gaming also requires players to read the grammar of visual icons (Subrahmanyam & Greenfield, 2006). College students who had prior experiences with video games were more skilled at understanding iconic representations, and those who played the game on a computer represented their learning in visual, iconic forms more so that those who played the game on a board (Greenfield, Camaioni, et al., 1994).

More recent video games, called exergames, require players to engage in gross motor movement during game play (Staiano & Calvert, 2011). This kind of game play over a period of several months resulted in increased executive function skills, which involve cognitive skills such as planning, in a sample of low-income youth (Staiano, Abraham, & Calvert, 2012). Recent developments in gaming, such as *Pokémon Go*, require players to move through space in augmented reality to capture characters. These kinds of games also have the potential to influence players' cognitive skills by increasing their physical movement, and potentially, their skills to deploy attention and spatial skills to move to specific locations to capture Pokémon who are located in their environments.

CONCLUSIONS

In conclusion, to engage children—to be invited into their everyday worlds—is a necessity before one can teach children cognitive lessons. Media characters are a ubiquitous presence in children's lives with vast untapped potential to educate children in informal settings. To accomplish that goal, characters must meet the developmental needs of the children who use them to become and to remain a part of their lives. Those needs change over time, and can be addressed, in part, through emotional, parasocial relationships that children develop with their favorite media characters.

Children who pay attention to a character that conveys educational content, who come back for more from their favorite media friend, are ideally situated to move forward to master the scientific knowledge that they need to succeed in our 21st century educational and work environments. Gaming experiences provide numerous opportunities for the player to be the character, resulting in the development of cognitive skills that involve attentional deployment, visual spatial and iconic representations, and executive function skills.

At an applied level, education now takes place in informal as well as formal contexts, and much informal learning now occurs in front of a screen. As a culture we have not developed a smooth transition for our children between in-classroom and out-of-classroom learning at this point in time. Approaches that maximize the use of these informal contexts to teach young children STEM concepts have the potential for educational innovation. Media characters can become teachers' allies in sustaining interest and in teaching fundamental STEM concepts to young children, which will get them off to the right start when they formally enter school to maximize their ongoing scholastic success.

Close relationships with media characters also have implications for the creation of supplemental learning materials as young children may be more attentive to materials that feature media characters with whom they have a parasocial relationship than with materials that use generic characters. Just as children learn more from their favorite teachers at school, in part because they trust them (see Harris & Corriveau, 2011), children also learn better from their favorite onscreen media characters, but only if they are accurate and credible. Thus, teachers could utilize existing and also develop new parasocial relationships with specific media characters to get children to view STEM character-based programs in classroom or in out-of-classroom settings to supplement and strengthen their curriculum in ways that are exciting and engaging to children. As we apply our knowledge about parasocial relationships to create intelligent agents and robots to teach STEM concepts, we can also provide supplementary teaching assistance that can be used either in the school or in home settings to improve STEM learning.

The digital landscape, in which our children traverse real and imaginary worlds in the blink of an eye, is one that can benefit their development if we have the vision to look beyond what media characters are now and imagine what they can be in the future—as entities that do not exist, yet can teach and educate children, can be their trustworthy friends and companions, and can provide comfort and emotional support. Children's gift for imaginative thought makes this kind of reality possible.

ACKNOWLEDGMENT

This chapter was supported in part by DRL Grant #1252113 from the National Science Foundation to Sandra L. Calvert.

REFERENCES

Anderson, D. R., Bryant, J., Wilder, A., Santomero, A., Williams, M., & Crawley, A. M. (2000). Researching *Blue's Clues*: Viewing behavior and impact. *Media Psychology, 2,* 179–194. http://dx.doi.org/10.1207/S1532785XMEP0202_4.

Anderson, D.R. & Kirkorian, H. (2015). Media and cognitive development. In L. Liben & U. Muller (Vol. Eds.), *Cognitive processes* (pp. 949-994). In R. Lerner (Ed.), *Handbook of child psychology and developmental science*, 7th ed., Hoboken, N.J.: Wiley.

Baroody, A. (1987). The development of counting strategies for single-digit addition. *Journal for Research in Mathematics Education, 18*(2), 141–157.

Baroody, A., Eiland, M., Purpura, D., & Reid, E. (2012). Fostering at-risk kindergarten children's number sense. *Cognition and Instruction, 30,* 435–470.

Bering, J., & Bjorklund, D. (2004). The natural emergence of afterlife reasoning as a developmental regularity. *Developmental Psychology, 40,* 217–233.

Bond, B. J., & Calvert, S. L. (2014a). A model and measure of U.S. parents' perceptions of young children's parasocial relationships. *Journal of Children and Media, 8,* 286–304. http://dx.doi.org/10.1080/17482798.2014.890948.

Bond, B. J., & Calvert, S. L. (2014b). Parasocial breakup among young children in the United States. *Journal of Children and Media, 8,* 474–490. http://dx.doi.org/10.1080/17482798.2014.953559.

Brunick, K. & Calvert, S.L. (2016). Color analysis of media characters and children's chang-ing parasocial relationships. *Poster presented at the Eastern Psychological Association, New York City, NY.*

Brunick, K. L., Putnam, M., Richards, M. N., McGarry, L., & Calvert, S. L. (2016). Chil-dren's future Parasocial relationships with media characters: The age of intelligent characters. *Journal of Children and Media.* http://dx.doi.org/10.1080/17482798.2015. 1127839.

Calvert, S. L. (1988). Television production feature effects on children's comprehension of time. *Journal of Applied Developmental Psychology, 9,* 263–273.

Calvert, S. L. (2001). Impact of televised songs on children's and young adults' memory of educational content. *Media Psychology, 3,* 325–342.

Calvert, S. L. (2015). Children and digital media. M. Bornstein, T. Leventhal, & R. Lerner (Eds.), *Handbook of child psychology and developmental science* (7th, pp. 375–415). *Ecological settings and processes in developmental systems*Hoboken, N.J.: Wiley.

Calvert, S. L., Brunick, K. L., Putnam, M. M., De Zamaroczy, Z., McCaffery, B., Nadeo, M., et al. (2017). Children's engagement with an intelligent game for learning early math skills. In *Poster presented at the Society for Research in Child Development, Austin, TX.*

Calvert, S. L., Brunick, K. L., Putnam, M. M., Mah, E., Richards, M. N., Horowitz, J., Richmond, E., Chancellor, S., & Barba, E. (2016). *Creating an intelligent character to teach early math skills. Paper presented at the society for research in child development special topic meeting on technology and media in children's development, Irvine, CA.*

Calvert, S. L., & Goodman, T. (1999). In *Enactive rehearsal for young children's comprehension of songs. Poster presented at the biennial meeting of the society for research in child development, Albu-querque, New Mexico.*

Calvert, S. L., Huston, A. C., Watkins, B. A., & Wright, J. C. (1982). The relation between selective attention to television forms and children's comprehension of content. *Child Development, 53,* 601–610.

Calvert, S. L., & Kotler, J. A. (2003). Lessons from children's television: Impact of the Chil-dren's Television Act on children's learning. *Journal of Applied Developmental Psychology, 24,* 275–335. Also published online via Science Direct: http://authors.elsevier.com/sd/ article/S0193397303000601.

Calvert, S.L. & Richards, M.N. (2014). Children's parasocial relationships with media char-acters. In J. Bossert (Oxford Ed.), A. Jordan & D. Romer (Eds.). *Media and the well being of children and adolescents.* Oxford: Oxford University Press.

Calvert, S. L., Richards, M. N., & Kent, C. (2014). Personalized interactive characters for toddlers' learning of seriation from a video presentation. *Journal of Applied Developmental Psychology, 35,* 148–155. http://dx.doi.org/10.1016/j.appdev.2014.03.004.

Calvert, S. L., Strong, B. L., Jacobs, E. L., & Conger, E. E. (2007). Interaction and partici-pation for young Hispanic and Caucasian children's learning of media content. *Media Psychology, 9*(2), 431–445.

Calvert, S. L., & Tart, M. (1993). Song versus prose forms for student's very long-term, long-term, and short-term verbatim recall. *Journal of Applied Developmental Psychology, 14,* 245–260.

Calvert, S. L., & Valkenburg, P. M. (2013). The influence of television, video, games, and the Internet on children's imagination and creativity. In M. Taylor (Ed.), *Oxford Handbook of the Development of Imagination.* Oxford University Press: New York, NY.

Cassell, J. (2016). *Winning (virtual) friends and influencing (virtual) people. Invited talk presented in the Department of Psychology.* Washington, D.C.: Georgetown University.

Corriveau, K., & Harris, P. L. (2009). Choosing your informant: Weighing familiarity and recent accuracy. *Developmental Science, 12,* 426–437.

Fernald, A. (1985). Four-month-old infants prefer to listen to motherese. *Infant behavior and development, 8*, 181–195.

Furman, W. & Rose, A.J (2015). Friendship, romantic relationships, and peer relationships. In M. Lamb (Vol. Ed.), *Socioemotional processes* (pp. 932–974). In R. Lerner (Ed.), *Handbook of child psychology and developmental science*, 7th ed., Hoboken, N.J.: Wiley.

Giles, D., & Maltby, J. (2004). The role of media figures in adolescence development: Relations between autonomy, attachment, and interest in celebrities. *Personality and Individual Differences, 36*, 813–822.

Gleason, T. R. (2013). Imaginary relationships. In M. Taylor (Ed.), *The Oxford Handbook of the Development of Imagination* (pp. 251–271). Oxford University Press: NY: NY.

Gola, A. A., Richards, M. N., Lauricella, A. R., & Calvert, S. L. (2013). Building meaningful relationships between toddlers and media characters to teach early mathematical skills. *Media Psychology, 16*, 390–411.

Green, C. S., & Bavalier, D. (2003). Action video game modifies visual selective attention. *Nature, 423*, 534–537.

Greenfield, P. A., Brannon, C., & Lohr, D. (1994). Two-dimensional representation of movement through three-dimensional space: The role of video game expertise. *Journal of Applied Developmental Psychology, 15*, 87–103.

Greenfield, P. A., Camaioni, L., Ercolani, P., Weiss, L., Lauber, B., & Perucchini, P. (1994). Cognitive socialization by computer games in two cultures: Inductive discovery or mastery of an iconic code? *Journal of Applied Developmental Psychology, 15*, 59–85.

Greenfield, P. A., deWinstanley, P., Kilpatrick, H., & Kaye, D. (1994). Action video games and informal education: Effects on strategies for dividing attention. *Journal of Applied Developmental Psychology, 15*, 105–123.

Harris, P. L., & Corriveau, K. H. (2011). Young children's selective trust in informants. *Philosophical Transactions of the Royal Society, 366*, 1179–1187.

Hartup, W. (1989). Social relationships and their developmental significance. *American Psychologist, 44*, 120–126.

Horton, D., & Wohl, R. R. (1956). Mass communication and parasocial interaction. *Psychiatry, 19*, 215–229.

Huston, A. C. (1983). Sex typing. In P. H. Mussen (Ed.), *Handbook of child psychology*. (4th). *Vol 4: Socialization, personality, and social behavior* New York: Wiley.

Huston, A. C., Wright, J. C., Wartella, E., Rice, M. L., Watkins, B. A., Campbell, T., et al. (1981). Communicating more than content: Formal features of children's television programs. *Journal of Communication, 31*, 32–48.

Jipson, J. L., & Gelman, S. A. (2007). Robots and rodents: Children's inferences about living and nonliving kids. *Child Development, 78*, 1675–1688.

Kahn, P. H., Friedman, B., Perez-Granados, D. R., & Freier, N. G. (2006). Robotic pets in the lives of preschool children. *Interaction Studies, 7*, 405–436.

Kahn, P. H., Kanda, T., Ishiguro, H., Freier, N. G., Severson, R. L., Gill, B. T., & Shen, S. (2012). "Robovie, You'll have to go into the closet now": Children's social and moral relationships with a humanoid robot. *Developmental Psychology, 48*, 303–314.

Kleeman, D. (2016). *PBS kids next generation*. Arlington, VA: Advisory Board Meeting.

Lauricella, A., Gola, A. A., & Calvert, S. L. (2011). Meaningful characters for toddlers learning from video. *Media Psychology, 14*, 216–232. http://dx.doi.org/10.1080/15213269.2011.573465.

Maccoby, E. (1999). *The two sexes: Growing up apart, coming together*. Boston, MA: Harvard University Press.

Melson, G. F., Kahn, P. H., Beck, A., Friedman, B., Roberts, T., Garrett, E., & Gill, B. T. (2009). Children's behavior toward and understanding of robotic and living dogs. *Journal of Applied Developmental Psychology, 30*, 92–102.

Mori, M., MacDorman, K. F., & Kageki, N. (2012). The uncanny valley [from the field]. *Robotics & Automation Magazine, IEEE, 19*, 98–100.

Noë, A. (2012). Storytelling and the 'uncanny valley'. NPR. Retrieved from http://www. npr.org/sections/13.7/2012/01/20/145504032/story-telling-and-the-uncanny-valley

Okagaki, L., & Frensch, P. (1994). Effects of video game playing on measures of spatial performance: Gender effects in late adolescence. *Journal of Applied Developmental Psychology*, *15*, 33–58.

O'Keefe, B. J., & Zehnder, S. P. (2004). Understanding media development: A framework and case study. *Journal of Applied Developmental Psychology*, *25*, 729–740.

Rafaeli, S. (1988). Interactivity: From new media to communication. In R. P. Hawkins, J. M. Wiemann, & S. Pingree (Eds.), *Advancing communication science: Merging mass and interpersonal processes* (pp. 110–134). Newbury Park, CA: Sage.

Richards, M. N., & Calvert, S. L. (2015). Toddlers' judgments of media character source credibility on touchscreens. *American Behavioral Scientist*, *59*, 1755–1775. http://dx. doi.org/10.1177/0002764215596551.

Richards, M. L., & Calvert, S. L. (2016a). Parent versus child report of young Children's Parasocial relationships. *Journal of Children and Media*, *10*, 462–480. http://dx.doi.org/ 10.1080/17482798.2016.115750.

Richards, M. L., & Calvert, S. L. (2016b). Media characters, parasocial relationships, and the social aspects of Children's learning from technology. In R. F. Barr & D. Linebarger (Eds.), *The new blooming, buzzing world: How content and context shape learning from media during early childhood*. NYC, NY: Springer.

Richards, M. L., & Calvert, S. L. (2017). Measuring young children's parasocial relationships: Creating a child self-report survey. *Journal of Children and Media*, *11*, 229–240.

Richert, R. A., Robb, M. B., & Smith, E. I. (2011). Media as social partners: The social nature of young children's learning from screen media. *Child Development*, *82*, 82–95.

Rosenthal-von der Putten, A. M., Kramer, N. C., Hoffmann, L., Sobieraj, S., & Eimler, S. (2013). An experimental study on emotional reactions toward a robot. *International Journal of Social Robotics*, *5*, 17–34.

Salomon, G. (1972). Can we affect cognitive skills through visual media? An hypothesis and initial findings. *AV Communication Review*, *20*, 401–422.

Singer, D. G., & Singer, J. L. (2005). *Imagination and play in the electronic age*. Cambridge, MA: Harvard University Press.

Staiano, A. E., Abraham, A., & Calvert, S. L. (2012). Competitive versus cooperative exergame play for African American adolescents' executive functioning skills. *Developmental Psychology*, *48*, 337–342. http://dx.doi.org/10.1037/a0026938.

Staiano, A. E., & Calvert, S. L. (2011). Exergames for physical education courses: Physical, social, and cognitive benefits. *Child Development Perspectives*, *5*, 93–98.

Subrahmanyam, K., & Greenfield, P. A. (1994). Effects of video game practive on spatial skills of girls and boys. *Journal of Applied Developmental Psychology*, *15*, 13–32.

Subrahmanyam, K., & Greenfield, P. M. (2006). Media symbol systems and cognitive processes. In S. L. Calvert & B. J. Wilson (Eds.), *Handbook of Children, media, and development*. Boston, MA: Wiley-Blackwell.

Valkenburg, P. M., & Calvert, S. L. (2012). Television and the child's developing imagination. In D. Singer & J. Singer (Eds.), *Handbook of children and the media*. (2nd ed.). Thousand Oaks, CA: Sage.

Wilson, B. J., & Drogos, K. L. (2007). In *Preschoolers' attraction to media characters. Paper presented at the annual meeting of the National Communication Association, Chicago, IL*.

Woolf, B., Burleson, W., Arroyo, I., Dragon, T., Cooper, D., & Picard, R. (2009). Affect-aware tutors: Recognizing and responding to student affect. *International Journal of Learning Technology*, *4*, 129–164.

Waytz, A., Klein, N., & Epley, N. (2013). Imagining other minds: Anthropomorphism is hair-triggered but not hare-brained. In M. Taylor (Ed.), *Oxford Handbook of the Development of Imagination* (pp. 272–287). Oxford University Press: New York, NY.

Children and Adolescents' Cognitive Skills as Enhanced Via Media

CHAPTER 6

Young Minds on Video Games

Thomas E. Gorman, C. Shawn Green
University of Wisconsin, Madison, WI, United States

Video games are one of the most heavily used forms of entertainment in the modern world. According to the most recent estimates, 155 million adults in the United States play video games (ESA, 2015). Furthermore, and counter to many common stereotypes, gaming is an activity that cuts across nearly all demographic categories, with females making up 44% of gamers, and 27% of gamers being older than 50 (ESA, 2015). Of all the demographic categories though, children, teens, and young adults are the group that has seen the most dramatic rise in video game play. In fact, video game play has become so ubiquitous within these groups that some surveys have found that up to 90% of teens play video games, with 8–18-year-old boys playing an average of 16 h per week, and girls playing an average of 9 h per week (see Gentile, 2009).

As is the case with any new technology that reaches such levels of use, questions naturally arise as to the possible consequences, especially among younger individuals. The fear that video games will lead to serious harm with regard to attention spans, cognitive abilities, and/or academic performance are similar to the fears society once raised toward television, movies, radio, and the phonograph. While none of these previous technologies led to the downfall of society (although this is not to say that they are totally benign—e.g., Gentzkow & Shapiro, 2008), the interactive and rewarding nature of video games makes this newest massively popular technology potentially more capable of altering the human brain (Gentile & Gentile, 2008). As such, the literature on the effects of video games is vast, and spans myriad disparate areas of psychology—from clinical (e.g., addiction—Gentile, 2009), to social (e.g., aggressive or pro-social behavior—Anderson & Bushman, 2001), to educational (e.g., the development of games to augment or replace classroom instruction—Charsky, 2010), to the main interest of this chapter, cognitive psychology.

Cognitive Development in Digital Contexts
http://dx.doi.org/10.1016/B978-0-12-809481-5.00006-7

NOT ALL GAMES ARE CREATED EQUAL

Before we begin our discussion of the cognitive impact of certain types of video games, it is critical to note that the label "video games" covers an incredibly broad range of quite dissimilar experiences. Games can vary enormously along tens or even hundreds of distinct dimensions. For example, some games involve extremely simple graphics (e.g., the game *Tetris* has only seven distinct shapes, with each shape constructed by four joined squares). Other games involve the creation of vast and detailed worlds (e.g., the game *Rise of the Tomb Raider,* where the level of graphical detail extends all the way down to the avatar's hair, which floats in water and clumps when wet). Some games are purely solitary experiences (i.e., engage only single player at a time), while others involve interacting with a myriad of other individuals in real-time experiences (e.g., *World of Warcraft*). Even within the broad group of games that involve interacting with other human players, some are purely cooperative (e.g., *Portal 2*, where two players must work together to solve puzzles), some are purely competitive (e.g., *StarCraft*, where two players compete over limited space and resources), and others involve mixtures of cooperative and competitive play (e.g., team-based competitive games such as *League of Legends*). All told, this wide-spread variation in game content, mechanics and dynamics, means that simply knowing that an individual has, for instance, played "two hours of video games," provides extremely little information regarding what that individual has actually experienced. Given that it is the actual experiences that drive changes in behavior, the enormous differences that exist across video games strongly suggest that not all games will affect behavior equally. As discussed next, there is one particular type of game that appears to drive changes in cognitive function to a greater degree than others.

VIDEO GAME RESEARCH

Action Video Games

The main video game genre of interest within the domain of cognitive psychology is what is known as the "action" video game genre. The distinguishing characteristics of action games include quickly moving target objects that must be tracked within a complex field of distracting objects; the need to frequently and efficiently switch between a diffuse attentional state, in which one monitors the broad environment, and a highly focused attentional state, where one locks in on a target and suppresses nontarget information; high cognitive and motor load, in that multiple objects must be tracked and often acted upon in quick succession, and multiple goals and or rules that constrain in-game behavior must be constantly updated and maintained (Spence & Feng, 2010). In practice, the games that are most commonly classified as "action" games are what are known as first-person shooter games (i.e., where the player looks through his/her avatar's eyes) and third-person shooter games (i.e., where the player looks at the back of his/her avatar).

METHODS
Correlational Methods

Research on the relationship between cognitive abilities and action video games has in general taken one of two different forms. The most commonly employed study design has been the correlational, or cross-sectional, design. Here researchers have taken advantage of the natural variation in different individuals' game playing habits (in particular the fact that some individuals play a great deal of action games, while other individuals play almost no action games). In these experiments, individuals who already avidly engage with action games (referred to as "Action Video Game Players" or AVGPs) are invited into the lab to undergo a series of diverse cognitive measures. These individuals are typically identified either through large-scale surveys administered to students in introductory psychology courses, or through recruitment posters or online advertisements that explicitly seek heavy action gamers. AVGP performance on the cognitive or perceptual tasks of interest is then compared against that of a group of individuals who rarely or never play action games (referred to as "Nonaction Video Game Players" or NVGPs). This methodology offers an easy and effective means of collecting data in adult populations, and it is quite viable given the large degree of natural variation in gaming habits across individuals. However, whereas the gaming habits of adults tend to be limited by their time and interests, the gaming habits of youth tend to be limited by their parents. In particular, given the violent content of many of the most popular action games (although not all—see Spence & Feng, 2010), some parents do not allow their children to play such games. This prohibition then limits the extent to which studies utilizing this type of video game can be conducted with children. As such, the number of correlational studies examining the impact of action video games in adults substantially outnumbers the number of correlational studies examining the impact of action video games in children and youth (Powers, Brooks, Aldrich, Palladino, & Alfieri, 2013).

Intervention/Experimental Methods

While correlational studies are certainly informative, they do not show how action video game play *causes* changes in cognitive or perceptual abilities. Indeed, AVGPs might be more likely to engage in some other activity than NVGPs, and this other activity may be the cause of their improved cognitive abilities. Similarly, individuals with innately superior cognitive abilities may be more drawn toward playing action games. Thus, to go beyond simple correlation, researchers typically perform an intervention study (i.e., a true experiment). In these studies, researchers first recruit individuals who have minimal video game experience. Next, pretest measures are taken of the participants' cognitive and/or perceptual abilities of interest. Importantly, these pretests measures do not remotely resemble video games (meaning that if improved performance is seen after video game training, it cannot be attributed to superficial/task specific improvements as discussed next). After pretesting, half of the participants are then trained on an action video game and half are trained on a nonaction video game (i.e., the control group). Importantly, the nonaction video game is carefully selected to be just as engaging and entertaining as the action game being used, to rule out subtle confounds, such as the possibility that engaging activities alone are sufficient to produce cognitive improvements. Total training durations have varied across the literature, but have typically been in the range of 10–50 h (with shorter durations used when performance on the tasks of interest is known to be more malleable—such as the case with visual search—and longer durations used when performance on the tasks of interest is more difficult to change via experience as is the case of contrast sensitivity). Importantly, researchers of quality studies in this domain have been sure to distribute training across time, rather than massing it together, as findings suggest that such distribution is essential for optimal learning of any skill (Baddeley & Longman, 1978). Finally, at least 24-h after the final training session (to ensure that any transient changes in the participants' internal state that could be induced by playing their respective video games have had time to dissipate), participants are posttested on the same measures of interest they were tested on prior to training. The final critical measure is whether the group trained on the action game improved more from pretest to posttest on the measure(s) of interest than the control group; see Green, Strobach, and Schubert (2014) for a more in-depth review on current issues in video game training research methodology.

Overall, intervention studies in this domain are far less common than correlational studies (Powers et al., 2013). While in adults this difference in prevalence is largely attributable to the considerable cost and difficulty associated with intervention studies, many additional issues are at play when considering younger populations. In particular, as noted above, action video games tend to contain violent content. Given that previous research suggests that exposure to such content may produce small, but, nonetheless, statistically reliable increases in aggressive tendencies, and that children may be particularly susceptible to such effects (Anderson et al., 2010), it would not be ethical to train individuals younger than 18 years old on most action video games (although see below for some solutions to this problem employed by researchers to date).

BRIEF REVIEW OF THE PERCEPTUAL AND COGNITIVE EFFECTS OF ACTION VIDEO GAMES IN ADULTS

Perception

A large portion of the work on action video games has examined the effects of such games on perceptual skills, in particular visual perception. One such study conducted by Li, Polat, Makous, and Bavelier (2009) examined the impact of action video games on low-level visual abilities—specifically contrast sensitivity (i.e., the ability to detect small changes in luminance across the visual field). These experimenters first conducted a correlational study (of the type previously described), comparing contrast sensitivity in AVGPs and NVGPs. Expert action gamers showed significantly superior contrast sensitivity. Then, to establish a causal relationship, the researchers performed a 50-h intervention study. Half of the participants were trained on an action game (*Unreal Tournament 2004* or *Call of Duty*), while the other half were trained on a nonaction game (*The Sims 2*). No improvements were observed in the control group. However, the action-game trained group showed significant improvements in their contrast sensitivity at posttest relative to their pretest scores. This finding is notable because contrast sensitivity is of great importance for many visual tasks (e.g., driving, reading), and has proven difficult to train (Sowden, Rose, & Davies, 2002).

Beyond contrast sensitivity, a number of other studies have similarly shown positive associations between action gaming and improved perceptual skills. For example, correlational studies have shown that AVGPs have superior peripheral vision (Buckley, Codina, Bhardwaj, & Pascalis, 2010), and an enhanced ability to process moving stimuli (Hutchinson & Stocks, 2013). Donohue, Woldorff, and Mitroff (2010) also showed that when AVGPs were presented with rapidly alternating visual and auditory stimuli, they demonstrated a superior ability to distinguish the correct temporal order of those stimuli, which is indicative of enhanced multisensory integration.

An Aside: Why Action Games Are Interesting—Transfer of Learning Is Rare

While one may not initially be surprised that training on a perceptually demanding task (like an action video game) results in improvements in perceptual skills (like contrast sensitivity), it is important to note that transfer of this nature is the exception, rather than the rule, within the domains of perception and cognition. Indeed, while humans are capable of improving at most perceptual and cognitive tasks, it is typically the case that such improvements are task specific and inflexible, and do not generalize to other, even very similar tasks (Fahle, 2005). A classic example of this phenomenon is the work of Fiorentini and Berardi (1980), who trained subjects to discriminate between two different types of visual patterns. Participants became very good at performing this discrimination, but then when the parameters of the task were changed in seemingly minor ways (i.e., the orientation of the patterns or the distance of the participants from the patterns), performance dropped back down to initial levels. Overall, this type of task-specific learning tends to be the most common result of perceptual and cognitive training. Because of this tendency toward learning specificity, the results of action game training are of particular note (i.e., improvements on tasks that share no clear surface features with the games).

Selective Attention

While there is significant overlap between those tasks thought to measure "selective attention abilities" and those thought to measure "perceptual abilities," in general attentional tasks are those that require participants to selectively enhance the processing gain of task-relevant information, while attenuating the processing gain of irrelevant information (i.e., the presence of some distracting information that must be suppressed is key).

A commonly utilized measure of visual selective attention is the Useful Field of View task, which requires participants to locate a target in their visual periphery (at varying degrees of eccentricity from 10 degrees to 30 degrees) from among a field of distractors. Performance on this task has been shown to be more predictive of the visual skills relevant to driving a car than performance on standard vision measures employed by most DMVs (e.g., standard eye charts—Owsley et al., 1998). Green and Bavelier (2003), found AVGPs to perform significantly better than NVGPs in this task. Then, in a follow-up training study, individuals trained 1 h per day for 10 days on an action video game (*Medal of Honor: Allied Assault*) improved significantly more on this task than did individuals trained on a nonaction game (*Tetris*).

While the Useful Field of View taps the ability to deploy attention across space, AVGPs have also been shown to have an advantage in their ability to deploy attention across time. The attentional blink, a popular measure of such ability, presents participants with a rapid stream of black letters, with a single white letter appearing at some point in the stream. On 50% of trials, a black "X" appears at some point after the white letter. Participants are tasked with first identifying the white letter, and then indicating whether an "X" was present in the stream. A wealth of studies have shown that if the "X" appears within 200–400 ms of the white letter, participants often fail to perceive it, and incorrectly report that it was not present (hence the term "attentional blink"—Raymond, Shapiro, & Arnell, 1992). Extended action video game experience has been associated with a shortened attentional blink, in both correlational and intervention studies (Dye & Bavelier, 2010; Green & Bavelier, 2003).

Beyond the deployment of attention in space and time, one final aspect of visual attention is the ability to attend to multiple stimuli simultaneously—often thought of as the "capacity" of visual attention. This capacity is often measured with the multiple object tracking (MOT) paradigm. This task requires participants to track several moving targets (i.e., blue dots) among a field of moving distractors (i.e., yellow dots). After several seconds, the blue target dots change color to appear the same as the yellow distractor dots, and participants are asked to continue tracking the original target dots. AVGPs have been shown to track a larger number of dots than NVGPs in correlational studies (Dye & Bavelier, 2010) with the causal relationship between action gaming and enhanced tracking abilities confirmed in an intervention study (Green & Bavelier, 2006).

Sustaining Attention, Impulsivity, Speed/Accuracy Tradeoffs

While selective attention refers to the capacity to focus on important information while filtering out distracting information, sustained attention refers to the ability to remain focused on a given task or stimulus for an extended period of time. Many of the concerns raised about possible negative outcomes of video games have come in the form of characterizing avid video gamers as "trigger happy," or arguing that the fast-paced nature of many games may make it difficult for children to remain focused in a relatively slow-paced classroom environment. However, the literature to date has offered little evidence in support of these concerns for adults (at least with respect to action games specifically, see next).

Two common measures of sustained attention are the Test of Variables of Attention (TOVA) and the AX-Continuous Performance Test (AX-CPT). In the TOVA, on each trial, participants are shown one of two stimuli—a square that appears on the top half of the screen or a square that appears on the bottom half of the screen. The participants are instructed that if they see the former stimulus (square on the top half), they are to press a button as quickly as possible (i.e., "go"). If they see the latter stimulus (square on the bottom half) they are to make no response (i.e., "no-go"). The overall task consists of two blocks that differ in the proportion of "go" to "no-go" trials that are present. In one block most of the trials contain squares in the upper half of the screen (i.e., "go" trials). The measure of most significant interest in this block is thus whether the individual can withhold a response when the rare "no-go" stimuli appear. In the second block, most of the trials contain squares in the bottom half of the screen (i.e., "no-go" trials). The measure of the most significant interest in this block is thus whether the individual can stay on task and respond quickly when the rare "go" stimuli appear. In cross-sectional work, AVGPs showed faster response times than NVGPs in both blocks of trials. Critically though, there was no difference in accuracy between the groups (i.e., the AVGPs were, if anything more capable of sustaining attention and were no more impulsive; Dye, Green, & Bavelier, 2009a). The AX-CPT is a similar task where participants respond as quickly as they can to a target stimulus under some conditions, and withhold the impulse to respond under other conditions. AVGPs have also been found to perform faster in this task, again with no harm to their accuracy (Cardoso-Leite et al., 2016).

In general, the pattern observed previously, with AVGPs responding faster to stimuli, but showing no corresponding decrease in accuracy, is consistent with the broader literature. To quantify this, Dye and colleagues

(Dye et al., 2009a) created what is known as a "Brinley plot" of the literature, wherein for each task reported in the literature, AVGP reaction time was plotted against NVGP reaction time. The authors found that across a wide range of average response times (i.e., from tasks where most participants responded in less than 300 ms, to tasks where most participants took more than 1 s to respond) AVGPs were approximately 12% faster than NVGPs, with no concomitant change in accuracy. This data is thus consistent with a true improvement in cognitive skill in AVGPs as a result of action video game experience, rather than, for instance, a simple speed–accuracy tradeoff.

Cognitive Control

A similar body of research has investigated the relationship between action video games and cognitive control abilities. Cognitive control refers to a variety of high-level cognitive abilities that require coordination of various sub-processes related to, for example, perception, memory, and planning. Task switching, or the ability to flexibly switch between different tasks, is thought to be one key aspect of cognitive control. This ability is typically measured by having participants alternate between two different tasks that are both performed on the same stimuli. For instance, participants might be presented with a global shape, composed of several smaller, local shapes (e.g., a square made of small circles), and be cued to identify either the global or local shape on different trials. Colzato, Van Leeuwen, Van Den Wildenberg, and Hommel (2010) used this task switching task to compare the cognitive-control abilities of AVGPs against that of NVGPs. While there was no significant group difference for overall reaction times, AVGPs reacted faster on trials that required them to switch to the alternate task. This same basic finding of action game-related advantages in task switching has been observed by a number of independent laboratories and indeed, is among the most consistently replicated findings in the field (Cain, Landau, & Shimamura, 2012; Green, Sugarman, Medford, Klobusicky, & Bavelier, 2012; Strobach, Frensch, & Schubert, 2012).

Another key aspect of cognitive control is dual-tasking/multitasking (i.e., wherein participants are given multiple tasks to perform at overlapping points in time, as opposed to in sequence as in task-switching paradigms). For example, Strobach et al. (2012) employed a dual-task measure wherein participants responded as quickly as possible to both a visual and an auditory stimulus that were offset from each other by a variable temporal delay (where shorter offsets make it more difficult to quickly perform the second task).

In both correlational and intervention designs, action gaming was shown to result in improved performance on this dual-tasking skill.

Practical Outcomes

The broad positive effects induced by action video game play have led many investigators to translate this research into practical applications. One such application has been to incorporate action video game training into treatment of individuals with amblyopia (colloquially termed "lazy eye"). This is a visual disorder wherein the brain disregards information from one, otherwise functional eye (usually due to issues such as strabismus or cataracts during early childhood). Previous research had struggled to produce effective treatments for adults with amblyopia; however, Li, Ngo, Nguyen, and Levi (2011) found significant improvements in visual acuity, and in some cases stereovision, in adult amblyopia trained on an action video game (note while the control group trained on a nonaction game also showed improvements, these effects were not as large). In addition to rehabilitation, action games have also been utilized in the training of both pilots and laparoscopic surgeons (McKinley, McIntire, & Funke, 2011; Schlickum, Hedman, Enochsson, Kjellin, & Felländer-Tsai, 2009).

Areas Where Little or No Improvements Have Been Observed

Action games lead to strong benefits in a large number of cognitive and perceptual areas. However, it is important to note that action games are not a panacea, and there are some cognitive domains where little to no evidence of improvement is found. For instance, exogenous attention (i.e., attention that is naturally drawn to salient stimuli such as flashes of light) has consistently failed to show change in response to action video game experience (Castel, Pratt, & Drummond, 2005; Dye, Green, & Bavelier, 2009b; Hubert-Wallander, Green, Sugarman, & Bavelier, 2011). This situation may reflect that this ability is at least partially subserved by less plastic subcortical brain regions, as compared to the more plastic cortical regions that underlie most of the selective attention/cognitive control abilities discussed previously. Furthermore, while there is not a great deal of research on the topic to date, it appears that those cognitive abilities that are not heavily utilized within action games, for instance, verbal cognition and fluid reasoning, are also not enhanced via action gaming (again speaking to idea that it is the nature of the experience that drives changes in cognitive function).

BRIEF REVIEW OF THE PERCEPTUAL AND COGNITIVE EFFECTS OF ACTION VIDEO GAMES IN CHILDREN

Genre Unspecific Studies From the 1990s and Early 2000s

Much of the early research on the cognitive effects of video games on children did not separate out the effects of different genres of video games and instead lumped all "gamers" together into a single group. For instance, Kuhlman and Beitel (1991) sorted a sample of 105 7- to 9-year-old children into three groups: non-, moderate-, and highly-experienced video game players. The experimenters found a main effect in their measure of interest, which was a coincidence anticipation task (i.e., a task that measures participants' ability to respond in rhythm with a dynamic stimulus), with highly experienced gamers outperforming nongamers. They also found an interaction between video game experience and gender, wherein female nongamers performed significantly worse than male nongamers, but there was no significant difference between female gamers and male gamers (an effect that was echoed in later work in action games—Feng, Spence, & Pratt, 2007). Along similar lines, Yuji (1996) separated a sample of 4- to 6-year-olds into video game playing and nonvideo game playing groups based on their responses to a simple 10-question survey of their possession of, and enthusiasm toward computer games. Children who were classified as video game players were found to have faster reaction times, with no loss in accuracy, than children classified as nonvideo game players.

While the two studies described previously are both correlational in nature, there is also some work from this time period that employed causal methods. For instance, Subrahmanyam and Greenfield (1994) split a cohort of 61 fifth graders (10.5–11.5 years old) into an action gaming, and a control gaming group. The action group was trained over three sessions with the video game *Marble Madness*, whereas the control group was trained on a simple word game. The authors found that *Marble Madness* training led to greater improvements between pretest and posttest in the outcome measures of spatial performance, with individuals with initially poor spatial skills showing the greatest improvements. Along similar lines, De Lisi and Wolford (2002) trained a group of 8- to 9-year-old students on either the video game *Tetris* (which is not an action video game, but was predicted to improve mental rotation ability), or the video game *Where in the World Is Carmen Sandiego* (as an entertainment-matched control game). Students in each group had equivalent mental rotation ability at pretest, but at posttest, students in the *Tetris* group performed significantly better, with the largest effect among female participants who had below-median performance at pretest.

Action Video Game Correlational Studies in Children

Because of the various ethical (e.g., action games are often violent) and logistical (e.g., fewer children have access to action video games than adults) issues, the majority of the research on action games specifically has been conducted using young adult participants. However, there is still a reasonable body of research on the effects of action video games on children and youth.

Trick, Jaspers-Fayer, and Sethi (2005) conducted one of the earliest studies examining the relationship between modern action video game experience and cognitive abilities in youth populations. In a correlational design, they compared performance in different groups of children on an MOT task. As is common in cognitive measures of younger children, the experimental task was "dressed up" in a gamified form so as to better hold the interest of the young participants. In the case of the MOT task, the gamification consisted of having participants track "spies" that disguised themselves in a crowd of "happy faces." as opposed to the adult version where colored target dots changed their color to appear indistinguishable from distractor dots. This study utilized five age groups (6, 8, 10, 12, 19), split between action video game players, action-sports players (i.e., players of real-life sports such as hockey or soccer), and nonaction players. For each age group, action game players were found to perform significantly better than nonplayers on the MOT task (with action-sports player performance lying in between those two groups).

Subsequent correlational studies found similar results wherein youth in age groups of 7–10, 11–13, 14–17, and 18–22 years old were tested on a variety of cognitive measures, and performance was compared between AVGPs and NVGPs within each age group. One such study (Dye et al., 2009b) utilized the Attentional Network Test (ANT), a commonly used task that provides reliable measurements on three components of attention: alerting, orienting, and executive control. This computerized task typically presents subjects with a row of arrows either above or below a fixation cross in the center of the screen, and the subject is tasked with indicating the direction of the central arrows. The arrows flanking the central arrow are either congruent (point in the same direction) or incongruent (pointing in the opposite direction), with the difference in reaction time between these two types of trials providing a measure of executive control/attentional spillover (see Dye et al., 2009b for additional discussion of this measure). Additionally, on some trials, the onset of the arrows is preceded by a cue that either alerts subjects to the upcoming presentation of the arrow (alerting network), or to the upcoming location of the arrow on the screen (orienting network). Similar to the modified MOT task above, the version of the ANT employed in this study was designed with fish pointing right or left, rather than arrows, so as to be more child friendly. Across all measures, action video game players were faster than nonaction players, without a concomitant decrease in accuracy. For the specific attentional networks, action gamers in each group exhibited greater benefits from orienting cues, and possessed increased attentional resources that spilled over to incongruent cues. No, difference in performance resulted from alerting cues, suggesting that some attentional networks are more susceptible to action game-related effects than others.

Another experiment, utilizing the same age groups as those described in the experiment above, found an advantage for action gaming in three different measures of cognitive skill described previously (Dye & Bavelier, 2010). In the Useful Field of View task, AVGPs in each age group had lower thresholds than their NVGP counterparts, whereby they could accurately identify the location of the target with a shorter presentation interval. In the attentional blink task, AVGPs were found to have smaller "blinks," whereby they needed less time for their attention to recover. In the MOT test, AVGPs in each age group were able to accurately track more objects than NVGPs, suggestive of a greater attentional capacity.

Along similar lines, researchers in Saudi Arabia recruited 156 children (mean age 9.2 years), and categorized them as either AVGPs or NVGPs based on the reported gameplay from both the children and their parents. Action gamers performed significantly better in numerous cognitive measures, including measures of spatial working memory, attention, and response inhibition (Al-Gabbani, Morgan, & Eyre, 2014). Of additional interest was that the fairly large sample size allowed the investigators to run a separate analysis of just the female participants, and found that the effect of action gaming remained.

Experimental Studies

Although most action games have a degree of violence that makes them unacceptable for training studies involving children, several groups have circumvented this issue by employing custom-made research video games. One such study by Rueda, Rothbart, McCandliss, Saccomanno, and Posner (2005) modified a training program previously used to train macaques for space travel into a gamified series of computer tasks, designed to tap various cognitive and executive functions. Over the course of five training days, children completed 9 or 10 different exercises that consisted of controlling or interacting with different objects or animals (e.g., observing a duck diving into a pond and, based on its trajectory, estimating where it would surface, or responding as fast as possible to sheep, while inhibiting responses if the sheep turned into wolves). This experiment employed a large battery of pretest/ posttest measures. Although many of the group comparisons were not significant, significant differences were found in intelligence measures of 4-year-olds in the training group, and a marginally significant intelligence advantage for 6-year-olds in the training group.

Another intervention study conducted by Mackey, Hill, Stone, and Bunge (2011), enrolled children ages 7–10, from low SES backgrounds. Children were assigned to one of two active training programs, a program designed to improve speed of processing, and a training group designed to improve reasoning and relational thinking. In sixteen 60-min sessions, both groups were trained with a variety of computerized (commercial video games on a computer and on a Nintendo DS) and noncomputerized games, selected by experimenters to tap the underlying skills of interest. Researchers were present during the training to provide encouragement and increase the difficulty level of the training games when appropriate. Both training groups saw improvements in the targeted skills, with the speed of processing group showing improvements in the cognitive speed tasks, but not the reasoning tasks. The reasoning group showed improvements in a test of nonverbal intelligence (TONI), with an average increase of 10 points in IQ, but no improvements in the cognitive speed tasks.

Practical Applications

In an example of a study that combined theoretical and translational work, Franceschini et al. (2013) examined the impact of action-game training on both standard attentional skills (of the type described previously) and on reading ability in a cohort of dyslexic children. As is standard in such studies, half of the children were assigned to train on an action game, while the other half were assigned to train on a control game. In a particularly clever twist though, both the action and control games were created from the same global "game"—*Rayman's Raving Rabbids*. The global *Rayman's Raving Rabbids* game contains a number of smaller "mini-games." The authors thus selected a subset of the mini-games that contained a great deal of action (i.e., the games had many quickly/unpredictably moving targets, high perceptual load, an emphasis on peripheral processing) for the action group to train on and selected a different subset of mini-games, that contained no action, for the control group to train on. After 12 h of training, those children trained on the action games showed improved visual attentional skills (replicating the standard effect seen in the field), and significantly improved reading ability, as compared to the controls. These reading improvements appeared to have been driven by increased reading speed, without any concomitant decrease in accuracy. A follow-up test 2 months after completion of the study suggested that the results had persisted.

Possible Negative Effects

While the research on action video games has tended to find either beneficial or in some cases, null effects across age groups, there has been some, broader level research that has found negative correlations between global video game use (i.e., not separated by genre) and attention. For instance, Swing, Gentile, Anderson, and Walsh (2010) tracked self- and parent-reported video game use, as well as teacher-reported attentional problems, of third, fourth and fifth graders over the course of 13 months. For each age group, controlling for gender, they found significant correlations between reported video game use and teacher-reported attentional problems. Importantly, these effects remained significant across time when controlling for previous attention problems (i.e., video game use at the first time point predicted attention problems at the final time point, independent of attention problems at the first time point). However, because this study was focused at the superordinate level of "video games," it remains difficult to discern what types of games may have been responsible for these correlations.

IMPACT OF OTHER EMERGING MEDIA INTERACTIONS

Whereas over the past two decades cognitive psychology research on the impact of technology has tended to focus on media such as video games and television, in recent years other forms of human-technology interactions have become of increasing interest. For instance, the phenomenon of media multitasking, wherein an individual engages with multiple media simultaneously (e.g., monitoring multiple browser windows on one's computer while also partially attending to one's phone, and listening to music in the background), has received growing scientific attention since the first major investigation into its effects was published in 2009 by Ophir, Nass, and Wagner. In their seminal study (Ophir, Nass, & Wagner, 2009), a comprehensive survey of media multitasking behavior was created, wherein participants are asked how often they engage with 11 different media types each week (e.g., listening to music or web browsing) as well as how often they use each type of media concurrently with each other type (e.g., listening to music while web browsing). This information was used to compute the media multitasking index (MMI). Ophir and colleagues administered their survey to a large body of Stanford undergraduates, and based on the results of that survey, separated students into two groups: (1) heavy media multitaskers (HMMs), consisting of individuals whose MMI scores were one standard deviation above the group mean and (2) light media multitaskers (LMMs), consisting of individuals whose MMI scores were one standard deviation below the group mean. HMM and LMM participants were then invited into the lab to undergo a series of cognitive tasks. HMMs were found to perform significantly worse than LMMs on numerous measures of attentional control, primarily on conditions that required effective filtering of distracting stimuli. Since this seminal investigation, numerous follow-up studies have found similar associations between excessive media multitasking and impaired attentional control (e.g., Cain & Mitroff, 2011; Cardoso-Leite et al., 2016; Gorman & Green, 2016; Lottridge et al., 2015; but see also Alzahabi & Becker, 2013; Minear, Brasher, McCurdy, Lewis, & Younggren, 2013).

Although there is, as of yet, little direct work on this phenomenon in young children, there is good reason to think that the general behavior is common among younger age groups. A 2009 survey by the Kaiser Family Foundation found that 8- to 18-year-olds spent on average over 10 h with media each day, with 29% of that time spent using more than one media type at once (Rideout, Foehr, & Roberts, 2010). In perhaps the most comprehensive examination of the effects of media multitasking on youth to date, Cain, Center, Leonard, Gabrieli, and Finn (2016) measured the media multitasking tendencies of a group of 12- to 16-year-olds, and administered a large battery of cognitive tests and personality measures, in addition to collecting the statewide standardized testing scores of these participants. Higher media multitasking scores were related to lower working memory capacity, as measured by both a count span and an N-back task. Media multitasking was also negatively related to academic performance (i.e., lower math and English test scores). Finally, media multitasking was negatively related to a measure of growth mindset (the belief that one's intelligence is malleable) and positively related to self-reported impulsivity. Notably, media multitasking was not related to certain other measures, such as speed of processing, manual dexterity, conscientiousness, and grit.

Another study examining the relationship between media multitasking and cognitive functioning in youth found a significant correlation between media multitasking and distractibility during a sentence congruency judgment task. This distractibility was associated with increased right prefrontal cortex activation during the task. As this brain region is thought to be associated with top-down attentional control, greater activation may be indicative of heavy media multitaskers needing to "work harder" when performing certain cognitive tasks (Moisala et al., 2016). Consistent with this view, youth media multitasking has also been found to correlate with self-reported attentional problems (Baumgartner, Weeda, van der Heijden, & Huizinga, 2014; though note that not all studies have seen negative effects—Lui & Wong, 2012).

TECHNOLOGICAL INTERVENTIONS DESIGNED FOR IMPROVING COGNITION IN YOUTH

The success of action video games at engendering general cognitive improvements has spurred many investigators to design their own custom-made training programs, often in the form of standard psychological tasks (such as those described previously) dressed up with some sort of reward structure and a leveling system (often referred to as "gamification"). However, this type of gamification has proven to be a more difficult task than one may have thought at the outset. For instance, Katz, Jaeggi, Buschkuehl, Stegman, and Shah (2014) created a training game (based on an N-back working memory task) with five distinct motivational elements: real-time scoring, theme changes, prizes, end of session certificates, scaffolding to explain lives, and a leveling system. They examined the effects of these elements on eighth grade students by employing (1) a version with all five elements, (2) a version with none of the elements, and (3) five other versions which each removed a single motivational element. The results demonstrated no positive effect of any of the gamification elements (in fact, the effects were negative). The authors suggested that this impaired performance resulted from the motivational elements distracting subjects from the task at hand.

In a more successful example of gamifying a training task in a training-transfer experiment, Jaeggi, Buschkuehl, Jonides, and Shah (2011) created a graphically rich working memory task with dynamic themes and engaging background stories linked to the themes. Importantly, the vocabulary and knowledge control training task was also dressed up in such a manner. Elementary and middle school children trained on this task showed improved fluid intelligence scores, compared to children trained on the control task. The observed gains in fluid intelligence were far larger in that half of the sample comprising participants whose performance improved the most at the working memory training task; the effect of training persisted even when accounting for baseline ability. The children who improved the most at the training task were those who rated the training task as challenging, without being overwhelming, suggesting that optimal task difficulty may be critical for producing transfer.

This data, in combination with numerous similar studies performed on adults (Melby-Lervåg & Hulme, 2013; Redick et al., 2013) ostensibly suggests that, while progress has been made, we are not yet at the point where we can reliably and effectively translate what we know about commercial games (such as action games) in to the realm of dedicated cognitive training programs.

ISSUES GOING FORWARD

Dynamic Game Genres

The research on the genre-specific effects of certain types of video games is quickly becoming complicated by the fact that the formerly reliable boundaries between many game genres have slowly begun to dissolve. Indeed, while it was previously the case that the fast-paced, attentional-demanding mechanics of action game were unique to that genre, these mechanics are now also being incorporated into a number of genres that traditionally were not considered "action" genres. These include role playing games (i.e., *The Elder Scrolls: Skyrim*) and adventure games (i.e., *Assassins Creed: Syndicate*). Action-based mechanics can now also be found in the newer genre of real time strategy and multiplayer online battle arena games (i.e., *StarCraft* and *League of Legends*). The fact that an ever-growing number of games include "action" components, combined with the fact that video game use among teens and young adults is now greater than 90%, means that it is increasingly difficult to find participants who qualify as "nonaction game players."

Complex Mixtures of Media Effects

As described earlier, action video game experience has been both associated with, and causally related to improved perceptual and cognitive abilities, whereas media multitasking behavior has been repeatedly associated with impaired cognitive abilities. Few researchers have examined these effects in conjunction with each other. However, the research that does exist suggests that the combined effects are nonlinear in nature. For example, Cardoso-Leite et al. (2016) replicated the base effects of both the action gaming and media-multitasking literatures, wherein action gamers performed better than nongamers, and heavy media multitaskers performed worse than light media multitaskers on diverse cognitive measurements. However, the positive effects of action video game experience were only found among intermediate media multitaskers, with heavy and light media multitaskers who were also action video gamers showing no advantage. This pattern of results may not have been obvious a priori, as one may have assumed that the beneficial effects of action games would have been sufficient to overcome the typically deleterious relationship between media multitasking and cognitive ability. The pattern also strongly suggests that it will be critical for researchers in both domains to measure participant experience with gaming and media multitasking.

Other Ethical Obstacles in Children

Thus far we have discussed only a few of the ethical issues inherent in training children with video games (e.g., as related to violence). However, while the violence issue is potentially solvable (i.e., by creating/utilizing nonviolent action games), another effect—known as the displacement effect—may not be. In essence, the displacement effect refers to the simple idea that any time spent on one activity (such as playing a video game) is time not spent on another activity (such as reading or doing school-work). Weis and Cerankosky (2010) attempted to examine this issue by first recruiting families who intended to purchase a video game system for their children in the future. The researchers then offered to purchase the video game system for the family in return for participation of the child in the study. Half of the children were randomly assigned to receive their video game system right away, while the other half received the system 4 months later. The children who received their video game system immediately were found to have weaker reading and writing skills at a posttest assessment, as compared to the other group, a difference that the authors attributed to the presence of the video game system. Thus, any future training studies in children need to ensure that the intervention is not displacing what are potentially more valuable activities.

CONCLUSIONS

As video games become increasingly popular, the importance of understanding their impact has increased as well. A key conclusion of this research has been that the genre of the video game is what matters when one examines the consequences of frequent play. Within the domain of cognitive psychology, the measurable effects of action video games in particular have tended to be positive for both children and adults. This research has already had some success in the translational sphere (i.e., as applied to amblyopia and dyslexia treatment, as well as training for pilots and surgeons). However, the research to date also suggests that translating what is known about action games to produce dedicated cognitive training tools will not be a trivial endeavor.

REFERENCES

Al-Gabbani, M., Morgan, G., & Eyre, J. A. (2014). In *Positive relationship between duration of action video game play and visuospatial executive function in children IEEE 3rd international conference on serious games and applications for health (SeGAH)* (pp. 1–4): IEEE.), May.

Alzahabi, R., & Becker, M. W. (2013). The association between media multitasking, task-switching, and dual-task performance. *Journal of Experimental Psychology: Human Perception and Performance, 39*(5), 1485.

Anderson, C. A., & Bushman, B. J. (2001). Effects of violent video games on aggressive behavior, aggressive cognition, aggressive affect, physiological arousal, and prosocial behavior: A meta-analytic review of the scientific literature. *Psychological Science, 12*(5), 353–359.

Anderson, C. A., Shibuya, A., Ihori, N., Swing, E. L., Bushman, B. J., Sakamoto, A., et al. (2010). Violent video game effects on aggression, empathy, and prosocial behavior in eastern and western countries: A meta-analytic review. *Psychological Bulletin, 136*(2), 151–173.

Baddeley, A. D., & Longman, D. J. A. (1978). The influence of length and frequency of training session on the rate of learning to type. *Ergonomics, 21*(8), 627–635.

Baumgartner, S. E., Weeda, W. D., van der Heijden, L. L., & Huizinga, M. (2014). The relationship between media multitasking and executive function in early adolescents. *The Journal of Early Adolescence, 34*(8), 1120–1144.

Buckley, D., Codina, C., Bhardwaj, P., & Pascalis, O. (2010). Action video game players and deaf observers have larger Goldmann visual fields. *Vision Research, 50*(5), 548–556.

Cain, M. S., Center, N., Leonard, M. J. A., Gabrieli, J. D., & Finn, A. S. (2016). Media multitasking in adolescence. *Psychonomic Bulletin & Review, 23*(6), 1932–1941.

Cain, M. S., Landau, A. N., & Shimamura, A. P. (2012). Action video game experience reduces the cost of switching tasks. *Attention, Perception, & Psychophysics, 74*(4), 641–647.

Cain, M. S., & Mitroff, S. R. (2011). Distractor filtering in media multitaskers. *Perception, 40*(10), 1183–1192.

Cardoso-Leite, P., Kludt, R., Vignola, G., Ma, W. J., Green, C. S., & Bavelier, D. (2016). Technology consumption and cognitive control: Contrasting action video game experience with media multitasking. *Attention, Perception, & Psychophysics, 78*(1), 218–241.

Castel, A. D., Pratt, J., & Drummond, E. (2005). The effects of action video game experience on the time course of inhibition of return and the efficiency of visual search. *Acta Psychologica, 119*(2), 217–230.

Charsky, D. (2010). From edutainment to serious games: A change in the use of game characteristics. *Games and Culture 5*(2), 177–198.

Colzato, L. S., Van Leeuwen, P. J., Van Den Wildenberg, W., & Hommel, B. (2010). DOOM'd to switch: Superior cognitive flexibility in players of first person shooter games. *Frontiers in Psychology, 1*, 8.

De Lisi, R., & Wolford, J. L. (2002). Improving children's mental rotation accuracy with computer game playing. *The Journal of Genetic Psychology, 163*(3), 272–282.

Donohue, S. E., Woldorff, M. G., & Mitroff, S. R. (2010). Video game players show more precise multisensory temporal processing abilities. *Attention, Perception, & Psychophysics, 72*(4), 1120–1129.

Dye, M. W., & Bavelier, D. (2010). Differential development of visual attention skills in school-age children. *Vision Research, 50*(4), 452–459.

Dye, M. W., Green, C. S., & Bavelier, D. (2009a). Increasing speed of processing with action video games. *Current Directions in Psychological Science, 18*(6), 321–326.

Dye, M. W., Green, C. S., & Bavelier, D. (2009b). The development of attention skills in action video game players. *Neuropsychologia, 47*(8), 1780–1789.

Entertainment Software Association (2015). 2015 essential facts about the computer and video game industry. *Social Science Computer Review, 4*(1), 2–4. Retrieved from http://www.theesa.com/facts/pdfs/ESA_EF_2008.pdf.

Fahle, M. (2005). Perceptual learning: Specificity versus generalization. *Current Opinion in Neurobiology, 15*(2), 154–160.

Feng, J., Spence, I., & Pratt, J. (2007). Playing an action video game reduces gender differences in spatial cognition. *Psychological Science, 18*(10), 850–855.

Fiorentini, A., & Berardi, N. (1980). Perceptual learning specific for orientation and spatial frequency. *Nature, 218*, 697–698.

Franceschini, S., Gori, S., Ruffino, M., Viola, S., Molteni, M., & Facoetti, A. (2013). Action video games make dyslexic children read better. *Current Biology, 23*(6), 462–466.

Gentile, D. (2009). Pathological video-game use among youth ages 8 to 18. A national study. *Psychological Science, 20*(5), 594–602.

Gentile, D. A., & Gentile, J. R. (2008). Violent video games as exemplary teachers: A conceptual analysis. *Journal of Youth and Adolescence, 37*(2), 127–141.

Gentzkow, M., & Shapiro, J. M. (2008). Preschool television viewing and adolescent test scores: Historical evidence from the Coleman study. *The Quarterly Journal of Economics*, 279–323.

Gorman, T. E., & Green, C. S. (2016). Short-term mindfulness intervention reduces the negative attentional effects associated with heavy media multitasking. *Scientific Reports, 6*.

Green, C. S., & Bavelier, D. (2003). Action video game modifies visual selective attention. *Nature, 423*(6939), 534–537.

Green, C. S., & Bavelier, D. (2006). Effect of action video games on the spatial distribution of visuospatial attention. *Journal of Experimental Psychology: Human Perception and Performance, 32*(6), 1465.

Green, C. S., Strobach, T., & Schubert, T. (2014). On methodological standards in training and transfer experiments. *Psychological Research, 78*(6), 756–772.

Green, C. S., Sugarman, M. A., Medford, K., Klobusicky, E., & Bavelier, D. (2012). The effect of action video game experience on task-switching. *Computers in Human Behavior, 28*(3), 984–994.

Hubert-Wallander, B., Green, C. S., Sugarman, M., & Bavelier, D. (2011). Changes in search rate but not in the dynamics of exogenous attention in action videogame players. *Attention, Perception, & Psychophysics, 73*(8), 2399–2412.

Hutchinson, C. V., & Stocks, R. (2013). Selectively enhanced motion perception in core video gamers. *Perception, 42*(6), 675–677.

Jaeggi, S. M., Buschkuehl, M., Jonides, J., & Shah, P. (2011). Short-and long-term benefits of cognitive training. *Proceedings of the National Academy of Sciences of the United States of America, 108*(25), 10081–10086.

Katz, B., Jaeggi, S., Buschkuehl, M., Stegman, A., & Shah, P. (2014). Differential effect of motivational features on training improvements in school-based cognitive training. *Frontiers in Human Neuroscience, 8.*

Kuhlman, J. S., & Beitel, P. A. (1991). Videogame experience: A possible explanation for differences in anticipation of coincidence. *Perceptual and Motor Skills, 72*(2), 483–488.

Li, R. W., Ngo, C., Nguyen, J., & Levi, D. M. (2011). Video-game play induces plasticity in the visual system of adults with amblyopia. *PLoS Biol, 9*(8), e1001135.

Li, R., Polat, U., Makous, W., & Bavelier, D. (2009). Enhancing the contrast sensitivity function through action video game training. *Nature Neuroscience, 12*(5), 549.

Lottridge, D. M., Rosakranse, C., Oh, C. S., Westwood, S. J., Baldoni, K. A., Mann, A. S., et al. (2015). In *The effects of chronic multitasking on analytical writing Proceedings of the 33rd annual ACM conference on human factors in computing systems* (pp. 2967–2970): ACM.

Lui, K. F., & Wong, A. C. N. (2012). Does media multitasking always hurt? A positive correlation between multitasking and multisensory integration. *Psychonomic Bulletin & Review, 19*(4), 647–653.

Mackey, A. P., Hill, S. S., Stone, S. I., & Bunge, S. A. (2011). Differential effects of reasoning and speed training in children. *Developmental Science, 14*(3), 582–590.

McKinley, R. A., McIntire, L. K., & Funke, M. A. (2011). Operator selection for unmanned aerial systems: Comparing video game players and pilots. *Aviation, Space, and Environmental Medicine, 82*(6), 635–642.

Melby-Lervåg, M., & Hulme, C. (2013). Is working memory training effective? A -meta-analytic review. *Developmental Psychology, 49*(2), 270.

Minear, M., Brasher, F., McCurdy, M., Lewis, J., & Younggren, A. (2013). Working memory, fluid intelligence, and impulsiveness in heavy media multitaskers. *Psychonomic Bulletin & Review, 20*(6), 1274–1281.

Moisala, M., Salmela, V., Hietajärvi, L., Salo, E., Carlson, S., Salonen, O., et al. (2016). Media multitasking is associated with distractibility and increased prefrontal activity in adolescents and young adults. *NeuroImage, 134*, 113–121.

Ophir, E., Nass, C., & Wagner, A. D. (2009). Cognitive control in media multitaskers. *Proceedings of the National Academy of Sciences of the United States of America, 106*(37), 15583–15587.

Owsley, C., Ball, K., McGwin, G., Jr., Sloane, M. E., Roenker, D. L., White, M. F., et al. (1998). Visual processing impairment and risk of motor vehicle crash among older adults. *JAMA, 279*(14), 1083–1088.

Powers, K. L., Brooks, P. J., Aldrich, N. J., Palladino, M. A., & Alfieri, L. (2013). Effects of video-game play on information processing: A meta-analytic investigation. *Psychonomic Bulletin & Review, 20*(6), 1055–1079.

Raymond, J. E., Shapiro, K. L., & Arnell, K. M. (1992). Temporary suppression of visual processing in an RSVP task: An attentional blink? *Journal of Experimental Psychology: Human Perception and Performance, 18*(3), 849.

Redick, T. S., Shipstead, Z., Harrison, T. L., Hicks, K. L., Fried, D. E., Hambrick, D. Z., et al. (2013). No evidence of intelligence improvement after working memory training: A randomized, placebo-controlled study. *Journal of Experimental Psychology: General, 142* (2), 359.

Rideout, V. J., Foehr, U. G., & Roberts, D. F. (2010). *Generation M^2: Media in the lives of 8-to 18-year-olds.* Henry J. Kaiser Family Foundation.

Rueda, M. R., Rothbart, M. K., McCandliss, B. D., Saccomanno, L., & Posner, M. I. (2005). Training, maturation, and genetic influences on the development of executive attention. *Proceedings of the National Academy of Sciences of the United States of America, 102* (41), 14931–14936.

Schlickum, M. K., Hedman, L., Enochsson, L., Kjellin, A., & Felländer-Tsai, L. (2009). Systematic video game training in surgical novices improves performance in virtual reality endoscopic surgical simulators: A prospective randomized study. *World Journal of Surgery, 33*(11), 2360–2367.

Sowden, P. T., Rose, D., & Davies, I. R. (2002). Perceptual learning of luminance contrast detection: Specific for spatial frequency and retinal location but not orientation. *Vision Research, 42*(10), 1249–1258.

Spence, I., & Feng, J. (2010). Video games and spatial cognition. *Review of General Psychology, 14*(2), 92.

Strobach, T., Frensch, P. A., & Schubert, T. (2012). Video game practice optimizes executive control skills in dual-task and task switching situations. *Acta Psychologica, 140*(1), 13–24.

Subrahmanyam, K., & Greenfield, P. M. (1994). Effect of video game practice on spatial skills in girls and boys. *Journal of Applied Developmental Psychology, 15*(1), 13–32.

Swing, E. L., Gentile, D. A., Anderson, C. A., & Walsh, D. A. (2010). Television and video game exposure and the development of attention problems. *Pediatrics, 126*(2), 214–221.

Trick, L. M., Jaspers-Fayer, F., & Sethi, N. (2005). Multiple-object tracking in children: The "catch the spies" task. *Cognitive Development, 20*(3), 373–387.

Weis, R., & Cerankosky, B. C. (2010). Effects of video-game ownership on young boys' academic and behavioral functioning a randomized controlled study. *Psychological Science, 21*(4), 463–470.

Yuji, H. (1996). Computer games and information-processing skills. *Perceptual and Motor Skills, 83*(2), 643–647.

CHAPTER 7

Playing With Virtual Blocks: *Minecraft* as a Learning Environment for Practice and Research

H. Chad Lane, Sherry Yi
University of Illinois, Urbana-Champaign, IL, United States

If we can discover a child's urgent needs and powers, and if we can supply an environment of materials, appliances, and resources—physical, social, and intellectual—to direct their adequate operation, we shall not have to think about interest. It will take care of itself—John Dewey (1913, pp. 95–96).

INTRODUCTION: WHAT IS IN A "GAME?"

Whether it be over violence, addiction, or cognitive and social development, debates on the impact of video games have proven extraordinarily difficult to characterize. Confirmation biases and personal opinions seem to dominate public discourse, with video game play often spuriously implicated after mass shootings and violent attacks (Ferguson, 2016). Despite consistent attention being paid to the problems and consequences associated with video game play, researchers have also examined the possible positive aspects of video game play, which include benefits in motivational, emotional, cognitive, and social aspects of one's life (Granic, Lobel, & Engels, 2014). The explosion of games and game genres over the last several decades have even made it difficult to conclude that video games comprise a coherent category suitable for methodological inquiry. In a position statement addressing how video game study findings are reported, Bavelier et al. (2011) remarked that "One can no more say what the effects of video games are, than one can say what the effects of food are" (p. 763). Indeed, the highly novel designs and mechanics present in many modern games, especially those coming from the Indie (or "Independent") market, make them resistant to clear boundaries or categories. Thus, we argue that references to video game play may be less critical in reviewing their impacts than the kinds of experiences that they provide.

Cognitive Development in Digital Contexts
http://dx.doi.org/10.1016/B978-0-12-809481-5.00007-9

145

Video games provide engineered experience generators that seek to engage players emotionally, cognitively, and socially (Sylvester, 2013). Our position is that researchers who study the impact of game play should seek to link changes in knowledge or behavior to the kinds of manufactured experiences they provide. It is not enough for parents to blame video games for their children's behavior as much as it is unreasonable for a teacher to blame a child for using a cell phone in class. While acknowledging that the child might have stepped out of the set boundaries, we must recognize the *intentions* of the child while using the digital tool. Was the child acting out for attention, and games make him or her feel more adequate? Was the child using his or her cell phone to perform menial calculations in order to solve a much more elaborate math problem? When would it be appropriate for adults to intervene? Therefore, it is important for researchers, educators, and parents to develop an understanding of, for example, what kinds of situations arise within games, what decisions players make, and what sorts of interactions they have before making bold claims about their consequences. We further suggest unpacking the thinking and decision making required to play a given game and consider how players feel about the experiences they have in that environment.

In this chapter, we pursue these goals with a focus on the very popular and influential game, *Minecraft*. Because research that investigates *Minecraft* is nascent, we make no broad claims regarding its impacts or consequences of play; however, we do lay out an argument for why we believe *Minecraft* to be a unique educational game among its mainstream kin and why researchers and educators should consider it as potentially transformative for fostering learning and cognitive skills. Since Markus Persson released an early version of the game in 2009 (with the official release in 2011 through his Swedish company, Mojang), millions of children across the world have chosen to spend hundreds of thousands of cumulative years playing (Thompson, 2016). Given this situation, we believe that it is probably influencing how children think about the world around them including how it works and how we build on it. We view *Minecraft* as an ideal target for research on learning and development, to summarize the kinds of activities involved in playing, to describe how and why children play, and discuss how educators are already using it in schools and other contexts around the world. We present arguments for pursuing research on how *Minecraft* may foster science learning, promote collaboration and creativity, and be used as a vehicle for the development of interest.

Minecraft: An overview. Why is *Minecraft* so relevant for education and learning? What makes it appealing for educators and parents who may be unsure about their own family's video game playing policies? The simplest observation is that interactions in *Minecraft* involve a broad range of educationally relevant content. For example, in *Minecraft*, players routinely engage in activities that involve:

- exploring and investigating different biomes and climates that match those on Earth, including deserts, forests, jungles, and taigas;
- navigating in and around different types of terrain, such as hills, mountains, caverns, caves, and oceans;
- interacting with a wide variety of wildlife and agricultural content, including animals, fish, birds, wheat, grass, fruits, vegetables, and diverse fictional content;
- searching for, mining, collecting, and combining many different resources such as different kinds of wood, stone, metal, and dirt; and
- designing and building electrical circuits, switches, and complex machines that can sense and modify the world.

Players have even reconstructed existing world wonders. Many of these works of engineering that can be found online (e.g., YouTube, dedicated servers) are virtual copies of actual structures such as the *Taj Mahal*, but many more can only exist virtually, such as *Westeros* from the television series *Game of Thrones* (see Fig. 1). To achieve such feats of engineering, players often work collaboratively by planning and coordinating their tasks. They assume roles (e.g., as resource collectors, planners, builders), work iteratively to refine and perfect their creations, and share their work with friends, family, and online communities.

The popularity of *Minecraft*. Since its release in 2009 and recent ascendance to the second most popular video game of all time (Peckham, 2016), *Minecraft* has achieved historic levels of use (see Table 1). Demographic data are difficult to gather given Mojang's privacy policies; however, one survey suggests that 20.59% (of the 100 M+ players) are less than 15 years of age.[1] With console and mobile app sales capturing more than 67% of total sales, the number of young players has grown since 2015: a recent analysis (Bryant & Levine, 2015) of mobile game play by children ages 6–14, found that 85% played at least several times a week, with almost half playing their favorite app every day. In the same age range, *Minecraft* tops the list of favorite apps for boys (with 16.3% indicating it as their favorite) and

---

[1] http://minecraft-seeds.net/blog/minecraft-player-demographics/.

Fig. 1 Minecraft recreations of the Taj Mahal (top) and Westeros (bottom; part of WesterosCraft.com, a mod devoted to the television show).

comes in third place for girls (with 8.5% indicating it as their favorite). For the youngest learners (ages 6–11), *Minecraft* finished in a clear first place again (over *Angry Birds*).

Given the massive size of the community, *Minecraft* has an enormous audience of players from many different age groups. Upon the release of touch-screen and mobile versions of the game, the number of younger players skyrocketed—this development is, in part, one of the motivations for investigating it as a unique learning tool. We contend that *Minecraft* is likely influencing these young learners, in terms of how they perceive the world and, relevant to national goals to improve students' achievement in STEM (science, technology, engineering, and math), how they learn science and math. With these data in mind, we describe below what it is like to play *Minecraft*, what players actually do when playing, and how they go about personalizing it for their own interests.

Table 1 How big is *Minecraft*?[a]

100,000,000+ players	19,000,000 PC downloads	54,000,000 units sold
241,000,000 logins per month (2011)	Purchased by Microsoft, $2.5B (2014)	2B+ hours played (Xbox alone)
18×10^{18} possible worlds	The Danish Geodata Agency built a 1:1 model of Denmark (1 T blocks) (2014)	*"Minecraft"* #2 YouTube search (2014)

[a]http://www.wired.com/2015/05/data-effect-minecraft/ Fallon, S. (May 27, 2015).

MINECRAFT 101

Minecraft is a video game that is relatively intuitive to play and capable of supporting incredibly complex interactions and experiences. It is frequently characterized as a "sandbox" style game, whereby it prioritizes open play such that players can roam freely and pursue self-generated goals using any means that the game allows (Lastowka, 2012; West & Bleiberg, 2013). With its decidedly lower resolution graphics and open approach to content development, its success has come as a surprise to the commercial games industry. It is widely believed that one of the key factors behind its rapid ascent was Mojang's, the company behind *Minecraft*'s creation, early embracing of user generated content and user modification (a highly uncommon practice for game studios at the time). Although *Minecraft* has evolved substantially since its official release, the core mechanics, interactions, and basic game play modes have remained stable.

A world made out of blocks. Simply put, *Minecraft* is played in a world made entirely of blocks. The various blocks encountered in the game have different compositions and functions, such as variants of stone, wood, and metal. Even liquids, such as water and lava, are modeled as block units, although they adhere to natural laws such as gravity and flow. Prior to starting a single-player game, the terrain (i.e., a virtual world) must be generated. These digital worlds are huge as the exact cubic volume of a *Minecraft* world is 262 quadrillion by 144 trillion blocks (West & Bleiberg, 2013). The terrain generation algorithm produces remarkable (block-style) landscapes and includes features found in the natural world, such as varying biomes (e.g., desert, forest), caves, mountains, oceans, rivers, and lakes (Fig. 2 shows two typical screenshots). No two *Minecraft* worlds are exactly alike, and the generation algorithm can be adjusted to meet entertainment or educational needs (such as favoring more deserts or oceans).

Two primary modes of play: Survival and creative. In stark contrast to a majority of commercial games, *Minecraft* does not include an active narrative or set game play objectives. Nor is there is a direct way to "win" or obvious ways to "level up," although some elements of experience points are used (e.g., items acquired during gameplay can be enhanced through "enchanting,"

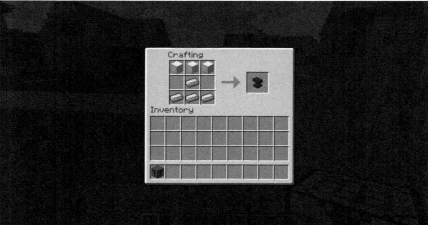

Fig. 2 Typical Minecraft interactions. The top screenshot shows an automatically generated village and farm, while the bottom screenshot shows a crafting screen, where the player can create new items (e.g., an anvil) from more basic components (e.g., iron ingots).

which is only possible after enough experience points have been earned). Although recent versions of *Minecraft* provide five different modes of play, the two most commonly used modes are survival mode, whereby the player must actively seek resources and forge tools to survive, while monsters spawn randomly during the night. The purpose of this mode is to survive by collecting, building, crafting, and defending. The creative mode grants the player invincibility, an unlimited supply of blocks and resources, the ability to fly, and places no active restriction on the player's imagination. Specifically, in this mode, players are gifted the power to create and destroy as they find necessary, goals are entirely self-generated, and the game introduces no obstacles to play. The creative mode is common for play-like activities, such as riding roller coasters, creating video recordings, exploring another player's world, interacting with and crafting their own modified objects.

At the start of a typical survival game, the player learns that she can gain wood by chopping at a tree barehanded. With wood, she can then make wooden planks and sticks through a process known as *crafting*. Four wood planks can be combined to create a *crafting table* (Fig. 2), which enables players to create more complicated tools and objects, such as an anvil as shown in the figure. Duncan (2011) explains that once the initial learning curve is mastered, the player learns how to create an even stronger axe, to construct tracks and mine carts to move ore, to make torches to light dark caves, and to recombine building blocks (stone, iron, glass) into fortresses that defend against nocturnal monsters (survival mode only). If the player gathers all the proper materials, it is possible to build working electrical circuits or coal-powered engines that function similarly to their real-life counterparts (West & Bleiberg, 2013). The pattern of collect, build, and improve repeats throughout the game, thus, enabling new tools and resources to be constructed.

The creative mode in *Minecraft* is vastly different. Players have access to an unlimited supply of the complete slate of, for example, blocks, tools, creatures, and objects. With no threats and no chance of harm from falling (your character is actually hurt when you fall too far in survival mode), players in creative mode normally build and engage in deeply elaborate and creative projects, such as recreating the Taj Mahal (shown in Fig. 1, which would have no real practical value in survival mode). Other key differences in creative mode include the ability to fly (which enables the player to view their work from a top view and explore terrains more quickly), ability to spawn creatures, such as chickens and polar bears (as many as desired), and to exert complete control over the environment, including rain and sunlight (via *Minecraft's* command line). The creative mode ultimately provides a construction and experimental playground where players can learn how to build in *Minecraft*, work on elaborate structures and inventions, and show off their work to peers and the world. Later, we discuss links between *Minecraft* and the development of creativity.

Customization and personalization. A common explanation given for *Minecraft's* remarkable success is that it is highly customizable as players create their own environment through design and construction of their own buildings, structures, and caves during normal game interactions and use a variety of external tools to make more substantive changes to the game. The three aspects of customization and personalization we address here are avatar design, world editing, and "modding" (i.e., game modification).

Avatars and skins. The "skin" of a character refers to the avatar's appearance, which is the representation of the player in the game. "Steve" (see Fig. 3) is the default character in *Minecraft* who has become a YouTube celebrity and the "face" of *Minecraft* on promotional materials. The simplest form of personalization entails adjusting or replacing the Steve skin to something more appealing to that player. Numerous Internet tools allow players to create their own skins from scratch (e.g., NovaSkin), or download existing avatars inspired, perhaps, by other interests (e.g., Darth Vader). Generally, avatar creation and selection can act as a window into a learner's identity and self-perceptions (Kafai, Fields, & Cook, 2010), and *Minecraft* is

Fig. 3 Steve, the default character in *Minecraft*, surrounded by a variety of animals and a "Creeper" (the four-legged creature to the right of Steve).

very similar to other games in this regard. For example, a player can create an avatar that, for example, sits in similarity or in opposition to their real-life persona. As with changing skins, players can also load "texture packs," which simply change the surface appearances of blocks, clouds, and other objects in the game.

Playing God: Map editors and modding. Other forms of customization of *Minecraft* are more sophisticated and involve making changes that involve use of external tools (i.e., that are not part of "Vanilla" *Minecraft*). Stepping back briefly to the early years of *Minecraft* development, one of the most noteworthy decisions that emerged was the decision to grant tremendous power to the player community to change the game in fundamental ways. This decision was atypical for game studios around 2009, but is now generally regarded as one of the most profound contributors to *Minecraft's* success. We describe two such forms of customization in the remainder of this section: map editor tools and game "mods" (or modifications).

With more than 1.8×10^{19} possible maps, *Minecraft* is capable of providing an essentially endless number of possible worlds to explore. The number of possible worlds is a topic of debate as it also depends on which version of *Minecraft* is used. Different kinds of blocks tend to become available in more recent releases. Normally, players begin with a random map and can provide a seed number, which can be used to guarantee replication of individual maps when the seed is reused (each generated world requires a random number "seed" which is used to guide terrain decisions, such as topographical features and biomes). If, however, a user wishes to have maps with specific features or characteristics, the *Minecraft* user community has produced a wide range of tools that allow players to create their own maps easily without programming. These tools, often called *map editors,* allow players to readily make broad-sweeping changes to worlds. They work much like a typical paint or publishing tool, with the exception that they are used to define a three-dimensional (3D) space through sculpting and manipulation of surface features of a map (e.g., mountains, basins, valleys, trees, sand, creatures), bodies of water (e.g., rivers, lakes, oceans), and underground structures (e.g., caves, lava). Different tools allow editing in both third person view (top down) and first person (similar to playing the game). Authored maps are easily loaded from inside *Minecraft* and played like any other map.

The most significant and powerful changes to *Minecraft* involve changing the code that controls the game, a process known as *modding* (i.e., "modifying"). The possibility for the player community to create and share new versions of *Minecraft* reflecting their own ideas has likely contributed greatly to its success. *Mods* (the product of modding) can be found on most imaginable topics and span the science and technology gamut. A large number of mods simply change the look and feel of *Minecraft*, add content, and provide new capabilities such as combining multiple tools into one (to save inventory space) or jumping higher than the programmed default. However, many others leverage the powerful simulation components of *Minecraft*. A few of these mods that are highly relevant to science learning include

- *Galacticraft:* Allows players to travel through the solar system, design and travel spaceships, explore planets and moons, experience different environments and gravities, use life-support technologies, and engage with friends in space races and other competitions.
- *ComputerCraft:* provides programmable turtles, essentially small robots, for automation of many game tasks, networking simulation, command-line interfaces, and more computing simulations.
- *Climate Control:* allows players to control environmental behaviors, including ocean sizes, biome frequencies, and other weather/environmental factors.
- *Agricraft:* provides a more detailed and complex agricultural system for *Minecraft*, including more crops, hybrid crops (mixing breeds), and irrigation tools.

Using mods is relatively simple whereby a user first needs a "mod loader," which is a separate program that helps players find new mods and manages the activation of the ones desired at any given time (many people play *Minecraft* with several mods active at once, and change frequently). Once loaded, a new game is started from within the chosen loader (documentation is typically provided when using the new resources from a mod may not be obvious). Notably, these mods are created by the community. Comparable to how *Wikipedia* grew and is now sustained, mods depend on user-generated content and donated time. The enormous range of mods available to the world represents a significant resource, for players seeking new kinds of experiences and educators who wish to focus on specific topics. So how can educators and researchers leverage these tools? How can *Minecraft* be applied in educational settings and used to answer questions about cognitive development and learning? The remainder of the chapter focuses on these questions.

MINECRAFT AS AN ENVIRONMENT FOR TEACHING AND LEARNING

Because *Minecraft* is essentially a simulation of the natural world and boasts high levels of popularity among children, educators around the world are rapidly embracing it for educational uses (Thompson, 2016). In this section, we describe several examples of how it can be used to promote learning and how teachers have leveraged these capabilities in the classroom.

Science and engineering in Minecraft. Minecraft's strong links to science topics imply that it is worthwhile to ask to what extent it might act as a proxy for the study of and experimentation with simple phenomena from the natural sciences, such as those performed in middle- or high-school science classes. Short (2012), a high-school science teacher who uses *Minecraft* extensively, identifies several techniques for teaching ecology, mathematics, and physics. He highlights students' ability to explore different biomes and identify the conditions in each biome that impact sustainable life (e.g., access to water, temperature). As an example, Short describes *Minecraft's* "smelting" feature, whereby a player can combine game objects in a furnace to create a new resource. The process has a rather direct mapping into combination reactions in chemistry, allowing students to witness and learn heat's key role in the combination or the alteration of multiple objects and elements. As another example, Short points to how colors can change based on environmental conditions and the sun's location in the sky. He describes how *Minecraft* simulates *atmospheric refraction*, which is the deviation of light from a straight line as it passes through the atmosphere and is impacted by variation in air density and height. Thus, *Minecraft* players see a red tinted sky at sunrise, just as they would in the natural world.

Many direct links between *Minecraft* and engineering are also present. When playing *Minecraft* in survival mode, one of the earliest tasks is to construct a building for protection. As the game progresses, it is common for this building (or fort) to become larger, stronger, and more complex. It is also common to see players build and design machines, either for the inherent challenge of doing so or with a specific purpose. These structures often require working with electricity, which is possible in *Minecraft* given a fictional resource known as "redstone." Simply put, redstone can be thought of as a source of energy that allows locomotion (Brand & Kinash, 2013). In combination with circuits, switches, repeaters, and other objects, redstone enables electrical signals and power to be incorporated into complex machines, enabling players to build everything from drawbridges to flying machines. Circuits can be attached to a variety of triggering mechanisms, such as pressure plates and sensors, which can set automated tasks into motion.

Redstone circuits are animated so that players can observe the signals moving over the created networks, the triggering actions, and the completion of their journeys. While unrealistic when compared to the actual world, slowing the signal down significantly helps the player to better isolate bugs and solve operational problems in their designs. Students equipped with redstone in *Minecraft* can solve complex automation problems at their own pace, learn how basic circuits operate through exploration, and watch their creations come to life repeatedly. We also note that using *Minecraft* as a virtual demo tool could potentially save schools, money, and time since once a *Minecraft* demonstration is set up, it can be saved, re-used, and modified easily.

Minecraft as a conduit to more advanced topics. A quick search on YouTube will reveal a seemingly endless list of remarkable and complex creations accomplished in *Minecraft*, much like the Taj Mahal and Westeros examples from earlier. Because of its richness and extendibility, *Minecraft* ostensibly provides a gateway for many learners worldwide to explore more advanced topics or new areas of interest. A number of mods exist for the singular purpose of exposing young learners to advanced topics—some that may be well beyond what is usually considered accessible at a young age.

One example of such a creation is *Circuit Madness*, a world designed to teach students logic through *Minecraft*. The player must learn the functions of basic logical operators (e.g., AND, OR, XOR) to find their way out of each room, and in the grander scope, escape from the game's entire maze (Duncan, 2011). *Circuit Madness* is an example of a mod that could be hypothesized to act as a trigger for interest (Hidi & Renninger, 2006), for example, in electronics and computer science, and enable sustained exposure to game content, while possibly motivating players to build circuits on their own. Game experiences such as those provided by *Circuit Madness* could also play a role in addressing gender and cultural imbalances in STEM areas. Computer science and engineering, in particular, are two fields with significant and persistent deficits in terms of female participation (Jenson & De Castell, 2010). The idea that digital technologies can contribute to a more level playing field for all learners (which *Minecraft* certainly can be) is supported by the possibility to be represented digitally: real-life features of our identities, such as gender and race, could take a back seat to content and learning. For example, Mimi Ito's *Connected Learning* framework

(Ito et al., 2013), which includes use of *Minecraft* camps and servers for collaborative learning, is a leading candidate for such a vision.

Educator uses of Minecraft to increase engagement in learning. Because of *Minecraft's* broad appeal, educators in both formal and informal contexts quickly adopted the game to suit a wide range of learning goals. Its usage by teachers in schools and afterschool programs has grown rapidly,[2] for topics as diverse as history, foreign languages, social studies,[3] and mathematics (Bos, Wilder, Cook, & O'Donnell, 2014). *Minecraft* clubs have formed across the world, such as "*Minecraft* Mania," at the Children's Museum of Houston[4] as well as larger coalitions, such as ThoughtSTEM, a statewide network of afterschool *Minecraft* programs in California.[5] Ito et al. (2013) have proposed a "connected learning" framework as a fresh take on peer-support that is often mediated by technology. They predict that education will (continue to) shift from singular learning to be interest-driven, specialized, and fueled by the support of like-minded peers. *Minecraft* is an example of a technology that exemplifies this vision since it is an environment where students can easily pursue academically oriented goals for learning with the help of their instructors, peers, and families. In addition to the ideas for science education described above by Short (2012) for engineering, ecology, chemistry, and physics, we provide two more concrete use cases.

Jeffrey Adams, a middle school science teacher in Toronto, used *Minecraft* to pursue such a goal. In a lesson to encourage students to learn about sustainable planning, he asked his students (80 seventh grade boys) to build their own model of a sustainable city in *Minecraft*. Students assumed roles, such as farmer, builder, or miner, and then were tasked with building a sustainable village. The products of their work including interviews and surveys suggested very deep engagement in the activity. Eighty-six percent of students expressed a preference to keep using games in their classes, and 80% of students in the class reported that *Minecraft* allowed them to "be more creative and do things [they] couldn't do before" (Adams, 2012, p. 11).

In a similar approach, teachers Karen Yager and Andrew Weeding (in Sydney, Australia) asked students in their science classes of 12- to 13-year-olds to design cities that minimized the use of energy and resources.

---

[2] http://fortune.com/2015/06/30/minecraft-teachers/.
[3] http://ww2.kqed.org/mindshift/2015/09/28/for-the-hesitant-teacher-leveraging-the-power-of-minecraft/.
[4] http://www.cmhouston.org/event/minecraft-houston.
[5] http://www.thoughtstem.com/home/programs/after-school-programs.

Here, students were given the choice of how to design, build, and present their models (e.g., physical vs. digital). Notably, 96% of the students chose *Minecraft*. Then, over the course of 5 days, students built out their virtual cities. To encourage students to think more broadly than engineering, students had daily in-world challenges covering multiple disciplines: English, mathematics, science, and foreign languages. At the end of the unit, students presented their cities to their classmates via a walking tour of their cities to show off their work, energy-saving features, and building designs. Yager and Weeding reported that their students primarily enjoyed the freedom *Minecraft* offered them and the ability to create functional models (West & Bleiberg, 2013).

These examples suggest that *Minecraft* has great flexibility when it comes to fulfilling the different needs of instructors. Further, in blogs and in person, educators often report increases in engagement, interest, and time-on-task with *Minecraft*-based assignments. To what extent these outcomes are due to Minecraft or teacher quality or other variables is unclear, warranting further examination. Given the popularity and flexibility of *Minecraft*, though, we view it as important to determine its efficacy alongside more traditional instructional methods. Some initial studies, however, suggest that *Minecraft*-based assignments positively impact noncognitive outcomes, such as attitude (Sáez-López, Miller, Vázquez-Cano, & Domínguez-Garrido, 2015) and creativity (Cipollone, Schifter, & Moffat, 2014).

MINECRAFT AS AN EDUCATIONAL RESEARCH TOOL

As educator uses reveal, the design of *Minecraft* makes it an appealing environment for thinking about teaching and learning. In this section, we discuss potential research foci whereby *Minecraft* could act as the learning environment. Specifically, we discuss three important areas that have already received some researcher attention but are poised for much larger research efforts: collaboration, creativity, and special education.

Collaboration and cooperation in Minecraft. Minecraft's open world approach resists the competitive edge that comes with games such as racecar or fighting games. Barron (2003) suggests that for collaboration in groups, the more competitive the environment, the more students will focus on themselves instead of "learning for the sake of learning" (p. 350). So, instead of withdrawing into themselves, sandbox platforms such as *Minecraft* may encourage students to view learning (in-game) as playing and enjoy exploration of the digital space. Another advantage of using *Minecraft* in the classroom setting is that it capitalizes on the relationships already established between the students. Friends are more productive in dialogue during learning activities and elaborate on ideas; their past experiences with each other motivate them to nurture their friendship (Barron, 2003). Random assignment or strategic pairing of students to play together also may enable new friendships to form.

Other research on collaboration has implications for the study of *Minecraft*. For example, when in groups, students are known to complete tasks for the sake of the group, rather than simply out of self-interest (Slavin, 2015). In a case study conducted by Walker (2012), students were assigned collaborative building or writing tasks that required information gathered from *Minecraft* worlds, from the classroom, or from course textbooks. Tasks in the study ranged from "exploring secret rooms and traps within the Great Pyramid" to "collaboratively writing a modern myth following the common stages of Greek mythology" (p. 5). Additional challenges were made available to students who wished to pursue them on their own or in groups. Walker encouraged students to explore the game's open world, for the sake of fun and entertainment and to pursue knowledge. The varied tasks assigned provided short-term goals for the students to meet while they pursued the overarching goal of better understanding history. The new information attained through *Minecraft* could then be reinforced through peers, classroom materials such as textbooks, and the teacher's reiteration.

Minecraft is an inherently collaborative game, with teams often able to accomplish more together than alone, and often pursuing entirely intrinsically motivated activities (such as building the Taj Mahal). Support for collaboration was a key aim of the recent release of *Minecraft: Education Edition*,[6] which greatly reduces the technical hurdles necessary for groups to work together on class projects, by eliminating the need for a server, for example, and allowing one computer on a local network to act as host. Further, it provided a suite of teacher resources, such as prebuilt maps and large-scale recreations of objects (such as the human eye, see Fig. 4). These recent developments have positive implications for teachers and suggest new ways of tracking and evaluating collaboration around learning tasks that will be possible in the very near future.

Cultivating and nurturing creativity. A growing body of evidence suggests that video game play is at least positively correlated with creativity, especially for children (Jackson et al., 2012). In some cases, frequent video game play has been causally linked to creativity either by way of game mechanics

---

[6] http://education.minecraft.net/.

Fig. 4 A recreation of a human eye in *Minecraft: Education Edition*. Groups of learners can go inside, witness the conversion of light into electrical impulses (that would then go to the brain), and even modify the eye's construction.

tapping into creative problem-solving skills or identity development (Bowman, Kowert, & Ferguson, 2015; Yeh, 2015); however, more research is needed to better understand what causal mechanisms are at play.

When positioned alongside over 50 years of research on creativity— which has focused on how to define, measure, and cultivate it (Sawyer, 2012)—*Minecraft* stands out from other video games in terms of its capacity for creative expression and uses of creativity in a science context (Garrelts, 2014). *Minecraft* has been frequently associated with *constructivism* and linked to Bruner's seminal work on the active construction (and co-construction) of knowledge (Bruner, 1991) as well as *constructionist* approaches to learning that emphasize constructivist principles in the context of interaction with and creation of artifacts (Papert & Harel, 1991; Schifter & Cipollone, 2015). In particular, constructionism challenges the idea that "verbally expressed formal knowledge" is a sufficient end point for education (Papert & Harel, 1991, p. 11). Rather, knowledge is seen as constructed by learners, in the context of creation, invention, and exploration. Brand et al. (2014) argue that *Minecraft* is ideally suited for constructivist learning and is likely to promote creative thinking because it shifts learning from experiences with predefined interactions to ones with a broad range of possible interactions. In particular, *Minecraft* "provides multiple depictions or perspectives of reality by allowing a variety of levels of detail and scale for building worlds in addition to full 3D freedom of exploration" (p. 61).

Arguably, *Minecraft* could promote creative thinking in at least two principle ways. First, it provides features that are known to promote creative thinking. For example, it combines the use of constraints (via the virtual world) with open-ended decision making, a combination that has been shown to promote creative thinking in a variety of contexts (Costello & Keane, 2000). Second, it is suitable for both collaborative and individual work, both essential for creative expression (Sawyer, 2012). Further, as a virtual world, *Minecraft* makes it easy to inspect anything in the game world from any perspective (inside, outside, upside down, etc.). The need for perspective taking and the skill to do so are known to be important for both empathy and creativity (Grant & Berry, 2011). Second, for decades researchers have pursued measures of creativity (Kerr & Gagliardi, 2003) leading to a wide range of approaches, such as tests of divergent thinking and problem-solving tasks that require insight. *Minecraft* presents a compelling context in which to pursue another prominent direction of assessment through the inspection of artifacts (Kaufman, Baer, Cole, & Sexton, 2008). In particular, because all activities in the game can be logged, it would be possible to inspect how learners change creations over time, how they make those changes (alone or together), and how they choose to express their ideas over time. While most measures tend to focus on traits or specific ways of thinking, *process* measures for creativity are often far more appropriate for learning and development, and the affordances of *Minecraft* align nicely with this need.

Minecraft for struggling learners. Because *Minecraft* offers a familiar interface (for many learners) and is vastly different from what students normally expect in school, some initial efforts are underway to use it as a tool for engaging struggling learners and to provide new avenues for participation. For example, Brian Kenney, a math teacher in Corona, California, set out to increase engagement of his special needs students by allowing them to explore geometry concepts in *Minecraft*. Specifically, his students created buildings and then labeled the geometric shapes and properties in their designs (e.g., parallel walls, right angles, complementary angles). Anecdotally, Kenney reported that it changed his students' willingness to engage in the material and also improved their attitudes toward the class.[7] Notably, there is strong evidence that preexisting *interest* in a topic increases engagement (Renninger, Nieswandt, & Hidi, 2015). Thus, whether that interest lies

---

[7] http://www.cta.org/Professional-Development/Publications/2013/10/October-2013-Educator/Games.aspx.

in *Minecraft* itself, or in the vast experiences it can provide, further research is needed to better understand the tradeoffs involved with *Minecraft*-based lessons, such as those related to time it takes to learn to play (if they don't already) and potentially negative impacts on students who do not normally play video games.

Going well beyond STEM, the *Minecraft* community has also produced content specifically focused on inviting autistic players to the game. One of the most well-known servers for players with Autism is *AutCraft*, a *Minecraft* server "dedicated to providing a safe and fun learning environment for children on the autism spectrum and their families."[8] The server addresses all relevant aspects of autism, including promoting healthy social interactions, establishing a "safe space," emphasizing anti-bullying principles, and providing a place of acceptance. Kate Ringland, a researcher, spent 60 h observing interactions between players to better understand how the server worked and why it was especially suited for players with autism. By analyzing how players searched for, practiced, and defined social skills, she found improvements in how players were interacting socially in the game (demonstration of transfer outside the game has not been studied as of this writing). She concluded that *Minecraft*, despite (or perhaps, because of) its lower-end graphics, was a suitable environment for learning social and emotional skills (Ringland, Wolf, Faucett, Dombrowski, & Hayes, 2016). These conclusions are supported by recent evidence that children with autism are better able to acquire social skills with robotic partners (Cabibihan, Javed, Ang, & Aljunied, 2013), whereby such interventions can act as practice for autistic learners in an environment that does not include direct, and potentially stressful interaction with humans.

CONCLUSION

We have described the game of *Minecraft*, how it is played, how and why educators are using it, and have provided suggestions on the kinds of research questions that are pertinent given these developments. We argued that *Minecraft* is unique as it does not fit the mold of other successful video games and is simultaneously flexible enough to be used for a wide range of educational purposes. In this final section, we briefly discuss the relationship between the *Minecraft* phenomenon and cognitive development, followed by a concluding discussion of possible future research directions.

[8] http://autcraft.com/.

Minecraft and cognitive development. While young children may consider watching *Minecraft* how-to videos or exploring the pixelated Arctic with friends as a hobby (a theme of popular YouTube shows filmed in *Minecraft*), their constant engagement is hypothesized to aid in forming emergent digital literacies (Holloway, Green, & Livingstone, 2013). In many ways, the use of *Minecraft* in curriculums is a nod to Vygotsky's theory of play in the mental development of the child. The theory calls attention to four aspects of play: the child's needs, inclinations, incentives, and motives to act. Vygotsky equates play with wish fulfillment. The desires of a toddler and a kindergartener are not comparable; the child's aspirations and self-perceptions change over social interactions and time (Vygotsky & Cole, 1978).

We have indirectly argued for multiple ways that *Minecraft* addresses Vygotsky's aspects of play, and how the game can be used to fulfill whatever goal or fantasy the child desires to craft. Perhaps the most prominent aspect lies in sociability, where time spent in the digital realm can spark a "sense of shared purpose and identity" among players in spite of the technological gap between generations (Brand & Kinash, 2013). We have emphasized *Minecraft*'s digital medium since it allows participants to experience a series of grand episodes and go well beyond what is possible in the classroom and the real world. Shane Asselstine, a featured educator from 2014 on *Minecraft Edu* (the predecessor to *Minecraft*: Education Edition), describes noted improvements on student group work:

> We have also used MinecraftEdu in survival mode maps. In these maps students are more focused on aspects of cooperation, citizenship, and resource management... They really learn the value of working together to accomplish a goal. I am also always amazed at the details students can remember from a close call, or a grand discovery of resources.

Our view is that teacher and parent reports of children accomplishing amazing feats in *Minecraft* are a signal that cognitive and developmental sciences should take note and work to incorporate more of it into the global education research agenda.

Beyond Minecraft. We have attempted to make a case for *Minecraft* as a unique game that has implications far beyond the small, entertainment goals it began with in 2009. As an open-ended game, *Minecraft* does not emphasize mastery or any of the traditional goals video games tend to impose on players, such as leveling up, unlocking content, or sharing through social interaction (Fullerton, 2007). Rather, the focus of the *Minecraft* community and its players rests on the ongoing possibility of doing things that have yet to be done. The phrase "sandbox box" game is based on an apt metaphor in that players have the chance to explore and play with ideas and are only bound by the tools made available to them. Deep links between *Minecraft and* science, communication, and engineering are being pursued very quickly by teachers, but too slowly by researchers. How we leverage this powerful tool and merge it with education to promote learning, engagement, interest, and in developmentally sound ways are all open questions.

What will the world look like 10–15 years from now? What will it mean to have an entire generation of scientists, engineers, and artists who grew up using *Minecraft* to express themselves? While it may not be possible to ever answer this question confidently, more research is needed to understand the impact dramatic use of *Minecraft* is having on children. Each time a child collects a resource, changes their avatar, discovers diamonds in a deep mine, designs a redstone circuit, coordinates what to build next with their friends, we should nudge them in ways that maximize the potential long-term value of the skills they are acquiring. But, we should also marvel that they do this by their own volition, and importantly, stay out of the way.

REFERENCES

Adams, J. (2012). Inquiry learning? Try a game. In D. Laycock (Ed.), *Teaching boys at the coal face: Mining key pedagogical approaches* (pp. 5–24). The International Boys' Schools Coalition. http://www.theibsc.org/about-ibsc/contact-us.

Barron, B. (2003). When smart groups fail. *The Journal of the Learning Sciences, 12*(3), 307–359.

Bavelier, D., Green, C. S., Han, D. H., Renshaw, P. F., Merzenich, M. M., & Gentile, D. A. (2011). Brains on video games. *Nature Reviews Neuroscience, 12*(12), 763–768.

Bos, B., Wilder, L., Cook, M., & O'Donnell, R. (2014). Learning mathematics through minecraft. *Teaching Children Mathematics, 21*(1), 56–59.

Bowman, N. D., Kowert, R., & Ferguson, C. J. (2015). The impact of video game play on human (and orc) creativity. In G. P. Green & J. C. Kaufman (Eds.), *Video games and creativity* (pp. 39–61). Amsterdam: Elsevier.

Brand, J. E., de Byl, P., Knight, S. J., & Hooper, J. (2014). Mining constructivism in the university. In N. Garrelts (Ed.), *Understanding Minecraft: Essays on play, community and possibilities* (pp. 57–75). Jefferson, NC: McFarland & Company, Inc.

Brand, J. E., & Kinash, S. (2013). Crafting minds in minecraft. *Education Technology Solutions, 55*, 56–58.

Bruner, J. (1991). The narrative construction of reality. *Critical Inquiry, 18*(1), 1–21.

Bryant, A., & Levine, P. (2015). Kid Appeal: An exploration of children's favorite digital games, how they select them, and why they engage with them. Retrieved from https://www.scribd.com/doc/274334646/PlayScience-Kids-Apps-and-Digital-Media.

Cabibihan, J. J., Javed, H., Ang, M., Jr., & Aljunied, S. M. (2013). Why robots? A survey on the roles and benefits of social robots in the therapy of children with autism. *International Journal of Social Robotics, 5*(4), 593–618.

Costello, F. J., & Keane, M. T. (2000). Efficient creativity: Constraint-guided conceptual combination. *Cognitive Science, 24*(2), 299–349.

Dewey, J. (1913). *Interest and effort in education*. Boston: Houghton Mifflin Co.

Duncan, S. C. (2011). Minecraft, beyond construction and survival. *Well Played: A Journal on Video Games, Value and Meaning, 1*(1), 1–22.

Ferguson, C. J. (2016. *Stop blaming violent video games*. U.S. News & World Report.

Fullerton, T. (2007). *Game design workshop, second edition: A playcentric approach to creating innovative games*. Burlington, MA: Morgan Kaufmann.

Garrelts, N. (2014). *Understanding minecraft: Essays on play, community and possibilities*. Jefferson, NC: McFarland.

Granic, I., Lobel, A., & Engels, R. (2014). The benefits of playing video games. *The American Psychologist, 69*(1), 66–78.

Grant, A. M., & Berry, J. W. (2011). The necessity of others is the mother of invention: Intrinsic and prosocial motivations, perspective taking, and creativity. *Academy of Management Journal, 54*(1), 73–96.

Hidi, S., & Renninger, K. A. (2006). The four-phase model of interest development. *Educational Psychologist, 41*(2), 111–127.

Holloway, D., Green, L., & Livingstone, S. (2013). *Zero to eight: Young children and their Internet use*. LSE, London: EU Kids Online.

Ito, M., Gutierrez, K., Livingstone, S., Penuel, B., Rhodes, J., Salen, K., et al. (2013). *Connected learning: An agenda for research and design*. Irvine, CA: Digital Media and Learning Research Hub.

Jackson, L. A., Witt, E. A., Games, A. I., Fitzgerald, H. E., von Eye, A., & Zhao, Y. (2012). Information technology use and creativity: Findings from the children and technology project. *Computers in Human Behavior, 28*(2), 370–376. http://dx.doi.org/10.1016/j.chb.2011.10.006.

Jenson, J., & De Castell, S. (2010). Gender, simulation, and gaming: Research review and redirections. *Simulation & Gaming, 41*(1), 51–71.

Kafai, Y. B., Fields, D. A., & Cook, M. S. (2010). Your second selves player-designed avatars. *Games and Culture, 5*(1), 23–42.

Kaufman, J. C., Baer, J., Cole, J. C., & Sexton, J. D. (2008). A comparison of expert and nonexpert raters using the consensual assessment technique. *Creativity Research Journal, 20*(2), 171–178.

Kerr, B., & Gagliardi, C. (2003). Measuring creativity in research and practice. In S. J. Lopez & C. R. Snyder (Eds.), *Positive psychological assessment* (pp. 155–169). Washington, DC: American Psychological Association.

Lastowka, G. (2012). Minecraft as Web 2.0: Amateur creativity in digital games. In D. Hunter, R. Lobato, M. Richardson, & J. Thomas (Eds.), *Amateur media: social, cultural, and legal perspectives* (pp. 153–169). London, UK: Routledge.

Papert, S., & Harel, I. (1991). Situating constructionism. *Constructionism, 36*, 1–11.

Peckham, M. (2016). '*Minecraft*' is now the second best-selling game of all time. *Time*. Retrieved from http://time.com/4354135/minecraft-bestelling/.

Renninger, K. A., Nieswandt, M., & Hidi, S. (2015). On the power of interest. In K. A. Renninger, M. Nieswandt, & S. Hidi (Eds.), *Interest in mathematics and science learning* (pp. 1–14). Washington, DC: American Educational Research Association.

Ringland, K. E., Wolf, C. T., Faucett, H., Dombrowski, L., & Hayes, G. R. (2016). In *"Will I always be not social?": Re-conceptualizing sociality in the context of a minecraft community for autism*. Paper presented at the Proceedings of ACM CHI Conference on Human Factors in Computing Systems 2016.

Sáez-López, J. -M., Miller, J., Vázquez-Cano, E., & Domínguez-Garrido, M. -C. (2015). Exploring application, attitudes and integration of video games: MinecraftEdu in middle school. *Educational Technology & Society, 18*(3), 114–128.

Sawyer, R. K. (2012). *Explaining creativity: The science of human innovation*. New York: Oxford University Press.

Schifter, C. C., & Cipollone, M. (2015). Constructivism vs constructionism: implications for minecraft and classroom implementation. In P. Isaías, M. J. Spector, D. Ifenthaler, & G. D. Sampson (Eds.), *E-learning systems, environments and approaches: Theory and implementation* (pp. 213–227). Cham: Springer International Publishing.

Short, D. (2012). Teaching scientific concepts using a virtual world—Minecraft. *Teaching Science—The Journal of the Australian Science Teachers Association, 58*(3), 55.

Cipollone, M., Schifter, C. C., & Moffat, R. A. (2014). Minecraft as a creative tool: A case study. *International Journal of Game-Based Learning, 4*(2), 1–14.

Slavin, R. E. (2015). Cooperative learning in elementary schools. *Education 3–13: International Journal of Primary, Elementary, and Early Years Education, 43*(1), 5–14.

Sylvester, T. (2013). *Designing games: A guide to engineering experiences* (1st ed.). Sebastopol, CA: O'Reilly.

Thompson, C. (2016). *The minecraft generation.* New York Times Magazine. Retrieved from http://www.nytimes.com/2016/04/17/magazine/the-minecraft-generation.html.

Vygotsky, L. S., & Cole, M. (1978). *Mind in society: The development of higher psychological processes.* Cambridge: Harvard University Press.

Walker, E. (2012). *Exploring the ancient, virtual world: Engagement and enrichment within a virtual historical learning environment.* Robert Morris University. Retrieved from http://faculty.rmu.edu/~short/research/minecraft-ct/references/Walker-E-2012.pdf.

West, D. M., & Bleiberg, J. (2013). Education technology success stories. *Issues in governance studies.* Retrieved from http://www.insidepolitics.org/brookingsreports/education_technology_success_stories.pdf.

Yeh, C. S. -H. (2015). Exploring the effects of videogame play on creativity performance and emotional responses. *Computers in Human Behavior, 53*, 396–407. http://dx.doi.org/10.1016/j.chb.2015.07.024.

CHAPTER 8

The Impact of Digital Media on Executive Planning and Performance in Children, Adolescents, and Emerging Adults

Alexander W. Fietzer, Stephanie Chin
Hunter College, CUNY, New York, NY, United States

Individuals in the United States have access to an unprecedented number of digital screens. National reports estimate that the average household has four digital screens and that consumers use them an average of 60 hours per week (Nielsen, 2014). For example, children between the ages of 2 and 11 are reported to watch more than 22 hours of television and play three hours of video games weekly, while adolescents between the ages of 12 and 17 watch more than 19 hours of television and play more than four hours of video games weekly (Nielsen, 2016). In addition, 24% of adolescents are online "almost constantly" (Pew Research Center, 2015). Questions regarding how this constant and extensive screen use might affect the development of cognitive functions such as executive functioning (EF) remain unanswered, which has been shown to mature throughout childhood and adolescence (see Best, Miller, & Jones, 2009).

EF refers to a specific set of cognitive functions that is related yet distinct from other cognitive functions such as intelligence (e.g., Arffa, 2007). EF broadly pertains to those aspects of cognition that require focused concentration, ignoring extraneous stimuli, and planning complex sequences of actions to achieve a goal. Given that various forms of screen media require these aspects (e.g., planning the shortest route to a goal in a video game, task switching in social media from consuming content to creating it), the ubiquity of screens and the reported frequency of their use, pose interesting questions in terms of their influence on the development of EF.

We review in the following, the impact of three different forms of screen media—video games, mobile technology, and social networking sites (also

Cognitive Development in Digital Contexts
http://dx.doi.org/10.1016/B978-0-12-809481-5.00008-0

167

known as social media)—on the development of EF in children and adolescents and special needs populations. Here, digital screen media is characterized as including any device that produces digitized images in applications used at an individual or small group level. We conceptualized EF from a clinical neuropsychological standpoint based on a modified framework initially articulated by Lezak, Howieson, Bigler, and Tranel (2012), whereby EF comprises: (1) attention, or the ability to focus on a stimulus without losing concentration; (2) working memory, or the ability to retain elements of a stimulus in a memory store while manipulating them in some novel way; (3) set shifting, or the ability to switch from one task to a different task without significant errors occurring in either task; (4) inhibition, or the ability to respond correctly to a target stimulus while preventing responses to distractor stimuli that are similar; (5) fluency, defined as correctly generating responses that fit into a predefined category (e.g., retrieving the names of as many vegetables as possible in a given amount of time); (6) planning/problem solving, or the ability to organize information about the rules or requirements of a task in order to facilitate its completion as efficiently as possible; and (7) metacognition, which refers to the ability to identify patterns of thinking, reasoning, and problem solving that one or the other uses, and to deduce logical rules about these patterns.

THE IMPACT OF SCREEN MEDIA ON EF

Video Games

Video games have been categorized into three broad and overlapping categories: "edugames," whereby the goal is to educate the player about some topic or skill; "commercial off-the-shelf games," which include all games that are sold commercially either online or in physical stores; and "exergames" that allow an individual to control the game using some type of gross motor movement (e.g., jumping) (Jiménez, Pulina, & Lanfranchi, 2015). A broad range of game genres are found in each category including puzzle games, wherein the goal is to solve logic problems, role playing, and strategy games that require planning and resource management, and action games that require quick reflexes in the navigation of the game space.

Given that the overwhelming majority of games require sustained attention, planning, monitoring, inhibition, and set shifting, it follows that EF may differ among individuals who avidly play video games and those who do not. However, there is a distinct lack of longitudinal experimental designs to provide clear evidence for or against this hypothesis. Instead, most research designs have been cross-sectional in nature.

Powers, Brooks, Aldrich, Palladino, and Alfieri (2013) conducted two meta-analyses that investigated the impact of commercially available video games in relation to information processing skills, including EF—with one meta-analysis focusing on the results of quasi-experiments, comparing individuals who avidly play video games with less-experienced players, and one focusing on true experiments, involving training with a commercially available game. The authors defined EF as including measures of inhibition, task-shifting, intelligence, working memory, as well as EF test batteries. The meta-analysis of quasi-experiments examining the effects on EF comprised 110 statistical comparisons involving 4395 participants in 22 studies. These cross-sectional studies included control groups of inexperienced video game players, players with little skill in playing video games, and players who played video games that differed from more action-oriented games (e.g., shooter games). The results demonstrated a small but statistically significant effect size of $d=0.44$ for a composite EF variable. Dividing the composite EF variable into its constituent parts revealed statistically significant small to medium effects sizes for all subcategories ranging from $d=0.29$ (inhibition) to $d=0.67$ (task-switching and dual/multitasking). However, only one study, by Li and Atkins (2004), was classified as examining the relationship between video games and EF in youth, and the authors found no relationship between the presence of computer games at home, and intelligence in a sample of 122 rural preschoolers.

A study by Dye, Green, and Bavelier (2009) was included in the first meta-analysis by Powers et al. (2013), but was classified as a visual processing task rather than as an EF task. However, Dye and colleagues considered their dependent variable to be a measure of EF, so we include it in this review. This study investigated the impact of playing predominantly action-oriented video games compared with other video game types such as puzzle-based and strategy games on attention in a cross-sectional study of 131 participants ranging from age 7 to age 22. The authors assessed attention using the Child Attention Network Task (ANT-C), a reaction-time task that requires a participant to identify correctly the direction in which a target stimulus (e.g., a fish) is pointing. Across trials, distractors (i.e., other fish identical to the target) appear on both sides of the target and either point in the same direction (congruent) or the opposite direction (incongruent) as the target. Incongruent trials presumably assess inhibitory responding, as one must ignore the contradictory stimuli and focus on the target. Dye and colleagues found that action game players outperformed players of other video games in terms of reaction time across all age groups without sacrificing accuracy.

They also found that reaction time increased with age. Thus, as the authors noted, action video game players appeared to process information more quickly than their nonaction game playing peers.

The second meta-analysis of experimental studies conducted by Powers et al. (2013) provided less support for the hypothesis that playing video games improves EF. These studies included either pretest/posttest within-groups designs or random assignment of naïve participants to video game training and control conditions. In studies that included a control group, typically participants with minimal exposure to video games would be randomly assigned to play a video game or engage in another comparable task. Aggregating 89 statistical comparisons from 13 experimental studies involving a total of 3721 participants, Powers et al. found a statistically significant but marginal effect size of $d=0.16$ across all studies. However, when deconstructing EF into its constituent domains, only inhibition was statistically significant, albeit with a small effect size of $d=0.39$. Notably, only two of the experimental studies included youth samples (defined as ranging in age from 3 to 17).

One study, by Staiano, Abraham, and Calvert (2012), examined whether competition in video games might affect EF. African-American teenagers of low socioeconomic status ($N=54$) were randomly assigned to a competitive exergame, cooperative exergame, or no-game control group. Both exergame groups played the same video game, but the competitive group sought to win the game while playing with a peer, while the cooperative group sought to achieve the highest total score with their peer. EF was measured with task-switching and fluency tasks before and after a 10-week exergame training regimen. Results revealed that the competitive exergame group outperformed the other two groups in EF. The other study, by Miller and Kapel (1985) used a within-groups pretest/posttest design with 95 middle schoolers completing both pre- and posttest measurements. Students played puzzle and strategy computer games for 50 min per day for 15 days. The authors examined the sequential thinking and visuospatial processing of the students. They found that participants' spatial abilities improved over time, but that their sequential reasoning did not.

Note that studies examining effects of proprietary (custom-made) as opposed to commercially available video games were not included in the Powers et al. (2013) meta-analyses. Such studies also show mixed results of the impact of video games on EF in children and adolescents. In one of the few studies using preschool participants, Thorell, Lindqvist, Bergman Nutley, Bohlin, and Klingberg (2009) investigated whether playing video games could enhance the working memory and inhibitory response ability of preschoolers. The researchers assigned a sample of 65 toddlers into one of the four groups: one that was trained to improve their EF using a proprietary video game developed by the authors that targeted working memory, another group that played a proprietary video game targeting inhibition, an active control group that played a commercially available game chosen because it did not tax either working memory or inhibition, and a passive control group that received no intervention. All groups received a pretest and posttest battery consisting of eight EF instruments measuring inhibition, interference control, spatial and verbal working memory, auditory and visual attention, problem solving, and processing speed. The authors found that training improved the working memory capacity of toddlers in the working memory group relative to the control groups only; training did not improve the inhibition of toddlers in any group. Thus, at least the working memory of toddlers showed improvement through training.

Goldin et al. (2014) examined whether repeatedly playing video games could improve the EF of 6- and 7-year-old Argentinian children of low socioeconomic status and result in improved academic performance in language and mathematics. Children were assigned to either an experimental or control group that played games in class for 15 min from 1 to 3 times per week for 10 weeks. The experimental group played each of three proprietary computer games that targeted either working memory, planning, or inhibition in an individual. The control group played computer games matched to the experimental group's games for motor input but requiring minimal use of EF to advance in the game. Findings showed that video game training improved children's inhibitory control and attention, but not their planning. These improved skills resulted in improved academic grades in math and literacy at the end of the third quarter of the school year as assessed by teachers who were blind to the study.

Similarly, Mackey, Hill, Stone, and Bunge (2011) investigated whether extensive cognitive training (i.e., playing video games for 1 h twice per week for 8 weeks) using commercially available video games would improve different cognitive domains (working memory, processing speed, or fluid reasoning) among children from low socioeconomic backgrounds between the ages of 7 and 10. Children were trained using either a video game that rewarded fast processing speed or one that rewarded fluid reasoning skills. Children exposed to video games that rewarded faster cognitive processing (i.e., speed training) improved on tasks of processing speed and children exposed to games that rewarded reasoning ability improved on measures of cognitive reasoning.

Studies also show that EF does not necessarily improve with exposure to video games. For instance, Best (2012) assessed whether video game playing and sedentary habits influenced inhibitory responding using a within-subjects design. Thirty-three US children between the ages of 6 and 10 participated in four groups that varied in cognitive engagement and physical activity. Low physical activity sessions were either high in cognitive engagement (the child played a video game) or low (the child watched a video on healthy living habits). Sessions high in physical activity also varied between high cognitive engagement, whereby children played an exergame that required reacting to random stimuli to progress, or low cognitive engagement whereby children played an exergame that required them to run in place. Children's inhibition and attention were measured using the ANT-C (described previously). Neither video games nor engagement significantly predicted EF processes, although participants in the high physical activity condition did show improved attention compared with those in the low physical activity condition. Syväoja, Tammelin, Ahonen, Kankaanpää, and Kantomaa (2014) also found that self-reported frequency of playing video games in a sample of Finnish fifth and sixth graders predicted worse performance on measures of spatial working memory and set shifting.

Extraneous variables may explain such discrepant results. The relationship among sleep, attention, and video games illustrates this possibility. Wolfe et al. (2014) examined whether playing video games might lead to EF deficits in adolescents and examined the role of sleep as a potential mediating variable. A sample of 21 adolescents participated in a sleep study in which they could play video games before going to bed. The authors found that the amount of time spent playing video games correlated highly negatively with sleep duration and with sustained attention the following day, but was uncorrelated with working memory.

Hartanto, Toh, and Yang (2016) illustrated another such possibility. The authors examined the impact of the age of onset of intensive video game playing on EF performance. A sample of 134 undergraduate students reported the age at which they had begun playing video games intensively. Intensive playing was characterized as the self-reported number of hours per week that an individual engaged in playing video games and the age at which the individual began actively playing video games. The authors assigned the participants into three groups based on their experience: nonvideo game players (individuals who had rarely or never played video games prior to the study), early video game players (participants who actively played video games starting before age 12), and late video game players (participants who actively played video games starting after age 12). Findings demonstrated that an earlier age of onset, but not hours played per week, predicted improved EF performance.

Taken together, it appears that video games at least modestly improve the EF of children and adolescents. Furthermore, no studies found that playing video games was pernicious to EF. However, it is clear that longitudinal studies are needed to understand the development of EF among children and adolescents further and the relationship of that development to video game play.

Video Games and Special Needs Populations

Given that video games may potentially improve EF, it is notable that there remains little research examining whether video game play improves EF among individuals with special needs. One of the few studies was conducted by Grynszpan, Martin, and Nadel (2007), who developed two educational video games to determine whether an educational game could be used to ameliorate specific EF deficits in autism and ADHD (such as response inhibition and planning). One game was a network planning game designed to train and evaluate visuospatial planning. This game required participants to determine the most efficient path between nodes. The other was a text-based game designed to assess language comprehension of subtleties of speech such as irony, sarcasm, or metaphors. The authors used an experimental cross-treatment design using ten children with autism and 10 matched controls. They found that the text-based game helped improve language comprehension, but the network planning game did not improve the planning ability.

Dovis, Van der Oord, Wiers, and Prins (2015) examined whether playing a game that engaged children in three EF domains (visuospatial working memory, inhibition, and task-switching) improved these domains compared with playing versions of the same game that engaged children in one or none of the tasks. The authors used *Braingame Brian*, which requires participants to help the inventor Brian create new objects by having children "design" blueprints (visuospatial working memory), forge new materials (inhibition), or sort objects according to changing rules (task-switching). Children played the game for 25 sessions over the course of 5 weeks. The researchers examined 89 children between the ages of 8 and 12 diagnosed with ADHD. Participants were assigned to one of three conditions: a full-active condition where the difficulty for each task increased as the child progressed, a partially active condition where the difficulty increased for only the inhibition and task-switching tasks, and a placebo condition where the difficulty never increased for any of the tasks. Participants in the full-active condition demonstrated the most improvement on measures of inhibition and working memory (both auditory and visuospatial) that remained 3 months after completion of the study. However, these gains did not translate to ADHD symptoms or problem behavior reduction according to self-report, teacher-rating, or parent-rating scales.

Commercially available video games also have been found to improve the EF functioning in special needs populations. Anderson-Hanley, Tureck, and Schneiderman (2011) examined the impact of exergaming on the EF (i.e., inhibition, auditory working memory, and task-switching) of adolescents with autism. Using two popular commercial exergames (*Dance, Dance Revolution* and *Dragon Chase*), they found that these games reduced the repetitive behaviors of autism and improved performance in working memory and inhibition compared with that of a control group.

Findings also show that there may be potential risks for children with special needs who play video games. For example, Gentile, Swing, Lim, and Khoo (2012) investigated the relationship between video games and self-reported deficits in EF among children with ADHD using a 3-year longitudinal correlational design. Among a sample of 3034 children and adolescents, the researchers found that the amount of video game exposure was predictive of self-reported inhibitory and attentional control problems, even when controlling for potential moderating variables such as age, gender, race, and socioeconomic status.

Overall, there is a dearth of controlled studies that investigate the effect of video games on special needs populations. As with video games and EF in general, more studies are needed to understand better how video games differentially affect the functioning of each subpopulation (such as ADHD, ASD, or learning disorders).

Mobile Technology

Mobile technology includes portable electronic devices (i.e., computers) that use a liquid crystal display to project digital images and are manipulated by touching the screen using a stylus, or by entry of characters from a digital keypad. Typically, mobile devices include tablets (e.g., iPad, LeapPad, Android tablets), smartphones, and laptop computers. Research regarding mobile devices and EF is still relatively new and focuses on whether mobile devices can be used to measure children's EF or how EF moderates children's learning via mobile technology.

For example, Howard and Okely (2015) adapted a go/no go task for use on an iPad and a desktop computer to understand how variations in the task affected preschoolers' inhibitory responding. In these tasks, 60 participants completed six trials of the go/no go task, wherein participants try to react to a target stimulus as quickly as possible by pressing a key or without pressing the key during the presentation of nontarget stimuli. Each task varied in its stimulus presentation time, whether it was animated or static, and whether it required a touchscreen (tablet) or button press (desktop computer). The authors found that using longer spaces between trials (greater than 1000 ms) and using the touchscreen of the iPad resulted in the best discrimination between children on the go/no-go task.

Marshall, Bouquet, Thomas, and Shipley (2010) examined a novel form of motor inhibition in young children. The authors predicted that social learning of a gross motor response (drawing an "S" shape in the air) would occur after having observed another human model the gesture. Marshall et al. (2010) conducted two studies among 4- and 5-year-olds. In each study, participants were told to draw a sinusoidal shape with either a vertical orientation or a horizontal orientation on a digital tablet. As they completed the task, the screen of the device showed a video of an adult drawing the same shape in the air. On some of the trials, the adult drew in a direction that was either congruent or incongruent with what the child was instructed to do. In the latter case, the child needed to inhibit what they saw the adult do. Results demonstrated that children experienced difficulty drawing in the correct direction during the incongruent trials. In a follow-up study, the authors varied the age of the model (between 4.5 and 36 years of age) shown drawing the shape on the screen across types of trials between a similarly aged child and an adult. The results indicated that more interference effects occurred during trials with adult models, suggesting that measurement of EF in young children may vary depending on the age of the model used.

Other researchers have examined whether mobile devices enhance learning. McEwan and Dubé (2015) explored whether tablet computers improved children's learning of mathematical content, using EF as a moderator variable. The authors used eye-tracking technology to collect information on where exactly the 30 Canadian second-graders looked on a screen as they played four educational mathematics games. The authors classified the games as either simple or complex. Simple games only focused on one type of mathematics content (e.g., number line estimation, probability), had one learning mechanic, and had many static visuals. Complex games involved multiple types of mathematics content (e.g., counting, magnitude comparison, and number identification), had multiple learning mechanics, and displayed many animated visuals. McEwan and Dubé found that all tablet games enhanced learning of mathematics. Furthermore, they found that a composite EF variable consisting of auditory working memory and response inhibition moderated how a child interacted with a particular game. Children with lower EF scores focused on the content that related directly to the mathematics topic presented in the program (i.e., number identification) when the presentation was simple, while children with high EF scores adjusted to the complexity of the program.

One question that arises when using tablets as teaching tools for use among child participants is whether they may provide too much extraneous stimulus for any meaningful learning to occur. Axelsson, Andersson, and Gulz (2016) examined whether preschoolers could inhibit attending to distracting stimuli (e.g., a glitch on the screen, irrelevant animated stimuli in the background) and benefit from a learning-by-teaching program (LBT). LBT allows the child to tutor a peer or, in this case, a digital "peer" that uses an algorithm to appear to "learn" from the child. A sample of 36 5-year-olds were pretested on their attention and inhibitory ability using go/no go and anti-saccade tasks. The authors found that children were able to inhibit attending to the distracting stimuli during the tasks. Axelsson et al. concluded that LBT software on tablet computers would likely benefit all children, even if their EF was not yet fully developed.

Buckner and Kim (2012) used mobile devices innovatively to measure the EF of children living in areas with few resources such as war-torn countries and refugee camps. The authors recruited a sample of 185 Palestinian children from either rural or urban backgrounds and who had either high or low risk exposure to traumatic events due to war. They used electronic applications of the Wisconsin Card Sort Test and Tower of London EF tasks, both of which assess planning and problem solving. Buckner and Kim found that children living in high-risk areas performed poorly on both EF measures than children from low-risk areas, and that children from rural areas performed poorly on these EF measures than children from urban areas.

Collectively, these results suggest that mobile devices generally enhance the learning of typically developing children. The next logical question is whether mobile devices can assist the learning of children with developmental delays or disabilities. In one of the few studies examining this population, Arthanat, Curtin, and Knotak (2013) conducted a pilot case study of four children with developmental delays (autism spectrum disorder with some children also diagnosed with intellectual disability). The authors examined whether using mobile technology would improve learning for these children compared with that of a desktop computer. Arthanat and colleagues found no difference in the learning of three of the four children based on the device used. Furthermore, all four children displayed attentional issues regardless of the type of technology used. Although clearly more evidence is needed, it appears that simply using mobile technology without further scaffolding may provide little benefit to learners with developmental disabilities.

Social Media

Social media can be described as an interactive electronic interface that facilitates the communication among individuals via creating, sharing, or exchanging information in virtual communities or networks. In terms of number of users, three of the most popular social networking sites in the United States are Facebook, Youtube, and Twitter (eBizMBA, 2016). Facebook enables an individual to create a personalized biographic site and post personal information, connect with friends, and share content such as news and events. Youtube is a video-sharing platform whereby people can watch others' videos or create their own channel. Twitter is most often used for reading, posting, updating, or sharing brief messages (140 characters or less), although recently those limits have been expanded.

According to two studies that examined the relationship between social media and EF, engagement of social media appears to affect the attention and working memory domains. Rosen, Carrier, and Cheever (2013) examined multitasking between studying and engaging in social media among 263 students aged 12–23. Participants who preferred to switch between multiple tasks exhibited a shortened attention span during the study period. Alloway, Horton, Alloway, and Dawson (2013) studied the length of engagement and type of engagement with Facebook and Youtube on cognitive skills among 103 adolescents. The results demonstrated that individuals who had used Facebook for more than 1 year scored better on working memory than individuals who had used it for less time. The authors also investigated whether particular activities (e.g., checking a friend's status updates) were predictive of working memory performance, but found no significant differences. Alloway and colleagues also examined whether type of engagement with social media significantly affected the working memory. Based on the quality of social media interaction, students were assigned to one of two groups: active use (e.g., posting an update or comment, uploading a video, or playing a game) and passive use (e.g., watching a video, looking at a friend's page). However, the authors found no differences in EF between social media interaction types.

These findings suggest that more social media use can increase working memory while multitasking between activities including social media can decrease attention. However, given the dearth of literature on these topics, further research focusing on social media and its impact on EF in children, adolescents, and those with special needs is needed.

CONCLUDING THOUGHTS

A number of broad themes can be gleaned from perusing the literature examining the impact of digital screen media on EF. The first is that not enough research has been done regarding the potential benefits of digital screen media on EF in children and adolescents. A second theme is that concern about the pernicious effects of digital media on the development of EF in children and adolescents has little evidence to support it. Third, currently no longitudinal studies exist that would clarify the effects of digital screen media on EF.

Based on these themes, we recommend that future research use more longitudinal methods to understand better how EF develops over time in children and adolescents. Research using longitudinal designs, although expensive, would have the added benefit of permitting comparison between generational cohorts. Thus, we could conceivably compare how EF in children and adolescents may be affected by early exposure to social media versus those who matured alongside video games. Another recommendation is that more unique measures for each latent EF factor could be used to more accurately and validly measure each facet of EF in applications that involve latent variable modeling. This is because using more than one measure per domain would reduce measurement error while permitting comparison across different administrative methods (such as pen-and-paper versus kinetic). Finally, we recommend that more investigative work be performed on populations with special needs to understand better whether digital media exacerbates or ameliorates clinical issues in children and adolescents.

REFERENCES

Alloway, T. P., Horton, J., Alloway, R. G., & Dawson, C. (2013). Social networking sites and cognitive abilities: Do they make you smarter? *Computers and Education*, *63*, 10–16. http://dx.doi.org/10.1016/j.compedu.2012.10.030.

Anderson-Hanley, C., Tureck, K., & Schneiderman, R. L. (2011). Autism and exergaming: Effects on repetitive behaviors and cognition. *Psychology Research and Behavior Management*, *4*, 129–137. http://dx.doi.org/10.2147/PRBM.S24016.

Arffa, S. (2007). The relationship of intelligence to executive function and non-executive function measures in a sample of average, above average, and gifted youth. *Archives of Clinical Neuropsychology*, *22*, 969–978. http://dx.doi.org/10.1016/j.acn.2007.08.001.

Arthanat, S., Curtin, C., & Knotak, D. (2013). Comparative observations of learning engagement by students with developmental disabilities using an iPad and computer: A pilot study. *Assistive Technology*, *25*, 204–213. http://dx.doi.org/10.1080/10400435.2012.761293.

Axelsson, A., Andersson, R., & Gulz, A. (2016). Scaffolding executive function capabilities via Play-&-Learn software for preschoolers. *Journal of Educational Psychology*, *108*(7), 969–981. http://dx.doi.org/10.1037/edu0000099 [Advance online publication].

Best, J. R. (2012). Exergaming immediately enhances children's executive function. *Developmental Psychology*, *48*, 1501–1510. http://dx.doi.org/10.1037/a0026648.

Best, J. R., Miller, P. H., & Jones, L. L. (2009). Executive functions after age 5: Changes and correlates. *Developmental Review*, *29*, 180–200.

Buckner, E., & Kim, P. (2012). Mobile innovations, executive functions, and educational developments in conflict zones: A case study from palestine. *Educational Technology Research & Development*, *60*, 175–192. http://dx.doi.org/10.1007/s11423-011-9221-6.

Dovis, S., Van der Oord, S., Wiers, R. W., & Prins, P. M. (2015). Improving executive functioning in children with ADHD: Training multiple executive functions within the context of a computer game. A randomized double-blind placebo controlled trial. *Plos One*. *10*(4). http://dx.doi.org/10.1371/journal.pone.0121651. e0121651.

Dye, M. W. G., Green, C. S., & Bavelier, D. (2009). The development of attention skills in action video game players. *Neuropsychologica*, *47*, 1780–1789. http://dx.doi.org/10.1016/j.neuropsychologia.2009.02.002.

eBizMBA (2016). *Top 15 most popular social networking sites, August, 2016*. Retrieved from http://www.ebizmba.com/articles/social-networking-websites.

Gentile, D. A., Swing, E. L., Lim, C. G., & Khoo, A. (2012). Video game playing, attention problems, and impulsiveness: Evidence of bidirectional causality. *Psychology of Popular Media Culture*, *1*(1), 62–70. http://dx.doi.org/10.1037/a0026969.

Goldin, A. P., Hermida, M. J., Shalom, D. E., Costa, M. E., Lopez-Rosenfeld, M., Segretin, M. S., et al. (2014). Far transfer to language and math of a short software-based gaming intervention. *Proceedings of The National Academy of Sciences of the United States of America*, *111*(17), 6443–6448. http://dx.doi.org/10.1073/pnas.1320217111.

Grynszpan, O., Martin, J., & Nadel, J. (2007). Exploring the influence of task assignment and output modalities on computerized training for autism. *Interaction Studies: Social Behaviour and Communication in Biological and Artificial Systems*, *8*(2), 241–266. http://dx.doi.org/10.1075/is.8.2.04gry.

Hartanto, A., Toh, W. X., & Yang, H. (2016). Age matters: The effect of onset age of video game play on task-switching abilities. *Attention, Perception & Psychophysics*, *78*(4), 1125–1136. http://dx.doi.org/10.3758/s13414-016-1068-9.

Howard, S. J., & Okely, A. D. (2015). Catching fish and avoiding sharks: Investigating factors that influence developmentally appropriate measurement of preschoolers' inhibitory control. *Journal of Psychoeducational Assessment*, *33*(6), 585–596. http://dx.doi.org/10.1177/0734282914562933.

Jiménez, M. R., Pulina, F., & Lanfranchi, S. (2015). Video games and intellectual disabilities: A literature review. *Life Span and Disability, 18,* 147–165.

Li, X., & Atkins, M. S. (2004). Early childhood computer experience and cognitive motor development. *Pediatrics, 113*(6), 1715–1722.

Lezak, M. D., Howieson, D. B., Bigler, E. D., & Tranel, D. (2012). *Neuropsychological assessment* (5th ed.). New York, NY: Oxford University Press.

Mackey, A. P., Hill, S. S., Stone, S. I., & Bunge, S. A. (2011). Differential effects of reasoning and speed training in children. *Developmental Science, 14,* 582–590. http://dx.doi.org/10.1111/j.1467-7687.2010.01005.x.

Marshall, P. J., Bouquet, C. A., Thomas, A. L., & Shipley, T. F. (2010). Motor contagion in young children: Exploring social influences on perception-action coupling. *Neural Networks, 23,* 1017–1025. http://dx.doi.org/10.1016/j.neunet.2010.07.007.

McEwan, R. N., & Dubé, A. K. (2015). Engaging or distracting: Children's tablet use in education. *Educational Technology & Society, 18*(4), 9–23.

Miller, G. G., & Kapel, D. E. (1985). Can non-verbal, puzzle type microcomputer software affect spatial discrimination and sequential thinking skills of 7th and 8th graders? *Education, 106*(2), 160–167.

Nielsen (2014). *The U.S. digital consumer report.* Retrieved from http://www.nielsen.com/us/en/insights/reports/2014/the-us-digital-consumer-report.html.

Nielsen (2016). *Facts of life: As they move through life stages, Millenials' media habits are different and distinct.* Retrieved from http://www.nielsen.com/us/en/insights/news/2016/facts-of-life-as-they-move-through-life-stages-millennials-media-habits-are-different.html.

Pew Research Center (2015). *Teens, social media & technology overview.* Retrieved from http://www.pewinternet.org/2015/04/09/teens-social-media-technology-2015/.

Powers, K. L., Brooks, P. J., Aldrich, N. J., Palladino, M. A., & Alfieri, L. (2013). Effects of video-game play on information processing: A meta-analytic investigation. *Psychological Bulletin and Review, 20,* 1055–1079. http://dx.doi.org/10.3758/s13423-013-0418-z.

Rosen, L. D., Carrier, L. M., & Cheever, N. A. (2013). Facebook and texting made me do it: Media-induced task-switching. *Computers in Human Behavior, 29,* 948–958. http://dx.doi.org/10.1016/j.chb.2012.12.001.

Staiano, A. E., Abraham, A. A., & Calvert, S. L. (2012). Competitive versus cooperative exergame play for African American adolescents' executive function skills: Short-term effects in a long-term training intervention. *Developmental Psychology, 48,* 337–342. http://dx.doi.org/10.1037/a0026938.

Syväoja, H. J., Tammelin, T. H., Ahonen, T., Kankaanpää, A., & Kantomaa, M. T. (2014). The associations of objectively measured physical activity and sedentary time with cognitive functions in school-aged children. *Plos One. 9*(7). http://dx.doi.org/10.1371/journal.pone.0103559. e103559.

Thorell, L. B., Lindqvist, S., Bergman Nutley, S., Bohlin, G., & Klingberg, T. (2009). Training and transfer effects of executive functions in preschool children. *Developmental Science, 12*(1), 106–113. http://dx.doi.org/10.1111/j.1467-7687.2008.00745.x.

Wolfe, J., Kar, K., Perry, A., Reynolds, C., Gradisar, M., & Short, M. A. (2014). Single night video-game use leads to sleep loss and attention deficits in older adolescents. *Journal of Adolescence, 37*(7), 1003–1009. http://dx.doi.org/10.1016/j.adolescence.2014.07.013.

CHAPTER 9

Immersive Virtual Reality and the Developing Child

Jakki O. Bailey, Jeremy N. Bailenson
Stanford University, Stanford, CA, United States

Virtual reality (VR) allows users to fly across the skies, swim through the depths of the ocean, and become mythical creatures with magical powers. Immersive virtual reality (IVR) places users directly into virtual scenarios by blocking out the physical world, creating vivid and personal environments (Bailey et al., 2015; Bainbridge, 2007). Ivan Sutherland developed one of the earliest forms of IVR in the 1960s. Small displays connected to an apparatus hanging from the ceiling were placed over participants' eyes, creating one of the first times that people fully entered a virtual space. In the same decade, Morton Heilig pushed the limits of humans in virtual spaces by creating the Sensorama, a machine that created multisensory experiences with haptic, olfactory, and visual feedback (see Blascovich & Bailenson, 2011). For many decades, IVR technology was only available to research institutions, governments, and universities. It is now becoming more accessible and available to the public, as giant media corporations invest billions of dollars in IVR hardware and software (Lamkin, 2015; Solomon, 2014).

Decades of research have examined the uses and effects of VR with adult samples, demonstrating its power to alter attitudes (e.g., Peck, Seinfeld, Aglioti, & Slater, 2013), behaviors (e.g., Blascovich et al., 2002), and physiology (Salomon, Lim, Pfeiffer, Gassert, & Blanke, 2013). However, little is known about IVR and children despite their frequent media use and willingness to adopt new technologies (Lauricella, Cingel, Blackwell, Wartella, & Conway, 2014; Rideout, 2013). Given that IVR technology is gaining traction in the consumer market, it will be important to consider the developmental implications of its use.

This chapter will define IVR from both a technological standpoint (i.e., tracking, rendering, embodiment of senses) and a psychological standpoint (i.e., immersion vs. presence). We discuss some of the unique

Cognitive Development in Digital Contexts
http://dx.doi.org/10.1016/B978-0-12-809481-5.00009-2

181

attributes of IVR, and how they relate to topics of cognitive development, as pertaining to the development of executive functioning (EF) in early childhood. We also discuss the trends in empirical studies regarding IVR use among child populations, and provide future research directions.

WHAT IS VIRTUAL REALITY (VR)?

In virtual environments, a person is represented by an avatar, a digital representation of that person that he or she controls in real-time. In general, an avatar refers to any entity, digital, or nondigital, that represents the user in real time. When embodying an avatar, a person can have a first-person view of the virtual environment ("through one's own eyes") or a third-person view (having an outside perspective as if looking at a third party). In contrast to an avatar, an embodied agent is a digital representation that is solely controlled by a computer algorithm. What controls the digital representation, a person or a computer, determines if the representation is an avatar or an embodied agent. For example, a digital representation that looks like someone's aunt and is controlled by a computer algorithm is an embodied agent. However, if that same aunt controls a digital representation that looks like a dinosaur, it would be considered her avatar.

In a technological sense, VR can be defined by the tracking and rendering of a computing system or technology (e.g., computer, phone, tablet). Tracking captures the movement of the user (pushing a button, movement of the wrist, or swiping of fingers on a screen) and renders or updates the virtual world based on that tracked movement (e.g., the jumping of a character). Actions are tracked and rendered using translations (movement along x-, y-, z-axis) and/or orientation (pitch, roll, and yaw). A tracking device such as a sensor or a joystick detects a user's physical movements or location, and then renders or updates the virtual environment accordingly. For example, in a video game the player pushes the joystick forward (tracking his or her motion), and the virtual character moves up on the screen. Tracking body movements can occur through physical devices worn or held by the user (e.g., joystick, game pad, LED light sensor) or without the user wearing a device (e.g., infrared cameras). Senses that can be rendered in virtual environments are sight, hearing, touch, smell, and taste. Sight is the most common sense rendered in VR, and has been shown to elicit powerful responses from users even when other senses (i.e., touch, smell) are absent (Blascovich & Bailenson, 2011).

From a psychological vantage point, VR can be defined as an environment (actual or simulated) in which the perceiver experiences it as real

(Blascovich & Bailenson, 2011; Steuer, 1992). Presence is one term that is used to describe VR's psychological effect. Presence refers to the sensation of being located in a media event (Bowman & McMahan, 2007; Lee, 2004; Steuer, 1992), and is often used as an indicator of how involved a person feels or acts in a given event (Lombard & Ditton, 1997). People respond to virtual stimuli as if it were real, in ways that are similar to everyday experiences (Slater & Wilbur, 1997). Thus, a person feeling high presence staring into the eyes of a lion on a virtual Savannah, for example, would feel an increase in heart rate and perspiration. The overall concept of presence contains specific subcategories such as self-presence, social presence, and spatial presence. Self-presence refers to the degree that users identify with their avatars (i.e., experienced them as their actual bodies). Social presence refers to how other virtual representations or characters that are present seem real to the user (e.g., having the amount of interpersonal distance toward a digital character similar to that of a real person). Spatial presence refers to the degree that the virtual environment feels real; this term is often used interchangeably with the general term presence.

IMMERSIVE TECHNOLOGY

Immersion refers to the extent that a computing system can create a surrounding environment that shuts out the physical world, utilizing sensory modalities to create a rich representational experience (Slater, 2009). Immersion is defined by the objective capabilities of the technology. Immersive features can include, but are not limited to, the field of view, body tracking, frame rate, sound quality, or realism (Bowman & McMahan, 2007; Cummings & Bailenson, 2016; Slater, 2009). Presence refers to a subjective psychological experience while immersion refers to objective capabilities of the technology. For example, a person may feel a greater presence reading a novel, a form of media that has low sensory fidelity as compared with a television screen that has greater visual sensory feedback.

IMMERSIVE VIRTUAL REALITY (IVR)

IVR can be defined as a technological system consisting of a computer and a display (i.e., computer screen, projection screen). IVR has a rich sensory fidelity and immersive features that block out the physical world, and enable users to feel psychologically located in the simulated environment by experiencing it as real. Two types of technology commonly used to create

IVR are Cave Automatic Virtual Environments (CAVEs) and head-mounted displays (HMDs). A CAVE is a specially designed room in which the walls, ceiling, and or floor are covered with a screen that projects virtual images (Cruz-Neira, Sandin, DeFanti, Kenyon, & Hart, 1992). Three-dimensional views are created by either donning special eyewear such as stereoscopic glasses or by using autostereoscopic screens. In highly immersive CAVEs, the user is surrounded by the virtual environment (via the walls, ceiling, and floor). An HMD is a VR headset that places small screens in front of the user's eyes that block out other visual stimuli. It utilizes stereoscopic or monoscopic views, offering varying degrees of the field of view.

The assumption of many scholars is that greater levels of technological immersion create greater levels of presence. In a meta-analysis by Cummings and Bailenson (2016), it was found that immersion had a moderate effect on presence. The immersive features most associated with increasing levels of presence were the levels of tracking, stereoscopic vision, and the field of view. Other features such as sound quality and resolution had less of an effect. IVR is one type of technological system that has features that can elicit high levels of presence: it has the capability of providing many levels of tracking (i.e., the number and type of degrees of freedom) and the ability to mimic the human visual system with stereoscopic vision and a wide field of view. By experiencing high levels of presence, users will treat experiences in IVR as real, potentially influencing their behaviors and psychology in the physical world (Blascovich et al., 2002; Slater et al., 2006).

WHAT MAKES IVR UNIQUE?

IVR can provide users with multisensory experiences that replicate the physical world or create scenarios that are impossible or dangerous in the physical world (Blascovich et al., 2002). In the following, we focus on the unique capabilities of an HMD, an IVR technology that completely blocks out the physical world, including the user's body. Although a CAVE has many immersive qualities, the user cannot change how his or her body is represented in the virtual space from a first-person perspective. In contrast, with an HMD, users can look down and see their digital representation as a different sex, ethnicity, or body size; they can even embody an animal or an imaginary creature.

Through the powerful affordances of IVR, people treat their virtual bodies (i.e., their avatars) as their own, influencing their attitudes, behaviors, and physiology. Research has demonstrated that people are able to map their body schema onto virtual representations (i.e., avatars), and treat those representations as if they were their physical bodies (Banakou, Groten, & Slater, 2013; Blanke, 2012; Petkova & Ehrsson, 2008; Slater, Spanlang, Sanchez-Vives, & Blanke, 2010). Virtual embodiment can influence the brain such as to reduce pain perception (Hoffman et al., 2008), facilitate retraining for stroke rehabilitation (You et al., 2005), and even reduce skin or body temperature (Salomon et al., 2013). Findings also show that people claim a sense of ownership and agency over virtual bodies that differ drastically from their physical bodies (e.g., with a functional tail; Steptoe, Steed, & Slater, 2013), and can influence perceptions and attitudes in the physical world. For example, adults tended to overestimate the sizes of objects when embodying an avatar resembling a 4-year-old child versus an adult scaled to the same height as the child (Banakou et al., 2013). Peck et al. (2013) found that controlling an avatar of a different race reduced implicit race bias.

IVR has also been shown to alter how people interact in a virtual environment, which can influence how they interact socially with others. These transformed social interactions (TSI) refer to behaviors in the physical world that are filtered through a computer algorithm that transform the social interactions users have in the virtual world. These transformed actions can (a) alter how an avatar or embodied agent is presented to others (e.g., match the height of another user), (b) enhance the user's sensory capabilities (e.g., having confused audience members appear larger to the speaker as a signal that further explanation is needed), and (c) modify the context of the virtual experience (learning about ancient Greece from the Parthenon; Bailenson et al., 2008; Bailenson, Beall, Loomis, Blascovich, & Turk, 2004).

In IVR, users can transform the appearance and behavior of avatars and embodied agents to fit specific contexts to influence others socially. For instance, a person can present different versions (i.e., different genders, race, age, and height) of their avatar to different people simultaneously (co-workers, friends, strangers) to appear more appealing to a wide audience. Or in a virtual classroom, students could see a teacher whose race, gender, or affective qualities best suited their comfort and learning needs. Algorithms that change the appearance and behavior of avatars or embodied agents can yield real-world effects. A study by Bailenson et al. (2008) found that participants viewed embodied agents that mimicked their head movements during a speech to be more persuasive than those that did not.

TSI can enhance users' sensory abilities such as augmenting their view within the virtual environment. If a teacher lecturing in front of a virtual classroom does not maintain enough eye contact with one student, IVR can make the appearance of that student visually fade until the teacher regains adequate eye contact with the student (Bailenson et al., 2008). By extending the abilities of teachers in virtual classrooms, TSI in IVR could help train teachers (or any speaker) to distribute attention more evenly among students to facilitate learning.

Finally, the context of a virtual environment can be altered spatially and/ or temporally. Users can always feel that they are at the front of a room regardless of where they are actually located in the virtual space to better see the speaker or they could pause the lecturer to catch up on note taking. In addition, altering the context could help students learn by interacting directly with course materials. For example, students in a marine biology class could interact with underwater plants and sea creatures in a virtual ocean ecosystem to learn about individual species, without the risk or cost of an actual scuba-diving expedition.

CHILDREN EXPERIENCING IVR AS REAL

Media effects scholars have demonstrated that the body responds to digital media-technology (e.g., computers, televisions, IVR) as if it were real (Reeves, 1989; Reeves & Nass, 1996), and that the mind has not evolved to respond to it any differently from the physical world (Reeves, 1989). When using IVR as adults, we may know that we are safely located in a room wearing an HMD, yet when looking over the edge of a virtual precipice, our hearts race and our palms sweat (Blascovich & Bailenson, 2011). We comfort ourselves by remembering that we are in the room, by holding in our minds both the physical representation of the room that we can no longer see and the virtual environment with its salient sensory features. Young children, in contrast, may respond cognitively and behaviorally to sensory salient and immersive media like IVR in ways that differ from adults. IVR places users directly into the media content, potentially making the experience very vivid and real for children. For example, Sharar et al. (2007), using an HMD, found children of 6–18 years of age reported higher levels of presence and "realness" of a virtual environment compared with adults 19–65 years of age. If young children experience IVR as more real than adults, they may be more likely to be influenced by the content in both positive (e.g., prosocial education) and negative ways (e.g., increased materialism).

Research suggests young children struggle with the representational nature of certain media (i.e., television) because of the medium or technology itself (Troseth & DeLoache, 1998). This is an issue related to dual representation, the ability to understand the relationship between a symbol and its referent:

> *A symbolic artifact such as a picture or a model is both a concrete object and a representation of something other than itself. To use such objects effectively, one must achieve dual representation, that is, one must mentally represent the concrete object itself and its abstract relation to what it stands for.*
>
> **(DeLoache, 2004, p. 69)**

Dual representation allows children to understand the symbolic nature of media, which can facilitate and influence learning. This ability develops around the age of 3 and begins to develop fully during a time when executive function significantly improves (Obradović, Portilla, & Boyce, 2012).

Even in less-immersive media like a two-dimensional (2D) television screen, young children experience the content as real to a greater extent than their older counterparts, and this can affect how they behave and what they learn (Richert, Robb, & Smith, 2011). For instance, television research has shown young children are more likely to view the content as real compared with older children (i.e., thinking that popcorn will fall out of a bowl, if the researcher tips over the television screen holding the image; Flavell, Flavell, Green, & Korfmacher, 1990). Furthermore, children will use the content and characters in television as sources of information for decision making, if they feel the content and characters are real (Claxton & Ponto, 2013). Although research with less-immersive technologies has shown how children cognitively and socially experience content, it is unclear how children respond to IVR compared to these less-immersive technologies. IVR can create realistic sensory-rich experiences that place children directly into the content, which could make it challenging for them to recognize that it is a representation. For example, a young child may think that an embodied agent is an actual person, not a digital representation; this could influence the type of decisions that they make or the intensity of emotions they feel. According to DeLoache (2000, 2004), the more salient or appealing the appearance of the symbol, the more difficult it is for children to achieve dual representation.

How children cognitively and socially experience IVR as real could be influenced by brain development. The mental capabilities and skills of children develop differently over time according to a hierarchy of neural circuits in the brain (Fox, Levitt, & Nelson, 2010). For instance, younger adolescents may be less sensitive to social cues such as exclusion than older adolescents because regions of the brain related to social cognition mature slowly

(Blakemore & Mills, 2014). With the different neural circuits developing at different stages, it would be expected that children of different ages would respond to the same virtual experience differently. Brain-imaging research by Baumgartner et al. (2008) and Baumgartner, Valko, Esslen, and Jäncke (2006) suggests that adolescent and adult brains process virtual environments differently from how younger children do. Specifically, both adolescent (13–17 years of age) and adult (21–43 years of age) brains recruited regions located in the prefrontal cortex, an area associated with higher-level brain functioning, while younger children (8–11 years old and 6–11 years old, respectively) showed less activation in this brain region. Overall, based on how higher-order cognitive skills develop, one's developmental level may influence how media are understood and interpreted, and immersion may be one component of media that could influence cognition and behavior.

The immersive affordances of IVR have the potential to challenge young children's automatic reactions, such as motor or attentional reactions, and cognitive abilities. IVR can stimulate cognitive immersion, a process in which the mind and body become integrated with a virtual experience, given the technological affordances of the system. Specifically, IVR connects human senses with the technology, creating the illusion of being embedded in the content. By mimicking realistic and compelling scenarios, IVR has the potential to contribute to how concepts are created. Even in nonimmersive environments such as television, young children will prioritize information from a virtual character that acts socially contingent; they treat the virtual character as a live person, and claim that the character can see them (Claxton & Ponto, 2013).

Previous research on brain development and presence suggests that the development of EF may explain why young children respond to IVR as if it were real more than older populations, and experience cognitive immersion. EF skills could be one area to consider when examining children's cognitive experience of IVR. The prefrontal cortex, which is associated with EF, begins to develop throughout the preschool years (from 3 to 5 years of age) (Garon, Bryson, & Smith, 2008; Obradović et al., 2012). EF refers to self-regulatory abilities, and is often characterized as comprising inhibitory control, working memory, and cognitive flexibility (Obradović et al., 2012). Inhibitory control refers to the ability to suppress impulsive thoughts or behaviors and to resist distractions and temptations. Working memory refers to the ability to hold and manipulate verbal or nonverbal information in the mind over a short period of time (Obradović et al., 2012). Cognitive flexibility refers to the ability to shift attention between different and often competing rules and stimuli appropriately. Because the cognitive abilities supporting EF develop during the preschool years, young children will likely behave differently in IVR from adults.

Experiencing IVR may further involve simultaneously holding the idea of the physical world in mind while experiencing the virtual world. Immersive technology that has very salient sensory features may compromise children's ability to maintain the rules of the physical world, particularly when wearing a VR headset like an HMD that blocks out the location of objects in the physical world. Thus, it may be challenging for children to realize that they may walk into a wall while cognitively immersed in a virtual world. More research is needed to understand better how IVR may affect children's EF skills.

CHILDREN'S DISCOVERY OF THE SELF IN IVR

Children find themselves represented in digital form more often than previous generations: with a click of a mobile phone, a digital camera, or a handheld game, children's images can be placed within a virtual environment. Are younger children able to make that leap to understand the self-represented in IVR or the various forms that an avatar can take (i.e., first-person vs. third-person view of the self)? Experiencing immersive media such as IVR places users directly into the content, pushing the boundaries of self-representation, and the meaning of an avatar and an embodied agent.

Over time, children develop a sense that the self that exists in the present is the same as the self in the past, and that it will be the same person in the future (Fivush, 2011; Nelson & Fivush, 2004). Infants and toddlers can identify themselves in a mirror, demonstrating self-recognition (Courage & Howe, 2002; Nielsen, Suddendorf, & Slaughter, 2006). An extension of the mirror self-recognition task uses a video or photograph to measure the infant's more complex sense of self. In these tasks, children look at a delayed video recording or a series of photographs in which they see a mark being placed somewhere on them. Children who attempt to remove the mark after looking at these images pass the self-recognition test. Many studies show that by 3–4 years of age children successfully complete these tasks (Skouteris & Robson, 2006; Suddendorf & Butler, 2013; Suddendorf, Simcock, & Nielsen, 2007). Some scholars argue that the mirror recognition test measures a sense of a present self, whereas the delayed video or photograph tests represent an understanding of an extended temporal self (Suddendorf & Butler, 2013). These differences in performance based on the medium may be related to brain development. Results from neural imaging studies indicate that the neural mechanisms used to recognize the self in photographs are different from those used to recognize the self in a mirror (Suddendorf & Butler, 2013). Even with a live video stream, young children can struggle to pass the self-recognition test suggesting that the medium may influence self-recognition, and it is not solely an issue of delayed versus live feedback. With extensive practice over time, children under the age of 3 are able to counteract the "video deficit" (Troseth, 2003).

One dimension of presence in IVR is children being psychologically transported to the virtual environment (Lombard & Ditton, 1997). The ability to be psychologically transported to a virtual environment could be related to children developing a sense of self and understanding dual representation, that the self can exist in different forms, at different time points, and in different locations. Research from autobiographical memory provides some evidence as to why a sense of self is important for feeling psychologically transported. Autobiographical memory is a form of memory that reflects personal emotions, goals, and meaning (other forms of memory can be related to facts, skills, or lists), and "involves a sense of self experiencing the event at a specific point in time and space" (p. 488; Nelson & Fivush, 2004). Autobiographical memory develops during the preschool years (Nelson & Fivush, 2004). To remember the past, children are psychologically transported to that time in their mind to relive what happened to themselves (Fivush, 2011). Before the age of 3, children have not fully developed a sense of self in time and space (Skouteris & Robson, 2006; Suddendorf & Butler, 2013). This could be one possible explanation of why few people have memories before the age of 2 (Nelson & Fivush, 2004). Autobiographical memory is still developing during the preschool years, during a time in which children are learning to develop a sense of self over time. IVR can create virtual scenarios of different places and different time periods (Blascovich & Bailenson, 2011; Lombard & Ditton, 1997), and if children don't have a fully developed sense of self, they may confuse IVR experiences of occurring in the physical world (see Segovia & Bailenson, 2009). In addition, children would need to know that the self exists and have a grasp of dual representation to understand that they can be represented in virtual spaces (i.e., via an avatar). However, what could happen when the virtual self deviates from the appearance or behavior of the user, potentially making it challenging for children to recognize it as an avatar or an embodied agent? Two examples of how virtual environments challenge the self and how it can be represented in real time are exemplified via virtual doppelgangers and the Proteus effect.

A virtual doppelganger is a special type of an embodied agent: It is a virtual representation that looks like an actual person that exists (or existed) in the physical world, but is controlled by a computer. A virtual doppelganger blurs the line between an avatar and an embodied agent: It looks like the user, but a computer algorithm controls it. Through virtual doppelgangers, users can see themselves from a third-person point of view, perform novel acts that they otherwise could not or would not perform. For example, children could see their photorealistic representation performing or saying things they never did in the physical world such as walking on the moon or consuming a specific brand of sports drink. Importantly, users highly identify with their virtual doppelgangers even when they know that computer algorithms control them (Blascovich & Bailenson, 2011; Fox, Bailenson, & Binney, 2009). Viewing the behaviors of their virtual doppelganger in IVR affects user's attitudes, physiological responses and behaviors more than seeing a virtual character that does not look like them engage in the same behaviors (Blascovich & Bailenson, 2011). Users in IVR have been shown to prefer product brands they see their virtual doppelganger use over those endorsed by a virtual other (Ahn & Bailenson, 2011), have increased skin conductance when they see their virtual doppelganger running (compared with standing; Fox, Bailenson, & Ricciardi, 2012), and were more likely to invest in their future after seeing an aged version of themselves (Hershfield et al., 2011).

Another way that digital representations can influence people is through the appearance of their avatar. The Proteus effect refers to the notion that an avatar's appearance can affect the user's behaviors and attitudes in the real world (e.g., Fox, Bailenson, & Tricase, 2013). The user controls the actions of the avatar, but the avatar's appearance differs from the user's appearance. Research shows that the body types people assume in IVR affect their attitudes and behaviors such as behaving more confidently during a negotiation task when embodying a taller avatar (Yee & Bailenson, 2007), feeling self-objected after controlling a hypersexualized female avatar (Fox et al., 2013), or decreasing implicit race bias after embodying an avatar of a different race (Peck et al., 2013). The Proteus effect differs from the virtual doppelgangers in two ways: (1) the Proteus effect involves an avatar and a virtual doppelganger is a type of embodied agent, and (2) users see their virtual doppelganger, from a third-person view, engage in behaviors outside of their control (that may or may not have happened). This is similar to users watching themselves act in a movie. In contrast, the Proteus effect is about how the appearance of users' avatar (typically controlled from a first-person point of view) influences their behaviors.

THE FLUIDITY OF THE COGNITIVE SELF IN IVR

Imagine being a young child, having developed a sense of self for only a few years, and then being immersed in a virtual space where self-representation remains fluid; a new developed sense of self may lower the threshold for responding to one's avatar and embodied agents, as if they were real. In the past, self-recognition tests have manipulated real time (i.e., via a mirror or live video feed) versus delayed time (i.e., video recording). However, virtual doppelgangers push the self-recognition test to the limit: it is a mirror image of the self, but the child never had control of it at any point in time. With virtual doppelgangers, children can see themselves engage in behaviors that never happened. For example, Segovia and Bailenson (2009) found that when young elementary children (i.e., 6- to 7-years old) watched their virtual doppelganger swim with orca whales, they confused that as happening in real life. They were more likely to have "false memories" in these contexts compared with a no exposure control group or seeing another virtual child swimming with whales. Through immersion, children's sense of self through time was altered.

Surprisingly, in Segovia and Bailenson's (2009) study, there were no significant differences between conditions among preschool age children (i.e., 4- to 5-year olds). During the preschool years, children's dual representation and sense of self in media is still maturing, which could explain why this group was susceptible to creating false memories after all conditions (i.e., imagining swimming with whales, seeing the self-swim with whales in IVR, seeing another child swim with whales in IVR). In contrast, the older children (6- to 7-year olds) may have had a stronger understanding of self-recognition, but understanding how the self was represented in IVR may have been particularly challenging. IVR provides immersion that allows virtual content and digital representations to appear real even when the virtual scenario is impossible in the physical world. How children experience IVR and how immersion affects children may vary according to age, cognitive abilities, and type of immersive media-technology used.

TRENDS IN RESEARCH WITH IVR AND CHILDREN

Although there have been a number of studies and examples of children using virtual environments via low immersive technology such as using a 2D computer or television screen, there are few empirical studies that include children (e.g., under the age of 18) and IVR, specifically using an

HMD or CAVE. There are even fewer studies with children under the age of 7 (possibly due to the limited availability of IVR to the public or the large size and heaviness of past IVR technology). An overview of the literature shows four broad research topics: (1) IVR as a pain distraction tool, (2) IVR as a learning environment, (3) IVR for assessment and measurement, and (4) IVR's affect on child development. Studies included both clinical and nonclinical populations.

As a pain distraction tool, IVR has been used successfully to help with pain management for a multitude of medical procedures such as for burn wound cleaning (e.g., Das, Grimmer, Sparnon, McRae, & Thomas, 2005; van Twillert, Bremer, & Faber, 2007), cancer treatment (e.g., Gershon, Zimand, Pickering, Rothbaum, & Hodges, 2004; Schneider & Workman, 1999), and dental work (e.g., Aminabadi, Erfanparast, Sohrabi, Oskouei, & Naghili, 2012). IVR has been used as a distraction tool both from emotional and physical pain. In fact, research suggests that IVR has special qualities that help with pain distraction: With little to no interactivity (i.e., passively viewing the prerecorded actions of a video game or a film), patients report less pain compared with usual care (e.g., Dahlquist et al., 2007; Law et al., 2011). A review of VR as a pain distraction tool is found in Shahrbanian et al. (2012).

IVR has also been used as a tool for education. It has been used to facilitate learning for various skills and content areas such as visualizing fractions (Roussou, Oliver, & Slater, 2006), learning about gorilla behaviors (Allison & Hodges, 2000), and cognitive training for children with ADHD (Cho et al., 2002) or with Autism Spectrum Disorder (ASD; Jarrold et al., 2013). Several studies exist that use nonimmersive virtual environments for teaching children with ASD (e.g., teaching and practicing social cognition skills; Parsons, 2015; Wass & Porayska-Pomsta, 2014). However, few studies exist specifically using IVR to teach children with ASD. For a review of research on children with ASD using IVR and nonimmersive VR see the work of Bellani, Fornasari, Chittaro, and Brambilla (2011), and for a review of nonclinical educational virtual environments that include both IVR and nonimmersive VR refer to Mikropoulos and Natsis (2011) and Hew and Cheung (2010).

IVR can track where participants look and how they move their bodies, collecting thousands of data points. Researchers have used this capability to capture large amounts of data as a method for assessment and measurement. For example, researchers have used IVR as a tool to effectively measure the attention patterns of children with brain injuries (Gilboa et al., 2015) and to identify children with ADHD by measuring their attentional focus and performance on cognitive tasks (e.g., Bioulac et al., 2012). Although IVR has been used for pain distraction, education, and assessment with children, little is known about the effects of IVR as a technology on child development (for a general discussion of children's use of online virtual worlds and some of the developmental implications, see Subrahmanyam, 2009). The few studies that have explored issues of IVR and child development have examined the effect of IVR on children's visual system and memories. More specifically, one study examined the short-term use of IVR on fatigue related to the visual system (Kozulin, Ames, & McBrien, 2009) and another study examined IVR's impact on children believing that events in IVR happened in the physical world (Segovia & Bailenson, 2009).

CONCLUSIONS AND FUTURE DIRECTIONS

IVR is a system that blocks out the physical world, providing rich sensory fidelity wherein the user feels and responds to the virtual world, as if it were real. However, little is known about how IVR relates to child development. The little research examining young children and IVR suggests that they may have experiences unique to their age range. Brain development, EF, dual representation, and self-recognition (i.e., avatars, virtual doppelgangers, and TSI) in virtual environment may be important topics to consider regarding research on children's experiences in IVR. Basic questions related to presence, safety, and virtual characters in IVR also need to be answered before taking the steps to create effective content. For example, in IVR, virtual characters can mimic the child's behaviors, provide varying degrees of eye contact, or vary in size, with each of these factors potentially influencing the child's social behavior and learning. While television research provides the foundation for children's VR research, IVR can create content not possible in the physical world, and could elicit unknown reactions (i.e., emotional responses to standing in front of a virtual character 3 times the child's size).

Children may have strong reactions to IVR because they are still developing the skill of experiencing fully immersive technologies. For instance, there is some speculation that older children's attention to television content is less susceptible to formal features (e.g., cuts, zooms, music) because through experience, they have learned when and how to watch content based on those features (Anderson & Kirkorian, 2013). Perhaps, as children gain more experience with IVR, they will learn a type of immersive "formal feature" skill that could help them navigate in and out of immersive technologies. How children experience IVR may relate to their higher-order cognitive skills such as EF and dual representation, because the salient sensory feedback in IVR could challenge their behavioral and emotional regulation. If IVR could easily pull children into the content and elicit automatic responses related to attention and action, it may be a platform to develop new ways of measuring EF skills such as inhibitory control.

On November 8, 2015, the New York Times gave their Sunday print subscribers access to VR (Somaiya, 2015; Wohlsen, 2015). Placed neatly and easily in their newspapers, more than a million people had an inexpensive piece of cardboard in which after just a couple of minutes they could fold into an HMD that uses their phone as the screen. For the first time, millions of people had access to VR at the same time. Wired magazine writer, Wohlsen (2015), highlighted the potential implications of children having greater access to IVR, he writes, "But for good or ill, [the cardboard HMD] is just good enough to imprint a new paradigm on a nation of 8-year-olds. From now on, kids who've had the VR experience have a new set of expectations of what it should mean to interact with a computer. Imagine what they'll expect by the time they're 18." Although it had limited content and on the lower end of some immersive features (i.e., level of tracking), the New York Times roll out of VR demonstrated the children's access to immersive technologies is here.

Research with adult populations has shown IVR to have powerful effects on attitudes, behaviors, and physiology. IVR can be a technology that provides high degrees of immersion placing users directly into digital content, creating the illusion that the experience is real. Some research suggests that young children may experience virtual content differently from adults. Researchers, scholars, and VR developers need to examine the developmental issues related to the intersection of the immersive features and content of IVR further to determine what use of the technology are appropriate for which ages and how IVR can be used to enhance youth's lives. Children and adolescents are avid and early adopters of media. With broad access to VR breaching the horizon, it is expected that all ages will be interacting with immersive virtual environments. More than ever, it is a time to understand what these technological experiences mean for being a kid and what it means for human development.

REFERENCES

Ahn, S. J., & Bailenson, J. N. (2011). Self-endorsing versus other-endorsing in virtual environments. *Journal of Advertising, 40*(2), 93–106. http://dx.doi.org/10.2753/JOA0091-3367400207.

Allison, D., & Hodges, L. F. (2000). Virtual reality for education? *Presented at the proceedings of the ACM symposium on virtual reality software and technology*, ACM, pp. 160–165. http://dx.doi.org/10.1145/502390.502420.

Aminabadi, N. A., Erfanparast, L., Sohrabi, A., Oskouei, S. G., & Naghili, A. (2012). The impact of virtual reality distraction on pain and anxiety during dental treatment in 4–6 year-old children: A randomized controlled clinical trial. *Journal of Dental Research, Dental Clinics, Dental Prospects, 6*(4), 117–124.

Anderson, D. R., & Kirkorian, H. L. (2013). In J. Bryant & P. Vorderer (Eds.), *Psychology of entertainment* (pp. 35–51). Mahwah, NJ: Routledge.

Bailenson, J. N., Beall, A. C., Loomis, J., Blascovich, J., & Turk, M. (2004). Transformed social interaction: Decoupling representation from behavior and form in collaborative virtual environments. *Presence Teleoperators and Virtual Environments, 13*(4), 428–441. http://dx.doi.org/10.1162/1054746041944803.

Bailenson, J. N., Yee, N., Blascovich, J., Beall, A. C., Lundblad, N., & Jin, M. (2008). The use of immersive virtual reality in the learning sciences: Digital transformations of teachers, students, and social context. *Journal of the Learning Sciences, 17*(1), 102–141. http://dx.doi.org/10.1080/10508400701793141.

Bailey, J. O., Bailenson, J. N., Flora, J., Armel, K. C., Voelker, D., & Reeves, B. (2015). The impact of vivid messages on reducing energy consumption related to hot water use. *Environment and Behavior, 47*(5), 570–592. http://dx.doi.org/10.1177/0013916514551604.

Bainbridge, W. S. (2007). The scientific research potential of virtual worlds. *Science, 317* (5837), 472–476. http://dx.doi.org/10.1126/science.1146930.

Banakou, D., Groten, R., & Slater, M. (2013). Illusory ownership of a virtual child body causes overestimation of object sizes and implicit attitude changes. *Proceedings of the National Academy of Sciences, 110*(31), 12846–12851. http://dx.doi.org/10.1073/pnas.1306779110.

Baumgartner, T., Speck, D., Wettstein, D., Masnari, O., Beeli, G., Jäncke, L., et al. (2008). Feeling present in arousing virtual reality worlds: Prefrontal brain regions differentially orchestrate presence experience in adults and children. *Frontiers in Human Neuroscience, 2*, 8. http://dx.doi.org/10.3389/neuro.09.008.2008.

Baumgartner, T., Valko, L., Esslen, M., & Jäncke, L. (2006). Neural correlate of spatial presence in an arousing and noninteractive virtual reality: An EEG and psychophysiology study. *CyberPsychology & Behavior, 9*(1), 30–45. http://dx.doi.org/10.1089/cpb.2006.9.30.

Bellani, M., Fornasari, L., Chittaro, L., & Brambilla, P. (2011). Virtual reality in autism: State of the art. *Epidemiology and Psychiatric Sciences, 20*(03), 235–238. http://dx.doi.org/10.1017/S2045796011000448.

Bioulac, S., Lallemand, S., Rizzo, A., Philip, P., Fabrigoule, C., & Bouvard, M. P. (2012). Impact of time on task on ADHD patient's performances in a virtual classroom. *European Journal of Paediatric Neurology, 16*(5), 514–521. http://dx.doi.org/10.1016/j.ejpn.2012.01.006.

Blakemore, S. -J., & Mills, K. L. (2014). Is adolescence a sensitive period for sociocultural processing? *Annual Review of Psychology, 65*(1), 187–207. http://dx.doi.org/10.1146/annurev-psych-010213-115202.

Blanke, O. (2012). Multisensory brain mechanisms of bodily self-consciousness. *Nature Reviews Neuroscience, 13*(8), 556–571. http://dx.doi.org/10.1038/nrn3292.

Blascovich, J., & Bailenson, J. (2011). *Infinite reality: Avatars, eternal life, new worlds, and the dawn of the virtual revolution.* New York, NY: William Morrow & Co.

Blascovich, J., Loomis, J., Beall, A. C., Swinth, K. R., Hoyt, C. L., & Bailenson, J. N. (2002). Immersive virtual environment technology as a methodological tool for social psychology. *Psychological Inquiry, 13*(2), 103–124. http://dx.doi.org/10.1207/S15327965PLI1302_01.

Bowman, D. A., & McMahan, R. P. (2007). Virtual reality: How much immersion is enough? *Computer, 40*(7), 36–43. http://dx.doi.org/10.1109/MC.2007.257.

Cho, B. -H., Ku, J., Jang, D. P., Kim, S., Lee, Y. H., Kim, I. Y., et al. (2002). The effect of virtual reality cognitive training for attention enhancement. *CyberPsychology & Behavior, 5*(2), 129–137. http://dx.doi.org/10.1089/109493102753770516.

Claxton, L. J., & Ponto, K. C. (2013). Understanding the properties of interactive televised characters. *Journal of Applied Developmental Psychology, 34*(2), 57–62. http://dx.doi.org/10.1016/j.appdev.2012.11.007.

Courage, M. L., & Howe, M. L. (2002). From infant to child: The dynamics of cognitive change in the second year of life. *Psychological Bulletin, 128*(2), 250–277.

Cruz-Neira, C., Sandin, D. J., DeFanti, T. A., Kenyon, R. V., & Hart, J. C. (1992). The CAVE: Audio visual experience automatic virtual environment. *Communications of the ACM, 35*(6), 64–72. http://dx.doi.org/10.1145/129888.129892.

Cummings, J. J., & Bailenson, J. N. (2016). How immersive is enough? A meta-analysis of the effect of immersive technology on user presence. *Media Psychology, 19*(2), 272–309. http://dx.doi.org/10.1080/15213269.2015.1015740.

Dahlquist, L. M., McKenna, K. D., Jones, K. K., Dillinger, L., Weiss, K. E., & Ackerman, C. S. (2007). Active and passive distraction using a head-mounted display helmet: Effects on cold pressor pain in children. *Health Psychology, 26*(6), 794–801. http://dx.doi.org/10.1037/0278-6133.26.6.794.

Das, D. A., Grimmer, K. A., Sparnon, A. L., McRae, S. E., & Thomas, B. H. (2005). The efficacy of playing a virtual reality game in modulating pain for children with acute burn injuries: A randomized controlled trial. *BMC Pediatrics, 5*(1), 1. http://dx.doi.org/10.1186/1471-2431-5-1.

DeLoache, J. S. (2000). Dual representation and young children's use of scale models. *Child Development, 71*(2), 329–338. http://dx.doi.org/10.1111/1467-8624.00148.

DeLoache, J. S. (2004). Becoming symbol-minded. *Trends in Cognitive Sciences, 8*(2), 66–70. http://dx.doi.org/10.1016/j.tics.2003.12.004.

Fivush, R. (2011). The development of autobiographical memory. *Annual Review of Psychology, 62*(1), 559–582. http://dx.doi.org/10.1146/annurev.psych.121208.131702.

Flavell, J. H., Flavell, E. R., Green, F. L., & Korfmacher, J. E. (1990). Do young children think of television images as pictures or real objects? *Journal of Broadcasting & Electronic Media, 34*(4), 399–419. http://dx.doi.org/10.1080/08838159009386752.

Fox, J., Bailenson, J., & Binney, J. (2009). Virtual experiences, physical behaviors: The effect of presence on imitation of an eating avatar. *Presence Teleoperators and Virtual Environments, 18*(4), 294–303. http://dx.doi.org/10.1162/pres.18.4.294.

Fox, J., Bailenson, J. N., & Ricciardi, T. (2012). Physiological responses to virtual selves and virtual others. *Journal of CyberTherapy & Rehabilitation, 5*(1), 69–72.

Fox, J., Bailenson, J. N., & Tricase, L. (2013). The embodiment of sexualized virtual selves: The Proteus effect and experiences of self-objectification via avatars. *Computers in Human Behavior, 29*(3), 930–938. http://dx.doi.org/10.1016/j.chb.2012.12.027.

Fox, S. E., Levitt, P., & Nelson, C. A., III (2010). How the timing and quality of early experiences influence the development of brain architecture. *Child Development, 81*(1), 28–40. http://dx.doi.org/10.1111/j.1467-8624.2009.01380.x.

Garon, N., Bryson, S. E., & Smith, I. M. (2008). Executive function in preschoolers: A review using an integrative framework. *Psychological Bulletin, 134*(1), 31–60. http://dx.doi.org/10.1037/0033-2909.134.1.31.

Gershon, J., Zimand, E., Pickering, M., Rothbaum, B., & Hodges, L. (2004). A pilot and feasibility study of virtual reality as a distraction for children with cancer. *Journal of the American Academy of Child & Adolescent Psychiatry*, *43*(10), 1243–1249. http://dx.doi. org/10.1097/01.chi.0000135621.23145.05.

Gilboa, Y., Kerrouche, B., Longaud-Vales, A., Kieffer, V., Tiberghien, A., Aligon, D., et al. (2015). Describing the attention profile of children and adolescents with acquired brain injury using the virtual classroom. *Brain Injury*, *29*(13–14), 1691–1700. http://dx.doi. org/10.3109/02699052.2015.1075148.

Hershfield, H. E., Goldstein, D. G., Sharpe, W. F., Fox, J., Yeykelis, L., Carstensen, L. L., et al. (2011). Increasing saving behavior through age-progressed renderings of the future self. *Journal of Marketing Research*, *48*, S23–S37.

Hew, K. F., & Cheung, W. S. (2010). Use of three-dimensional (3-D) immersive virtual worlds in K-12 and higher education settings: A review of the research. *British Journal of Educational Technology*, *41*(1), 33–55. http://dx.doi.org/10.1111/j.1467-8535.2008.00900.x.

Hoffman, H. G., Patterson, D. R., Seibel, E., Soltani, M., Jewett-Leahy, L., & Sharar, S. R. (2008). Virtual reality pain control during burn wound debridement in the hydrotank. *The Clinical Journal of Pain*, *24*(4), 299–304. http://dx.doi.org/10.1097/ AJP.0b013e318164d2cc.

Jarrold, W., Mundy, P., Gwaltney, M., Bailenson, J., Hatt, N., McIntyre, N., et al. (2013). Social attention in a virtual public speaking task in higher functioning children with autism. *Autism Research*, *6*(5), 393–410. http://dx.doi.org/10.1002/aur.1302.

Kozulin, P., Ames, S. L., & McBrien, N. A. (2009). Effects of a head-mounted display on the oculomotor system of children. *Optometry and Vision Science*, *86*(7), 845–856. http://dx. doi.org/10.1097/OPX.0b013e3181adff42.

Lamkin, P. (2015, June 18). Virtual reality devices: $4 billion+business by 2018. Retrieved September 11, 2016 from http://www.forbes.com/sites/paullamkin/2015/06/18/ virtual-reality-devices-4-billion-business-by-2018/#53d8c14cfd92.

Law, E. F., Dahlquist, L. M., Sil, S., Weiss, K. E., Herbert, L. J., Wohlheiter, K., et al. (2011). Videogame distraction using virtual reality technology for children experiencing cold pressor pain: The role of cognitive processing. *Journal of Pediatric Psychology*, *36*(1), 84–94. http://dx.doi.org/10.1093/jpepsy/jsq063.

Lauricella, A. R., Cingel, D. P., Blackwell, C., Wartella, E., & Conway, A. (2014). The mobile generation: youth and adolescent ownership and use of new media. *Communication Research Reports*, *31*(4), 357–364. https://doi.org/10.1080/08824096.2014.963221.

Lee, K. M. (2004). Presence, explicated. *Communication Theory*, *14*(1), 27–50. http://dx.doi. org/10.1111/j.1468-2885.2004.tb00302.x.

Lombard, M., & Ditton, T. (1997). At the heart of it all: The concept of presence. *Journal of Computer-Mediated Communication*. *3*(2). http://dx.doi.org/10.1111/j.1083-6101.1997. tb00072.x.

Mikropoulos, T. A., & Natsis, A. (2011). Educational virtual environments: A ten-year review of empirical research (1999–2009). *Computers & Education*, *56*(3), 769–780. http://dx.doi.org/10.1016/j.compedu.2010.10.020.

Nelson, K., & Fivush, R. (2004). The emergence of autobiographical memory: A social cultural developmental theory. *Psychological Review*, *111*(2), 486–511. http://dx.doi.org/ 10.1037/0033-295X.111.2.486.

Nielsen, M., Suddendorf, T., & Slaughter, V. (2006). Mirror self-recognition beyond the face. *Child Development*, *77*(1), 176–185. http://dx.doi.org/10.1111/j.1467-8624.2006.00863.x.

Obradović, J., Portilla, X. A., & Boyce, W. T. (2012). Executive functioning and developmental neuroscience: Current progress and implications for early childhood education. In R. C. Pinta, L. Justice, W. S. Barnett, & S. Sheridan (Eds.), *Handbook of early childhood education* (pp. 324–351). New York, NY: Guilford. Retrieved from http://cepa.stanford. edu/content/executive-functioning-and-developmental-neuroscience-current-progress-and-implications-early-childhood-education.

Parsons, S. (2015). Learning to work together: Designing a multi-user virtual reality game for social collaboration and perspective-taking for children with autism. *International Journal of Child-Computer Interaction*, *6*, 28–38. http://dx.doi.org/10.1016/j.ijcci.2015.12.002.

Peck, T. C., Seinfeld, S., Aglioti, S. M., & Slater, M. (2013). Putting yourself in the skin of a black avatar reduces implicit racial bias. *Consciousness and Cognition*, *22*(3), 779–787. http://dx.doi.org/10.1016/j.concog.2013.04.016.

Petkova, V. I., & Ehrsson, H. H. (2008). If I were you: Perceptual illusion of body swapping. *PLoS ONE*, *3*(12), e3832. http://dx.doi.org/10.1371/journal.pone.0003832.

Reeves, B. (1989). Theories about news and theories about cognition: Arguments for a more radical separation. *The American Behavioral Scientist*, *33*(2), 191–198.

Reeves, B., & Nass, C. I. (1996). *The media equation: How people treat computers, television, and new media like real people and places: (Vol. xiv)*. New York, NY, US: Cambridge University Press.

Richert, R. A., Robb, M. B., & Smith, E. I. (2011). Media as social partners: The social nature of young children's learning from screen media. *Child Development*, *82*(1), 82–95. http://dx.doi.org/10.1111/j.1467-8624.2010.01542.x.

Rideout, V. (2013). *Zero to eight: Children's media use in America 2013*. Common Sense Media. Retrieved from https://www.commonsensemedia.org/research/zero-to-eight-childrens-media-use-in-america-2013.

Roussou, M., Oliver, M., & Slater, M. (2006). The virtual playground: An educational virtual reality environment for evaluating interactivity and conceptual learning. *Virtual Reality*, *10*(3–4), 227–240. http://dx.doi.org/10.1007/s10055-006-0035-5.

Salomon, R., Lim, M., Pfeiffer, C., Gassert, R., & Blanke, O. (2013). Full body illusion is associated with widespread skin temperature reduction. *Frontiers in Behavioral Neuroscience*, *7*, 65. http://dx.doi.org/10.3389/fnbeh.2013.00065.

Schneider, S. M., & Workman, M. L. (1999). Effects of virtual reality on symptom distress in children receiving chemotherapy. *CyberPsychology & Behavior*, *2*(2), 125–134. http://dx. doi.org/10.1089/cpb.1999.2.125.

Segovia, K. Y., & Bailenson, J. N. (2009). Virtually true: Children's acquisition of false memories in virtual reality. *Media Psychology*, *12*(4), 371–393. http://dx.doi.org/ 10.1080/15213260903287267.

Shahrbanian, S., Ma, X., Aghaei, N., Korner-Bitensky, N., Moshiri, K., & Simmonds, M. J. (2012). Use of virtual reality (immersive vs. non immersive) for pain management in children and adults: A systematic review of evidence from randomized controlled trials. *European Journal of Experimental Biology*, *2*(5), 1408–1422.

Sharar, S. R., Carrougher, G. J., Nakamura, D., Hoffman, H. G., Blough, D. K., & Patterson, D. R. (2007). Factors influencing the efficacy of virtual reality distraction analgesia during postburn physical therapy: Preliminary results from 3 ongoing studies. *Archives of Physical Medicine and Rehabilitation*, *88*(12 Suppl. 2), S43–S49.

Skouteris, H., & Robson, N. (2006). Young children's understanding of photo self-representations. *Australian Journal of Educational & Developmental Psychology*, *6*, 50–59.

Slater, M. (2009). Place illusion and plausibility can lead to realistic behaviour in immersive virtual environments. *Philosophical Transactions of the Royal Society of London B: Biological Sciences*, *364*(1535), 3549–3557. http://dx.doi.org/10.1098/rstb.2009.0138.

Slater, M., Antley, A., Davison, A., Swapp, D., Guger, C., Barker, C., et al. (2006). A virtual reprise of the Stanley Milgram obedience experiments. *PLoS ONE*, *1*(1), e39. http://dx. doi.org/10.1371/journal.pone.0000039.

Slater, M., Spanlang, B., Sanchez-Vives, M. V., & Blanke, O. (2010). First person experience of body transfer in virtual reality. *PLoS ONE*, *5*(5), e10564. http://dx.doi.org/10.1371/ journal.pone.0010564.

Slater, M., & Wilbur, S. (1997). A framework for immersive virtual environments (five): Speculations on the role of presence in virtual environments. *Presence Teleoperators and Virtual Environments*, *6*(6), 603–616. http://dx.doi.org/10.1162/pres.1997.6.6.603.

Solomon, B. (2014, March 25). Facebook buys oculus, virtual reality gaming startup, for $2 billion. Retrieved August 15, 2016, from http://www.forbes.com/sites/briansolomon/2014/03/25/facebook-buys-oculus-virtual-reality-gaming-startup-for-2-billion/.

Somaiya, R. (2015, October 20). The times partners with google on virtual reality project. *The New York Times*. Retrieved from http://www.nytimes.com/2015/10/21/business/media/the-times-partners-with-google-on-virtual-reality-project.html.

Steptoe, W., Steed, A., & Slater, M. (2013). Human tails: Ownership and control of extended humanoid avatars. *IEEE Transactions on Visualization and Computer Graphics*, *19*(4), 583–590. http://dx.doi.org/10.1109/TVCG.2013.32.

Steuer, J. (1992). Defining virtual reality: Dimensions determining telepresence. *Journal of Communication*, *42*(4), 73–93. http://dx.doi.org/10.1111/j.1460-2466.1992.tb00812.x.

Subrahmanyam, K. (2009). Developmental implications of children's virtual worlds protecting virtual playgrounds: Children, law, and play online. *Washington and Lee Law Review*, *66*, 1065–1084.

Suddendorf, T., & Butler, D. L. (2013). The nature of visual self-recognition. *Trends in Cognitive Sciences*, *17*(3), 121–127.

Suddendorf, T., Simcock, G., & Nielsen, M. (2007). Visual self-recognition in mirrors and live videos: Evidence for a developmental asynchrony. *Cognitive Development*, *22*(2), 185–196. http://dx.doi.org/10.1016/j.cogdev.2006.09.003.

Troseth, G. L. (2003). TV guide: Two-year-old children learn to use video as a source of information. *Developmental Psychology*, *39*(1), 140–150. http://dx.doi.org/10.1037/0012-1649.39.1.140.

Troseth, G. L., & DeLoache, J. S. (1998). The medium can obscure the message: Young children's understanding of video. *Child Development*, *69*(4), 950–965. http://dx.doi.org/10.1111/j.1467-8624.1998.tb06153.x.

van Twillert, B., Bremer, M., & Faber, A. W. (2007). Computer-generated virtual reality to control pain and anxiety in pediatric and adult burn patients during wound dressing changes. *Journal of Burn Care & Research: Official Publication of the American Burn Association*, *28*(5), 694–702. http://dx.doi.org/10.1097/BCR.0B013E318148C96F.

Wass, S. V., & Porayska-Pomsta, K. (2014). The uses of cognitive training technologies in the treatment of autism spectrum disorders. *Autism*, *18*(8), 851–871. http://dx.doi.org/10.1177/1362361313499827.

Wohlsen, M. (2015, November 9). Google cardboard's New York Times experiment gave a bunch of kids their first glimpse of the future. Retrieved September 11, 2016, from https://www.wired.com/2015/11/google-cardboards-new-york-times-experiment-just-hooked-a-generation-on-vr/.

Yee, N., & Bailenson, J. (2007). The proteus effect: The effect of transformed self-representation on behavior. *Human Communication Research*, *33*(3), 271–290. http://dx.doi.org/10.1111/j.1468-2958.2007.00299.x.

You, S. H., Jang, S. H., Kim, Y. -H., Hallett, M., Ahn, S. H., Kwon, Y. -H., et al. (2005). Virtual reality–induced cortical reorganization and associated locomotor recovery in chronic stroke an experimenter-blind randomized study. *Stroke*, *36*(6), 1166–1171. http://dx.doi.org/10.1161/01.STR.0000162715.43417.91.

CHAPTER 10

Digital Childhoods and Literacy Development: Is Textspeak a Special Case of an "Efficient Orthography"?

Clare Wood*, Helen Johnson†
*Nottingham Trent University, Nottingham, United Kingdom
†Coventry University, Coventry, United Kingdom

Over the past decade, the use and ownership of mobile phones and other personal digital devices have become increasingly common for adults, children, and adolescents. The advent of more affordable handsets with full keyboards and touchscreens has enabled a younger generation to embrace this technology (Skierkowski & Wood, 2012). The increased use of personal digital technology has changed the way in which people communicate. Holtgraves (2011) has observed that text messaging (SMS) is a particularly interesting phenomenon as it merges features of written and oral communication. That is, texting and instant messaging are mobile, highly interactive, and can take place in real time. They also *extend* opportunities for social contact and interaction, providing a means of remaining in contact with others where the technology is supported (Skierkowski & Wood, 2012). These methods of communication enable users to coordinate activities, maintain social networks, and share information, as well as offer a distracting activity in itself by filling dead time (Tossell et al., 2012). For example, some children have noted that they find themselves sending digital messages at times when they would not normally phone or otherwise interact with people (Wood, Kemp, & Plester, 2014).

For children in the United Kingdom, the use of mobile phones, texting, and other forms of digital messaging is now commonplace. In 2005, Jackie Marsh suggested that "Digikids" would spend their preschool years familiarizing themselves with mobile phones and would therefore enter school with extensive experience of this type of technology. Consistent with this

Cognitive Development in Digital Contexts
http://dx.doi.org/10.1016/B978-0-12-809481-5.00010-9

prediction, toy versions of mobile phones for preschool children are easily found, and there is evidence that some children now own their own phones at 5 years of age (Wood, Kemp, & Plester, 2014) with other preschoolers well versed in their use through exposure to preschool apps available on smartphones.

As mobile devices have become increasingly commonplace, concerns have been raised by the media about the use of such technology by children and young people (see Crystal, 2008; Thurlow, 2006; Thurlow & Bell, 2009, for overviews). Some media coverage has included concerns about children not getting enough sleep due to late night phone use and even the dangers associated with inattention when crossing roads. However, the primary concern has centered on the impact that the growing use of text messaging could have on language itself (e.g., Humphrys, 2007) and children's language development in particular. For example, suggestions have been made that the use of abbreviations and alternative spellings, which are a feature of communication via text and instant messaging, ultimately pose a threat to children's spelling and grammatical development (e.g., see Woronoff, 2007). Such assertions have not been made tentatively; rather, they have been asserted as inevitable truths, despite the lack of evidence at the time to support such strong claims.

However, our own work and that of others working in this field have not supported these concerns and have in fact either shown positive or null associations between the use of texting slang and literacy development (e.g., Coe & Oakhill, 2011; Plester, Wood, & Joshi, 2009; Wood, Jackson, Hart, Plester, & Wilde, 2011; Wood, Meachem, et al., 2011; Wood, Kemp, Waldron, & Hart, 2014; Wood, Kemp, & Waldron, 2014). The question of why there has been little evidence of any detrimental impact is one that we have explored in our papers. However, there is scope to understand further the findings we obtained in these studies if we consider the proposition that the linguistic forms that many children use when writing in digital contexts represent a type of "efficient" orthographic system.

AN EFFICIENT ORTHOGRAPHY

An "efficient orthography" is one that affords optimal conditions for individuals to decode new words effectively and which also enables automatized reading for experienced readers. To permit these dual affordances, an efficient orthography is one that comprises distinct and specific word units with a consistent orthographic configuration. In other words, an efficient orthography is one that permits self-teaching to occur because of the transparency and predictability of its orthographic units and their correspondences with phonology (Share, 1995). Through repeated exposure to texts in such orthographies, readers become more proficient and efficient at decoding texts, and when new words are encountered, the features of the orthographic system permit its users to successfully decode and extract meaning from these novel items and to easily acquire and retain the spellings of those new items. The efficiency of an orthographic system can account for cross-linguistic variations in levels of literacy difficulties and speed of literacy acquisition (e.g., Seymour, Aro, & Erskine, 2003; Ziegler, Perry, Ma-Wyatt, Ladner, & Schulte-Korne, 2003), and in particular can explain why the levels of reading difficulty experienced by children learning to become literate in English are so pronounced.

The concept of an efficient orthography is one that is particularly relevant in the context of literate activity within digital media. That is, over the last 20 years, we have seen the emergence, development, and maintenance of an orthographic system referred to as *textspeak*. Textspeak is a version of an established orthography (such as English) where alternative, abbreviated, and simplified spellings are used (see Crystal, 2008, for examples of textspeak across different language contexts). Within English textspeak, users typically employ alternative representations of words or sentences (known as "textisms") alongside more conventional orthographic units (e.g., "Hi! Hope everything OK. U goin out 2nite?"). Textisms can be phonetic in nature (e.g., "2nite" for "tonight") but can also comprise truncated and abbreviated word forms that represent words or entire phrases (e.g., "U" for "you," and "imho" for "in my humble opinion"). Table 1 summarizes the different types of textisms that have been identified, to illustrate the range of adaptations that are used. These forms were originally used to keep text messages short and therefore within the character restrictions of the early mobile phones. Contemporary phones no longer restrict text message length in the same way, and the prevalence of standard keyboard interfaces on phones (as opposed to the original "multipress" numerical keypads) led to speculation that the use of such abbreviations would decline and eventually disappear. However, this situation has not occurred, and textisms continue to be readily observable in text messages and other forms of written digital communication, such as instant messaging, social media posts, and even email communications. Moreover, as Crystal (2008) has noted, the use of similar abbreviations has been noted in examples of writing that predate digital technologies.

As Table 1 shows, even within phonetic textisms, the standard English orthographic system is disrupted through the use of numerical characters as

Table 1 Examples of types of text abbreviation or "textisms" used

Category of textism	Examples
Shortenings	Feb, bro
Contractions	txt, chldrn
g-Clippings	shoppin, sleepin
Other clippings	shal (shall), hav (have), Cov (Coventry)
Omitted apostrophes	wont, didnt, mums
Acronyms	GB, ITV
Intialisms	rofl (rolling on the floor laughing),
Symbols	☺ @ & x o
Emoji	
Letter/number homophones	2nite (tonight), U (you), R (are)
Nonconventional spellings	nite, fone
Accent stylization	sup (what's up), kewl (cool), wiv (with), innit (isn't it)

graphemes (e.g., *l8r* for "later") and through the representation of national and regional accents rather than received pronunciation (e.g., "anuva" for "another," "kewl" for "cool"). Even punctuation can be substituted by novel markers such the use of emoticons and emojis, which have been observed to be used consistently as substitutes for full stops or commas (e.g., Wood, Kemp, Waldron & Hart, 2014), and which are arguably more successful than conventional punctuation at conveying and disambiguating any nonliteral meanings intended by the author.

As such, it can be argued that the use of textspeak and of textisms in particular, affords a particular context for examining the claims of self-teaching theory. That is, young people who are new to texting are exposed to an orthographic environment that shares some regularities and tokens from their more familiar language system, but which also incorporates novel items. It should be noted that in English textspeak, phonetic textisms tend to be the most frequently used type (Plester, Wood, & Bell, 2008; Wood, Kemp, & Plester, 2014), and in published studies of naturalistic (as opposed to elicited) text messages, there have been no reported examples of young people writing all their text messages in textisms only. Therefore, a typical primary school aged child's text message might comprise a sentence in which approximately 30–40% of the words are textisms (e.g., Wood, Meachem, et al., 2011) and of which the majority of those textisms will be phonetic in nature (Plester et al., 2008; Wood, Kemp, & Plester, 2014). As a result, in English at least, the use of textisms should facilitate self-teaching as they usually follow a more transparent and simplified set of orthographic principles than the opaque orthographic system from which they have been derived. However, just as in normal reading, some novel words may be characterized as "foreign" in the sense that they are based on a set of orthographic principles that are not consistent with the regularities of the language in which they are contextualized (e.g., symbols and initialisms).

TEXTISM USE AND LITERACY SKILLS

Research into the use of text abbreviations has shown that the children's use of textisms in SMS messages is positively associated with literacy outcomes and with growth in spelling ability in particular (e.g., see Plester et al., 2009; Wood, Jackson, et al., 2011; Wood, Meachem, et al., 2011). It was originally suggested that textism use may contribute to children's reading and spelling acquisition because it affords children an environment in which they can rehearse their understanding of letter–sound correspondences and improve their phonological processing abilities. What we did not consider at the time was the possibility that by augmenting their writing with textisms, children were potentially creating a more optimal orthographic environment for self-teaching of standard English words to occur within, and that it could have been this factor that explained the apparent additional benefits of textism use on children's attainment in reading and spelling.

Other explanations were originally offered for the benefits of text messaging on literacy, but these were not substantiated. For example, one of the explanations that we suggested when trying to account for the results from our early studies was that perhaps the children were increasing their exposure to print when sending and receiving texts (e.g., see p. 156 of Plester et al., 2009) and that this situation led to the positive association between texting and reading performance. This argument was presented in the context of an apparent decline in the United Kingdom in schoolchildren reading for pleasure outside of school and the rise in mobile phone ownership and texting behavior in school-age populations. In Wood, Jackson, et al. (2011), we were able to examine directly this explanation. That is, in this study, we recruited 114 9- and 10-year-old children in the United Kingdom who did not own a mobile phone (these children were sampled from a range of different schools). The children within each school were then randomly allocated to one of two conditions: a control group (business as usual) and an intervention group that was provided with basic mobile phones topped up with texting credits for use over weekends and during a weeklong half-term school break. Each week, we collected the phones from the children and transcribed each text message they had sent, and we also noted how many text messages each child had sent and received. These "traffic" data provided us with a direct measure of the additional exposure to print that each child was afforded by his/her mobile phone. When we considered these data in our analyses, we found that there was no evidence of an exposure to print contribution to the literacy outcomes of the children we studied. And yet, within the group of children who were given mobile phones (i.e., novice texters), we saw textism use that explain significant growth in spelling ability over time, even after controlling for individual differences in IQ, after just one term (10 weeks) of phone use.

This relationship between children's spelling development and their use of textisms was not an isolated finding. We also conducted a longer-term (September to July) longitudinal study of textism use and literacy outcomes in a cohort of 8- to 12-year-old children who were preexisting mobile phone users (Wood, Meachem, et al., 2011). In this study, we assessed the children at the beginning and end of an academic year on their reading, spelling, general cognitive ability, rapid naming, and phonological aware- ness. Like Plester et al. (2009), we found positive associations between use of textisms and concurrent reading and spelling scores. Of particular interest was the finding that the children's use of textisms at the start of the year could account for growth in their spelling ability over the academic year, even after controlling factors such as phonological awareness, verbal intelligence, and age. Moreover, we found that the nature of this relation- ship was unidirectional. That is, textism use at the beginning of the year could account for unique variance in spelling development over the course of the academic year, but reading and spelling scores at the beginning of the year could not account for growth in textism use over the academic year. Therefore, it could not be claimed that the observed relationships between textism use and literacy were attributable to the fact that it was the children with well-established literacy levels who were simply more proficient at textism use.

So, for some time now, we have speculated about the nature of the "value added" contribution of textism use to children's literacy skills. What we have learned from studies such as Wood, Jackson, et al. (2011) and Coe and Oakhill (2011) is that the contribution of textspeak to literacy develop- ment is specifically rooted in children's use of textisms rather than the frequency of texting behavior. Clearly, the contribution of textism use to children's phonological development is part of this explanation; in Wood, Meachem, et al. (2011), we presented regression analyses that demonstrated this contention. However, the use of textisms seems to add something distinctive to children's literacy development. For example, in Plester et al. (2009), there was a positive concurrent association between reading and textism use that remained significant even after controlling for individual differences in age, short term memory, vocabulary, phonological awareness, and length of mobile phone ownership. In our earlier work, we suggested that engagement with textisms may motivate children to engage in playful exploration of language (Plester et al., 2009), which could be beneficial on a number of counts. It seems equally plausible to suggest that what textism-based literate activity affords children is an orthographic environment that is more "efficient" than conventional English orthography, and following Share's ideas, this may be promoting more effective literacy acquisition via the self-teaching mechanism.

SELF-TEACHING THEORY

In his (1995) paper, David Share outlined how orthographic representations were acquired through a process of self-teaching. He explained that although there were other potential routes to acquiring orthographic representations, phonological recoding was the most important because it enabled all readers (children and adults) to learn the orthographic representations needed for fluent word reading. Within self-teaching theory, it is proposed that the development of phonological recoding skill is achieved incrementally, item-by-item (as opposed to a stage-based progression), and is primarily applied to unfamiliar words, as the orthographic representations of high-frequency words are likely to be rapidly acquired:

> *Because orthographic information is acquired rapidly… high frequency items are likely to be recognized visually with minimal phonological processing from the very earliest stages of reading acquisition. Novel, and less familiar items for which the child has yet to acquire orthographic representations will be more dependent on phonology.*
>
> **(Share, 1995, p. 155).**

However, orthographic knowledge will increasingly constrain phonological recoding processes because as a child's lexicon grows, regularities in that language system will be identified and used to make phonological recoding more efficient:

> *The process of phonological recoding becomes increasingly "lexicalized" in the course of reading development. Simple letter-sound correspondences become modified in the light of lexical constraints imposed by a growing body of orthographic knowledge. The expanding print lexicon alerts the child to regularities beyond the level of simple one-to-one grapheme–phoneme correspondences, such as context-sensitive, positional and morphemic constraints. The outcome of this process of "lexicalization" is a skilled reader whose knowledge of the relationships between print and sound has evolved to a degree that makes it indistinguishable from a wholly lexical mechanism that maintains sublexical spelling-sound correspondence rules.*
>
> **(Share, 1995, p. 156).**

According to Share (1995), the acquisition of a small initial set of simple grapheme–phoneme correspondences may be sufficient.

INDIVIDUAL DIFFERENCES IN PHONOLOGICAL PROCESSING WILL IMPACT SELF-TEACHING

So from this account, for self-teaching to occur, two component processes are warranted—one phonological and one orthographic. Both make an independent contribution to literacy acquisition, but Share is careful to stress that it is the phonological recoding process that is dominant as research has shown that it can account for most of the variance in reading ability. The orthographic processing system is therefore seen as secondary. Moreover, there will be individual differences in an individual's ability to engage in phonological recoding and orthographic processing, and these individual differences will also impact the extent to which an individual draws on phonological or visual processing during self-teaching. Consistent with this idea, we can predict that in the context of text messaging, we should see evidence of reduced phonological engagement and increased reliance on more visual forms of text abbreviation in populations where phonological processing abilities are more compromised.

This prediction is supported by the findings of Veater, Plester, and Wood (2010). In this study, children with developmental dyslexia were compared to reading age and chronological age-matched control groups on their use of textisms and their performance on measures of general ability and literacy-related skills. Veater et al. observed that the children with dyslexia were similar to controls in the overall proportion of text abbreviations that they used when texting, but the types of textism that they favored were different. In particular, they appeared to use fewer phonetic text abbreviations and more initialisms and symbolic forms. In line with this, we also observed that there was no significant association between the dyslexic children's use of textisms and phonological skills, whereas such a relationship was observed for the children in the control groups. Veater et al. also found no association between textism use and reading ability in the group with dyslexia, whereas there was one for the control groups. Similarly, Durkin, Conti-Ramsden, and Walker (2011) compared the texting behaviors of 47 adolescents with Specific Language Impairment (SLI) to 47 age-matched controls who were typically developing readers. They observed that the teenagers with SLI were less likely to reply to text messages, and those who did reply, wrote shorter texts and use fewer textisms than the control group.

From Veater et al. (2010), we can see evidence of reduced use of phonetic text abbreviations compared to controls and no link between overall levels of textism use and literacy for the children with developmental dyslexia. In contrast, for the control children, there was an association between textism use and literacy skills. It should be recalled that the proportion of textisms used, although slightly lower in the dyslexic group, did not differ significantly from the textism levels observed in controls. Thus, where the textisms used afforded better opportunities for self-teaching to occur, given their phonetic transparency, we see a link between their use and reading attainment.

SELF-TEACHING THEORY AND SPELLING

Another reason to consider textism use as a beneficial route to self-teaching comes from Shahar-Yames and Share (2008), whose work demonstrated that learning to spell novel items is a more powerful route to self-teaching than reading. This is because during spelling acquisition the need for phonological recoding at the item level is unavoidable. Thus, we can predict that within our text messaging studies, we should see greater evidence of a link between textism use and spelling development than we do between textism use and reading. This is, in fact, what we do observe. Although in the Plester et al. (2009) study, there was a stronger relationship between reading and textism use than there was between spelling and textism use, it should be noted that the data in this study were concurrent whereby the text messages were elicited rather than spontaneously produced outside of the research setting. When we focus on the studies where we sampled actual messages sent by the children "in real life," we see significant but weaker relationships between textism use and reading compared to the relationships between textism use and spelling scores. Moreover, there was evidence that textism use could explain variance in the development of spelling over time, which was not replicated for reading development (Wood, Meachem, et al., 2011; Wood, Jackson, et al., 2011).

A GOOD ENOUGH ORTHOGRAPHY

It is important to recognize that textspeak is not a perfect orthography: it is not perfectly transparent to read and spell once the code is unlocked. As noted, some textisms are not readily decodable through phonological recoding, and textisms are not used 100% of the time, or even most of the time, when textspeak is used. Semantic access is compromised if too many textisms are used relative to recognizable words. However, these features are permitted within self-teaching theory:

> Too great a number of unfamiliar words will disrupt ongoing comprehension processes…but the occasional novel string will provide relatively unintrusive self-teaching opportunities.
>
> **(Share, 1995, p. 158)**

Textisms that are frequently used are often very simplified phonetic spellings, which may be unconventional spellings in the sense of not being the accepted forms, but they usually do conform to the underlying orthographic rules of English in terms of legal letter combinations and positions. In this sense, a word like "nite" is acceptable as it follows the same pattern as "site," and "wot" is orthographically acceptable just as "hot" and "got" are. Clearly these spellings are oversimplifications, but they do offer children the ability to communicate before they may have grasped more unfamiliar or complex orthographic forms such as "-ight" or "wh-" and may also be observed in children's early attempts at spelling in formal school work. Rather than representing a threat to children's literacy development, it would seem that such spellings provide an entry point to a more complete conventional orthography by permitting the learning of an initial set of orthographic representations which kick start the self-teaching process.

> … there is a considerable volume of reading and spelling data indicating that an initially incomplete and oversimplified representation of the English spelling-sound system becomes modified and refined in the light of print experience.
>
> **(Share, 1995, p. 165)**

Although print experience in textspeak will expose children to an increased number of simplified spellings than they would usually see in print, they will be interacting with other children and adults whose responses in textspeak may include the conventional spellings of these items, and it is important to acknowledge that children are not entirely dependent upon digital texts for exposure to conventional orthographic forms.

If we accept textspeak as a recently developed example of an efficient orthography (or at least a more efficient orthography than Standard English), we also can consider its utility in the context of reading instruction. Children's familiarity with textisms affords teachers a new context in which to explore their students' understanding of phonic principles with real world validity. For example, the use of nonwords in the United Kingdom nationally implemented reading test for 6-year-olds has been viewed controversially by primary school teachers because children at such an early stage of reading instruction may be confused by being asked to "read" words which have no semantic content. Phonetically based textisms, however, in this age group, have the orthographic properties of nonwords but could be employed in the context of lessons to introduce students to the idea of alternative (nonconventional spellings), as in "these words are used as a quick and friendly way of writing when we are talking to our friend on the computer or on our phones." They could also be potentially used to reinforce phonics-based instruction for children who perhaps need more extended exposure to simplified orthographic forms. This exposure would permit a wider range of semantic content to be accessed for the purposes of storytelling as in the case of reading books in which textisms are used as a story device for characters to interact with each other, thereby permitting older readers who experience reading delays to read more age appropriate content in a simplified orthographic environment. Experimental evidence from Dixon and Kaminska (2007) has shown that we do not need to be anxious about encouraging children who are in the acquisition phase of reading development to read alternative spellings as they do not undermine their memories for the conventional "correct" forms of those words (although it should be noted that the same is not true for adults who have consolidated understanding of conventional word spellings).

Textism use is, of course, not something that should replace conventional reading instruction, which we are not suggesting here. But what we can say is that it can support children's literacy development by providing a "real" linguistic environment that children engage with outside of the classroom on a frequent basis. It is also the one that could be employed and manipulated if necessary to guide children to successful phonological recoding skills and full orthographic representation of English where increased exposure to a more simplified set of orthographic conventions is needed to establish phonological recoding processes. Care would need to be exercised in relation to students whose phonological processing abilities are limited, as in the case of dyslexia, but the potential is there.

WIDER TEXTING BEHAVIORS AND ACADEMIC PERFORMANCE

The use of digital technologies by young people has also raised concern in terms of its potential impact on wider academic skills and behaviors. For example, there have been a number of negative reports of its impact, with excessive texting (i.e., texting frequency rather than textism use) being linked to poor academic performance and ultimately students falling behind on schoolwork (Espinoza & Juvonen, 2011). It would appear that for schools ownership of mobile phones by their pupils has proven a difficult transition to navigate. That is, schools want to integrate these technologies into the curriculum, but they can be viewed as disruptive to quality teaching and learning. Purcell et al. (2012), in a survey of high school teachers, found that the majority of parents and teachers believed that young people were now more easily distracted than previous cohorts of students had been, and that they also had shorter attention spans. Similarly, technologies such as text messaging are seen as a distraction to students, rather than a resource with the potential to support learning. However, arguably, such distractions are now an inevitable part of modern-day life and should be seen as something to be managed successfully rather than a problem to be overcome.

One suggestion as to why young people's general academic attainment may be adversely affected by the use of personal digital technology is the compulsion to multitask. The rise of technology has made multitasking the norm. How often do we, as adults, sit on the sofa in the evening "watching" television while at the same time checking our phones for a text message or browsing the Internet on a tablet or computer? It has been suggested that such multitasking (transference between activities) can not only lead to an inevitable increase in the amount of time it takes to complete tasks and more errors but also more "shallow thinking" in place of deeper, more reflective cognitive activity (Carr, 2010). It has been suggested that the desire to multitask is driven by the emotional rewards gained through reading the text messages even if this is at the cost of learning (Wang & Tchernev, 2012).

It is however important to consider whether, as we have seen before, these anecdotal accounts about the impact of text messaging are actually correct. In one study, Rosen, Lim, Carrier, and Cheever (2011) sent college students none, four, or eight text messages during a lecture. The results were perhaps surprising in that the students who received the most text messages only performed 11% worse than the group of students who received no texts. The group who received four text messages did not do any worse than the group that received no texts. However, Rosen also found that during 15-min observation periods, participants were only able to maintain on-task behavior for a short time (approximately 6 min). Those who received text messages more often were more easily distracted from their primary task activity. Rosen, Carrier, and Cheever (2010) suggest that young people should be allowed to multitask particularly when the task demands of the secondary task are low or when the tasks require different sensory modalities.

Rosen, Cheever, and Carrier (2012) have further argued that rather than banning the use of mobile phones, schools could consider a policy of providing "technology breaks." Young people would be permitted to check their phones before a lesson started and place them on their desks on silent upside down so that they were in sight. This, it is argued, would prevent young people from being interrupted but would provide a stimulus to remind them that they will be able to check their phones on their next technology break. It was found this method boosted attention and focus and enhanced learning.

CONCLUDING REMARKS

Overall, the world of the young person has changed; the extent of their online behaviors outside school does have an impact on their educational performance, and these impacts can be positive. We need to mobilize this environment to support young people through the teaching of new skills and the development of new rules. It is suggested that young people need to be taught metacognitive strategies regarding how best to exploit and manage their use of technology in the context of learning to mitigate its more negative effects (Rosen et al., 2011).

As we have noted elsewhere (Wood, 2017), the nature of children's literacy experiences and practices are fundamentally changing (if not already changed) as a result of the digital mediation of childhood and of information in society. Textspeak has its own currency and utility for young people and is arguably providing them with a linguistic environment in which their written language acquisition is supported and facilitated rather than damaged and diminished. The ideas from self-teaching theory enable us to contextualize the learning process of children engaging with textisms outside of school and to understand the reasons as to why the use of such alternative forms do not represent a threat to conventional learning, instruction, or development. Furthermore, there is scope to use textisms in experimental work to examine the ideas behind self-teaching theory and even to test the ideas put forward here regarding the efficiency of textspeak. For example, it would be a simple matter to construct an experiment in which reading speed and comprehension are assessed in the context of a standard English passage containing some unfamiliar word tokens compared to the same passage with the unfamiliar words replaced by textism versions (phonetic in one condition, visual/symbolic in another, if further comparison is desired). The participants' memory for the spelling and meaning of the novel items could be compared across conditions as a further examination of self-teaching principles.

Use of digitally mediated texts by children and young people is on the increase and the nature of literacy is changing in many ways, but the fundamentals of learning to read and spell remain. The issue is that, for many practitioners, digitally mediated literacy is seen to have a lower value than conventional literacy practice, and as a result its affordances are overlooked. In this chapter, we hope that we have shown that even the most "problematic" forms of digital text exposure have a potential positive function that can be understood in very conventional terms, and as with all resources and technology, it is through understanding their application that we can mobilize them to achieve the greatest benefits.

ACKNOWLEDGMENTS

The work conducted by the first author referred to in this chapter has been supported by research grants from the British Academy, Becta, and Nuffield Foundation.

REFERENCES

Carr, N. (2010). *The shallows: What the internet is doing to our brains.* New York, NY: W. W. North & Company.

Coe, J. E. L., & Oakhill, J. V. (2011). 'txtN is ex f u no h2 rd': The relation between reading ability and text-messaging behaviour. *Journal of Computer Assisted Learning, 27,* 4–17.

Crystal, D. (2008). *Txtng:the gr8 db8.* Oxford: Oxford University Press.

Dixon, M., & Kaminska, Z. (2007). Does exposure to orthography affect children's spelling accuracy? *Journal of Research in Reading, 30*(2), 184–197.

Durkin, K., Conti-Ramsden, G., & Walker, A. J. (2011). Txt lang: Texting, textism use and literacy abilities in adolescents with and without specific language impairment. *Journal of Computer Assisted Learning, 27,* 49–57.

Espinoza, G., & Juvonen, J. (2011). The pervasiveness, connectedness, and intrusiveness of social network site use among young adolescents. *Cyberpsychology, Behaviour, and Social Networking, 14*, 705–709.

Holtgraves, T. (2011). Text messaging, personality, and the social context. *Journal of Research in Personality, 45*, 92–99.

Humphrys, J. (2007). I h8 txt msgs: How texting is wrecking our language. *The Daily Mail*, Viewed 23 November 2016. Available from http://www.dailymail.co.uk/news/article-483511/I-h8-txt-msgs-How-texting-wrecking-language.html#ixzz2CCCC4TJH.

Plester, B., Wood, C., & Bell, V. (2008). Txt msg n school literacy: Does texting and knowledge of text abbreviations adversely affect children's literacy attainment? *Literacy, 42*, 137–144.

Plester, B., Wood, C., & Joshi, P. (2009). Exploring the relationship between children's knowledge of text message abbreviations and school literacy outcomes. *British Journal of Developmental Psychology, 27*, 145–161. http://dx.doi.org/10.1348/026151008X320507.

Purcell, K., Raine, L., Heaps, A., Buchanan, J., Friedrich, L., Jacklin, A., et al. (2012). How teens do research in the digital world. Retrieved from http://pewinternet.org/Reports/2012/Student-Research.

Rosen, L. D., Carrier, L. M., & Cheever, N. A. (2010). *Rewired: Understanding the iGeneration and the way they learn.* New York, NY: Palgrave Macmillan.

Rosen, L. D., Cheever, N. A., & Carrier, L. M. (2012). *iDisorder: Understanding our obsession with technology and overcoming its hold on us.* New York, NY: Palgrave Macmillan.

Rosen, L. D., Lim, A. F., Carrier, M., & Cheever, N. A. (2011). An empirical examination of the educational impact of text message-induced task switching in the classroom: Educational implications and strategies to enhance learning. *Psicologia Educative, 17*(2), 163–177.

Seymour, P. H. K., Aro, M., & Erskine, J. M. (2003). Foundation literacy acquisition in European orthographies. *British Journal of Psychology, 94*, 143–174.

Shahar-Yames, D., & Share, D. L. (2008). Spelling as a self-teaching mechanism in orthographic learning. *Journal of Research in Reading, 31*, 22–39.

Share, D. L. (1995). Phonological recoding and self-teaching: Sine qua non of reading acquisition. *Cognition, 55*, 151–218.

Skierkowski, D., & Wood, R. M. (2012). To text or not to text? The importance of text messaging among college-aged students. *Computer in Human Behaviour, 28*, 744–756. http://dx.doi.org/10.1016/j.chb.2011.11.023.

Thurlow, C. (2006). From statistical panic to moral panic: The metadiscursive construction and popular exaggeration of new media language in the print media. *Journal of Computer Mediated Communication, 11*, 667–701.

Thurlow, C., & Bell, K. (2009). Against technologization: Young people's new media discourse as creative cultural practice. *Journal of Computer Mediated Communication, 14*, 1038–1049.

Tossell, C. C., Kortum, P., Shepard, C., Barg-Walkow, L. H., Rahmati, A., & Zhong, L. (2012). A longitudinal study of emoticon use in text messaging from smartphones. *Computers in Human Behaviour, 28*, 659–663.

Veater, H. M., Plester, B., & Wood, C. (2010). Use of text message abbreviation and literacy skills in children with dyslexia. *Dyslexia, 17*, 65–71.

Wang, Z., & Tchernev, J. M. (2012). The "myth" of media multitasking: Reciprocal dynamics of media multitasking, personal needs, and gratifications. *Journal of Communication, 62*, 493–513.

Wood, C. (2017). Early literacy practice: More than just knowing how to read and write. In N. Kucirkova, C. Snow, V. Grover, & C. McBride (Eds.), *The Routledge international handbook of early literacy education: A contemporary guide to literacy teaching and interventions in a global context.* London: Routledge.

Wood, C., Jackson, E., Hart, L., Plester, B., & Wilde, L. (2011). The effect of text messaging on 9- and 10-year-old children's reading, spelling and phonological processing skills. *Journal of Computer Assisted Learning, 27*, 28–36.

Wood, C., Kemp, N., & Plester, B. (2014a). *Text messaging and literacy—The evidence.* London: Routledge.

Wood, C., Kemp, N., & Waldron, S. (2014b). Exploring the longitudinal relationships between the use of grammar in text messaging and performance on grammatical tasks. *British Journal of Developmental Psychology, 32,* 415–429.

Wood, C., Kemp, N., Waldron, S., & Hart, L. (2014c). Grammatical understanding, literacy and text messaging in school children and undergraduate students: A concurrent analysis. *Computers and Education, 70,* 281–290.

Wood, C., Meachem, S., Bowyer, S., Jackson, E., Tarczynski-Bowles, M. L., & Plester, B. (2011). A longitudinal study of children's text messaging and literacy development. *British Journal of Psychology, 102,* 431–442.

Woronoff (2007). *Cell phone texting can endanger spelling.* Retrieved 23 November 2016 from http://www.articlesbase.com/cell-phones-articles/cell-phone-texting-can-endanger-spelling-276413.html.

Ziegler, J. C., Perry, C., Ma-Wyatt, A., Ladner, D., & Schulte-Korne, G. (2003). Developmental dyslexia in different languages: Language-specific or universal? *Journal of Experimental Child Psychology, 86,* 169–193.

CHAPTER 11

Bridging Theory and Practice: Applying Cognitive and Educational Theory to the Design of Educational Media

Shalom M. Fisch
MediaKidz Research & Consulting, Teaneck, NJ, United States

Within the field of children's educational media, there is all too often a dis-
connect between the academic researchers who study children's interaction
with media and the producers who create these media. This presents an
unfortunate missed opportunity, as both communities have a great deal to
learn from each other.

Having straddled the line between academia and industry for decades,
I have seen firsthand how knowledge from each of these communities
can enhance the efforts of the other. Established theories of education, cognitive development, and social development can provide a firm foundation
for educationally valid, age-appropriate approaches to the design of educational media. Understanding how children think about, interact with, and
learn from media can help producers enhance the quality and effectiveness
of educational media by creating media products that are tailored to fit the
needs, abilities, and limitations of their users.

At the same time, because children in the United States (and, perhaps, elsewhere) spend more time using media than in any other activity except sleep-
ing (e.g., Rideout & Saphir, 2013), the ubiquitous role of media in children's
lives presents a meaningful context in which researchers can study applied
aspects of children's cognitive and social development. Indeed, even the
knowledge gained in developing educational media, as well as applied research
conducted to inform production or assess impact, can itself carry implications
that reach beyond a media product, to lend insight into the nature of children's
broader development. Recall, for instance, that even the research that
informed the creation of Bandura's seminal social learning theory (which later

Cognitive Development in Digital Contexts
http://dx.doi.org/10.1016/B978-0-12-809481-5.00011-0

217

evolved into social cognitive theory) was media-based research on children's modeling of filmed aggression (e.g., Bandura, Ross, & Ross, 1963).

To illustrate the value of bridging the gap between theory and practice, this chapter presents examples of ways in which educational and developmental theory have been applied to the creation of effective educational television series, digital games, and projects that span multiple media platforms. The chapter will consider, first, the application of theoretical approaches that were not originally developed with media in mind, and then, more specific theories that were devised to explain aspects of children's interactions with and learning from media. (The inverse role of product-based research and practice in informing broader theory and research is also worthy of discussion, but is beyond the scope of this chapter.)

FROM THEORY TO PRACTICE

The applicability of broader theory within the context of educational media should not be surprising, because humans do not have a unique part of their brains that is devoted exclusively to processing media; rather, humans process media through the same cognitive mechanisms and social schemas that they employ in every other aspect of their lives. For example, while subjects watch television commercials, physiological research has shown evidence of brain activation associated with episodic memory, attention control, and working memory (Smith & Gevins, 2004), and adults' interactions with inanimate television sets and computers are influenced by many of the same social norms that have been found to guide interactions with other people (Reeves & Nass, 1996). Indeed, even on the most primitive level, Pratt, Radulescu, Guo, and Abrams (2010) adopted an evolutionary perspective to conduct a series of experiments (outside the context of media) on the effects of motion on visual attention. Using the stimuli of animated dots on a screen, Pratt et al. consistently found shorter reaction times for animate motion (i.e., motion that suggested a conscious actor, such as changing speed or direction without colliding with another dot) than for inanimate motion (changing direction or speed only in response to a collision). They explained their findings as an evolutionary vestige of primitive humans' need to quickly identify and attend to potential predators and prey in the wild. This attentional advantage for animate forms of visual movement in the context of animated dots on a screen parallels the long-established finding that children's attention is captured more easily by visual action on television than by dialogue among "talking heads," and that children prefer programs with visual action (e.g., Lesser, 1974; Valkenburg & Janssen, 1999). Might similar perceptual and cognitive mechanisms contribute to both phenomena?

Some classic theories have become so ingrained in the production of educational media, that they are applied almost universally—even if the producers who apply them are not necessarily aware that they are doing so. Applications of Bandura's (2009) concept of modeling are evident throughout most current educational television series, in which characters model targeted concepts and skills in the course of narrative stories, instead of lecturing directly to the audience. Vygotsky's and Bruner's notions of scaffolding are critical to designing increasingly challenging levels in well-designed educational games (Vygotsky, 1978; Wood, Bruner, & Ross, 1976). Moreover, beyond the basic approaches to production that they have inspired, these theories carry a host of specific, concrete implications for design as well. For instance, to maximize the educational impact of a television program among a diverse audience, modeling suggests the need for a diverse cast of characters to encourage identification with characters who are seen as being "like me." Scaffolding points to the need for each level of a digital game to build upon the knowledge acquired in earlier levels, gradually increase difficulty across levels, and increase hints and feedback if a player makes repeated errors that indicate a failure to understand (e.g., Revelle, 2013).

EDUCATIONAL TELEVISION

Historically, the creation of educational television has always been rooted in producers' personal notions of how children learn and grow. For example, the producers of the 1960s television series *Captain Kangaroo* intended to promote manners and the Golden Rule of "Do unto others as you would have them do unto you" (Keeshan, 1989), and the experiments demonstrated on the 1950s science series *Mr. Wizard* were gathered from a library of 1000 science textbooks, encyclopedias, and other academic publications (Herbert, 1988). However, these early series typically were not guided by any sort of formal educational curriculum or empirical research with children. That changed in the late 1960s, when the Children's Television Workshop (now "Sesame Workshop") pioneered the formal of curriculum and research into television production via the *CTW Model* or *Sesame Workshop Model* (e.g., Fisch & Truglio, 2001; Lesser, 1974), an interdisciplinary approach to television production that brought together educational content experts, television producers, and developmental researchers, who worked hand in hand at every stage of production. Curriculum seminars brought leading educators in direct contact with producers to lay the foundation for the educational approaches that were the basis for *Sesame Street*, while in-house content and research staff collaborated closely with the production team on an ongoing basis to ensure the effective implementation of these approaches. Indeed, *Sesame Street* continues to employ these same strategies today, as the series continues to evolve so that it can remain relevant to its current audience.

Even today, there is a broad spectrum of models through which educational television is produced, ranging from little or no involvement by educators and researchers to the intensive involvement exemplified by *Sesame Street* and its peers. When skilled educators and researchers are brought into the process of production, either as periodic advisors or as members of the ongoing production team, evidence-based educational practice can be woven into an educational television series. For example, noted mathematics educators have been involved in the production of math series such as *Cyberchase* and *Odd Squad*, literacy experts have contributed to series such as *The Electric Company* and *Between the Lions*, and scientists and science educators have informed the production of series such as *3-2-1 Contact* and *The Magic School Bus*. Summative research has shown that viewing each of these series produces significant educational gains among its target audience (e.g., Fisch, 2004; Wartella, Lauricella, & Blackwell, 2016).

Naturally, though, theories of education and child development are not static entities that are universally held forever. Even within a single television series, as theories of learning and child development have evolved over time, so too have the curricula, educational approaches, and research designs that they inform. For instance, when *Sesame Street*'s curriculum was first developed, the field of education was still greatly influenced, not only by Piagetian views on cognitive development (e.g., Piaget & Inhelder, 1969) but also by a focus on behavioral outcomes that grew out of the behaviorist approaches of Skinner (1971) and others. This was reflected accordingly in the language of the original *Sesame Street* curriculum, which centered on behavioral outcomes, such as "The child can recognize such basic symbols as letters, numbers, and geometric forms." In subsequent decades, both the content and language of the curriculum evolved in response to changes in the state of theory and research concerning children's growth, development, and learning, as well as changes in the demographics of the audience and societal concerns (Kotler, Truglio, & Betancourt, 2016; Lesser & Schneider, 2001).

Changes in theoretical trends were reflected in the formative research methods used to inform *Sesame Street*'s production too. Originally, the appeal of *Sesame Street* segments was assessed via a behavioral "distractor method" in which children were seated between two screens to chart individual children's attention to *Sesame Street* material versus unrelated slides that served as visual distractors. Subsequently, this approach evolved into an "eyes on screen" method that replaced the slides with the natural distractions that arise among groups of children watching together, and eventually grew into an "engagement" measure that took into account, not only visual attention but also other indicators of engagement such as laughing or moving in time to music (Fisch & Bernstein, 2001).

GAMES AND DIGITAL MEDIA

Just as there is a wide range of models for the production of educational television (from intensive involvement by educators and researchers to little or none), the same is equally true for digital media. Although the App Store currently features more than 80,000 apps that are labeled "educational," a content analysis of 2400 literacy apps found that fewer than one-third (29%) were presented as based on any sort of established curriculum, and only 2% mentioned that research was conducted to evaluate children's learning from the app (Vaala, Ly, & Levine, 2015).

Perhaps this is not surprising, considering the expense of research or educational consultants, and the fact that anyone can post an app to the App Store, regardless of their credentials or whether they are employed by a production company with adequate resources for product evaluation. Yet, among digital media too, theory and research can contribute significantly to the quality of an educational game. For example, drawing on inquiry-based approaches to education (e.g., Bybee, 2000), the National Science Education Standards (NGSS Lead States, 2013), and the theoretical construct of distributed cognition (e.g., Hollan, Hutchins, & Kirsh, 2000)—a perspective through which cognitive processes such as learning and reasoning are shared among several learners who work together as a group—the multiplayer game *River City* was designed to engage middle school students in inquiry-based science learning. In this game, players work in teams to develop, investigate, and test hypotheses about one of several illnesses plaguing a town. In the course of playing the game, children exercise inquiry skills and acquire knowledge about ecosystems and the role of microorganisms in spreading disease (e.g., Ketelhut, Dede, Clarke, Nelson, & Bowman, 2007).

Even outside the context of such obviously instructional games, existing theory and research can also play an important role in more surprising products, such as digital plush dolls. Strommen and Alexander (1999) have recounted how developmental research on children's emotional interaction helped shape the development of Microsoft Actimates interactive plush dolls of PBS characters such as Barney and Arthur. By incorporating elements of naturalistic social interactions among children into the dolls' prerecorded speech and including variations on responses, these talking and moving dolls were able to interact with their users through interfaces that more closely mimicked human social interaction, thus making them appear more lifelike.

In some cases, interactive educational media can grow out of multiple generations of theory as well. For instance, one of the pioneers in the study and use of digital media for education, Seymour Papert, studied with Jean Piaget early in his career. Later, Papert drew heavily on Piaget's theory of *constructivism* (in which children are seen as constructing their own knowledge, rather than passively receiving it; e.g., Piaget & Inhelder, 1969) to formulate his own theory of *constructionism*, which extended constructivism to digital media and posited that children learn best through the process of actively constructing something themselves (Papert, 1980). The theory of constructionism, in turn, directly motivated Papert's students and collaborators to create numerous prominent digital media products for education, such as LEGO Mindstorms programmable building sets (e.g., Resnick, Martin, Sargent, & Silverman, 1996), the online MamaMedia platform for children to make and share digital media (e.g., Harel Caperton, 2010), and the children's programming language Scratch (e.g., Resnick et al., 2009).

THEORIES OF LEARNING FROM MEDIA

In the preceding examples, the theories and research that were applied to TV or digital production were broad theories of development or education that had not been formulated specifically with regard to media. If these theories hold implications for the design of educational media, then all the more so, theories designed specifically to explain children's processing of educational media should hold implications for design.

In particular, from a cognitive perspective, any television program or digital game can be conceptualized as a complex audiovisual stimulus. As such, processing cognitive input from a TV program or game is subject to the limited capacity of working memory. Thus, it is not surprising that working memory limitations play a central role in several theories of children's processing of media (e.g., Fisch, 2000, 2004; Lang, 2000; Mayer, 2005, 2014), as well as in applications of Sweller's Cognitive Load Theory to problem solving in digital games (e.g., Sweller, 1988, 2010).[1] Let us consider several theories that directly address children's comprehension of and learning from media, and their implications for creating educationally effective television programs and digital games.

COMPREHENSION OF EDUCATIONAL TELEVISION

Whereas the cognitive demands of processing audiovisual information in real time pose challenges for processing any television program (educational or noneducational), Fisch's (2000, 2004) Capacity Model posits that children face even greater processing demands when watching educational television programs because these programs typically present narrative (i.e., story) content and educational content that must be processed simultaneously. For example, consider the example of a program about a boy who wants to join a band (narrative content) and, in the process, learns how different musical instruments create sound through vibration (educational content). The capacity model proposes that comprehension of educational content depends, not only on the cognitive demands of processing the educational content itself but also on the demands presented by the narrative in which it is embedded. In addition, the model argues that comprehension is affected by distance, that is, the degree to which the educational content is integral or tangential to the narrative (Fig. 1). To understand the notion of distance, imagine a television mystery in which the hero suddenly stops to give a lesson on mathematical rate-time-distance problems. If the mathematical content is not directly relevant to the mystery, it would be tangential to the narrative and distance would be large. Conversely, if the hero uses the rate-time-distance concept to prove that only one suspect was near enough

[1] Originally, research by Sweller (e.g., 1988) and his colleagues investigated the impact of cognitive load on performance and learning in abstract problem-solving tasks, such as trigonometry problems, with increased load inhibiting performance on concurrent tasks. Later, Sweller (e.g., 2010) and others applied the principle of cognitive load (as Cognitive Load Theory) to applied contexts, including educational games and other forms of multimedia instruction. In particular, this work identified factors contributing to several types of cognitive load that stem from either the intrinsic difficulty of the embedded task, the design of the materials, or amount of invested mental effort, as will be discussed later.

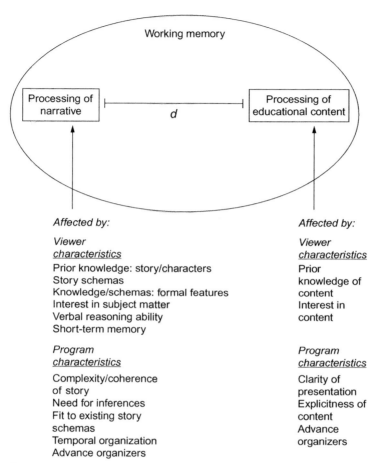

Fig. 1 The capacity model, as applied to educational television. *(From Fisch, S.M. (2000). A capacity model of children's comprehension of educational content on television.* Media Psychology, 2, *63–91; Fisch, S.M. (2004). Children's learning from educational television: Sesame Street and beyond. Mahwah, NJ: Lawrence Erlbaum Associates.)*

to commit the crime (i.e., if it provides the key clue to solve the mystery), then the mathematical content is integral to the narrative and distance would be small.

According to the capacity model, if distance is large, the mental resources needed for comprehension are devoted primarily to the narrative, with less resources available for processing the educational content. However, if the educational content is integral to the narrative, then the two complement, rather than compete with, each other; the same processing that permits comprehension of the narrative simultaneously contributes to comprehension of the educational content. Thus, comprehension of educational content typically would be stronger under any of the following conditions: (1) when the processing demands of the narrative are relatively small (e.g., because few inferences are needed to understand the story or the viewer's language skills are sufficiently sophisticated to follow the narrative easily; see Fig. 1 and Fisch, 2004, for a full list of contributing factors), (2) when the processing demands of the educational content are small (e.g., because it is presented clearly or the viewer has some knowledge of the subject already), or (3) when distance is small. The predictions of the model have been tested and confirmed empirically in several studies, most directly by Aladé and Nathanson (2016), Nichols (2011), and Piotrowski (2014).

Applied to the production of educational television, the Capacity Model points to several factors that can be incorporated into a television program to help maximize young viewers' comprehension: The program should be appealing and interesting to children so that they will attend to the program and devote more cognitive resources to understanding it. To reduce the demands of processing educational content, the educational content should be presented clearly and explicitly, with advance organizers used to orient viewers and encourage the activation of relevant schemas. To reduce the demands of processing narrative, the story should be clear and sequential, without requiring extensive inferences to untangle implicit content, and the structure of the story should conform to established story schemas. Finally, and perhaps most critically, the educational content should be well integrated at the heart of the story (i.e., the distance should be small)—what Sesame Workshop has referred to as "content on the plotline" (e.g., Hall & Williams, 1993)—so that the narrative and educational content do not have to compete for limited cognitive resources. In working with television writers and producers, I typically explain the concept of content on the plotline via this rule of thumb: If a viewer tells a friend what the story in the program was about, he or she should not be able to do it without mentioning the embedded educational concept. If the main points of the plot can be related without mentioning the educational content, then the content is not on the plotline.

LEARNING FROM DIGITAL GAMES

The Cognitive Theory of Multimedia Learning, or CTML, is intended to describe the processing by which users encode and learn from digital multimedia (e.g., Mayer, 2005, 2014; Moreno, 2006). CTML has its roots in three assumptions that grow out of the research literature in cognitive psychology: that humans take in visual and auditory information through two separate information-processing channels, that each channel has a limited capacity for processing information at any given time, and that active learning entails carrying out a coordinated set of cognitive processes during learning. Since multimedia presentations typically present information via more than modality (e.g., visual images and auditory narration, or on-screen text and animated images), the model tracks the processing of elements of information through the visual and auditory channels as they make their way through the three classic cognitive structures of cognition and memory: sensory memory (responsible for the initial encoding of external stimuli), working memory (in which active processing of information occurs), and long-term memory (where information is stored beyond a matter of moments). CTML posits that, when a user engages with an instructional message via multimedia, bits of visual and auditory information are encoded and processed separately, to yield a pictorial mental model of the visual information and a verbal mental model of the auditory information. These two models are then integrated into a single representation in which corresponding elements of the pictorial and verbal models are mapped onto each other (see Fig. 2).

Under this model, an effective piece of educational software must be clear and well organized, with little extraneous information. Drawing on Sweller's (2010) Cognitive Load Theory, CTML predicts that, just as a child may fail to learn if the educational content in a digital game is too complex (what Mayer, 2014 refers to as *essential overload*), the child also may fail to learn if the software includes too much extraneous material (e.g., unnecessary animation, text, graphics, or music), or requires users to engage in too much extraneous cognitive processing (which Mayer terms *extraneous*

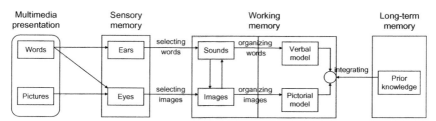

Fig. 2 Cognitive theory of multimedia learning. *(From Mayer, R.E. (2005). Cognitive theory of multimedia learning. In R.E. Mayer (Ed.), The* Cambridge handbook of multimedia learning *(pp. 31-48). New York, NY: Cambridge University Press.)*

overload). In either case, the cognitive load posed by the game exceeds the limited capacity of working memory, and the material will not be well learned (or, perhaps, even well understood).[2]

Parallel to the Capacity Model, CTML can be applied to the production of educational games, with concrete implications for design. Growing out of CTML, Mayer and his colleagues have conducted an extensive program of research to identify game features that either support or inhibit learning from games (see Mayer, 2014, for a review). Their data indicate that players learn better from games when words in the game are spoken rather than written (i.e., presented as auditory information instead of visual, to avoid interfering with visual processing of other elements of the game screen), when words are in conversational style, when pretraining is used so that in-game learning builds on prior knowledge, when players receive advice or explanations throughout the game, and when players are asked to explain their choices (i.e., think reflectively) during the game.

APPLYING THE CAPACITY MODEL TO EDUCATIONAL GAMES

As is evident from the preceding discussion, CTML, Cognitive Load Theory, and the Capacity Model share much in common. All three are grounded in the limited capacity of working memory. All three view comprehension of educational content as impacted, not only by the cognitive demands of the educational content itself but also by the demands of the surrounding material in which the educational content is embedded. All three identify program or game features that can increase or reduce cognitive load, with concrete implications for the design of effective educational media.

However, a key aspect of the Capacity Model that differentiates it from CTML and Cognitive Load Theory is the Capacity Model's construct of distance, which does not appear in either of the other two theories. When the distance between narrative and educational content is high (i.e., educational content is tangential to the story), all three models predict that comprehension of educational content will be impaired. But, when distance is small (i.e., the educational content is "on the plotline" or at the heart of

---

[2] The distinction between essential and extraneous processing (e.g., Mayer, 2014) is very much in line with the Capacity Model's distinction between educational and narrative content. However, neither Cognitive Load Theory nor CTML includes a construct parallel to distance, which leads to differences in both theoretical constructs and predictions, as will be discussed shortly.

gameplay, as will be discussed shortly), the Capacity Model no longer views narrative content as "extraneous" material that must compete with educational content for limited cognitive resources in working memory.

Yet, the original Capacity Model (Fisch, 2000, 2004) was devised to explain comprehension of educational television, not digital games. Although many aspects of processing may be common to television and games, each medium presents its own unique issues as well. Thus, a modified version of the Capacity Model, applicable to digital games, is currently being developed (Fisch, 2016).

Because of the unique nature of digital games, the new model differs from the original in several ways. First, whereas the original model has two components (narrative and educational content), the new model has three, reflecting the demands of processing educational content, narrative (which can be substantial in a virtual world, or minimal in a smaller "casual game"), and gameplay (i.e., cognitive demands of playing the game itself, which rest on factors such as usability, well- vs. ill-defined problems, and so on). Second, the original model predicts that priority is given to processing narrative over educational content [as confirmed empirically by Nichols (2011) and Aladé and Nathanson (2016)]; in the new model, priority during an educational game is given instead to gameplay—that is, to the thinking and behavior that are necessary to use the interface and play the game. Third, distance between narrative and educational content is a critical component of the original model, but three types of distance are central to the new model: the distance between gameplay and educational content, between educational content and narrative, and between narrative and gameplay (see Fig. 3). The most pivotal type of distance is between gameplay and educational content—the degree to which the game requires players to exercise the targeted educational concept and/or skills in order to play the game successfully.

When applied to the production of educational games, many of the new model's implications are similar to those of the original model, as well as Cognitive Load Theory and CTML: the need to present educational content clearly, minimize extraneous cognitive load, and so on. A unique implication of the new model is the need to minimize, not only distance between narrative and educational content by embedding "content on the plotline" but also the distance between educational content and gameplay by placing "content at the heart of gameplay." Just as content on the plotline requires that television viewers should not be able to recount the story of a program without mentioning the educational content, content at the heart of gameplay requires that players should not be able to play a game without employing the targeted content or skills. As an example of deceptively high distance

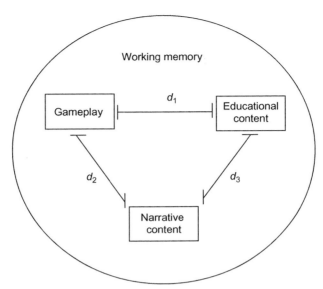

Fig. 3 The capacity model, as applied to educational games. *(From Fisch, S.M. (2016). The capacity model, 2.0: Cognitive processing in children's comprehension of educational games. Paper presented at the Society for Research in Child Development special topic meeting: Technology and Media in Children's Development, Irvine, CA.)*

between educational content and gameplay, consider a game that I once tested with preschool children: In this game, to help children learn how to count by 2, players clicked once to remove two obstacles at a time. Children played the game with little difficulty, but comprehension of the math was poor. Although the designers' intent was that children would practice counting by 2 as they played the game (which would comprise a small distance between educational content and gameplay), this was not actually the case. Rather, because children only had to keep clicking until all of the obstacles were gone, the computer counted by 2 *for* them—the gameplay never actually required children to count by 2 themselves. Thus, although the educational content was clearly shown on the screen, it was not integral to gameplay and was not clearly understood.

Subsequently, when working with a different client on the development of several games about counting by 2, 5, and 10, we took the lesson of the earlier experience. In the subsequent games, players had to jump between numbered or unnumbered objects by 2, 5, or 10 s while skipping the objects in between. In this way, players were forced to count the objects and/or think about numbered labels on the objects in order to win the games (Fisch, Damashek, & Aladé (2016).

CROSS-PLATFORM LEARNING

Until this point, we have considered the two media of television and digital games separately. Today, however, producers often do not create "just" a television series or "just" a game. Amid industry buzzwords, such as *multiplatform*, *convergence*, and *transmedia*, it is increasingly common for projects to span several media platforms, so that an educational television series might be accompanied by related digital games, hands-on outreach materials, or a museum exhibit or live show. My colleagues and I use the term *cross-platform learning* to refer to a child's learning from combined use of multiple, related media platforms (e.g., a television program and digital game) that address the same educational concept, using the same characters and world.

Data from several empirical research studies have indicated that cross-platform approaches have the potential to promote significantly greater learning than the use of any one media component in isolation. By applying established theories and educational practices, we can suggest some mechanisms that may underlie these effects. Cross-platform approaches provide multiple entry points to informal educational materials, accommodate children with diverse interests and learning styles, provide repetition and reinforcement of educational content, and allow content creators to match each particular educational concept to the medium through which it can be conveyed most effectively. Perhaps most importantly, cross-platform approaches also can facilitate transfer of learning (i.e., the ability for learners to apply concepts or skills acquired in one context to a new problem or context): children can take what they have learned from one medium (e.g., an educational television program) and apply it to support and enrich their performance while they are in the midst of learning from a second medium (e.g., while playing a related digital game). This richer engagement contributes to greater learning of the targeted concepts and/or skills (see Fisch, 2013, for a review).

However, the same research studies also suggest that to obtain the benefits of cross-platform learning, it is not sufficient to simply flood children with a greater number of media products; "more" is not always better. To maximize the potential for cross-platform learning, educational media must be designed in ways that take advantage of the unique strengths and affordances that each medium presents (e.g., using video narrative to explain and model concepts or digital games to provide opportunities to practice emergent skills). In addition, the various media should be integrated in ways that make the components complementary to each other. For example, in the multimedia mathematics project *UMIGO*, interactive moments are integrated into animated video adventures. When characters in the video encounter a problem, an embedded interactive moment requires children to apply a targeted math concept to help the characters solve their problem. In this way, the video motivates children to do the task in each interactive moment (and explains and models the necessary math concepts); conversely, solving the interactive task helps to advance the story in the video narrative (Fisch et al., 2016).

CONCLUSION

As demonstrated throughout this chapter, the application of theory—both broad theories of education and child development, and more focused theories of the cognitive processing of educational media—can provide a firm foundation for the production of educationally effective media, and point to specific techniques that can be incorporated into a given media product to maximize learning. The Capacity Model and CTML alone suggest guidelines for the production of educational television series, such as:

- Both the story and the underlying program should be appealing and interesting to children.
- Educational content should be presented clearly and explicitly.
- The story should also be clear, without requiring extensive inferences to untangle implicit content.
- The structure of the story should be sequential, conforming to established story schemas.
- Advance organizers can be used to orient viewers and encourage the activation of relevant schemas.
- Perhaps most critically, the distance between narrative and educational content should be small ("content on the plotline").

Guidelines for the creation of digital games include:

- Instructions, dialogue, and other words should be spoken rather than written.
- Instructions and dialogue should be presented in conversational style.
- Pretraining can be used to allow in-game learning to build on prior knowledge.
- Players can be supported by advice or explanations throughout the game.
- Players can be asked to explain their choices, to encourage reflective thinking during the game.

- As above, gameplay should require players to apply the targeted concepts and skills, so that the distance between educational content and gameplay is small ("content at the heart of gameplay").

For cross-platform projects, guidelines include the following:

- Media components should be combined in ways that build upon the strengths and affordances of each medium (e.g., video for explanation and modeling, games to practice emerging skills).
- Media components should also be integrated in ways that make them complementary to each other.

To apply theory effectively to production, however, it is not sufficient for theories to be well grounded or carry value, since media producers generally cannot be expected to wade through complex, highly technical theoretical models and extract practical design implications on their own. In some of the examples discussed earlier (e.g., Scratch or *River City*), the producers have been academics or researchers themselves. However, this typically is not the case. Indeed, that is where the value of collaboration lies, with producers and researchers each bringing their unique skills and knowledge to complement each other.

Yet, when academics and producers attempt to collaborate, they often quickly discover that they are essentially speaking different languages, with little accomplished through the effort. Rather, for theory to be applied effectively in production, abstract theoretical models must be translated into specific, concrete, practical recommendations that are feasible to implement within the design of the media product being developed (e.g., Fisch & Bernstein, 2001). If such an approach is implemented in a collaborative atmosphere, with mutual respect among the participants, it can give rise to educational media that are educationally impactful and well suited to the needs and abilities of their target audience.

REFERENCES

Aladé, F., & Nathanson, A. I. (2016). What preschoolers bring to the show: The relation between viewer characteristics and children's learning from educational television. *Media Psychology, 19*, 406–430.

Bandura, A. (2009). Social cognitive theory of mass communication. In J. Bryant & M. B. Oliver (Eds.), *Media effects: Advances in theory and research* (3rd ed., pp. 94–124). New York, NY: Routledge.

Bandura, A., Ross, D., & Ross, S. A. (1963). Imitation of film-mediated aggressive models. *Journal of Abnormal and Social Psychology, 66*, 3–11.

Bybee, R. (2000). Teaching science as inquiry. In J. Minstrell & E. H. van Zee (Eds.), *Inquiring into inquiry learning and teaching in science* (pp. 20–46). New York, NY: American Association for the Advancement of Science.

Fisch, S. M. (2000). A capacity model of children's comprehension of educational content on television. *Media Psychology, 2,* 63–91.

Fisch, S. M. (2004). *Children's learning from educational television: Sesame Street and beyond.* Mahwah, NJ: Lawrence Erlbaum Associates.

Fisch, S. M. (2013). Cross-platform learning: On the nature of children's learning from multiple media platforms. *New Directions for Child and Adolescent Development, 139,* 59–70.

Fisch, S. M. (2016). The capacity model, 2.0: Cognitive processing in children's comprehension of educational games. *Paper presented at the Society for Research in Child Development special topic meeting: Technology and Media in Children's Development, Irvine, CA.*

Fisch, S. M., & Bernstein, L. (2001). Formative research revealed: Methodological and process issues in formative research. In S. M. Fisch & R. T. Truglio (Eds.), *"G" is for growing: Thirty years of research on children and Sesame Street* (pp. 39–60). Mahwah, NJ: Lawrence Erlbaum Associates.

Fisch, S. M., Damashek, S., & Aladé, F. (2016). Designing media for cross-platform learning: Developing models for production and instructional design. *Journal of Children and Media, 10,* 238–247.

Fisch, S. M., & Truglio, R. T. (Eds.), (2001). *"G" is for growing: Thirty years of research on children and Sesame Street.* Mahwah, NJ: Lawrence Erlbaum Associates.

Hall, E. R., & Williams, M. E. (1993). Ghostwriter research meets literacy on the plot-line. B. J. Wilson (Chair) (Ed.), *Formative research and the CTW model: An interdisciplinary approach to television production. Symposium presented at the annual meeting of the International Communication Association, Washington, DC.*

Harel Caperton, I. (2010). Toward a theory of game-media literacy: Playing and building as reading and writing. *International Journal of Gaming and Computer-Mediated Simulations, 2,* 1–16.

Herbert, D. (1988). Behind the scenes of Mr. Wizard. In M. Druger (Ed.), *Science for the fun of it: A guide to informal science education* (pp. 51–56). Washington, DC: National Science Teachers Association.

Hollan, J., Hutchins, E., & Kirsh, D. (2000). Distributed cognition: Toward a new foundation for human-computer interaction research. *ACM Transactions on Computer-Human Interaction, 7*(2), 174–196.

Keeshan, B. (1989). *Growing up happy: Captain Kangaroo tells yesterday's children how to nurture their own.* New York, NY: Doubleday.

Ketelhut, D. J., Dede, C., Clarke, J., Nelson, B., & Bowman, C. (2007). Studying situated learning in a multi-user virtual environment. In E. Baker, J. Dickieson, W. Wulfeck, & H. O'Neil (Eds.), *Assessment of problem solving using simulations* (pp. 37–58). New York, NY: Routledge.

Kotler, J. A., Truglio, R. T., & Betancourt, J. (2016). R is for responsive: How Sesame Street meets the changing needs of children in the United States. In C. F. Cole & J. H. Lee (Eds.), *The Sesame effect: The global impact of the longest street in the world* (pp. 71–91). New York, NY: Taylor & Francis.

Lang, A. (2000). The limited capacity model of mediated message processing. *Journal of Communication, 50,* 46–70.

Lesser, G. S. (1974). *Children and television: Lessons from Sesame Street.* New York, NY: Vintage Books/Random House.

Lesser, G. S., & Schneider, J. S. (2001). Creation and evolution of the Sesame Street curriculum. In S. M. Fisch & R. T. Truglio (Eds.), *"G" is for "growing": Thirty years of research on children and Sesame Street* (pp. 25–38). Mahwah, NJ: Lawrence Erlbaum Associates.

Mayer, R. E. (2005). Cognitive theory of multimedia learning. In R. E. Mayer (Ed.), *The Cambridge handbook of multimedia learning* (pp. 31–48). New York, NY: Cambridge University Press.

Mayer, R. E. (2014). *Computer games for learning: An evidence-based approach.* Cambridge, MA: The MIT Press. pp. 31–48.

Moreno, R. (2006). Learning in high-tech and multimedia environments. *Current Directions in Psychological Science, 15*, 63–67.

NGSS Lead States. (2013). *Next generation science standards: For states, by states.* Washington, DC: The National Academies Press.

Nichols, C. A. (2011). How fast can they learn? Testing educational and narrative content acquisition through the capacity model. In *Paper presented at the 2011 meeting of the International Communication Association, Boston, MA.*

Papert, S. (1980). *Mindstorms: Children, computers, and powerful ideas.* New York, NY: Basic Books.

Piaget, J., & Inhelder, B. (1969). *The psychology of the child.* New York, NY: Basic Books.

Piotrowski, J. T. (2014). The relationship between narrative processing demands and young American children's comprehension of educational television. *Journal of Children and Media, 8*, 267–285.

Pratt, J., Radulescu, P. V., Guo, R. M., & Abrams, R. A. (2010). It's alive! Animate motion captures visual attention. *Psychological Science, 21*, 1724–1730.

Reeves, B., & Nass, C. (1996). *The media equation: How people treat computers, television, and new media like real people and places.* New York, NY: Cambridge University Press.

Resnick, M., Maloney, J., Monroy-Hernandez, A., Rusk, N., Eastmond, E., Brennan, K., et al. (2009). Scratch: Programming for all. *Communications of the ACM, 52*(11), 60–67.

Resnick, M., Martin, F., Sargent, R., & Silverman, B. (1996). Programmable bricks: Toys to think with. *IBM Systems Journal, 35*(3–4), 443–452.

Revelle, G. (2013). Applying developmental theory and research to the creation of educational games. *New Directions for Child and Adolescent Development, 139*, 31–40.

Rideout, V. J., & Saphir, M. (2013). *Zero to eight: Children's media use in America 2013.* San Francisco, CA: Common Sense Media.

Skinner, B. F. (1971). *Beyond freedom and dignity.* New York, NY: Bantam/Vintage.

Smith, M. E., & Gevins, A. (2004). Attention and brain activity while watching television: Components of viewer engagement. *Media Psychology, 6*, 285–305.

Strommen, E. F., & Alexander, K. (1999). Emotional interfaces for interactive aardvarks: Integrating affect into social interfaces for children. *Paper presented at the annual ACM CHI conference on human factors in computing systems, Pittsburgh, PA.*

Sweller, J. (1988). Cognitive load during problem solving: Effects on learning. *Cognitive Science, 12*, 257–285.

Sweller, J. (2010). Cognitive load theory: Recent theoretical advances. In J. L. Plass, R. Moreno, & R. Brünken (Eds.), *Cognitive load theory* (pp. 29–47). New York, NY: Cambridge University Press.

Vaala, S., Ly, A., & Levine, M. (2015). *Getting a read on the app stores: A market scan and analysis of children's literacy apps.* New York, NY: Joan Ganz Cooney Center, Sesame Workshop.

Valkenburg, P. M., & Janssen, S. C. (1999). What do children value in entertainment programs? A cross-cultural investigation. *Journal of Communication, 49*(2), 3–21.

Vygotsky, L. S. (1978). *Mind in society: The development of higher psychological processes.* Cambridge, MA: Harvard University Press.

Wartella, E., Lauricella, A. R., & Blackwell, C. K. (2016). *The ready to learn program: 2010-2015 policy brief.* Evanston, IL: Northwestern University School of Communication.

Wood, D., Bruner, J., & Ross, G. (1976). The role of tutoring in problem solving. *Journal of Child Psychology and Child Psychiatry, 17*, 89–100.

Media Literacy as a Cognitive Skill

CHAPTER 12

Understanding the Technical and Social Complexity of the Internet: A Cognitive Developmental Resource Perspective

Samantha Bordoff, Zheng Yan
University at Albany, SUNY, Albany, NY, United States

The Internet is a special artifact system that is rapidly changing and complex, both technically and socially. The Internet has enormous technical complexity given its gargantuan nature as a special system that connects millions of networks and computers and billions of users worldwide. This complexity is almost invisible to the human eye but includes multilayer communication protocols (e.g., TCP/IP and MSTP), many physical connection devices (e.g., cables and satellites), and an abundance of application programs for users (e.g., email and web browsing). The vast number of networks is the primary technological feature of the Internet (Ralson, Reilly, & Hemmendinger, 2000). The Internet also is characterized by social complexity, given the multiple positive and negative effects of the Internet on an individual's life, such as facilitating communication across the globe while potentially breaching one's security and privacy.

Not surprisingly, children may find it challenging to understand the Internet through direct experience given these multiple facets of complexity. One reason for this difficulty may reflect the relative newness of the Internet and that it remains an emerging concept. There is a lack of formal education to teach children about the Internet and limited social scaffolding provided by adults, who may have inadequate understanding of the Internet themselves. Another reason is that the Internet is virtual. As an entire virtual world, it is not immediately accessible for children to experience through their senses (e.g., children cannot use their eyes to directly see the entire virtual space or use their hands to hold the gigantic virtual world), making

Cognitive Development in Digital Contexts
http://dx.doi.org/10.1016/B978-0-12-809481-5.00012-2

237

it challenging for children to imagine its complexity. Further, the Internet is highly connective and extremely open to everyone. Therefore, by design, the Internet is essentially free from control by an authority so that, in principle, any individual throughout the world can post materials online at any time at a high speed and low cost—another unique feature hard for children to imagine. Collectively, these qualities make it difficult for children to understand accurately the complexity of the Internet through their direct, hands-on experiences.

Similarly, there are perceptual and conceptual challenges faced by children when interacting with the Internet that compromise their ability to understand its complexity. To understand a concept, we generally rely on both perceptual processes and conceptual processes. Our perceptual processes rely on sensory-motor experiences to support us to understand a concept; our conceptual processes rely on abstract reasoning to go beyond the direct sensory-motor experiences (Dewart & Brace, 2006; Eysenck & Keane, 2000; Margolis & Laurence, 1999). When interacting with the Internet, perceptual knowledge is formed through direct experience with the computer screen, mouse, and keyboard. Typically, the external and internal features of an artifact are quite similar, such as with balls or books whereby their surface features (e.g., a round shape or a book cover) match their internal functions (e.g., bouncing up and down of the ball with a force or specific contents of the book to read) so that individuals can recognize a ball by its shape or know a book by its cover. Thus, children can develop considerable knowledge about artifacts through their sensory-motor direct experiences with them. However, the Internet is perceptually misleading, as a complex and virtual universe that is practically invisible to the user who only interacts with its simple interface on a computer screen. Additionally, the Internet does not have a fixed or distinctive interface. Instead, a computer screen becomes a single node of the Internet only when the Internet is accessed and it seamlessly switches back to a computer once the Internet is turned off. Consequently, as a perceptually misleading artifact, the Internet is a challenging concept for children to understand.

Conceptual knowledge, by comparison, develops later as the user interacts with various aspects of the Internet, including visiting websites or sending emails or instant messages. One conceptual challenge in understanding the Internet is its profound social and technical complexity. A second conceptual challenge is that the Internet is an artifact that is different from other physical, social, or psychological entities (Keil, 1989). Children's rich domain-specific knowledge about various concepts, such as those in biology (e.g., alive or dead) or physics (e.g., matter or speed) may not be a useful intellectual resource for understanding the Internet. This situation may result in ontological confusion for children when attempting to integrate their domain-specific knowledge in biology or physics with knowledge about the Internet (Wellman & Gelman, 1998). A third conceptual challenge is that the Internet is a virtual artifact that is not physically accessible in the real world. Other artifacts that children encounter on a daily basis, such as television, telephones, and computers, are physically accessible and allow the child to directly interact with them in the real world (e.g., Cameron & Lee, 1997; Huston & Wright, 1998; Marsh, 2006; Scaife & van Duuren, 1995). As a virtual artifact, the Internet can only be accessed indirectly, which makes it challenging to develop an accurate conceptual understanding of it, not only for young children but also for ordinary adults.

EARLY RESEARCH ON HOW INDIVIDUALS UNDERSTAND THE INTERNET

At present, there is very little research on developmental differences pertaining to children's understanding of the Internet as compared to the well-studied concept of television (e.g., Anderson et al., 2001; Calvert & Kotler, 2003; Huesmann, Moise-Titus, Podolski, & Eron, 2003; Huston & Wright, 1998; Singer & Singer, 2001). Denham (1993) conducted one of the few studies that examined children's understanding of computers. In this well-cited study, 9- to 14-years-old children were asked to draw pictures of the inner workings of a computer in a series of three studies. The top five inner workings that children drew were a communication link, a computer chip, input and output features, memory, and transport (Denham, 1993). Older children were more likely than younger children to include more or all of these top five components. Ostensibly, older children were more likely to view a computer as multifaceted than younger children.

One of the earliest efforts to examine how children understood the Internet was conducted by Luckin, Rimmer, and Lloyd (2001). These researchers investigated differences between children's understanding of the Internet before and after their school gained Internet access during the school year 1998–99. Prior to the school going online, none of the 9-year-old children in the study viewed the Internet as having complex connectivity. After going online, only 10% of these children viewed the Internet as complex, despite having gained more online experience at school. Similarly, the percentage of children who considered the Internet as having simple connectivity just between two computers decreased slightly from 35% to 28% during the school year. Further, whereas 66% of the children in the study initially saw the Internet as merely a computer, 62% presumed as such after the school went online. These findings suggested that young children's increased Internet experience only slightly increased their understanding of its complexity.

Few studies have investigated adults' understanding of the Internet. Thatcher and Greyling (1998) had 51 University students and faculty members in South Africa with different amounts of experience with computers and the Internet draw mental models of the Internet to examine their conceptualization of it. Findings showed that the more experience participants had using the Internet the more complex were their conceptualizations. Similarly, Philleo (1995) had graduate students participate in a 5-week course to learn about the Internet. Afterwards, the graduate students were asked to draw a picture of their conceptualization of it. Students in the course showed a more complex understanding of the Internet than those not in the course. Levin, Stuve, and Jacobson (1999) later found differences in college students' understanding of the Internet that persisted after one semester of being exposed to it. Thus, direct experience with the Internet can lead to a slightly greater understanding of the Internet for adults. This line of research with adults yields results similar to those found among children, as presented above, and provides initial but interesting evidence for how children and adults understand the Internet as a unique concept.

THREE MAJOR STUDIES ON HOW INDIVIDUALS UNDERSTAND THE INTERNET

In a series of studies Yan (2005, 2006, 2009a) systematically investigated developmental differences in children's understanding of the Internet. In the first of these studies, Yan (2005) explored differences among children aged 5- to 12-years old (split into three groups: 5- to 8-year-olds, 9- and 10-year-olds, and 11- and 12-year-olds) and adults in their understanding of the technical and social complexity of the Internet. Participants completed a survey (for older children who had basic reading skills) or interview (for young children who did not yet have basic reading skills) concerning three variables: online experience, understanding of the technical complexity of the Internet, and understanding of the social complexity of the Internet. To examine the first variable, participants were asked about their experience with a variety of Internet applications, such as email, the number of years of experience with the Internet, and how often they used the Internet. To investigate their understanding of the technical complexity of the Internet, participants were asked open-ended questions such as "what is the Internet?," "where is the Internet?," and "how big is the Internet?" To explore their understanding of the social complexity of the Internet, the participants were questioned about the possible negative and positive social consequences and about safety concerns.

Based on whether and how much participants perceived the Internet perceptually or conceptually (a computer-like interface or a complex network system), participants' technical understanding as demonstrated through these surveys and interviews was coded as reflective of one of four levels: minimal (perception-based), partial (perception-bounded), extended (conception-bounded), and correct (conception-based). Minimal Understanding represented completely perception-based knowledge about the Internet. It was assigned to those who perceived the Internet as one computer (e.g., saying that Internet is a computer or drawing a picture of one computer). Partial Understanding represented perception-bounded knowledge about the Internet. It was assigned to those who perceived the Internet as either several computers with no indication of connections among them or simple connections of several computers (e.g., saying that the Internet has only two computers or drawing several computers connected with a straight line). Extended Understanding represented conception-bounded understanding of the Internet. It was assigned to those who considered the Internet a network-like system in which a computing center links with multiple computers (e.g., saying that the Internet is a network or drawing a picture of a computer network). Correct Understanding represented completely conception-based understanding of the Internet. It was assigned to those who correctly understood the Internet as a system with multiple connected networks, demonstrating a scientifically sound understanding of technical complexity (e.g., saying that the Internet is a network of networks or drawing a picture of multiple networks).

Like their technical understanding, participants' social understanding was coded at four levels: minimal (perception-based), partial (perception-bounded), extended (conception-bounded), and correct (conception-based). Minimal Understanding indicated that an individual knew very little about the positive or negative social consequence of the Internet (e.g., concerned only about the slowness of opening web pages) and expressed little precaution when using the Internet (e.g., claiming that the Internet would never hurt a person). Partial Understanding indicated that an individual had a general but limited sense of the positive or negative social consequences (e.g., reporting only 1–2 superficial social consequence(s) such as seeing too many popup advertisements and spending too much time in a chat room) and made reference to vague precautions related to using the Internet (e.g., believing that a bad thing could happen when emailing someone). Extended Understanding indicated a clear understanding of the profound social consequences of the Internet (e.g., discussing two or three important societal concern(s) such as online privacy or the digital divide) and a proper attitude towards Internet use (e.g., explicitly expressing precautions in using email and browsing websites). Correct Understanding indicated a balanced and comprehensive understanding of the profound positive and negative social consequences of the Internet (e.g., explicitly specifying various serious problems on the Internet, such as teenage pornography websites, stealing personal information, posting false advertisements, and online attacks by hackers) and a thoughtful attitude towards Internet use and online safety (e.g., discussing password protection and filtering programs), showing a scientifically sound understanding of the social complexity of the Internet.

As expected, there were significant differences among the age groups in online experience, with 11- to 12-year-olds and adults reporting the most experience and the 5- to 8-year-olds, the least. For understanding of the technical complexity, a significant difference between the 9- to 10-year-old group and the 11- to 12-year-old group was found as 68% of the former group showed a minimal understanding. Among the 11- to 12-year-old group, few showed a minimal understanding of the technical complexity (23%); the majority showed either partial (43%) or extended understanding (29%). Only two participants in the 11- to 12-year-old group and one adult showed correct scientific understanding of the Internet's technical complexity. For understanding the social complexity, significant age differences between the 9- to 10-year-old group and the 11- to 12-year-old group were found, as well as between the 11- to 12-year-old group and adults. Similarly, the majority of 9- to 10-year-olds (68%) showed a minimal understanding of the Internet's social complexity. However, the majority of 11- to 12-year-olds (53%) showed a partial understanding. Almost all adults showed either a partial understanding (36%) or an extended understanding (61%). Only one adult showed a correct scientific understanding of the social complexity of the Internet. These findings indicated that children showed development in their understanding of the complexity of the Internet between the ages of 9- to 12-years-old. However, even adults rarely showed a correct scientific understanding of the technical and social complexity of the Internet.

Furthermore, age and online experience were both significant predictors of understanding the technical complexity of the Internet, with age serving as a better predictor than experience. Thus, older children and adults generally showed significantly greater understanding of the technical complexities of the Internet than younger children did, while their online experience played only a secondary role rather than a primary one. However, for understanding the social complexity of the Internet, only age was a significant predictor. These findings highlight developmental differences in understanding the complexity of the Internet.

Yan (2006) then examined the relationship between age, online experience, and the understanding of the technical and social complexity of the Internet. He hypothesized that an individual's understanding of the technical and social complexity of the Internet would be influenced by factors including: direct online experience (e.g., years using the Internet, hours using the Internet per week), indirect online experience (e.g., experience gained through informal Internet classes or media exposure), demographic variables (e.g., age and gender), and psychological variables (e.g., reasoning and personality). Participants were fourth through eighth graders.

A symmetric reciprocal effect was not found between technical understanding and social understanding based on two key pieces of statistical evidence. First, a model with two reciprocal paths between technical understanding and social understanding showed a good fit to data, indicating that there existed some significant relationships between these two paths. However, neither of the reciprocal paths were found to be significant; note also that the path from social understanding to technical understanding was negative and much weaker. This model indicated that there were no symmetric reciprocal relationships between social and technical understanding of the Internet; otherwise, these two paths would have been statistically significant and relatively equal in their path coefficients. Second, after removing the weaker path from social understanding to technical understanding, the model showed both better fit indices and more parsimonious evidence, with a significant path from technical understanding to social understanding, $b_{\text{tech-soc}} = .197$, $p < .001$, indicating that children's understanding of the technical complexity of the Internet influenced their social understanding, but not vice versa. Thus, the Internet is a technological system, and understanding its technological complexity helps children understand its social complexity (e.g., knowing that the Internet is a gigantic system of various networks linking to millions of different users helps one to understand how cyber predicators could abuse the Internet in various sophisticated ways); however, understanding its social complexity may have no ramifications for understanding its technical complexity (e.g., hearing a scaring story about a cyber predicator might not automatically make one understand how complex computational networks work technically).

Age remained the most powerful predictor of Internet understanding. On average, children showed a partial understanding of the social and technical complexity of the Internet (Yan, 2005, 2006). Specifically, in terms of direct effects of age, both the path from Age to Technical Understanding and the path from Age to Social Understanding were statistically significant. Further, while there was no indirect effect of age on technical understanding, there were multiple indirect effects of age differences on social understanding through a variety of pathways (e.g., via Frequency of Internet Use, Internet Classes, and Technical Understanding). In short, older children showed a greater understanding of the social and technical complexity of the Internet than younger children. Further, children's understanding of the complexity of the Internet was more a reflection of their age than other factors related to Internet use, such as both the duration and frequency of Internet use, or having attended informal classes about the Internet. In contrast, no gender effects were found for either type of understanding. Collectively, Yan (2005, 2006) show that preadolescents show an adult level of understanding of the technical and social complexity of the Internet. However, correct scientific understanding of the complexity of the Internet remains rare. These findings conform to those addressing children's conceptual understanding of other natural, social, and mental systems, whereby their understanding becomes more sophisticated over the course of development (e.g., Carey, 1985; Keil, 1989; Wellman & Gelman, 1998).

The effect of age on understanding raises a more general issue seen in the study of conceptual development concerning how children learn to understand these very new and highly complex concepts. Because Yan's participants were raised in New York, a state with one of the highest Internet penetration rates in the country, many had four to five years of direct online experience at home and at school and also had attended at least one informal Internet class. This experience was likely self-guided (e.g., children learn about the Internet by themselves rather than from a good book) (Kuhn, 1989) and the social scaffolding provided by their parents may not have been optimal (Fischer & Bidell, 1998; Yan & Fischer, 2002), thereby limiting their understanding of the complexities of the Internet. Educational scaffolding as provided via Internet workshops offered by schools or public libraries also may not be effective for learning about the Internet (Dawson, 2002).

Similarly, the novel concepts to be learned may be too new to allow children to use their existing fundamental knowledge, such as fundamental concepts of theory of mind or early numbers (Wellman & Gelman, 1998), or core knowledge (Spelke, Breinlinger, Macomber, & Jacobson, 1992). Thus, children may rely on domain general resources, such as maturity, to enhance their understanding of the Internet (Carey, 1999).

Yan (2005, 2006) was limited because three types of criteria were used to assess participants' knowledge of the complexities of the Internet. First, the 2005 and 2006 studies compared understanding in relation to other age levels, which reflects a norm-referenced approach to assessment rather than a criterion-referenced approach to assessment (Cronbach, 1970; Glaser, 1963). Norm-referenced assessments are appropriate for examining differences across age groups (e.g., Kalish & Cornelius, 2007; Shtulman & Carey, 2007). However, they do not assess how well individuals actually understand the complexity of the Internet. Second, the reference system used to judge understanding was adults. Typically, adults represent the most sophisticated level of understanding in developmental research so they are a good reference group to use when determining the understanding of children and adolescents (Coley, 2000; Kelly & Church, 1998; Notaro, Gelman, & Zimmerman, 2001). However, the Internet appears to be a unique artifact in that adults may not hold correct scientific understanding of the Internet. This method again is a norm-referenced approach that measures children's understanding in comparison to adults but does not measure how well individuals actually understand the complexity of the Internet. Third, how correct their understanding of the Internet is was also used as a reference of understanding. This method is a criterion-reference approach since it compares the actual understanding of the Internet to a set of criteria. Different assessment approaches will lead to different conclusions. For instance, while the peer-referenced assessment suggested significant improvement across age, the adult-referenced assessment indicated adult-like understanding among children, and the correctness-referenced assessment suggested very limited understanding among both children and adults. Thus, the mixed use of three different assessment methods in the studies made it difficult to determine how well individuals understood the Internet.

In a follow-up study, Yan (2009a) chose to use correctness-referenced assessments to assess how well individuals understood the Internet among 786 participants, including children aged 9- to 17-years old and adults. Based on whether and how much participants perceived the Internet perceptually or conceptually (a computer-like interface or a complex network system), participants' technical understanding was coded at four levels: (1) Level 1 was Minimal Understanding, representing completely perception-based knowledge about the Internet which was assigned to those who perceived the Internet as one computer; (2) Level 2 was Partial Understanding, representing perception-bounded knowledge about the Internet. It was assigned to those who perceived the Internet as either several computers with no indication of connections among them or simple connections of several computers; (3) Level 3 was Extended Understanding, representing conception-bounded understanding of the Internet. It was assigned to those who considered the Internet a network-like system in which a computing center linked with multiple computers; and (4) Level 4 was Correct Understanding, representing completely conception-based understanding of the Internet. It was assigned to those who correctly understood the Internet as a system with multiple connected networks, demonstrating a scientifically sound understanding of technical complexity.

Like their technical understanding, participants' social understanding was coded at four levels: (1) Level 1 was Minimal Understanding, indicating that an individual knew very little about the positive or negative social consequence of the Internet and expressed little precaution when using the Internet; (2) Level 2 was Partial Understanding, indicating that an individual had a general but limited sense of the positive or negative social consequence, and a vague precaution related to using the Internet; (3) Level 3 was Extended Understanding and indicated a clear understanding of the profound social consequences of the Internet and a proper attitude towards Internet use; and (4) Level 4 was Correct Understanding, indicating a balanced and comprehensive understanding of the profound positive and negative social consequences of the Internet and a thoughtful attitude towards Internet use and online safety, collectively reflecting a scientifically sound understanding of the social complexity of the Internet.

There are two major findings of the study. First, no 9- to 13-year-olds showed correct technical understanding; only about 5% of 14- and 15-year-olds had correct technical understanding, and only 12% of 17-year-olds and adults had correct technical understanding. At all ages, a considerable number of participants showed minimal or partial technical understanding, essentially perception-based or perception-bounded knowledge about the Internet. Second, no 9- to 13-year-olds showed correct social understanding, except for one 11-year-old. Less than 5% of the 14- to 17-year-olds showed correct social understanding, and only 10% of adults showed correct social understanding. Again, at all ages, many participants showed limited social understanding, essentially perception-based or perception-bounded knowledge about the Internet.

These findings are surprising because of the vast experience these participants had had with the Internet, with many indicating that they use the computer on a daily or weekly basis and have attended multiple informal Internet classes. These findings are even more surprising because children show much lower levels of understanding the Internet compared to their levels of understanding of other concepts. A plethora of evidence indicates that children understand basic concepts in a variety of domains, such as physics, psychology, and biology in early childhood (e.g., Carey, 1985; Gopnik, Meltzoff, & Kuhl, 1999; Harris, Brown, Marriott, Whittall, & Harmer, 1991; Siegler & Thompson, 1998; Vosniadou & Brewer, 1992; Wellman & Gelman, 1998). Typically, this knowledge improves greatly during middle childhood (e.g., Carey, 1985, 1999; Hatano & Inagaki, 1994; Simons & Keil, 1995; Smith, Solomon, & Carey, 2005). Children then tend to have a correct understanding of normally unobservable scientific concepts and spiritual concepts by 10 years of age (Harris & Koenig, 2006). Most 9-year-olds have a conceptual understanding of the world around them, including their own brain, life, and earth. In contrast, Yan's work overall indicates that children's understanding of the Internet as a system with enormous technical complexity and social complexity may lag about 2 to 5 years behind their understanding of other concepts, since children in the study did not reach an adult-like understanding of the Internet until 12 to 15 years of age.

The lag phenomenon observed in these studies can be interpreted through the lens of developmental resources theory (Carey, 1999). According to this theory, there are basically two resources of information relevant for conceptual development, *internal* sources (e.g., mathematical-logic ability and perspective taking capacity, Piaget, 1983) and *external* sources (e.g., language competence and cultural knowledge, Vygotsky, 1978). The internal sources can be domain-*general* (e.g., metacognition) or domain-*specific* (e.g., knowledge in core domains, such as biology). The external sources can be attained through either *direct* experiences (e.g., daily life experiences) or *indirect* experiences (e.g., learning from testimony from adults).

As an internal resource for understanding the Internet, only age appears to be a direct dominant influence. As a new and emerging concept, there is a lack of domain-specific knowledge about the Internet, and domain-general knowledge may not be applicable to understanding the Internet given the mismatch between perceptual features and the conceptual reality of the

Internet. With respect to external resources, children, adolescents, and adults all have had plenty of direct experience with the Internet. However, these direct experiences tend to involve essentially a trial-and-error process, with much self-observation and self-exploration, but without good support and scaffolding. They do have access to various educational opportunities (such as through informal Internet classes) as a way to develop their indirect experience and to learn about the Internet. However, these indirect experiences are found to be an ineffective tool for learning about the complexity of the Internet.

Thus, given these unique circumstances, both children and adults are left to learn about the Internet only through their own internal domain-general resources. This has led to a surprisingly limited and perception-bounded understanding and knowledge about the Internet. In short, the limited internal and external resources likely lead to the limited understanding of the technical and social complexity of the Internet for both children, as exemplified in the 2- to 5-year lag in understanding the Internet compared to children's understanding of other concepts, and adults, as only few adults show a scientific understanding of the Internet.

CONCLUSIONS

In this chapter, we have synthesized empirical evidence, indicating that adults and children demonstrate a limited understanding of the technical and social complexity of the Internet and have limited resources to help them understand the Internet as a highly complex and newly emerged artifact. It is still a long way for the cognitive development community to develop a solid scientific understanding of how people understand the Internet. Nevertheless, this line of research might stimulate and motivate future developmental research in two major directions. First, within the area of artifact research, it should be particularly promising to conduct a series of comparative studies to examine individuals' understanding of a wide variety of artifacts, including simple artifacts (e.g., teapots or books) vs. complex artifacts (e.g., the Internet and mobile phones), existing artifacts (e.g., telephones and television) vs. emerging artifacts (e.g., the Internet of things or wearable devices), static artifacts (e.g., buildings and furniture) vs. moving artifacts (e.g., cars and airplanes), and biological artifacts (e.g., artificial hearts and artificial eyes) vs. nonbiological artifacts (e.g., solar systems and nanomaterials). A systematic developmental investigation of understanding artifacts can help build a new important research program, similar to the highly productive research programs of understanding the natural, social, and mental world in developmental science.

Second, in terms of cyber behavior, it should be critical to build a research program systematically examining three core areas of research: Internet understanding, Internet decision making, and Internet behavior among adults and children. To guide and protect Internet users, developmental researchers should examine how adults and children understand the Internet, and more importantly, explore how they make online decisions intuitively or rationally and eventually how they take actions in the cyber world. A few years ago just after he won the Noble Prize in Economics, Daniel Kahneman pointed out the special need for studying online intuitive and rational decisions as an emerging area (D. Kahneman, personal communication, April 16, 2008). These three areas of research are sequentially interconnected as the three major pieces of a chain of cyber behavior, from the top to the bottom. Developmental researchers should and will make unique and important contributions to this program by examining how people, especially young Internet users, develop their abilities over time in understanding the Internet, making decisions online, and taking actions in the cyberspace.

REFERENCES

Anderson, D. R., Huston, A. C., Schmitt, K. L., Linebarger, D. L., Wright, J. C., & Larson, R. (2001). Early childhood television viewing and adolescent behavior: The recontact study. *Monographs of the Society for Research in Child Development, 66*(1), 1–147.

Calvert, S. L., & Kotler, J. A. (2003). Lessons from children's television: The impact of the Children's Television Act on children's learning. *Journal of Applied Developmental Psychology, 24*(3), 275–335.

Cameron, C. A., & Lee, K. (1997). The development of children's telephone communication. *Journal of Applied Developmental Psychology, 18*(1), 55–70.

Carey, S. (1985). *Conceptual change in childhood.* Cambridge, MA: MIT Press.

Carey, S. (1999). Sources of conceptual change. In E. K. Scholnick, K. Nelson, S. A. Gelman, & P. Miller (Eds.), *Conceptual development: Piaget's legacy* (pp. 293–326). Mahwah, NJ: Lawrence Erlbaum Associates.

Coley, J. D. (2000). On the importance of comparative research: The case of folkbiology. *Child Development, 71*(1), 82–90.

Cronbach, L. J. (1970). *Essentials of psychological testing.* New York, NY: Harper & Row.

Dawson, T. L. (2002). New tools, new insights: Kohlberg's moral judgement stages revisited. *International Journal of Behavioral Development, 26*(2), 154–166.

Denham, P. (1993). Nine-to fourteen-year-old children's conception of computers using drawings. *Behaviour & Information Technology, 12*(6), 346–358.

Dewart, H., & Brace, N. (2006). *An introduction to cognitive psychology* (2nd ed.). New York, NY: Taylor & Francis.

Eysenck, M. W., & Keane, M. T. (2000). *Cognitive psychology: A student's handbook.* New York, NY: Taylor & Francis.

Fischer, K., & Bidell, T. (1998). Dynamic development of psychological structures in action and thought. In R. M. Lerner (Ed.), *Handbook of children psychology: Vol. I. Theoretical models of human development* (5th ed., pp. 467–561). New York, NY: Wiley.

Glaser, R. (1963). Instructional technology and the measurement of learning outcomes: Some questions. *American Psychologist, 18*(8), 519–521.

Gopnik, A., Meltzoff, A. N., & Kuhl, P. K. (1999). *The scientist in the crib: Minds, brains, and how children learn.* New York, NY: William Morrow & Co.

Harris, P. L., Brown, E., Marriott, C., Whittall, S., & Harmer, S. (1991). Monsters, ghosts and witches: Testing the limits of the fantasy—Reality distinction in young children. *British Journal of Developmental Psychology, 9*(1), 105–123.

Harris, P. L., & Koenig, M. A. (2006). Trust in testimony: How children learn about science and religion. *Child Development, 77*(3), 505–524.

Hatano, G., & Inagaki, K. (1994). Young children's naive theory of biology. *Cognition, 50*(1), 171–188.

Huesmann, L. R., Moise-Titus, J., Podolski, C. L., & Eron, L. D. (2003). Longitudinal relations between children's exposure to TV violence and their aggressive and violent behavior in young adulthood: 1977-1992. *Developmental Psychology, 39*(2), 201–221.

Huston, A. C., & Wright, J. C. (1998). Mass media and children's development. *Handbook of child psychology* (pp. 999–1058). Vol. 4 (pp. 999–1058). New York: John Wiley & Sons.

Kalish, C. W., & Cornelius, R. (2007). What is to be done? Children's ascriptions of conventional obligations. *Child Development, 78*(3), 859–878.

Keil, F. C. (1989). *Concepts, kinds, and cognitive development.* Cambridge, MA: MIT Press.

Kelly, S. D., & Church, R. B. (1998). A comparison between children's and adults' ability to detect conceptual information conveyed through representational gestures. *Child Development, 69*(1), 85–93.

Kuhn, D. (1989). Children and adults as intuitive scientists. *Psychological Review, 96*(4), 674–689.

Levin, J. A., Stuve, M. J., & Jacobson, M. J. (1999). Teachers' conceptions of the Internet and the World Wide Web: A representational toolkit as a model of expertise. *Journal of Educational Computing Research, 21*(1), 1–23.

Luckin, R., Rimmer, J., & Lloyd, A. (2001). *"Turning on the Internet": Exploring children's conceptions of what the internet is and does.* Brighton: School of Cognitive and Computing Sciences, University of Sussex.

Margolis, E., & Laurence, S. (1999). *Concepts: Core readings.* Cambridge, MA: MIT Press.

Marsh, J. (2006). Emergent media literacy: Digital animation in early childhood. *Language and Education, 20*(6), 493–506.

Notaro, P. C., Gelman, S. A., & Zimmerman, M. A. (2001). Children's understanding of psychogenic bodily reactions. *Child Development, 72*(2), 444–459.

Philleo, T. J. (1995). Visualizing the internet: Examining images constructed by beginning users. *Paper presented at the 27th Annual conference of the International Visual Literacy Association, Chicago, IL.* October.

Piaget, J. (1983). Piaget's theory. In P. H. Mussen (Ed.), *Handbook of child psychology, Vol. 1. History, theory, and methods* (pp. 103–126). New York, NY: Wiley.

Ralson, A., Reilly, E. D., & Hemmendinger, D. (2000). *Encyclopedia of computer science* (4th ed.). London: Nature Publication Group.

Scaife, M., & van Duuren, M. (1995). Do computers have brains? What children believe about intelligent artifacts. *British Journal of Developmental Psychology, 13*(4), 367–377.

Shtulman, A., & Carey, S. (2007). Improbable or impossible? How children reason about the possibility of extraordinary events. *Child Development, 78*(3), 1015–1032.

Siegler, R. S., & Thompson, D. R. (1998). "Hey, would you like a nice cold cup of lemonade on this hot day": Children's understanding of economic causation. *Developmental Psychology, 34*(1), 146–160.

Simons, D. J., & Keil, F. C. (1995). An abstract to concrete shift in the development of biological thought: The insides story. *Cognition, 56*(2), 129–163.

Singer, D. G., & Singer, J. L. (2001). *Handbook of children and the media.* Sage: Thousand Oaks, CA.

Smith, C. L., Solomon, G. E., & Carey, S. (2005). Never getting to zero: Elementary school students' understanding of the infinite divisibility of number and matter. *Cognitive Psychology, 51*(2), 101–140.

Spelke, E. S., Breinlinger, K., Macomber, J., & Jacobson, K. (1992). Origins of knowledge. *Psychological Review, 99*(4), 605–632.

Thatcher, A., & Greyling, M. (1998). Mental models of the internet. *International Journal of Industrial Ergonomics, 22*(4), 299–305.

Vosniadou, S., & Brewer, W. F. (1992). Mental models of the earth: A study of conceptual change in childhood. *Cognitive Psychology, 24*(4), 535–585.

Vygotsky, L. (1978). *Mind in society: The development of higher psychological processes.* Cambridge, MA: Harvard University Press.

Wellman, H. M., & Gelman, S. A. (1998). Knowledge acquisition in fundamental domains. W. Damon (Ed.), *Handbook of child psychology: Vol. 2* (5th ed., pp. 523–573). New York, NY: Wiley.

Yan, Z. (2005). Age differences in children's understanding of the complexity of the internet. *Journal of Applied Developmental Psychology, 26*(4), 385–396.

Yan, Z. (2006). What influences children's and adolescents' understanding of the complexity of the Internet? *Developmental Psychology, 42*(3), 418–428.

Yan, Z. (2009a). Limited knowledge and limited resources: Children's and adolescents' understanding of the internet. *Journal of Applied Developmental Psychology, 30*(2), 103–115.

Yan, Z., & Fischer, K. (2002). Always under construction. Dynamic variations in adult cognitive development. *Human Development, 45*(3), 141–160.

CHAPTER 13

Measuring the Digital and Media Literacy Competencies of Children and Teens

Renee Hobbs
University of Rhode Island, Kingston, RI, United States

Arguably, media literacy entered the mainstream of public education when educational testing companies began including media literacy themes in their testing regimes. For example, in 2011, the College Board's essay test included a prompt about reality TV in which the question read:

> *Reality television programs, which feature real people engaged in real activities rather than professional actors performing scripted scenes, are increasingly popular. These shows depict ordinary people competing in everything from singing and dancing to losing weight, or just living their everyday lives. Most people believe that the reality these shows portray is authentic, but they are being misled. How authentic can these shows be when producers design challenges for the participants and then editors alter filmed scenes? Do people benefit from forms of entertainment that show so-called reality, or are such forms of entertainment harmful?*

The *Washington Post* and some other media outlets critiqued the College Board's choice of question, wondering whether an intimate knowledge of reality shows would give an essay-writer an advantage in presenting examples and vivid details about TV shows like *Jersey Shore* and reality TV celebrities like Snooki. Because the essay test invites students to take one side of an issue and develop an argument, such questions are valuable to learners. However, students were likely interested in the underlying issues covered in the prompt, that include the effects of television on society, the desire for fame and celebrity on the part of ordinary people, and the authenticity and value of various realistic representations. Indeed, issues of representation are central to the study of all the arts, including media, painting, film, drama, and literature (Bunin, 2011).

The framing of the College Board essay question is structured such that it embodies the mainstreaming of the empowerment-protection dialectic of

Cognitive Development in Digital Contexts
http://dx.doi.org/10.1016/B978-0-12-809481-5.00013-4

media literacy. For most of the 20th century, media literacy has been alternately framed in one of two ways: empowerment is a form of taste discrimination enabling people to make good decisions about evaluating the quality of media content, while protection is rooted in the idea that critical thinking about media reduces people's likelihood of negative influence to media content, including violence, sexuality, propaganda, and misrepresentation. By embracing the empowerment-protection dialectic, media literacy advocates conceptualize the audience as simultaneously active as constructors of messages and meanings and also passive and potentially vulnerable to media's cultural influence on attitudes, beliefs and values, including potential risks and harms associated with negative media effects, including gender, race and ethnic stereotyping, materialism, desensitization to media violence and bystander effects, and more (Hobbs, 2011b). As will be discussed below, both empowerment and protectionist paradigms underlie the measurement of digital and media literacy competencies. In this chapter, I outline research and scholarship that has made progress in refining the measurement of media literacy through competency-based and self-report approaches to measurement and consider the need for some new strategies that connect cognitive and affective domains while being sensitive to the role of the teacher in shaping the learning context.

CONTEXT AND BACKGROUND

Contemporary framing of children's use of media and technology has been undergoing a transformation that has resulted from the rise of the Internet and the availability of ubiquitous wireless broadband (Aspen Institute Task Force on Learning and the Internet, 2014). Children's immersion in digital media texts and technologies and the larger media culture in which they circulate has interested professionals in human development, communication and media studies, and education (Anderson & Hanson, 2010; Bawden, 2007; Bazalgette, 1991). Although social norms for media use at home and school are quite varied, most American children have a television in their bedroom and by the age of 10 have access to a tablet, computer, and/or cell phone for their personal use (Lenhart, 2015). Although some scholarship in media studies frames youth media use as uniformly active and participatory, a nationally representative sample of children and youth ages 8–17 found that preadolescents and adolescents spent about 40% of their time in *passive* media consumption, including the watching of online videos, TV, reading, and listening to music. *Interactive* consumption, including playing games and browsing websites, represented about 37% of preadolescents' time with media and 25% of a teen's daily media use. *Communication* activities, including using social media and video chatting, represented 26% of teen's daily media use. Children and young people today use media to access entertainment and information, interact with content, and socialize with peers. By contrast, findings show that creative digital media *production* activities including making art or music or writing represented only 3% of time spent with media (Common Sense Media, 2015).

Parents, classroom educators, and researchers may differ in their perceptions of the risks and rewards of integrating digital media into the context of public education (Howard, 2010; Livingstone, 2012). Although quality of access is still uneven, schools are increasingly likely to provide learners with wireless Internet access throughout the K–12 spectrum. Increasing numbers of schools use tablets, laptops, and other digital media as a part of instruction, encouraging children to use information sources and interact with digital texts and technologies (Bakia, Murphy, Anderson, & Trinidad, 2011). Since the birth of social media in 2007, widespread understanding is emerging among parents, educators, and future employers that *digital literacy* competencies are required to use the Internet and digital technologies effectively (Belshaw, 2012).

Among educators, there is a growing awareness that the concept of literacy is expanding to include mass media, popular culture, and digital media (Felini, 2014). The term *media literacy* intentionally transforms and expands the concept of literacy from a narrow focus on reading and writing of alphabetic text to a broader focus on the sharing of meaning through symbolic forms. By expanding the concepts of text and authorship to include images, video, infographics, and popular culture, media literacy is gradually becoming a mainstream part of English instruction (Behrman, 2006; Bruce, 2012; Hobbs, 2007). People who are media literate can "access, analyze, evaluate, and communicate messages using a wide variety of forms" (Aufderheide & Firestone, 1993; p. 1). Media literacy education is aligned with inquiry learning and emphasizes the practice of "asking critical questions about what we watch, see, and read" (Hobbs, 2010, p. iii). By analyzing and deconstructing messages through asking "how" and "why" questions, learners come to recognize the constructed nature of symbol systems. Media literacy education focuses on critical analysis and inquiry through a pedagogy of asking questions about media form and content, including issues of authorship, ownership, distribution, and impact while the term *digital and media literacy* includes the skills, knowledge, and

competencies associated with the Internet and social media (Hobbs, 2010).
Advocates want learners to

> acquire a basic understanding of the ways media representations structure our
> perceptions of the world; the economic and cultural contexts in which mass media
> is produced and circulated; the motives and goals that shape the media they con-
> sume; and alternative practices that operate outside the commercial mainstream.
> (**Jenkins, Purushotma, Weigel, Clinton, & Robison, 2006, p. 20)**

APPROACHES TO MEASUREMENT

Digital and media literacy have been called "a constellation of life skills"
(Hobbs, 2010, p. vii) given the diverse definitions, uses, purposes, and contexts in which these literacies are applied. Accordingly, in the scholarship
within the discipline of education, there is as yet no consensus as to how
these competencies should be measured. Academic researchers have been
especially challenged to create research that meets the needs of educators
in the field. Competency-based or performance measures of media literacy
are appealing to both educators and pragmatic researchers: the use of naturalistic measurement of tasks resembling school assignments may help link
academic research on media literacy with assessment of student learning,
increasing the perceived relevance of academic scholarship among K–12
educators. However, researcher-initiated interventions that rely on large-
scale surveys and self-report measures are useful for developing theoretical
models and testing some of the explicit and implicit benefits of media literacy
education. Martens (2010) wrote: "It has become widely accepted that evaluating and explaining effectiveness is one of the most profound challenges
for contemporary research on media literacy education" (p. 9).

Theoretically, the measurement of media literacy competencies has been
influenced by the development of perspectives from both the humanities
and the social sciences. Humanistic approaches to media literacy tend
to emphasize ideas from semiotics, meaning, interpretation, and political
economy; social scientific approaches to media literacy emphasize media
effects. The core concepts of media literacy are a set of humanistic principles
developed at the Aspen Institute Leadership Conference on Media Literacy
in the early 1990s. The concepts emphasize that: (1) all media messages
are constructed; (2) media messages are constructed using a creative language
with its own rules; (3) different people interpret the same media message
differently; (4) media have embedded values and points of view; and (5) most
media are organized to gain profit and/or power. These ideas serve as foundational understandings that media literate individuals use as both consumers

and producers of media messages (Center for Media Literacy, 2002). In synthesizing the core ideas of media literacy, information literacy, visual literacy, and new literacies, Hobbs (2006) structured key humanistic ideas around the theoretical frames of authors and audiences (AA), messages and meanings (MM), and representations and reality (RR). Reflecting the British media education tradition, Buckingham (2007) identifies the concepts of language, production, audience, and representation as reflecting the core theoretical ideas that serve to focus critical inquiry.

Social scientific perspectives to media literacy education generally emphasize the negative effects of media and efforts to use media literacy education to mitigate those effects. Some examples include a focus on media violence, sexual representation, and body image (Potter, 2010). In the social science conceptualization of media literacy, since the mass media have the potential to exert a wide range of potentially negative (and positive) effects, the purpose of media literacy is "to help people to protect themselves from the potentially negative effects" (Potter, 2010, p. 681). Scholars working in this tradition tend to target a specific "problem" whereby a particular vulnerability to media messages is identified and an intervention is designed. This work often relies on survey research to measure digital and media literacy competencies and test hypotheses about the relationships between variables that assess the impact of advertising, news media, media violence, racism, sexism and issues of representation, and perceptions of credibility of news and information.

Children's vulnerability to advertising and persuasion has long been a concern of media literacy educators (Rozendaal, Lapierre, van Reijmersdal, & Buijzen, 2011). As a result of deregulation of media industries in Great Britain, media literacy has become the official remit of the British media regulator, OFCOM (Wallis & Buckingham, 2013). There, government researchers have examined how British children interpret a variety of new forms of advertising. For example, research has shown that many children and young people are relatively unfamiliar with how to recognize online advertising. In one performance-based measure of media literacy, children were shown a picture of the results returned by Google for an online search for "trainers," the British term for athletic shoes, and then asked to identify advertising displayed in online search results. Although the sponsored links were presented in an orange box with the word "Ad" written in them, less than one in five children and only one-third of teens were able to identify correctly these sponsored links as a form of advertising. Half of British teens were aware of personalized advertising, by recognizing that some people might see ads that differ from those they see when visiting the same website or app. However, less than half of the teens were aware of the potential for vloggers (creators of video blogs) to be paid for endorsing products or brands (OFCOM, 2016). This evidence suggests that media literacy competencies are still not developed fully among British children and teens, although media education has had a long and distinguished tradition in the context of English instruction.

In recent years, performance-based empirical research on media literacy measures have been outstripped by qualitative research studies that dominate the education literature. In many studies of digital media and learning, researchers develop a short-term (often), grant-funded intervention and report on informal learning practices that involve children and youth who participate in digital media literacy programs or online communities (Barron, Gomez, Pinkard, & Martin, 2014). Numerous case studies of practice also fill practitioner journals, such as the *Journal of Adolescent and Adult Literacy*, demonstrating the varied contexts in which teachers, and those working in afterschool settings, have developed programs and activities that blend critical thinking and creative media production using digital media and technologies. Case studies of individual learners/classrooms help scholars and educators visualize the learning process inside the classroom and advance theory about digital and media literacy education pedagogy but may not elucidate how to evaluate, scale, or assess the quality of school-wide or district level initiatives.

Below, I identify the distinctive characteristics of performance or competency-based measures of media literacy and measures that rely on self-report of attitudes and knowledge. Performance-based measures represent the "gold standard" because they precisely capture dimensions of media literacy competencies using tasks that are highly similar to the everyday practices of analyzing and creating media in the real world. Self-report measures can help researchers test theories by asking users to self-assess their knowledge, skills, attitudes, and behaviors, and by considering the relationship between media literacy competencies and other variables. Each of these approaches has value to practitioners and scholars. I now examine some characteristics of competency-based and self-report measures to assess media literacy education.

COMPETENCY-BASED MEASURES

Competency-based measures of digital and media literacy have generally focused on behaviors within the cognitive domain, engaging learners in using, analyzing, and creating media texts. Specifically, users are asked to demonstrate their analysis and creative skills, often via questions requiring students to analyze media or create media. Measuring media literacy through performance tasks is a practice that is well aligned with classroom routines, as elementary and secondary teachers routinely create assignments where demonstration of critical analysis is required. Among the first to develop such methods were Quin and McMahon (1995) who studied two tests that were developed by a panel of Australian teachers to measure students' media literacy learning. High-school students were asked to analyze the language, narrative, and target audience of print advertisements and an excerpt from a situation comedy. After receiving media instruction as a part of their standard curriculum, students could identify compositional elements and analyze the impact of those elements on the mood of a piece. Students were less skilled in analyzing the more complex relationships among issues of authorship, purpose, cultural context, and audience. The authors acknowledged that this measurement tool may have been biased in favor of girls and native English speakers, who scored higher relative to the other subgroups.

In studying teens in American high schools, Hobbs and Frost (2003) used a quasi-experimental design to compare a group of 11th graders who were involved in a year-long media literacy curriculum to students in a matched control school who were exposed to a traditional literature-based English curriculum. The researchers examined students' ability to critically analyze print advertising, radio, and television news, via their ability to identify the purpose, target audience, point of view, and construction techniques used in media messages. Students were also asked to identify omitted information as a means to measure their ability to recognize a message's distinctive point of view. Pre- and posttest responses of students in the two schools showed that students enrolled in the media literacy program showed higher levels of comprehension and analysis of media messages, including print, video, and audio messages as compared to the control group. Students in the media literacy group also produced longer paragraphs in their writing, perhaps because they had a better understanding of how to critically analyze a news media message as compared to students who did not receive instruction in media literacy.

Performance-based measures of media literacy generally require hand scoring and decisions about scoring test responses may involve examining the variation in student responses to an expert group (for example a panel of high-school teachers) or by examining individual responses in relation to the range of responses within a particular peer group of those who completed the test. For example, in the Hobbs and Frost (2003) study, after watching a TV news segment about hurricanes, students were asked, "What values or points of view were presented in this message?" A response such as,

"Much of this story was presented from the point of view of the people who were affected by the storm" was deemed a higher-level answer than a responses such as, "Hurricanes are destructive, dangerous, and unpredictable." Hand scoring generally involves the construction of a codebook, training of two or more coders, and careful attention to language, inferential meaning, and interpretation in judging responses.

Other researchers have used performance-based measures of media literacy to demonstrate its correlation with traditional measures of critical thinking. Arke and Primack (2009) found, with a small sample of college students, good internal consistency among the five subscales of the measure: recall, purpose, viewpoint, technique, and evaluation. In their measures, closely adapted from the work of Hobbs and Frost, "recall" assesses basic comprehension of the media message, "purpose" assesses understanding of the author's intent, "viewpoint" assesses whether the participant can identify the sender of the message, and what points-of-view may be omitted from the message, "technique" assesses an individual's ability to analyze the production techniques that were used to attract attention, and finally, "evaluation" assesses how individuals evaluate that message in comparison to their own perspective. These measures of media literacy were found to correlate strongly with the California Critical Thinking Skills Test (CCTST), which assess critical thinking and reasoning skills.

As noted earlier, the for-profit testing industry has also explored the value of measuring digital and media literacy competencies. The pressure for accountability in higher education has inspired the development of various instruments designed to measure learners' ability to navigate, understand, and critically evaluate information available through digital technology (ETS, 2003). The iSkills test is a performance-based measure that utilizes real-world scenarios to measure the ability to navigate, critically evaluate, and make sense of the wealth of information available through digital technology. These scenarios are set in the context of the humanities, social sciences, natural sciences, business/workplace, practical affairs, and popular culture, and assess information, communication, and technology (ICT) content areas, including task types aligned with the ACRL standards: define, assess, evaluate, manage, integrate, create, and communicate (Educational Testing Service, 2004).

For example, one task entails reviewing information sent by seven people about training courses taken by people in an organization and creating a memo to summarize information and data. To perform the task, users must read the material, identify the relevant data and information about training course attendance, and summarize key themes, using both word processing and spreadsheet software tools. In another scenario, users are asked to evaluate medical information about arthroscopic surgery to repair a tennis injury. This task requires test takers to use a search engine to locate sites that have articles about connective-tissue injuries, anterior cruciate ligament tears, arthroscopic surgery, and rehabilitation programs. Users must effectively and efficiently locate information, evaluate its sufficiency for the purpose, and to evaluate the degree to which the source is trustworthy (Somerville, Smith, & Macklin, 2008).

After completing a series of simulation tasks like this one, students receive a score based on their ability to evaluate the usefulness and sufficiency of information for a specific purpose; create, generate, or adapt information to express and support a point; communicate information to a particular audience or in a different medium; define an information problem or formulate a research statement; and access, summarize, and integrate information from a variety of digital sources (Educational Testing Service, 2014).

The measurement of digital and media literacy has revealed important gaps between self-assessment (measured by self-report) and actual performance (measured by competency tasks). For example, when implementing the iSkills test with undergraduate students, researchers found a significant gap between the skills students believe they possess and their actual competencies. Before taking the iSkills test, a sample of Purdue University freshmen ($N = 262$) were asked to self-assess their information and communication skills; 90% rated themselves highly skilled users of information technologies. However, 52% of these students performed scored lower on the iSkills test than 50% of the population who took the test. Thus, more than half of these students believed they were competent at information and communication skills yet unable to demonstrate the skills when asked to perform them (Somerville et al., 2008).

Although the iSkills test seemed a promising approach to the measurement of digital and media literacy, in 2016, ETS decided to discontinue because it did not sell well in the education market. They were, perhaps, ahead of their time. The company had designed the test for students in the last 2 years of high school and the first 2 years of college. Given the rapidly changing nature of information technology, it is also likely that, over time, the interface for completing the performance tasks was perceived by users as clunky and unattractive. However, it is also true that as technology changes, the practice and nature of digital and media literacy competencies also change. ETS admitted that without a large enough sample of users, the test simply lost both its psychometric and its economic viability. Indeed, performance-based measures of digital and media literacy are expensive to develop, score, and maintain over time. Thus, many researchers rely on self-report measures to provide an inexpensive approximation of the competencies that embody some aspects of media literacy.

SELF-REPORT MEASURES OF MEDIA LITERACY

The use of self-report to measure media literacy has a long history as researchers have recognized the value of finding ways to identify how people make critical judgments about media (Brown, 1991). In the 1980s, researchers used *perceived realism* as a proxy for media literacy, examining how learners evaluated the realism of television programs, asking them to explain why they perceived particular programs as realistic and others as unrealistic. In general, audiences are thought to perceive media content as realistic if they judge it to be like real life in some meaningful way or if they respond to it as though it were real (Hall, 2009). Perceptions of realism differ among individuals as people use different criteria to make realism judgments, including factual realism, social realism, and narrative coherence. Such judgments may occur at different stages of the interpretation process: some people begin interpreting a specific media text based on the format or genre, while others evaluate as they read or view, and still others evaluate realism retrospectively (Busselle & Greenberg, 2000).

Many scholars have examined how media literacy may support healthy lifestyles among children and teens (Domine, 2015). In evaluating the impact of media literacy program, Austin and her colleagues incorporated perceived realism into the development of the Message Interpretation Process (MIP) model (Austin & Knaus, 2000) to trace factors that may lead to increased cognitive involvement with media messages through both reasoning and affective pathways of decision making. The model builds on social cognitive theory and expectancy theory and extends dual-process theories of persuasion. Levels commonly analyzed using the MIP framework include desirability; perceived realism, norms, and perceived similarity; identification; expectancies; and behavior.

In one study that used this model, Pinkleton, Austin, Cohen, Chen, and Fitzgerald (2008) explored how a teen-led media literacy curriculum focusing on sexual portrayals in the media might increase adolescents' awareness of media myths concerning sex, decrease the allure of sexualized portrayals, and decrease positive expectancies for sexual activity.

A posttest-only quasi-experiment with control groups was conducted with 522 middle-school students at 22 school and community sites in Washington. Significant differences were found in the knowledge gained by those in the media literacy program as compared to control-group participants. Students in the media literacy group were less likely to overestimate sexual activity among teens, more likely to think that they could delay sexual activity, less likely to expect social benefits from sexual activity, more aware of myths about sex, and less likely to consider sexual media imagery desirable. Thus, as part of a sex education program, media literacy instruction may provide adolescents with a cognitive framework necessary to understand and resist the influence of media on their decision-making concerning sex.

In addition to asking people to self-assess their competencies, data on media use behaviors and knowledge of media industries, institutions, or economics have also been considered as important variables in the development of media literacy competencies (Potter, 2010). Some of this research has resulted from government mandate. For example, in Britain, the media regulator OFCOM has taken responsibility for measuring the media literacy competencies of British children and adults. Although the government agency generally focuses on gathering data about people's media use (the frequency of media activities involving laptops, cell phones, radio, and television), they also include a mix of self-report behaviors and knowledge measures as a dimension of media literacy competencies.

In 2015, a random survey of 500 children aged 8–15 who used the Internet at home or elsewhere were surveyed about their critical understanding, a concept used in England to describe the skills and knowledge children needed to understand, question, and manage their media environment. OFCOM did not find evidence that these skills and knowledge were increasing among British children. In 2015, when asked to judge the truthfulness of content, British children were more likely than in 2014 to think that various kinds of online information were "always true." Surprisingly, 23% of children aged 8–11 and 14% of children aged 12–15 answered that all the information on news and information sites was true. One in five teenage users of search engines believed that if a search engine listed information it must be true. Only one-third of 12- to 15-year-old viewers of television gave the correct response when asked how the BBC was funded (OFCOM, 2016).

Self-report measures of media literacy have also been used by public health and communication researchers to examine how media literacy education may help modify attitudes and knowledge that contribute to behavior change (Austin & Johnson, 1997; Domine, 2015). As an example, Primack et al. (2006) developed and validated the Smoking Media Literacy (SML) scale, a self-report Likert scale with items representing the three theoretical frames of AA, MM, and RR mentioned earlier. Items include: "To make money, tobacco companies would do anything they could get away with," "Cigarette ads try to link smoking to things that people want like love, beauty and adventure," and "Cigarette ads show scenes with a healthy feel to make people forget about the health risks." These measures have been found reliable with both high-school and middle-school students and have been used in evaluating web-based programs for media literacy (Shensa, Phelps-Tschang, Miller, & Primack, 2016).

Other self-report measures of media literacy ask users to reflect on their critical thinking about both media sources and message content. Austin, Muldrow, and Austin (2016) evaluated critical thinking about the source of the media message on a seven-point Likert scale, where users respond to statements like "I think about the purpose behind alcohol advertisements I see," "I think about what the creator of alcohol advertisements wants me to believe," "I think about who created the alcohol advertisements I see," and "I think about the truthfulness of alcohol advertisements before I accept them as believable." Participants respond to items that invite them to reflect on their evaluation of the content of the message, responding to statements like "I think about what the creator of a message wants me to think," "I look for more information before I believe something I see in messages," and "It is important to think twice about what messages say." The authors found that critical analysis of sources was a precursor to critical thinking about media content and that both skills were associated with personality factors, including the need for cognition and the need for affect.

Many studies have used scaled self-report measures of the media literacy competencies of learners to examine what Scharrer (2002) has called the implicit assumptions about the benefits of media literacy education. In an important meta-analysis of 51 quantitative studies of media literacy interventions involving learners ranging from elementary school to college students, Jeong, Cho, and Huang (2012) found a moderate overall effect size ($d = 0.37$), indicating a positive role of media literacy in shaping these outcomes. Interventions that were longer resulted in larger effect sizes and those interventions with more instructional components (including, for example both analysis and creative media production activities) resulted in smaller effect sizes. A closer review of this study suggests that differences between academic research and program evaluation may partly explain these findings. In well-controlled researcher-centric programs, simple experimental manipulations target short-term attitude, knowledge or behavior change, and researchers are more successful measuring a limited number of learning outcomes with precision (Grafe & Breitner, 2014). For those who design, implement, and assess more complex and real-world oriented media literacy programs in the field, which often include multiple goals and outcomes as per the needs of diverse stakeholders including educators, parents, and researchers, measurement challenges may result from differential program completion rates and other challenges associated with field-based research. In field-based collaborations between schools and university research partners, there is substantial negotiation inherent in the process of collaboration (Hobbs & Moore, 2013).

MEDIA KNOWLEDGE AND MEDIA LITERACY

How important is knowledge of media industries, media theories, and media effects in the development of media literacy competencies? Potter's (2004) theory of media literacy posits that knowledge about media content, industries, and effects is key to identifying people's level of media literacy. In particular, he claims that people with more knowledge of how media institutions operate will be more media literate than those with less knowledge. Potter also distinguishes between low-level information such as knowing the lyrics to television show theme songs and knowledge gained from personal experience, noting that "people who have played sports will be able to appreciate the athletic accomplishments they see on television to a greater depth than those who have not physically tested themselves on those challenges" (p. 34).

In exploring the relationship between knowledge of the news media and usage or consumption of news, Ashley, Maksl, and Craft (2013) developed an index to assess media knowledge as a dimension of news media literacy. They used multiple-choice questions to test college students' knowledge of the structure of the US media system, focused on knowledge of business, ownership and regulatory systems, media effects, and content frames. Items included knowing that: CNN.com employs reporters whereas Google News does not; journalists are not required to be individually licensed in the United States; FOX News is generally thought to have a politically conservative bias; and only about five companies own the majority of major media outlets today compared to 50 companies in the early 1980s. Other knowledge items included knowing that people who watch a lot of television news tend to think the world is more violent and dangerous than it really is.

Some researchers doubt the relative value of media knowledge as a dimension of media literacy. In framing media literacy as a set of critical competencies, Hobbs and Moore claim that intellectual curiosity and the ability to ask "how" and "why" questions are far more important than either having digital technology usage skills or possessing knowledge about the media industry. They argue that when instructors are over-focused on transmitting knowledge in a media literacy program, the instructional strategies used may not advance critical thinking competencies. Still, they acknowledge that contextual information about media industries, economics, and effects may shape people's interpretation and inquiry processes (Hobbs & Moore, 2013).

Scholars who have measured the impact of media literacy curricula on young people's civic engagement have found that exposure to a media literacy presentation can mitigate perceptions of bias (Vraga, Tully, & Rojas, 2009) and that learning about the economic and political structure of the US media system can increase skepticism as measured by credibility ratings of news stories (Ashley, Poepsel, & Willis, 2010). McDevitt and Kiousis (2006) observed how effects of a grade 5–12 civics curriculum passed from students to their families. Using a primary-group model, the family was conceptualized "as mitigating the influence of social structural institutions such as schools and mass media" (p. 261). The civics curriculum stimulated increased political knowledge and information seeking from news media among students, who in turn, stimulated increased political knowledge and information seeking from news media among their parents. The impact was greater for low-income families, thus narrowing the knowledge gap related to political issues.

Democracy depends on people caring about the accuracy of information used to make political decisions. For this reason, researchers have examined the relationship between political knowledge, critical analysis of media, and exposure to media literacy education. Because people's judgment of truth is shaped more by their preexisting beliefs rather than the evidence itself, researchers have long examined how confirmation bias may intersect with reasoning processes (Johnson, Hashtroudi, & Lindsay, 1993). Concern about "fake news" has made this topic especially timely to American citizens. Recently, Kahne and Bowyer (2017) conducted a field experiment to determine how directional motivation and accuracy motivation affect young people's judgments of truth claims. They embedded an experiment inside a survey of a large, nationally representative sample of 2101 young people aged 15–27. Some participants were randomly assigned to view one of six posts (political cartoon or graph) on the topics of income inequality and tax policy. These posts were manipulated in two ways: (1) type of evidence: some verbal content was emotive (subjective with no evidence presented), some was evidence-based, and some included misinformation; and (2) political ideology: liberal (referencing "the rich") and conservative (referencing "successful Americans"). Participants were asked to rate the accuracy of the post on a four-point scale and as part of the survey, they were also identified as liberal or conservative by asking their opinions on whether government should be involved in reducing income inequality. Also, a three-question survey that was deemed a reliable indicator of political knowledge was used.

To measure exposure to media literacy education, participants were asked two questions: how often they had discussed in school how to tell if the information found online was trustworthy and how often they discussed the importance of evaluating the evidence that backs up people's opinions. Not surprisingly, the researchers found that participants' judgment of accuracy was associated with their preexisting political beliefs. Further, 67% of participants who saw a post that aligned with their preexisting views rated it as accurate as compared with only 39% of people who saw a post that did not align with their political views, demonstrating that directional motivation affects judgments of accuracy. Political knowledge did not improve judgment: those with more political knowledge were, in fact, were more likely to judge posts that they agreed with as accurate despite the presence of misinformation. However, subjects who reported high levels of media literacy education showed no differences in directional motivation and ostensibly made a clear distinction between a post with misinformation and one with accurate evidence, even when it agreed with their preexisting political beliefs (Kahne & Bowyer, 2017).

Media literacy education may disrupt other forms of bias. Babad, Peer, and Hobbs (2012) examined teens' nonverbal processing of political news, building upon previous research which has shown that viewers judge a TV interviewee more favorably when the interviewer's nonverbal behavior toward the interviewee is friendly rather than hostile. High-school students who participated in a media literacy course were compared to a control group within the same school to determine susceptibility to this particular form of media bias. Participants were randomly assigned to view a brief interview in which the interviewer's nonverbal behavior was either friendly or hostile toward the interviewed politician. Results showed that the control group showed a nonverbal media bias effect and judged the interviewee more favorably when the interviewer was friendlier, whereas this effect disappeared among media literacy students. It is possible that increased awareness of the constructed nature of media representations is the underlying factor at work here.

Theoretical arguments position media literacy competencies as situated within the development of more general reasoning and cognitive development. For younger children, the ability to use reasoning to justify one's media preferences has been identified as a precursor skill supporting future development of critical analysis skills. This trajectory was supported in work by Hobbs and RobbGrieco (2012), who examined differences in 156 African-American children, ages 9–11, comparing a group of high-achieving students to those enrolled in a regular education program. The construct of "active reasoning" was defined as the process of engaging in inference-making, reasoning, or metacognitive thinking about media texts, tools, and technologies in response to a prompt asking children to identify their favorite media and give reasons to explain why they liked it. High-achieving children were more likely than regular education students to engage in active reasoning when asked to offer an explanation for why a particular TV show, video game, or music was one's favorite by identifying the genre, describing compositional elements, making a link between elements, identifying the purpose or meaning of a message, or identifying the social purpose of a media message. Clearly, children's emotional responses to media may provide opportunities to help them reflect on the formal elements of the content and the characteristic features of the media they enjoy (Nichols, 2006; Nyboe & Drotner, 2008). However, researchers are just beginning to explore how media literacy competencies may develop in relation to the affective domain.

MEDIA LITERACY AND THE AFFECTIVE DOMAIN

In his comprehensive review of the literature, Martens notes that affective mechanisms are likely to interact with cognitive and behavioral dimensions of media literacy, "raising many additional methodological challenges" (Martens, 2010, p. 15). Fortunately, academic researchers have begun to examine affective dimensions of media literacy competencies (Ranieri, 2016). For example, Scharrer and Wortman Raring (2012) examined children's journal entries in response to a media literacy intervention exploring media violence. In a program where undergraduate students provided media literacy education to elementary school students, the researchers found that a protectionist orientation to media literacy, which focused on negative media effects, could be introduced in ways that "encourage complexity and nuance" (p. 4). Analysis of children's written homework revealed that media literacy activities helped them reflect on moral and ethical values regarding the depiction of media violence. In another study, Friesem (2015) examined how affect was incorporated within video production lessons designed to engage elementary school-age learners and promote their collaboration in the context of a year-long technology integration initiative. Findings showed that when students were involved in media making, teachers became more sensitive to the individual needs of learners, recognizing the unique contributions of children who may not have strong academic backgrounds but thrive when presented with collaborative media production learning opportunities.

Affective dimensions of media literacy have also been measured in relation to teacher motivations for the use of media and technology in school. In reflecting on the results of a 3-year university-school partnership in media literacy implemented in an urban elementary school, Hobbs and Moore (2013) described the kind of "messy engagement" that occurred when children were empowered to create and analyze popular culture and digital media in ways that connected the classroom to the local neighborhood and community. They posited that teacher motivations for digital and media literacy might differentially shape instructional practices, as some teachers brought more student-centered orientations into their approach to media literacy while others were more attentive to the content or the form of various media genres, the expressive dimensions or the political economic context in which media messages circulate. Building on this research, a 48-item measure of teacher motivations for digital and media literacy was tested and validated among a large sample of 2800 teachers in Turkey (Hobbs & Tuzel, 2017). This measure showed substantive differences in motivation between language arts, social studies, and technology teachers. For example, teachers who self-identified as *activists* (those who see media literacy as helping contribute to making society more just and equitable) showed a different attitudinal profile than those who identified as *demystifiers* (those who emphasize asking critical questions about media) or *spirit guides* (those who value talk about media as a means to enhance children's socioemotional development). Future research is needed to examine how differences in teacher motivations regarding digital and media literacy may shape instructional choices in the classroom, and how these instructional choices then may affect students' media literacy learning outcomes.

IMPLICATIONS FOR THE FUTURE

As American children spend time with entertainment media each day, they engage in widely varying patterns of media use including those who can be classified as light media users, readers, mobile gamers, heavy viewers, video gamers, and social networkers (Common Sense Media, 2015). Children's immersion in digital and media culture continues to rise and discourses of empowerment and protection will continue to attract attention from parents, teachers, and others with interests in the developmental needs of children and teens (Tyner, 1998). The measurement of media literacy competencies by educators, academic, and professional stakeholders is conceptualizing the new competencies, skills, and habits of mind that are necessary for full participation in a media–saturated and technologically intensive world.

Because media content is ever-changing and the devices we use are transforming continually, the measurement of media literacy competencies is a fast-moving target. The use of both self-report and performance-based measures arises from the increasing variety of disciplinary perspectives, including human development, public health, media studies, cultural studies, information science, and media psychology. This reflects the growing hyper-specialization of the field of children, media, and education. The changes occurring in the media sector, with new apps, games, platforms, and genres rapidly emerging, have contributed to the instability of meaning of the concept of media literacy and added to the measurement challenges (Wallis & Buckingham, 2013). Which specific competencies are worth measuring and how are these practices contextualized in relation to at-home and in-school uses of media and technology? At the present time, I believe that new theory is needed to support the development of new measures to better understand the development of children's reasoning, critical thinking and reflective competencies over the span of childhood and adolescence. We also need to learn more about how measurement challenges are exacerbated when considering media literacy competencies in relation to the developmental trajectories of children and youth.

Protectionist paradigms offer important insight into the ways in which media and technology reflect and shape cultural values, including attitudes about aggression, sexuality, race, gender, and commodity culture. Media literacy education offers the potential to reveal how media reproduce inequalities. Critical inquiry practices help learners gain distance from their everyday and often unquestioned media use, seeing their own behavior in a new way. Such forms of learning may potentially contribute to renewing active citizenship for participation in democratic societies (Mihailidis, 2014). By strengthening the competencies of reflection and social action, protectionist paradigms enable people of all ages to build importance meta-cognitive and social communication skills.

Empowerment perspectives, including the paradigms of digital media and learning, visual literacy, information literacy, and new literacies, all focus on competencies that enable people to access, analyze, and create media, using an iterative learning process where learning-how-to-learn predominates. Media literacy educators bring a deep appreciation of the dynamic relationship between reading and writing, speaking and listening, and media analysis and media production; this long-standing feature of the discourse community should contribute more to the development of both new theoretical formulations of media literacy and of innovative practices for measuring media literacy competencies (Garcia & Morrell, 2013; RobbGrieco, 2012; Rogow, 2013).

In this brief review of approaches to measuring digital and media literacy competencies, it is clear that researchers and practitioners differ in how they prioritize learning outcomes. Because of the challenge of designing valid and reliable measures, this chapter has shown that both performance, or competency-based, measures of media literacy and self-report measurement tools can be useful. The research community must continue to explore other variables, including media knowledge, habits of mind like intellectual curiosity, and the impact of teacher motivations. As yet, researchers are just beginning to explore how media literacy may support development in the affective domain, particularly the development of empathy and socioemotional development. Future research is needed to conceptualize and measure the intersectionality of these important concepts.

Because they are responsible for integrating digital and media literacy competencies into existing curriculum, elementary and secondary educators have an orientation to the identification of learning outcomes that is different from approaches used by academic researchers. For another Kuhnian paradigm shift to occur in this field, close examination of how teachers themselves aim to capture the full range of digital and media literacy competencies may be useful. It is possible that teacher creativity and reflexive practice have much insight to offer to academic researchers who advance new knowledge in the field.

REFERENCES

Anderson, D. R., & Hanson, K. G. (2010). From blooming, buzzing confusion to media literacy: The early development of television viewing. *Developmental Review, 30*(2), 239–255.

Arke, E., & Primack, B. (2009). Quantifying media literacy: Development, reliability, and validity of a new measure. *Educational Media International, 46*(1), 53–65.

Ashley, S., Maksl, A., & Craft, S. (2013). Developing a news media literacy scale. *Journalism & Mass Communication Educator, 68*(1), 7–21. http://dx.doi.org/10.1177/1077695812469802.

Ashley, S., Poepsel, M., & Willis, E. (2010). Media literacy and news credibility: Does knowledge of media ownership increase skepticism in news consumers? *Journal of Media Literacy Education, 2*(1), 37–46.

Aspen Institute Task Force on Learning and the Internet. (2014). *Learner at the center of a networked world.* Washington, DC: Aspen Institute. Available at: http://bit.ly/2oV51KR.

Aufderheide, P., & Firestone, C. (1993). *Media literacy: A report of the national leadership conference on media literacy.* Queenstown, MD: Aspen Institute.

Austin, E., & Johnson, K. (1997). Effects of general and alcohol-specific media literacy training on children's decision making about alcohol. *Journal of Health Communication, 2,* 17–42.

Austin, E. W., & Knaus, C. (2000). Predicting the potential for risky behavior among those "Too Young" to drink as the result of appealing advertising. *Journal of Health Communication, 5*(1), 13–27.

Austin, E., Muldrow, A., & Austin, B. W. (2016). Examining how media literacy and personality factors predict skepticism toward alcohol advertising. *Journal of Health Communication, 21*(5), 600–609. http://dx.doi.org/10.1080/10810730.2016.1153761.

Babad, E., Peer, E., & Hobbs, R. (2012). Media literacy and media bias: Are media literacy students less susceptible to nonverbal judgment biases? *Psychology of Popular Media Culture, 1*(2), 97–114.

Bakia, M., Murphy, R., Anderson, K., & Trinidad, G. E. (2011). *International experiences with technology in education: Final report.* Washington, DC: US Department of Education, Office of Educational Technology.

Barron, B., Gomez, K., Pinkard, N., & Martin, C. K. (2014). *The Digital Youth Network: Cultivating digital media citizenship in urban communities.* Cambridge, MA: MIT Press.

Bawden, D. (2007). Origins and concepts of digital literacy. In C. Lankshear & M. Knobel (Eds.), *Digital literacies: Concepts, policies and practices* (pp. 17–32). New York, NY: Peter Lang.

Bazalgette, C. (1991). Media education. In M. Alvarado & O. Boyd-Barrett (Eds.), *Media education: An introduction.* London: Open University Press.

Behrman, E. (2006). Teaching about language, power, and text: A review of classroom practices that support critical literacy. *Journal of Adolescent and Adult Literacy, 49*(6), 490–498.

Belshaw, D. (2012). *What is digital literacy? A pragmatic investigation* (PhD dissertation). Durham University.

Brown, J. A. (1991). *Television "Critical Viewing Skills" education: Major media literacy projects in the United States and selected countries.* Mahwah, NJ: Lawrence Erlbaum Associates.

Bruce, D. (2012). Video grammar: A multimodal approach to reading and writing video texts. In S. Miller & M. McVee (Eds.), *Multimodal composing in classrooms: Learning and teaching for the digital world* (pp. 32–43). New York, NY: Routledge.

Buckingham, D. (2007). *Beyond technology.* London: Polity Press.

Bunin, L. (2011). SAT head defends reality-TV question. *Daily Beast,* March 18.

Busselle, R., & Greenberg, B. (2000). The nature of television realism judgments: A reevaluation of their conceptualization and measurement. *Mass Communication and Society, 3,* 249–268.

Center for Media Literacy (2002). *Media Lit Kit. Literacy for the 21st century.* Retrieved on January 30, 2016 from: http://medialit.org/sites/default/files/01a_mlkorientation_rev2.pdf.

Common Sense Media. (2015). *The Common Sense census: Media use by tweens and teens.* Available from http://bit.ly/1rI5Fx4.

Domine, V. (2015). *Healthy teens, healthy media: How media literacy education can renew education in the United States.* New York, NY: Roman and Littlefield.

Educational Testing Service. (2003). *Succeeding in the 21st century: What higher education must do to address the gaps in information and communication technology proficiencies.* Princeton, NJ: Educational Testing Service. Retrieved from https://www.ets.org/Media/Tests/Information_and_Communication_Technology_Literacy/ICTwhitepaperfinal.pdf.

Educational Testing Service. (2004). *ICT literacy assessment: An issue paper from ETS*. Princeton, NJ: Educational Testing Service. Retrieved from https://www.ets.org/Media/Tests/Information_and_Communication_Technology_Literacy/0202heapaper.pdf.

Educational Testing Service (2014). *The i-skills assessment*. Retrieved January 30, 2016 from https://www.ets.org/iskills/about.

Felini, D. (2014). Quality media literacy education: A tool for teachers and teacher educators of Italian elementary schools. *Journal of Media Literacy Education*, 6(1), 28–43.

Friesem, J. (2015). *Media production as learning: Exploring elementary school teachers' motivation and practice of media literacy* (PhD dissertation). University of Rhode Island.

Garcia, A., & Morrell, E. (2013). City youth and the pedagogy of participatory media. *Learning, Media and Technology*, 38(2), 123–127. http://dx.doi.org/10.1080/17439884.2013.782040.

Grafe, S., & Breitner, A. (2014). Modeling and measuring pedagogical media competencies of pre-service teachers (M3K). In C. Kuhn, T. Miriam, & O. Zlatkin-Troitschanskaia (Eds.), *Current international state and future perspectives on competences assessment in higher education* (pp. 76–80). Berlin: Humboldt University of Berlin.

Hall, A. (2009). Realism and reality TV. In R. Nabi & M. B. Oliver (Eds.), *The SAGE handbook of media processes and effects* (pp. 423–438). Thousand Oaks, CA: Sage.

Hobbs, R. (2006). Multiple visions of multimedia literacy: Emerging areas of synthesis. M. McKenna, L. Labbo, R. Kieffer, & D. Reinking (Eds.), *Handbook of literacy and technology: Vol. II* (pp. 15–28). Mahwah, NJ: Lawrence Erlbaum Associates.

Hobbs, R. (2007). *Reading the media: Media literacy in high school English*. New York, NY: Teachers College Press.

Hobbs, R. (2010). *Media literacy: A plan of action*. Washington, DC: Aspen Institute and John and James L. Knight Foundation.

Hobbs, R. (2011a). *Digital and media literacy: Connecting culture and classroom*. Beverly Hills, CA: Corwin/Sage.

Hobbs, R. (2011b). The state of media literacy: A response to Potter. *Journal of Broadcasting and Electronic Media*, 55(3), 419–430.

Hobbs, R., & Frost, R. (2003). Measuring the acquisition of media-literacy skills. *Reading Research Quarterly*, 38, 330–352.

Hobbs, R., & Moore, D. C. (2013). *Discovering media literacy: Digital media and popular culture in elementary school*. Thousand Oaks, CA: Corwin/Sage.

Hobbs, R., & RobbGrieco, M. (2012). African-American children's active reasoning about media texts as a precursor to media literacy. *Journal of Children and Media*, 6(4), 502–519.

Hobbs, R., & Tuzel, S. (2017). Teacher motivations for digital and media literacy: An examination of Turkish educators. *British Journal of Educational Technology*, 48(1), 7–22. http://dx.doi.org/10.1111/bjet.12326.

Howard, S. (2010). Affect and accountability: Exploring teachers' technology-related risk perceptions. *Educational Media International*, 48(4), 261–283.

Jenkins, H., Purushotma, M., Weigel, K., Clinton, K., & Robison, A. (2006). *Confronting the challenges of a participatory culture: Media education for the 21st century*. Cambridge, MA: MIT Press.

Jeong, S. H., Cho, H., & Huang, Y. (2012). Media literacy interventions: A meta analytic review. *Journal of Communication*, 62, 454–472.

Johnson, M. K., Hashtroudi, S., & Lindsay, D. S. (1993). Source monitoring. *Psychological Bulletin*, 114(1), 3–28.

Kahne, J., & Bowyer, B. (2017). Educating for democracy in a partisan age: Confronting the challenges of motivated reasoning and misinformation. *American Educational Research Journal*, 54(1), 3–34.

Lenhart, A. (2015). *Teens, social media and technology*. Retrieved January 30, 2016 from http://www.pewinternet.org/2015/04/09/teens-social-media-technology-2015/.

Livingstone, S. (2012). Critical reflections on the benefits of ICT in education. *Oxford Review of Education, 38*(1), 9–24.

Martens, H. (2010). Evaluating media literacy education: Concepts, theories and future directions. *Journal of Media Literacy Education, 2,* 1–22.

McDevitt, M., & Kiousis, S. (2006). Deliberative learning: An evaluative approach to interactive civic education. *Communication Education, 55*(3), 247–264.

Mihailidis, P. (2014). *Media literacy and the emerging citizen: Youth, participation and empowerment in the digital age.* New York, NY: Peter Lang.

Nichols, J. (2006). Countering Censorship: Edgar Dale and the film appreciation movement. *Cinema Journal, 46*(1), 3–22.

Nyboe, L., & Drotner, K. (2008). Identity, aesthetics and digital narration. In K. Lundsby (Ed.), *Mediatized stories* (pp. 161–176). New York, NY: Peter Lang.

OFCOM (2016). *Children and parents: Media use and attitudes report.* November (pp. 4–203). Retrieved from https://www.ofcom.org.uk/__data/assets/pdf_file/0034/93976/Children-Parents-Media-Use-Attitudes-Report-2016.pdf.

Pinkleton, B. E., Austin, E. W., Cohen, M., Chen, Y. C., & Fitzgerald, E. (2008). Effects of a peer-led media literacy curriculum on adolescents' knowledge and attitudes toward sexual behavior and media portrayals of sex. *Health Communication, 23*(5), 462–472. http://dx.doi.org/10.1080/10410230802342135.

Potter, J. (2004). *Theory of media literacy.* Thousand Oaks, CA: Sage.

Potter, J. (2010). The state of media literacy. *Journal of Broadcasting and Electronic Media, 54*(4), 675–696.

Primack, B. A., Gold, M. A., Switzer, G. E., Hobbs, R., Land, S. R., & Fine, M. J. (2006). Development and validation of a smoking media literacy scale. *Archives of Pediatric & Adolescent Medicine, 160,* 369–374.

Quin, R., & McMahon, B. (1995). Evaluating standards in media education. *Canadian Journal of Educational Communication, 22*(1), 15–25.

Ranieri, M. (2016). *Populism, media and education: Challenging discrimination in contemporary societies.* New York, NY: Routledge.

RobbGrieco, M. (2012). *Media for media literacy: Discourses of the media literacy education movement in Media&Values magazine, 1977–1993* (PhD dissertation). Temple University.

Rogow, F. (2013). *Intersections: Media literacy education and Common Core ELA standards.* Available from http://www.kidsplay.org/NAMLE13/intersect_grid.pdf.

Rozendaal, E., Lapierre, M. A., van Reijmersdal, E., & Buijzen, M. (2011). Reconsidering advertising literacy as a defense against advertising effects. *Media Psychology, 14*(4), 333–354.

Scharrer, E. (2002). Making a case for media literacy in the curriculum: Outcomes and assessment. *Journal of Adolescent and Adult Literacy, 46,* 354–357.

Scharrer, E., & Wortman Raring, L. (2012). A media literacy curriculum on violence in the United States: Studying young people's written responses for evidence of learning. *Journal of Children and Media, 6*(3), 351–366. http://dx.doi.org/10.1080/17482798.2012.693050.

Shensa, A., Phelps-Tschang, J., Miller, E., & Primack, B. (2016). A randomized crossover study of web-based media literacy to prevent smoking. *Health Education Research, 31*(1), 48–59. http://dx.doi.org/10.1093/her/cyv062.

Somerville, M., Smith, G., & Macklin, A. (2008). The ETS iSkills assessment: A digital age tool. *The Electronic Library, 26*(2), 158–171. http://dx.doi.org/10.1108/02640470810864064.

Tyner, K. (1998). *Literacy is a digital world.* Mahwah, NY: Erlbaum.

Vraga, E. K., Tully, M., & Rojas, H. (2009). Media literacy training reduces perception of bias. *Newspaper Research Journal, 30*(4), 68–81.

Wallis, R., & Buckingham, D. (2013). Arming the citizen-consumer: The invention of "media literacy" within UK communications policy. *European Journal of Communication, 28*(5), 527–540. http://dx.doi.org/10.1177/0267323113483605.

CHAPTER 14

Risks, Opportunities, and Risky Opportunities: How Children Make Sense of the Online Environment

Leslie Haddon, Sonia Livingstone
London School of Economics and Political Science, London, United Kingdom

As homes, schools, and the wider society increasingly adopt and find ways to appropriate online, convergent, mobile, and networked media, children figure prominently in debates about the likely benefits and harms that will result. Children are the digital natives, say some, ahead in their understanding and uses of new technologies and thus leaving behind the adults who have, traditionally, supported and guided them. Children are the vulnerable victims of the digital age, say others, exploited for their innocence by commercial bodies and abusive adults alike. Children are the future, say a further group, and thus merit educational technologies so they can develop the 21-century skills that future employers will demand. And yet despite this abundance of claims about children's online experiences and potential, relatively few policy makers, practitioners, or journalists actually listen to children as they articulate their own views, concerns, hopes, and demands. This is the power of empirical research, for researchers do not just consult the "usual suspects" (the typically privileged children invited to participate in policy consultations). Nor do they refer to their own children as a touchstone for children's experiences in general. And nor do they conduct quick-and-dirty "polls" to gather dramatic claims for a media headline.

It is fortunate, then, that underpinning the growing edifice of policy and practice regarding children's online risks and opportunities, the research effort is also growing apace (Cortesi & Glasser, 2015; Livingstone, Mascheroni, & Staksrud, 2017; OECD, 2011; UNICEF, 2012), even if too easily overlooked by those who might make best use of the findings (Donoso, Verdoodt, van Mechelen, & Jasmontaite, 2016; O'Neill, Staksrud, & McLaughlin, 2013).

Cognitive Development in Digital Contexts
http://dx.doi.org/10.1016/B978-0-12-809481-5.00014-6

Thus, as parents, teachers, and children are acquiring, learning how to use, and finding a purpose for the Internet within their daily lives, a range of stakeholders—governments, schools, industry, child welfare organizations, and families—are seeking more or less evidence-based ways to maximize online opportunities while minimizing the risk of harm associated with Internet use. However, research with children throws up challenges of its own. This chapter addresses the ways in which children work out what risks face them online. We show that they do not always agree with adults in the prioritization or even in the classification of risks and opportunities, as their experiences, opinions, and understandings do not fit neatly into such a seemingly obvious binary scheme.

Understanding children's perspectives is important because parents and teachers seek to prioritize online opportunities (after all, this is the reason why they invest in the technology in the first place) while trying to control or reduce the risk of harm as if they and the children they are responsible for see eye-to-eye about which is which. In the parental mediation literature, while it is sometimes acknowledged that children and parents have different motivations for using media, it seems not to be noticed that they may interpret risks and opportunities differently. Some simple examples can make the point: meeting a new person online is generally an opportunity as children see it but a risk to their parents; giving out personal information online enables children to pursue new opportunities but worries their parents; looking up sexual information is vital for many teenagers but can seem like an obsession with pornography, and something to be filtered or blocked, to many parents.

As danah boyd (2014) has shown, if parents and children do not agree, then children are likely to try to circumvent and undermine parental efforts at mediating the Internet. Children find benefits from activities that adults do not anticipate; for example, children wish—sometimes with good justification—to explore forms of knowledge forbidden to them, or they wish to test themselves against challenges that adults fear they cannot withstand (Willett & Burn, 2005). As the realization grows that adults cannot "wrap children in cotton wool" online but must, instead, find ways to build their resilience against possible adversity (Young Minds, 2016), it is important to examine how children themselves perceive online risks, opportunities and, somewhere in between, "risky opportunities" (Livingstone, 2008). This will help to understand how children themselves find ways—and may be better supported in finding ways—to cope with them (Vandoninck, d'Haenens, & Segers, 2012; Weinstein et al., 2016). For, as research has shown over and again, children are unlikely to tell parents or, especially, teachers if something untoward happens to them online precisely because they think adults do not understand the problem and will overreact in a punitive fashion (Haddon, 2015; Pasquier, Simões, & Kredens, 2012).

This chapter analyses how British children aged 9–16 discuss their online experiences more broadly, listening for their conceptions of online risk, opportunity, risky opportunity, and their thoughts on whether adult intervention or support is required and why. Specifically, our research questions are:

- In what forms do children encounter online risks and opportunities?
- How do they make sense of these experiences, for example, in terms of evaluating risks and contextualizing them in relation to their broader experiences?
- Beyond the normal risk agenda, what other online experiences do children regard as being negative and why?
- What strategies do they use to prevent or cope with potentially negative online experiences?

METHODOLOGY

The EU Kids Online project aimed to enhance the knowledge of European children's and parents' experiences and practices regarding risky and safer use of the Internet. After the EU Kids Online I project (2006–09) had reviewed existing European data in this field, the EU Kids Online II project (2009–11) conducted a pan-European survey (Livingstone, Haddon, Görzig, & Ólafsson, 2011; see Livingstone, Haddon, Görzig, & Ólafsson, 2010 specifically for the UK findings). Some of the same questions were asked in the Net Children Go Mobile survey in 2013 providing comparative data over time for the United Kingdom (Livingstone, Haddon, Vincent, Mascheroni, & Ólafsson, 2014).

The follow-up EU Kids Online III (2011–14) project examined the qualitative and quantitative dimensions of children's online risks and opportunities as part of a network now encompassing researchers across 33 countries. This included a substantial qualitative study of children's perspectives, asking about risks but also other experiences online that children may perceive as problematic. The pan-European results (from Belgium, the Czech Republic, Greece, Italy, Malta, Portugal, Romania, Spain, and the United Kingdom) are reported in Smahel and Wright (2014).

This chapter looks specifically at the experiences of the UK children who took part in that wider European project. In the UK pilot, interviews were conducted in January 2013 and the main interviews took place between March and September 2013 in four schools—two primary and two secondary. This consisted of interviews with two boys and two girls from each age group (9–10, 11–13, 14–16), and one boys' and one girls' focus group from each of the three age bands, with each group consisting of five people. There was one extra interview with a boy aged 9–10. This made a total of 13 interviews and 6 focus groups—with 43 children aged 9–16 years old in total. While this is a fairly modest study in terms of UK children, it gains strength from being part of the larger European study which, in all, encompassed 378 children aged 9–16, recruited through schools and youth centers, and interviewed in 56 focus groups and 114 individual interviews. In discussing the UK qualitative findings, we contextualize these in relation to the EU Kids Online and Net Children Go Mobile survey findings.

CHILDREN'S PERCEPTIONS OF PROBLEMATIC SITUATIONS
Sexual Content

The Net Children Go Mobile[1] survey found that UK children were less likely than the European average to have seen sexual images in general (17% vs. 28%) (Livingstone et al., 2014). What did children have to say about the possibility and reality of such experiences? In the qualitative study, most of the UK children interviewed, especially the younger ones, had learned to use the term "inappropriate" to describe the content that their parents had told them they were not supposed to view online. Sometimes this could mean violent content, mainly for games, and it could also mean bad language, but most commonly it referred to sexual images. Some of the youngest, the 9- to 10-year-olds, also characterized some of this material as "disgusting" (Livingstone, Kirwil, Ponte, Staksrud, & the EU Kids Online Network, 2013; Smahel & Wright, 2014).

To put this into perspective, from the EU Kids Online survey data only 3% of children in the United Kingdom had both seen sexual images online and been bothered by this (Livingstone et al., 2010). This was reflected in many of the qualitative interviews, the main example of someone being bothered coming from one of the focus groups with younger boys:

---

[1] Where the Net Children Go Mobile UK report covered the same ground as the EU Kids Online I, the former's data are reported because they are more recent.

Joseph: There are some really disgusting adverts like the ladies in bikinis. It's so annoying. It's really inappropriate.
Interviewer: So, what type of things?
Joseph: Well, it's like…on YouTube…on [?] it's just a giant picture of ladies' boobs [Joseph puts his hand to his forehead, the other boys all laugh] …and next you see men staring at it…eyeballs like that [gestures to show eyes coming out of the head] …That's disgusting… [he buries his head in his arms, the others laugh] Switch off the laptop! That's just out of order! And that happened to my cousin once…and he called me…and I said 'Why did you call me for such a thing like that, that's disgusting'.

(Boy, 10)

For some of the children, it was clear that they personally might not be particularly worried by encountering "inappropriate" content, whatever their parents said, but they nevertheless thought that it was "inappropriate" for younger siblings and relatives such as cousins who might be adversely affected by the content. Some 14- to 16-year-olds might say this referring to relatives who could be 9–10, but 9- to 10-year-olds might say the very same thing about siblings even younger than them. It was clear that even young children understood the nature of sexual content. In fact, sometimes they expressed quite a sophisticated appreciation. For example, Lewis understood the principle that sexual images in adverts are used to sell products, but was mystified why they were used to sell this particular product.

Lewis: Sometimes they have adverts of these ladies around poles…you know those ladies who… [mimics rubbing up a pole in pole dancing] …like fashion models…advertising a pint of milk! And I was thinking [opens his eyes very wide] …basically what they did…all these ladies coming down the catwalk show [mimics them moving his thighs and with his hand behind his head] …and then suddenly one came along with a pint of milk [holds his two hands out in front, mimicking carrying the milk] And I was thinking 'Is that all! They're advertising milk!'… [moves his shoulders up and down as if walking down the catwalk] …'You milk' [imitates pouting and kissing the milk, others laugh]

(Boy, 10)

Slightly older children are often even more reflective and articulate about inappropriate content. Melanie talked about her encounter with sexual content starting when she was visiting a gaming site. Many children mentioned online gaming sites where the material "popped up." In fact, the EU Kids Online survey showed that pop-ups in general were the most common way of encountering such material—with 46% of children who saw online sexual images saying it happened in this way (Livingstone et al., 2010), and accidently encountering such material was frequently noted in the European qualitative report (Smahel & Wright, 2014). On the one hand, Melanie, like

Joseph, initially referred to the material as "disgusting," but then went on to ask why online sexual content should exist, not in terms of it being bad, but in terms of questioning why this would be interesting. This looks less like a view handed down from adults, but more a position she was trying to work out for herself.

> Melanie: I went on this gaming site and it came up...like... 'Click here to see free [um] porn'. And I didn't want to click it...but then... it looked disgusting! Like, we've all got the same bodies, sort of. Maybe different skin colours, yeah...but that don't mean nothing. 'Cos, like...what's the point of putting, literally, a body on the Internet for other people with the same body to watch it?
>
> **(Girl, 12)**

For some of the boys, the particular area where they raised questions about the nature of sexual images was in relation to games, given the importance of gaming in boys' culture. So their comments would drift between the games offline for consoles and those played online. For example, one typical comment was to question whether something should be counted as, for example, a nude image since you would have to be looking very closely to see anything, and most of the time boys would be more engaged in game-play. Or, as Zyan noted:

> Zyan: When it comes to nudity on that game, basically you can't even see them naked. They will be pixelated and you can't see any of their body parts. I don't know why they say there's nudity even though the body parts are pixelated. It doesn't make any difference, it's like they're still wearing clothes.
>
> **(Boy, 12)**

The other area of questioning was to argue that children can see forms of nudity in daily life in other media, like topless girls in newspapers, and that was "real life," as Shiv (Boy, 12) put it. So what was all the fuss about as regards much less ostentatious nudity in games? As Shiv put it, "*it doesn't really make sense, to be honest.*"

As regards the rationale for their own reactions to sexual images, Candice (Girl, 12) talked about encountering sexual videos on YouTube, and why at this stage in her life she would consciously prefer to remain "relatively" innocent of these things, even if she had some formal knowledge of sexual matters:

> Candice: It could get you thinking about all these things (...) that you don't really want to know, because I'm 12. I wouldn't want to know about inappropriate things (...) if there was a particular video about sex, for example, then I'd find that inappropriate, because I'm at the age, where I know what sex is, but if I want to find information, I'd probably ask my mum for starters. I don't know what these people are going to say, they could put the wrong ideas in my head.
> [Later, she continued...]

Candice: Boys, especially my age, they seem to be very into videos that are not really for their age, but they come from particular websites. The things they watch are a man and a woman having sex, or a woman stripping. But I wouldn't really watch that, because it's not very interesting, it's not for my age. I don't want to grow up really fast, I like being 12. I wouldn't watch it because my mum wouldn't like it either.
Interviewer: How do you know the boys are watching this type of stuff?
Candice: Because they talk about it nearly all the time.
Interviewer: And they're quite willing to talk about it, when the girls are around them as well?
Candice: They don't care. (…) Sometimes, you can't help what you hear. Maybe you heard this person saying it to another boy or maybe they're talking loudly. Most of them will say this, when we're having a break. Most of them have videos on their phones that they have downloaded. Last year, there was a group of boys looking at one person's phone and I didn't know what they were looking at. One of the boys told me, it was actually a woman stripping.

Candice's observations about her male peers fit with the EU Kids Online survey data that UK boys were more likely than girls to have encountered sexual images online (14% vs. 8%; Livingstone et al., 2010). However, not all boys were so engaged in watching sexual content, and in the interviews, even older boys could take a moral view on why pornography should have age restrictions, and what effects it might have, in terms of influencing their perspectives of sexuality. Consider these boys, aged 15–16:

David: Hopefully none of us at school will have sex before a good age so we shouldn't really, no one should really be seeing pornography yet. But then there probably are those odd one or two people who are watching it and while getting kind of ideas or something in their heads which will then kind of ruin the rest of their lives.
Jack: They shouldn't really be watching it because they just get ideas because if you're 18 you wouldn't get such ideas as you would if you're 13.
Interviewer: You think it's too easily available, the pornography, or is it okay? Maybe it should be available, maybe that's also part of life?
Roland: Okay, when you're, like, 18 or something you've never done it before, then it could, I guess, make you more aware, but at this age it's just not right because everyone's too young.

In fact, sometimes the objection is that sexual content can be a distraction, taking time away from doing more worthwhile things, such as preparing for General Certificate of Secondary Education (GCSE) exams:

Logan: I think there should be an age limit on it, because it could distract you from your work. Like, you wouldn't get the right level…it could affect you when you're doing GCSEs

(Boy, 15)

The survey had asked whether sexual material "bothered" the children. The answers from Candice and from the older boys suggest that some young people might not go as far as to suggest it actually upset them (and so they would not be reflected in EU Kids Online findings specifically on self-reported harm). But nevertheless, they had a viewpoint on this material and might choose to avoid it. In sum, while some, especially younger, children might be bothered by sexual content, others were clearly not—although they thought it might be an issue for children younger than them. Some of their reflections showed that even younger children can have a sophisticated understanding of why sexual content exists online, they can raise questions about why it should exist, or they question why there should be so much adult concern about sexuality online considering the sexual content they encounter elsewhere.

Making and Posting Sexual Content

Apart from looking at encountering sexual content, the EU Kids Online survey had also examined the practices of "sending" and "receiving" sexual images and messages in order to throw light on contemporary discussions of the "sexting" practices of young people. The more recent Net Children Go Mobile survey data showed that few children and young people in the United Kingdom have received sexual messages or images (4%), which is lower than the European average (11%) (Livingstone et al., 2014). But most of the qualitative interviews generated some spontaneous examples of sexting practices among the peer group, if not necessarily by the young person being interviewed. This included often lively discussions of what happens when images start off being sent to a particular person but are then posted online for a wider audience to see or otherwise distributed person-to-person.

In the United Kingdom, some of the 14- to 16-year-olds in particular knew of examples of this from their own schools, or from their friends, including the type of situation sometimes cited in media reporting of sexting, where a boy had solicited a sexual image of a girlfriend and subsequently passed it on to male friends. But it is clear that practices relating to sending and receiving sexual content are a little more varied. For example, Elsie (Girl, 15) had received pictures from a boy posing in his underwear (which she judged to be narcissistic) while a friend had received a more revealing picture from another boy. Both Huzaifah's (Boy, 12) friend and cousin had received unsolicited topless pictures from girls.

As regards images posted online, the European qualitative study had noted that some girls posted provocative photos of themselves in order to receive "likes" on social networking sites (SNSs) (Smahel & Wright, 2014). In keeping with this, a group of girls aged 12–13 commented on the way some of their peers posted pictures of themselves with "make-up and few clothes" to win "Friends." Christine (Girl, 15) also introduced a critical note about her peers when observing that the pictures some girls posted of themselves (e.g., in bikinis) were a little too revealing. However, the example below shows another route to the posting of such images. Past research on mobile phones had shown how young people sometimes take pictures of their peers, often of their faces with unusual expressions (otherwise known as "mugshots") and post them in order to tease or embarrass the victims (Haddon & Vincent, 2009). Here we see that posting sexual images can be an extension of this practice of embarrassing peers, when in this case the perpetrator is actually a girlfriend rather than the boyfriend discussed in some of the sexting cases. Girls aged 12–13 told us:

> Melanie: Once I stayed round my friend's house and like…I was…taking my top off [gestures to show what she means, imitates pulling it over her head] …in the bathroom to change into my pyjamas…and she come in and she took a picture of me like this [others laugh as Melanie poses] …and she posted it all over BBM…and I thought, like 'You really did that'. [Laughs]
> Interviewer: So was that embarrassing?
> Melanie: It was, yeah…it was (…)
> Interviewer: So when you were on the receiving end of this, did you ask for this picture to be taken down?
> Jane: You don't just say [in a polite voice] 'Can you take that picture down?' [Others laugh] Well, I wouldn't, but she might.
> Melanie: All I said, yeah…you know, like when they looked at the picture, yeah…and I had a Blackberry at the time and everyone was saying, 'Oh Melanie, I saw that picture'. And I said like … 'Yeah, I know. You like my body'.

Apart from Melanie's ability to cope with the dissemination of the topless image by laughing it off, it is interesting to note that Jane's comment is typical of these discussions of managing embarrassing pictures—part of the tease is to resist the request to take down the image when the "victim" asks them to do so. Lastly, Mary cites the case of a male peer, revealing her judgement that those who create such content should have known better. Again, this is framed in terms of there being an embarrassing picture and this led to teasing:

Mary: There was an incident about a year ago, in which someone sent a rather revealing photograph of themselves to someone else. It was really, like, this poor guy had to endure teasing for ages about it. It was all over the place (...) That's happened a couple of times to people, and it's just really bad, because they should know, by now, what's going to happen (...) it's going to get shared and stuff. And what's quite lucky with this case is that everyone was quite sensible and didn't post it on Facebook, which is what they might have done. I wasn't really interested too much in it, but it is a very silly thing to do.

(Girl, 15)

In this case, it looks as if the image was circulated more mobile to mobile, rather than being posted online. To sum up, reflecting the survey data we found that children's personal experience of sexting was limited, but their awareness of the practice and other people's experiences was more widespread. Sexting came in various forms with unsolicited pictures from boys and girls, as well as posting revealing pictures to win approval—although some of the girls were critical when their female peers did this. In one case, a victim reported that the perpetrator was actually another girl, but in this and other cases, perhaps the more interesting point is that the sexual images were framed in terms of the wider practice of taking, posting, or forwarding pictures as a tease or to embarrass.

"Bad Language" in Content

Sexual material was not the only form of inappropriate online content identified by the UK interviewees. Another was the use of bad language or swearing—and this was certainly content to which many parents objected, according to their children. This section differentiates this from swearing in interpersonal communication online, to be discussed in the next section. The younger children were more critical of such content, such as when Lewis (Boy, 10) had encountered the word "fuck" when looking up the "flag of Spain" on Google Image: *I don't think they should allow people to do really rude images or films...*

The word "rude" was also used to refer to this content, and so did not always mean sexual. As with Lewis, Shami (Girl, 10) questioned why this happened:

Shami: And also if you click on something, you think it's perfectly fine, but then it's...very rude (...) bad words. Swear words. I don't know why they do that but they just do... Which is strange. Because they don't need to.

The older children were more likely to question whether it was possible to avoid such language given that it was present in the offline world, and hence, as in the case of games and sexual images, they questioned the logic of parents trying to protect them from this just in the online world:

> *David: There's all these people telling my parents kind of: 'Oh, yes, you should make sure that your kids don't know any swearwords or anything until they're at an appropriate age.'*
> *Jack: It's hard to protect it from me because they go to school and the other kids there already know the stuff.*
> *David: Yes, the first time I ever came across the 'F' word (…) there was this bridge and I was just looking underneath it and someone had sprayed kind of the 'F' word along the wall.*
> *Jack: And just, like, staying out one night, one night really late, you just see so much stuff.*
>
> **(Boys, 15–16)**

In fact, some, like Damien (Boy, 15), observed that even when he could watch versions of films on YouTube with the swearing beeped out, he preferred to watch the "normal" version, where it was retained.

It is generally clear from the children's accounts that bad language in online content is an issue for parents, perhaps more so for parents of younger children. While some, especially younger, children simply shy away from such content, we saw examples of how these same children can comment critically on this material. On the whole, the older children were more likely to view such language as being an inevitable part of offline life, and hence sometimes had doubts about parental attempts to single out bad language online as a problem.

Aggressive Communication, Harassment, and Cyberbullying

While the EU Kids Online survey had concentrated on cyberbullying as a key risk, following the literature on this topic, the EU Kids Online European qualitative study broadened the focus to cover a range of negative forms of online interaction, including various forms of aggression (Černíková & Smahel, 2014). The rationale for this was that children would talk about these experiences of aggression, which were important to them, but they did not necessarily think about the experiences as constituting "cyberbullying." For example, Mohammed was among a number of children who objected to others swearing at him and, like his European counterparts, he felt angry about this rather than upset.

> *Mohammed: It was from this kid on this game that I was playing… […] he was using bad language to me and towards my friends (…) so I reported him and we got him banned straightaway.*

Interviewer: So he was on this chat thing you can do when you're on games? Okay. Was it a surprise, or have you had things like that in the past?

Mohammed: Yes, it was a surprise to me because nobody had spoken to me like that. I wasn't upset. I was just like angry because he was being rude and I hadn't done anything to him.

(Boy, 10)

But also it is not just strangers who could be aggressive. Children can also be generally nasty and mean to each other (and in the examples below, threatening as well).

Jane: Or they'll say 'if you don't BC someone I will haunt you'...and then they'll say 'They'll be someone at the end of your bed and he will come and chop your head off'.

Linda: It's like on X-Factor [TV competition] ...Jill wrote a BC...like if you don't vote for XXXX then this little girl's gonna come to your bed and kill you...or something like that.

Jane: Or 'You'll have bad luck'.

Melanie: And the 'You won't get a boyfriend' or something like that...how stupid!

(Girls, 12)

Sometimes the children felt this aggressive behavior occurred more online than offline precisely because it was not face-to-face, as when Josie (Girl, 12) noted: *Because you don't see the person's face, you don't see the person's reaction, so you just...and you're only typing...*

The EU Kids Online survey showed that only 8% of UK children who go online had received nasty or hurtful messages online, slightly above the European average (Livingstone et al., 2010). But as with the other risk areas, once the children were asked in the qualitative research to comment on cases of which they knew, quite a few could give examples, including those they identified as a form of cyberbullying. Sometimes incidents that were perhaps more thoughtless than intentionally harmful got out of hand in the online world. For example, several interviewees noted how comments made online were sometimes taken the wrong way: *"They don't think that they're saying anything mean but the other person finds it offensive"* (Pamela, Girl, 15). Others observed how something that started out as teasing—either in terms of a comment made or a picture posted—could easily *"escalate from being a joke to being quite abusive"* (Nathaniel, Boy, 12).

The European qualitative report also considered one particular case of online aggressive behavior—breaking into people's accounts and pretending to be them, then making nasty comments about other people, or sending nasty messages to friends of the victim while pretending to be them. In the Net Children Go Mobile Survey, this was covered in the section on the misuse of personal data, where 9% of children had experienced someone breaking into their profile and pretending to be them. A few of those interviewed in the United Kingdom had experienced this themselves, or else knew people who had. This was indeed particularly awkward to deal with, as the victim had to try to repair the social damage by assuring friends that the message was not from them.

Overall, online aggression, wider and more common than cyberbullying, was experienced by a range of the children interviewed, and could come from peers as well as strangers. Several of those interviewed agreed with a theme from the cyberbullying literature that there might be more aggression online because of fewer inhibitions when social clues present in face-to-face action are removed. But it is equally clear that some incidents that do not start out as intentionally aggressive, and indeed may come from the teasing practices identified earlier, may escalate, reflecting previous research observations about the power of the Internet to amplify social dramas (boyd, 2010).

Strangers

Meeting strangers online is certainly something parents worry about and advise against. Many of the children, especially the younger ones, were very wary of this risk. For instance, there were many examples across all age groups of children declining an invitation to be a "Friend" from someone unknown. Hence, few children interviewed in this research had had "negative" experiences of strangers precisely because they had refused attempts at contact. There were no cases in this sample of someone going to meet an online contact. The main example of some negative outcome, noted earlier and mostly experienced by boys, was encountering someone in games who used bad language. The Net Children Go Mobile survey had shown that 17% of children in the United Kingdom (compared to the European average of 26%) had made contact with someone online that they had not met face-to-face (Livingstone et al., 2014). However, the question arises as to why there is even this degree of contact in the face of parental and teacher advice not to talk to strangers. There are some clues from the interviews with children.

One pattern more common with but not unique to boys is meeting people through games, usually chatting to them via a headset while playing. The aural aspect is important because it means the voice of the other person can be heard and a judgement made as to whether they sound like another child. Sometimes the discussion is more focused on commenting on the game, but others take the contact further. For example, Mohammed (Boy, 12) was one of a number of boys who had met someone when playing; eventually they added each other as "Friends." Apart from talking about the game, they had chatted about such things as what they had done the day before, what they had watched on TV, and what they thought about various sports. They had kept in touch for some time and swapped email addresses, but then Moham-med had lost his "Friends'" details and they had lost contact.

In the early days of the Internet, one of the attractions sometimes cited for going online was to meet new people, and this is, to some extent, the same appeal for children. Most of Irene's (10) contacts were people she only encountered online, but she explained: *I know that might be dangerous, because my mum's warned me about it. But sometimes these people that have a lot in common with me. But I don't give all my personal details.* Meanwhile, Roland gave an example of talking to people from other countries, although like Irene, he was aware of the risks and was careful:

> Roland: ...they'll think that there's going to be like paedophiles and stuff on it. But it's actually quite nice people because it's sort of a lot of people your own age so you just talk to them because they, like, they want to hear your accent because you're from England and they're from, like, America so...yes.
>
> **(Boy, 15)**

To summarize, among the UK children interviewed there was little contact with strangers, in large part because of the awareness of risk and refusal to accept contacts online from people unknown. The notable exception, more so for boys, was contact made while gaming, and this often involved an aural element rather than text. The children were still careful, some more than others, but for the most part the often fleeting encounters were innocuous.

Rumor, Social Drama, and Unnecessary Communication

There are a whole set of practices related to the Internet that would not usu-ally be termed "risks" but which, to varying degrees, irritated the children, or else they found the experiences to be problematic. For example, one of the points made about the Internet is that while social drama always exists among young people (as well as adults), it can be amplified when online (boyd, 2010). We saw this process of escalation in the discussion of aggres-sive behavior and cyberbullying, but arguably it occurs in other forms as well, for example, through the spread of rumor. For example, Rawan (Girl, 12) told her closest friend that she liked a boy and the information was passed on online until she felt as if the whole school knew about it. While the infor-mation was true, she would have preferred it if it had not spread to the extent that it did and it was certainly embarrassing when the boy in question found out. In this second example below, the rumor was false, but it had major negative consequences that had to be sorted out. It started when Josie's friend, though not one of her really close friends, had just dyed her hair green:

> Josie: I was online with one of the other girls, and I was like: 'Have you seen her hair?' And the girl was like, 'Yeah, I don't really like the colour'. I was like, 'Oh. It suited her a bit, but she went too far this time'. And then I think the other girl went to tell another girl that I said I didn't like the [friend's] hair, and I think she's ugly. Then the next day at school, everyone was giving me the certain look, and I went up to one of my other friends…and she was really close to me. And she was like, 'Is it true you said all of these things about [this friend]?' And I was like, 'No, I never said anything about [her].' And then the girl came…the girl who dyed her hair green. She came crying to me, and then she was like, 'Oh, I thought we were close, you were like one of my best friends, and I can't believe you'd say these things about another person. Why didn't you just come say it to me?' I was like, 'What did I say?' And she explained to me everything that's been going around. I was like, 'No, I didn't say that.' It got to the point where she wanted to slap me, but we sat in this room. The teacher was like, 'We have to settle this', and we sat in a room, and she literally won't talk to me. So I explained everything, and she was listening, but she wasn't saying anything. And then after, she was like, 'Okay, I believe you. If you say you never said it, I believe you, because you haven't lied to me before.'
>
> **(Girl, 12)**

There is clearly potential for distorting reports of what has been said online, perhaps sometimes maliciously, and broadcasting this, which can sour relationships. In the story above, this might have led to physical aggression had the teacher not intervened. Sometimes these rumors, accounts of what other people had done, are not even solicited, and young people like Ade below simply did not want to know these types of things, in the same way as some children are not interested in offline gossip:

> Ade: Some people I might not even know…will just message me and say: 'Do you know someone's done this? And I'll just I'll ask them: 'Why do you need to tell me?' It's none of my business. And I just tell them 'Don't tell me any more secrets because I don't really need to know.'
>
> **(Boy, 12)**

Rumor is not the only type of communication that can come to be perceived in a negative light. Candice was among those children who got tired of Facebook because of the sheer amount of communication. At first she recounts a theme mentioned by others—that there was simply too much communication as people were supplying so many updates about themselves. But then she shifts to critically commenting on the nature of

communication, the gossip, speaking online behind other people's backs—
that was putting her off because of its negative consequences:

> Candice: At first, since everybody was going onto Facebook, when I wasn't
> allowed back in primary school, it was the most wonderful website ever. They
> were all using it and I wasn't allowed to and I didn't want to do it before my
> mum said that I could. At first it was really good, because I could see all my
> friends and photos and after a while, it's not very interesting. [...] It's just that
> it gets annoying when you have people updating their status every two minutes
> (...) I don't really want to know your life that much. You can tell me this in per-
> son, not over the Internet (...) it was exciting at the beginning (...) (your profile)
> was something that's really personal, you can put your favourite singers. It didn't
> really interest me after a while I think they were using it for the wrong reasons.
> Friends of mine, reasons for bashing people (i.e. talking about someone behind
> their back). I think it's immature that you would do that (...) (also) if something
> happens in real life in school, it has to be said on Facebook. If somebody's seen
> this fight in school, they'll say, 'I've seen this fight with so-and-so'. And then more
> people see the status. If they didn't know about it, then they'll ask the particular
> person who was in that fight, about it the next day. That person won't be very
> happy.
>
> **(Girl, 12)**

Apart from the notifications from other status updates and the online back-
stabbing, the other issue identified here is that, in Candice's eyes, too much
of the offline world can be reported online. Again, there is the potential for a
negative experience offline to be amplified when broadcast online. Return-
ing to the theme of there being simply too much communication, too many
notifications, expressed by a number of those interviewed, the boys below
give examples of what those communications might include, from emotional states to banal consumption—unnecessary and unwanted communications in their eyes:

> Shiv: People just put anything up. They put unnecessary things up that people don't
> want to hear. They just put anything up if they're bored, they'll just write 'I'm bored'.
> On BBM they'll just write 'Eating pasta'...they'll probably take a picture of their food
> and put it under their picture.
> Interviewer: [Speaking to Nathaniel who was nodding] Same type of experience?
> Nathaniel: Yes, when people make statuses and they say random stuff. There's a
> button and you just type in what you want, pick an emoticon and it could be eat-
> ing breakfast, and then they say 'Feeling hungry'. It's just like no one really wants to
> know, people keep bugging you and then more people do it.
>
> **(Boys, 12–13)**

And finally, there were the types of communication, not gossip, but nevertheless comments that people could more easily make because of anonymity

online which were in other senses inappropriate. For example, Abe (Boy, 12) thought that it was in very bad taste when "trollers" had made negative comments and jokes about someone who had died in an accident.

This section has outlined experiences, some associated with social drama, beyond those normally associated with more standard typologies of risks, that collectively appear to be far more common and which are perceived to be negative, to various degrees. One was rumor, which, whether based on truth or distortions, can be negative in its consequences. Indeed, some children try to avoid rumors or even feel negatively about SNSs because of the amount of (negative) rumors there. Then there are the other, sometimes distasteful, negative comments encountered online. Finally, adults sometimes see children's communications as banal when the children see them as being important. But here we see how even children sometimes find some of their peers' communications to be a waste of time and tedious, creating too much "traffic" online.

Excessive Use

In the Net Children Go Mobile survey, UK children were more likely than the European average to report various forms of excessive use (Livingstone et al., 2014). For example, 41% agreed that they have very or fairly often spent less time with family and friends or doing schoolwork than they should because of the time they spend on the Internet. In the qualitative study, most of those interviewed did not think their own use was problematic in this respect, but a few of the older children referred to the issue. Mary (15), like the other girls in the group interview, checked her Facebook every day, and had earlier mentioned that she missed Internet access and got annoyed when she could not go online while on holiday. However, she was also already worried that the time she spent on Facebook was affecting her schoolwork. Hence, she did not want to engage with any other forms of SNS since this would make things worse.

> Mary: I won't let myself on Tumblr. From what I can gather it's like people who are just blogging and stuff, and you never, ever get out of it. And I'm already, sort of, in a pit with Facebook, and I'd rather not dig myself into a deeper hole, especially with my GSCEs coming up … (for example) last night, I was babysitting my little brother, and was, like, with him for about two hours, and I got, like, five minutes' worth of homework done. The rest was spent on Facebook or on my account. And if I was on Tumblr, that time would just double, so… (…) I know what the appeal is, but with my GCSEs and stuff coming up, I really can't afford to get sucked into anything else.

In fact, it was not just schoolwork—she later noted that she would like to follow-up her other hobby of fan fiction writing, but social media were also taking time from that creative outlet:

> I have an account on a writing website, and I post my work on there, and I get reviews and, like, stuff, and it's really interesting. And if I didn't have Facebook, I'd actually spend a lot of time on there, as well, just, like, reading through other people's work.

Logan also saw it as a potential distraction, even referring to Facebook as potentially addictive. But like some of the other young people, this was more from observing others than from his own experience.

> Logan: It distracts you a bit…because once you get on it, you can't really get off it. Because my cousin's got it and he's on it all the time. And you're sort of boring after a while because all you're doing is just uploading pictures and talking to people and doing stuff like that.

> **(Boy, 15)**

In this case, Logan was clearly critical of the type of "boring" person that SNSs use can lead to—something from which he wanted to distance himself.

In this section, we have seen examples of how older children can be reasonably reflective about the appeal of SNSs, they can understand it, and in one case have experienced becoming locked in to using it. But they also recognized that heavy use of social media has costs, in terms of schoolwork and other interests, and in terms of the type of person you become, or are seen to become.

Commercial Content

While the survey had sought information about a range of risks identified in the literature on children's use of the Internet, the qualitative research also asked about other things that were problematic from the child's perspective. As with their European counterparts, UK children were often frustrated and irritated by commercial material on the Internet, often citing it early in the interview and with some feeling—even if they were also willing to talk about some of more standard risk areas covered previously.

> Francis: But the annoying things that come up are pop-ups. Say you want to click on that game. You click on it but before the game comes up…some big 'Sign up here and you get loads of money'…comes up. That's annoying (…) …and you have to wait ages for it to load before you can click the off button and close the window (…) And it takes forever!

> **(Boy, 12)**

Children, like many adults, do not like things that interrupt and waste their time. And Francis was not alone in being particularly peeved when commercial material suddenly appeared in the middle of playing a game, disrupting the flow. Pop-up adverts were the worst culprits. Some pop-ups did relate to risks areas, for example: *"I was typing what I wanted to listen to, and then suddenly this pop-up screen came up of like dating and naked ladies over there, and then I'm like 'What!'"* (Rawan, Girl, 12). Or "…the pop-up said *'Sign up for this website where you can talk to a woman and tell her to do anything you want. You can tell her to take off her clothes and stuff'"* (Huzaifah, Boy, 12). However, these were exceptions, and the more common complaint was that adverts were simply a distraction and/or inconvenience if they were difficult to get out of, or else if the children were redirected to a different site when they tried to close the pop-up down. *"Some of them, when you click on the X, it still ends up going on to the website"* (Shelley, Girl, 12).

Others resented the fact that adverts were often trying to mislead them, as in claims that they had won something (or could win something): *"They try to trick you, saying something is free and then saying it costs something"* (Cath, Girl, 10). In fact, some children noted that they could get into trouble with their parents if they did not read these adverts carefully (Robin, Girl, 10). Younger children in particular, but also older ones, could be indignant that people or companies online were trying to cheat them. For the younger ones, this was simply not fair, while older ones could be a little more worldly wise and cynical.

Other concerns were that adverts asking you to fill in something were trying to get hold of personal details, they might contain viruses, and there was a danger when typing quickly that an advert came up and it was easy to click on something inadvertently that would start a download. And some children were aware that if they did show an interest in some advert and clicked on it, the resultant cookie could attract yet more adverts. Lewis graphically characterized the experience of adverts below:

> Lewis: It's a bit like if you're trying to walk down the road and all your friends are coming up to you and saying 'Have you heard of this'… [makes the gesture of trying to push them out of the way and push past them] 'Excuse me, out the way, I'm trying to get somewhere'. And then someone else comes along and says… [mimics the same 'have you heard of this'] …like that, in your face!
> **(Boy, 10)**

In this section, we have seen that children can be at least as annoyed as adults about unwanted commercial content, and for many of the same reasons. And compared to other risks, they clearly encountered disruptive, unsolicited commercial content often. The interviews convey a sense that every child could complain about this if asked, and most, in practice, did, volunteering these as some of the first examples of negative experiences online. At the very least, they were irritating and sometimes offended their sensibilities that someone was intentionally lying to them, and they had to be careful in case mishandling them or inadvertently clicking at the wrong time could cost money and get them into trouble at home.

PREVENTATIVE MEASURES

Reflecting the high degree of eSafety training[2] in the United Kingdom, the children interviewed were, in general, careful. When searching for something or checking out a peer's recommended websites, many of the younger children (aged 9–10) asked parents to check these out first. Younger children usually asked permission to download things. Since even the younger ones had had some digital literacy training, they were aware that some websites were misleading, they often checked them twice, evaluated the information online against what they had been told in school, searched several times and compared answers on several websites. When asked to supply personal information on a site they would usually ignore the request (reflecting the 87% in the EU Kids Online UK survey who said this) or else they would give false information, as in the case of Jane (Girl, 12), who imaginatively supplied names and addresses from the *Harry Potter* stories. Sometimes giving false names is associated with accessing an SNS under-age, but here it is a tactic used by children to protect themselves. In addition, some children developed their own strategies, as in the case of Lawrence (Boy, 10) who specifically used the platform *Spotify* to download music because it did not have the versions remixed with swearing. Meanwhile Robin had developed her own search procedure:

> Robin: I always put 'For kids' (in the search) as well (…) If it either says in the title or in the little paragraph (afterwards), 'For kids,' I would click on it. I would probably check with my mum first of all.

> **(Girl, 10)**

Although the research provided a few examples of young people talking to strangers, on the whole the children did not talk to them, following school (and parental) advice. Most children, and all the younger children, did not communicate with people they did not know, and they turned down

[2] All those interviewed had had eSafety lessons, sometimes for several years.

Friend requests from strangers. Even those older children who were willing to make contact often took some precautions, as in the case of Roland who wanted to see via a webcam that he was actually talking to another young person, and tended to make contact when other friends were physically around:

> Roland: Oh, no, I don't go on the one where you can't see them because it's then kind of dodgy.
> Interviewer: Right, so you can see who you're talking to?
> Roland: Yes, but I only go when I'm with mates because then I, it feels kind of weird when you're just on your own.
>
> **(Boy, 15)**

Again, some developed their own communication strategies, such as Robin (Girl, 10), who would send a text message to friends warning them in advance that she was going to email them. And as in the *Spotify* example, some chose certain platforms rather than others because they were safer in some way. Hence Cath (Girl, 9–10) chose to use Club Penguin because it had rules about swearing and threatening behavior, and Theo chose Twitter over Facebook for a .related reason—because of their respective reputations:

> Theo: The reason I chose Twitter over Facebook was I heard kind of people saying 'Oh, Facebook, so-and-so has said this about me'...and it kind of sounded as if people are using it on purpose to either bully people, other people or something. But on Twitter I haven't heard that much kind of criticism about it.
>
> **(Boy, 15)**

Lastly, even though they could describe cases when hasty comments had been made or teasing had led to a situation that had "got out of hand," a number of those interviewed indicated that they personally tried to be cautious and reflective, and not do something online that was going to create problems for others:

> Ade: I don't want to put up something that's so bad that it can be harmful to other people, like something racist that can hurt other people's feelings, so I need to know where the limit is and where's the line to push the boundaries (...) If I'm not sure, I don't do it, just in case. So I just stay away from trouble.
>
> **(Boy, 12)**

In sum, although not claiming that all UK children are as careful as the ones in this research, their range of preventative measures was impressive, indeed sometimes inventive, and would make many of those who provide eSafety training proud. And while the previous sections on rumor and perhaps aggression may reflect some children being insensitive when online, here we have examples, and they were by no means the only ones, demonstrating thoughtfulness and empathy.

COPING

As regards encountering unwanted websites or pop-ups, most of those over the age of 11 dealt with them by technical means—often, deleting the pop-ups or simply moving on. So, when Fahima (Girl, 12) encountered a pop-up for a dating website, she deleted it, and when the system then offered her an option to block pop-ups, she took it. Younger children sometimes did this: when Mohammed (Boy, 10) recognized the site was "trying to trick him," he left it. Meanwhile, Abe's (Boy, 12) brother installed some software that stopped his pop-ups. Sometimes pressing the X-button to close a pop-up did not work, which was itself frustrating, and a number of children mentioned that they had to resort to closing the computer down in those cases. However, others admitted that their patience was really being strained:

> Francis: As soon as a pop-up comes up...I don't like it...because pop-ups will become more pop-ups...and it'll just become a big pop-up mess.
> Interviewer: Right. And as you said before, that irritates you.
> Francis: Yes. So much. I almost broke my laptop (...) I almost...ripped the screen in half... ...I was holding the middle of it...and you could see little cracks appearing...and then I stopped and I thought 'No, no, better not'.
>
> **(Boy, 12)**

Incidents like this, when there is such a strong reaction that the child almost destroys the machine, make it understandable that when asked in an open-ended way "what bothers them" or "what is negative about the Internet," sometimes the first thing volunteered is not the higher profile risks identified in eSafety teaching. Those can sometimes seem distant from their own personal experience, albeit important, whereas something like the frustrations, built up over time, of pop-ups can feel really immediate.

If younger children (aged 9–10) received a communication that they were not sure about or decided was negative, they usually told a parent. As regards aggressive communication, it was clear that many children of different ages had been warned by parents and/or teachers to tell someone if this happened, but also not to reply in order to avoid escalating the problem. Most did exactly this, or else used the "report" mechanism (e.g., if someone was swearing at them). In the example below, where Jane was threatened, not only did she report the case, but she also received social support from her friends.

> *Jane: There was the guy and he said that he was going to kill me and then all of my friends. So I reported him… All my friends were calling him names because of this.*
>
> **(Girl, 12)**

We only had one UK example of what the coping section of the European qualitative report identified as a "retaliation" response, here responding to aggression with aggression:

> *Keith: Yes, and some kid on there, he called me a bad name and I sort of hacked his Penguin account (…) I kept on making the guy crash into walls, yes, and he got really annoyed and called me a name.*
>
> **(Boy, 13)**

Apart from this case, the more mainstream and immediate response of ignoring aggression, or in the example below, virtually "walking away," can sometimes be followed up by measures to prevent this situation happening again. As the European qualitative report noted, additional new "preventative measures" can be a response to a previous negative experience. Here, Fahima's friend took an additional longer-term measure after an incident, no longer adding names she did not know to her Facebook account:

> *Fahima: I was talking to my friend on Facebook…and then all of a sudden…you know people sometimes invite themselves to a chat? (…) And me and my friend was talking, and they start saying rude things to her. And I was like, 'Just stop it'… I was like, 'You know, what. Don't reply back.' And we just both left the group chat. I think they just added her on her Facebook before that thing started. So then she went on her Facebook and she deleted all of them that she didn't know. So she got a lesson. She said that she never did it again…if she doesn't know anyone she never adds them.*
>
> **(Girl, 12)**

As noted earlier in the section on aggressive communication, the case of hacked accounts could be a particular problematic case of aggressive behavior. Note in the story below how Elsie "freaked out" when she got messages from her friend Isadora's account because it had been hacked. In our small sample of interviews several children reported that their account had been hacked in this way, and that often it required a serious effort to try to apologize to friends, convince them they were not to blame, and to generally sort it out afterwards.

Isadora: I got a virus on my Twitter, and they were, like...
Elsie: And then they were...she was sending me, like, really horrible messages. I was, like: 'What the...?'
Isadora: Like, nasty messages. 'It wasn't me. It wasn't me'.
Interviewer: So it looked like Isadora was sending Elsie really horrible...
Isadora: Nasty messages, but I wasn't... I got the virus, so I deleted my account, but the virus reactivated it. [...]
Elsie: I got really freaked out when I first got it.
Interviewer: And then you just have to close your whole account, and start all over?
Isadora: Yes, but then, because of the virus, it reactivated my account, so I can't make a new one on that email. So I just don't do Twitter anymore. I kind of gave up with it.

(Girls, 15–16)

The issue of how to deal with teasing that had the potential to escalate required more subtle social responses. The young people interviewed talked of mixed responses from peers when they asked them to remove posted photos that they were unhappy about. Below, Mary reports the case of two boys who had been photographed in such a way that it made it look like they were kissing. She was impressed by the way they successfully managed to deal with the teasing by laughing it off since she admitted that in their shoes, she might not have managed that coping response.

Mary: We lightly teased them about it, for about a few days, and it, sort of, just wore off. Like, the best part was, they were able to take the joke. If they hadn't...if it had been me, I might not have been able to take the joke, but they were able to, so it was all right.

(Girl, 15)

In general, it is clear that children do often heed much of the Internet safety advice to which they are exposed. In terms of content, they often dealt with content by technical means—deleting unwanted items, or if all else fails, turning the device off. However, unwanted content (which includes much commercial material, not just sexual content) was often one of the most frustrating and annoying experiences voiced by children, evoking some emotion. As regards communication, many children, especially younger ones, did tell parents about aggressive online contact, and tried not to escalate such confrontations. One of the most problematic of these to cope with was when the account was hacked, spoiling a child's reputation with peers. One other tricky situation to handle, which some managed better than others, was the posting of socially embarrassing (but not necessarily sexual) photos.

CONCLUSIONS

The value of research such as this lies in hearing children's voices directly. Thus, we have tried to capture just how children experience the online environment, including the clear risks of harm that adults (usually parents and teachers) have often warned them about and also the more ambiguous or contextual risky situations that they must navigate online. We have been most struck by the fact that children are indeed listening to adult advice but they are also struggling to make sense of it. The touchstone against which they judge the advice they receive is whether or not it illuminates their own experience. For example, if adults worry about online sexual content or swearing or rudeness while similar content is readily available and little noted offline, children are concerned at the discrepancy.

Then, children face a host of minor yet troublesome daily irritations and worries regarding their online experiences on which adults rarely comment or advise. These include commercial, technical, and interactional frustrations. Conversely, adults worry a good deal about rare albeit severe risks—by and large, it seems children have grasped these concerns loud and clear. However, children may not seem to act wisely in risky situations—at least as adults see it—because for children it can be difficult to match the advice given and the online situations they face. Online situations are often ambiguous or confusing. Clear rights and wrongs are difficult to determine, and children can find adult advice to be more confusing than clarifying. Moreover, the trickiest risks are posed not by strangers but by peers, complicating children's lives. For instance, it is striking that children are often concerned with the offline consequences of online interactions, finding it necessarily to put right or repair their or others' peer relationships face to face because of something that got misinterpreted online.

To conclude, we suggest three key implications for policy and practice that are supported by the evidence presented here. First, children are applying their intelligence in undertaking lively conversations among themselves in relation to online risks and safety. In seeking to guide and support them, parents and teachers would do well to recognize these conversations and, where possible, join in on occasion. They would necessarily be broaching new topics or raising new concerns with children, although children's level of understanding varies; rather, opening a conversation about online risks with children could recognize and validate their already-existing understanding, and thereby ease the task for parents and teachers of further supporting the development of children's understanding and approaches to coping.

Second, online risk of harm to children is simultaneously widespread and rare. By this we mean that most if not all children are now aware of, thinking about and responding emotionally to the array of risks within their purview, if not their direct experience. This leads them to reflect, often critically, on the behavior of adults in general as well as their teachers, parents, and peers in particular. In addition to being exposed to a generally risky environment, many children, especially as they become teenagers, know of someone among their peers who has encountered or been adversely affected by online risks of one kind or another, and the peer conversations are often focused on what they know or heard of a particular incident in their school or wider circle, this incident (whether true, embellished or frankly mythical) serving to stimulate children's thinking about what can happen, and inviting them to rehearse how they might cope in such circumstances. As survey statistics show, the proportion of children directly affected by online risks is much smaller, and we suggest that this generalized conversation about online risks and coping is productive in helping to ensure that most direct experience of risk does not become personally harmful, though some does.

Third, children's responses to online risk run the full gamut from humor to horror. Sexual risks in particular occasion ambivalence disgust, curiosity, moral approbation, humor, and pleasure. In exploring their mixed feelings, children are working out how to understand the world, their peers, and themselves. In doing so, they are also working out what is a risk or an opportunity—a sexual threat or an opportunity for sexual expression, for instance. In their offline lives, children are significantly protected from visible expressions of sexuality, and thus it is unsurprising that they are curious to explore and discuss the much more visible expressions of sexuality online. Rather than penalizing such curiosity as "too old for them" or seeing this as motivated by personal sexual desire, parents and teachers might do better to regard this as a curiosity about the world, like any other except that it is the dimension of life that adults are the most reluctant to discuss with children. What is striking about the conversations we have presented in this chapter—in relation to sexual risks but also other risks—is that children are seeking to understand both *what is* (i.e., the range of behaviors that actually occur in the wider world) and *what should be* (i.e., how the wider world, and they and their reference group more particularly, will or should judge what occurs, in moral terms).

As suggested at the outset of this chapter, such insights are important because, provided children are not given to think that their Internet access might be either removed or intrusively monitored, it seemed to us that children are broadly accepting that their online activities will be subject to adult advice, supervision, and support. For the most part, they even welcome this and it is particularly encouraging that the youngest children welcome adult support and intervention. Perhaps, if adults can intervene and guide children when they first go online—at ever younger ages—their advice will be accepted, children will learn to act wisely, and a positive dynamic can be established between child and adult that will stand them in good stead as they become teenagers deserving of greater privacy and independence.

ACKNOWLEDGMENTS

The authors thank the EU Kids Online network and its funder, the European Commission Better Internet for Kids Programme.

REFERENCES

boyd, d. (2010). Friendship. In M. Itoet al. (Eds.)*Hanging out, messing around and geeking out: Kids living and learning with new media* (pp. 79–116). Cambridge, MA: The MIT Press.

boyd, d. (2014). *It's complicated: The social lives of networked teens.* New Haven: Yale University Press.

Černíková, M., & Smahel, D. (2014). *Aggressive communication, harassment, cyberbullying and related feelings. In D. Smahel & M. Wright (Eds.), The meaning of online problematic situations for children: Results of cross-cultural qualitative investigation in nine European countries.* London: EU Kids Online Network. http://eprints.lse.ac.uk/56972/.

Cortesi, S., & Gasser, U. (Eds.), (2015). *Digitally connected: Global perspectives on youth and digital media.* Harvard: Berkman Center Research. Available at http://papers.ssrn.com/sol3/papers.cfm?abstract_id=2585686.

Donoso, V., Verdoodt, V., van Mechelen, M., & Jasmontaite, L. (2016). Faraway, so close: Why the digital industry needs scholars and the other way around. *Journal of Children and Media, 10*(2), 200–207.

Haddon, L. (2015). Children's critical evaluation of parental mediation. *Cyberpsychology: Journal of Psychosocial Research on Cyberspace, 9*(1). http://eprints.lse.ac.uk/63261/.

Haddon, L., & Vincent, J. (2009). Children's broadening use of mobile phones. In G. Goggin & L. Hjorth (Eds.), *Mobile technologies: From telecommunications to media* (pp. 37–49). Abingdon: Routledge.

Livingstone, S. (2008). Taking risky opportunities in youthful content creation: Teenagers' use of social networking sites for intimacy, privacy and self-expression. *New Media & Society, 10*(3), 393–411.

Livingstone, S., Haddon, L., Görzig, A., & Ólafsson, K. (2010). *Full findings from the EU Kids Online survey of UK 9-16 year olds and their parents.* London: EU Kids Online Network. http://eprints.lse.ac.uk/33730/.

Livingstone, S., Haddon, L., Görzig, A., & Ólafsson, K. (2011). *Risks and safety on the Internet: The perspective of European children. Full findings.* London: EU Kids Online Network. http://eprints.lse.ac.uk/33731/.

Livingstone, S., Haddon, L., Vincent, J., Mascheroni, G., & Ólafsson, K. (2014). *Net children go mobile: The UK report.* London: London School of Economics and Political Science. http://eprints.lse.ac.uk/59098/.

Livingstone, S., Kirwil, L., Ponte, C., Staksrud, E., & the EU Kids Online Network (2013). *In their own words: What bothers children online?* London: EU Kids Online Network. http://eprints.lse.ac.uk/50228/.

Livingstone, S., Mascheroni, G., & Staksrud, E. (2017). European research on children's Internet use: Assessing the past, anticipating the future. In *New Media & Society.*

O'Neill, B., Staksrud, E., & McLaughlin, S. (Eds.), (2013). *Towards a better Internet for children? Policy pillars, players and paradoxes.* Göteborg: Nordicom.

OECD (Organisation for Economic Co-operation and Development). (2011). *The protection of children online: Risks faced by children online and policies to protect them.* Paris: OECD Publishing.

Pasquier, D., Simões, J. A., & Kredens, E. (2012). Agents of mediation and sources of safety awareness: A comparative overview. In S. Livingstone, L. Haddon, & A. Görzig (Eds.), *Children, risk and safety on the Internet: Research and policy challenges in comparative perspective* (pp. 219–230). Bristol: The Policy Press.

Smahel, D., & Wright, M. (Eds.), (2014). *The meaning of online problematic situations for children: Results of cross-cultural qualitative investigation in nine European countries.* London: EU Kids Online Network. http://eprints.lse.ac.uk/56972/.

UNICEF. (2012). *Child safety online: Global challenges and strategies.* Florence: UNICEF Innocenti Research Centre.

Vandoninck, S., d'Haenens, L., & Segers, K. (2012). Coping and resilience: Children's responses to online risks. In S. Livingstone, L. Haddon, & A. Görzig (Eds.), *Children, risk and safety on the Internet: Research and policy challenges in comparative perspective* (pp. 205–218). Bristol: The Policy Press.

Weinstein, E. C., Selman, R. L., Thomas, S., Kim, J. -E., White, A. E., & Dinakar, K. (2016). How to cope with digital stress: The recommendations adolescents offer their peers online. *Journal of Adolescent Research, 31*(4), 415–441. http://dx.doi.org/10.1177/0743558415587326.

Willett, R., & Burn, A. (2005). 'What exactly is a paedophile?': Children talking about Internet risk. *Jahrbuch Medienpädagogik, 5,* 237–254.

Young Minds (2016). *Resilience for the digital world: Research into children and young people's social and emotional well being online.* Retrieved from London http://www.youngminds.org.uk/assets/0002/5852/Resilience_for_the_Digital_World.pdf.

Policy and Practice Recommendations for Facilitating Learning From Media

CHAPTER 15

Children's Learning in a Mobile Media Environment: Policies, Practices, and Possibilities

Sarah E. Vaala*, Amy B. Jordan[†]
*Joan Ganz Cooney Center at Sesame Workshop, New York, NY, United States
[†]University of Pennsylvania, Philadelphia, PA, United States

Societal opinions regarding the role of digital media in the lives of youth are often polarized and impassioned. Many feel that children are growing up in a golden age of media, in which opportunities to learn, create, and communicate are abundant and unencumbered by time or geographical constraints (e.g., Ito et al., 2013; Lieberman, Bates, & So, 2009). Others contend that digital media are threatening childhood by dominating children's time and attention and exposing them to harmful content and other dangers (Christakis & Zimmerman, 2006). The unprecedented scope and complexity of today's mobile media in the lives of youth necessitate and complicate the development and implementation of effective public policy surrounding children's uses of new and emerging media.

There is no question that mobile media have become a part of children's lives. A 2015 Common Sense Media survey of over 2600 US youth between 8 and 18 years of age indicated that about two-thirds of teens (aged 13–18 years) and nearly a quarter (24%) of 8- to 12-year-old "tweens" had their own smartphone (Rideout, 2015). Many had their own tablet device (53% and 37%, respectively) or laptop computer (45% and 19%). Tweens aged 8–12 years in this study spent 4.6 h a day with screen media on average (outside of school), while teens aged 13–18 years spent 6.7 h. A sizeable portion of that screen media time consisted of mobile media use, specifically, 41% of time for tweens and 46% of time for teens on average. Younger children are also increasingly mobile media users. In a 2013 Common Sense Media poll of US parents with children aged birth through eight years, 72% of parents reported that children of age 8 years and younger had used mobile media devices, and that 17% did so daily. Most children

Cognitive Development in Digital Contexts
http://dx.doi.org/10.1016/B978-0-12-809481-5.00015-8

begin using smartphones or tablets before their first birthday (Kabali et al., 2015). Common activities in which young children engage on mobile devices include watching television or video content and using games and other entertainment or educational apps (Kabali et al., 2015).

The mobility of these devices means they are often with children constantly. The size of many mobile technologies renders them personal devices, free from the prying eyes of parents who might wish to monitor or restrict their children's exposure to certain types of content or activities. These same features boost the potential for children's "anytime, anywhere" media-based learning and communication in ways that have not been possible from traditional media such as television sets or desktop computers.

Consider also the shift in the attention-grabbing features that have accompanied new digital media. While children actively seek out devices and particular content at times, their attention can also be recruited by media itself. Parents and child advocates have long worried about the time spent by children in viewing television (e.g., Hess & Goldman, 1962; Villani, 2001; Wartella & Jennings, 2000); yet to watch television a child (or someone else) must turn the TV set on and choose a program or channel. Contrast to that scenario with the buzz of a smartphone telling a teen that she was mentioned in a tweet, a pop-up urging her to resume play in her favorite game, or the ding that alerts her to an incoming text message. In short, mobile media are often vying actively for children's attention in ways that prior media have not.

Finally, the quantity and diversity of media available through mobile devices have increased dramatically. Given the development and growth of Internet-based services such as Netflix and Hulu and broadcast channel websites such as HBO Go, nearly any television content can now be accessed through Internet-connected mobile devices. Moreover, there are now literally thousands of children's apps for families to choose from. With regard to educational apps alone, the Apple Store boasts that, as of 2016, the store "features over 80,000 educational apps…that cover a wide range of subjects for every grade level and learning style" (apple.com, 2016). The 2015 Common Sense Media report on teens and tweens found that the activities in which youth engage using mobile technologies reflect a variety of purposes, including passive media consumption (such as watching TV content), communication (such as social media), interactive consumption (such as video games), and creation (such as blogging or editing videos).

The scope of content and program options available through mobile media is at once exciting and intimidating. Work by the Joan Ganz Cooney Center and New America has shown a lack of guidance available to parents for directing them toward high quality, educational products and programs and away from lower quality or even harmful offerings (Guernsey, Levine, Chiong, & Severns, 2012; Vaala, Ly, & Levine, 2015). Yet, emerging research, including some studies described in this book (see Dore, Zosh, Hirsh-Pasek, & Golinkoff), indicates that well-designed mobile media with clear educational goals do exist and can be a boon for children's learning (e.g., Falloon, 2016; Falloon & Khoo, 2014; Homer et al., 2014; Neuman & Neuman, 2014).

Of primary concern, then, are policy efforts to harness mobile media resources for youth learning and positive development and to reduce potential negative effects on well-being. The body of research on this topic is nascent, the result of the relatively recent emergence of these media combined with their rapid proliferation. In this chapter, we chart current policies in the United States surrounding childrens' and adolescents' access to and use of mobile media, with a particular focus on educational media. We employ a broad definition of policy, including investment in research, guidance and outreach to families, and school- and community-based programs and initiatives, in addition to federal regulations. We begin by describing regulatory policies aimed at reducing the possible negative influence of mobile media on youth and then turn to highlighting policies oriented toward boosting or leveraging the positive potential of mobile media for childrens' and adolescents' learning and well-being.

REGULATORY POLICIES: REDUCING THE NEGATIVE IMPACT OF MOBILE MEDIA

Parental and societal concerns about children's media tend to fall into four broad domains. These include worries about: (1) the time youth spend with media, (2) exposure to inappropriate or harmful content, (3) privacy and safety, and (4) exposure to marketing content.

Time. The American Academy of Pediatrics (AAP) publishes research-based guidelines for parents regarding a number of child health and development topics, including media use. The 2013 AAP media policy recommended that parents discourage all screen media use for children under age 2 years and to limit screen media use among older youth to 2 h or less per day (AAP, 2013). Parents are also encouraged to keep media technologies out of children's bedrooms, to monitor children's media use, and to coview TV and movies. The AAP has since acknowledged that the widespread use of mobile media by even very young children complicates their prior guidelines, which "must evolve or become obsolete" (Brown, Shifrin, & Hill, 2015, p. 1). In 2015, they convened a symposium of experts in 2015 to advise them on "how to provide thoughtful, practical advice to parents based on the evidence" (p. 1). In May 2016, the AAP published an article subtitled, "When advising families on media, remember all screens not created equal" (Mendelson, 2016). Specifically, the AAP Council on Communications and Media Executive Committee reminds parents of the value of face-to-face communication, the importance of shared digital media use, and an acknowledgement that "It's OK for pre-teens and teens to form and participate in online relationships" (2016, n.p.)

Harmful/inappropriate content. Surveys of parents and youth suggest that many parents have greater concerns and rules about the content of the media their children use than the time children spend using them (e.g., Rideout, 2015; Rideout, Foehr, & Roberts, 2010). Notably, general parental concern regarding exposure to inappropriate or harmful Internet content (such as violence or sex) seems to have surpassed concerns over TV content for many, particularly among parents of older children and teenagers (Bleakley, Vaala, Jordan, & Romer, 2014).

With regard to older media, such as television programming and video games, an uptick in parental and societal concerns about children's exposure to negative content has often been followed by threats of regulation, followed in-turn by preemptive industry self-regulation (Jordan, 2013). For example, when the Federal Trade Commission (FTC) and Federal Communication Commission (FCC) began considering whether food marketing in media was contributing to childhood obesity, food marketers (including manufacturers and broadcast media) created voluntary guidelines under the auspices of the Children's Advertising Review Unit of the Better Business Bureau. Yet, follow-up studies on the effectiveness of the voluntary practices revealed virtually no change in children's exposure to unhealthy food products (Kunkel, Castonguay, & Filer, 2015).

The media industry has, over the years, created ratings systems for parents to use, which indicate the age appropriateness and content of their products. Currently, separate rating systems exist for motion pictures, television programming, music lyrics, and video games. The goal of these systems is to help parents easily identify and select educational or developmentally appropriate content, while avoiding inappropriate content. For television programs, sets manufactured after 2000 have a built-in blocking device (the "V-Chip"), which can be programmed to block shows with particular content ratings. For movies, the ratings are provided so that parents can judge the appropriateness content for their children. However, it is up to the movie theaters to implement practices from keeping children out of PG-13 and R-rated films (Motion Picture Association of America). Similarly, although videogames may be labeled as inappropriate for children, they can still be sold to children under the Supreme Court decision, Brown v. Entertainment Merchants Association and 564 U.S. 08-1448 (2011).

No industry-wide ratings systems or blocking technologies yet exist for mobile media content aimed at children (e.g., apps). Such regulations are difficult to enact without sufficient public demand, and legislation mandating censorship or blocking technologies is particularly difficult given the media's right to free speech (Jordan, 2013). As described above, policies are typically considered and enacted platform by platform (e.g., regulations and ratings systems for television programming do not apply to video games). This system becomes more complicated and perhaps less useful for mobile devices, through which numerous types of content converge (e.g., children can play video games and watch television content on the same device; Jordan, 2013). Moreover, decades of research on the efficacy of ratings systems and blocking technologies have found that they are often not used or useful to parents (Vaala, Bleakley, Jordan, & Castonguay, 2017). The various content and age descriptors used between different media are not applied consistently by producers and become a confusing "alphabet soup" to parents (Greenberg, 2001). Many parents either do not know about blocking technologies such as the "V-chip" in television sets or find them too difficult to program (Scantlin & Jordan, 2006). Tech-savvy youth are also able to find ways around the V-chip and other blocking devices and strategies (Jordan, 2008).

Beyond ratings, there are resources to aid parents who wish to learn more about the mobile media content aimed at children. Several organizations (e.g., Common Sense Media; Children's Technology Review) issue their own independent ratings of children's media products, including apps and websites. These expert reviews can help guide parents toward educational and developmentally appropriate apps and other mobile media, while helping them to avoid negative content. However, the quantity of apps, websites, and other media for children means that these sites are able to rate only a relatively small proportion of what is available. App stores such as iTunes have created "family accounts" that enable parents to view, block, or delete apps on their children's devices. The AAP also advocates parental monitoring and mediation of children's Internet and mobile media use (AAP, 2013). Strategies such as monitoring what children are watching, co-using media with children, and actively restricting children from using particular content have been linked to favorable outcomes for youth, such as mitigated impact of unhealthy food marketing, reduced negative influence of media aggression, and greater positive impact of prosocial content (Buijzen, 2009; Gentile, Reimer, Nathanson, Walsh, & Eisenmann, 2014).

In the early days of the Internet, particular concern over youth exposure to sexual content led to efforts to restrict Internet pornography through proposed legislation known as the Communications Decency Act of 1996 (Jordan, 2013; Levesque, 2007). However, the bulk of this legislation was soon struck down by the Supreme Court in Reno v. American Civil Liberties Union which ruled that the measures infringed on the rights of adults to access sexual content online and on the premise that other measures, such as media education and blocking technology, would be more effective for shielding children (Jordan, 2013; Levesque, 2007). One aspect of the legislation did remain, however. Today, it is "illegal to knowingly transmit obscene or indecent messages to any recipient under 18 years of age" (Jordan, 2013, p. 11). This statute has been applied recently in efforts to curb teenage "sexting" (sharing sexual photos via text message) (Jordan, 2013). Some argue that the measure is too harsh to handle a behavior occurring primarily among adolescents, although parents and child advocates agree that sending and sharing explicit photos are a risky phenomenon that may carry a variety of negative repercussions for youth (Jordan, 2013).

Privacy and consumer protections. Parents' concerns about youth privacy in digital media use have also been salient in the digital media era. In 1998, in an effort to give more control to parents over what information was collected from children online, the FTC enacted the Children's Online Privacy Protection Act (COPPA). COPPA stipulates that any website which knowingly has or targets users under age 13 must first obtain parental consent for the collection and use of all personal information before children can create an account (see Boyd et al., 2011). In 2013, the FTC clarified that the law applies to mobile apps in addition to websites. Moreover, the personal information covered by COPPA now includes photos, geolocation, and identifiers such as computer IP addresses, which are tracked across websites and services (Magid, 2013). To avoid the complications and legal implications of having to comply with these regulations, many producers of websites, services, and apps choose to restrict the use to individuals 13 years or older. A notable example is the social media platform Facebook.

However, the efficacy of COPPA in practice has been questioned. A study of Android apps conducted by Hong and colleagues at Carnegie

Mellon University (see Patel, 2014) found that apps varied considerably in how much their data collection and use behaviors differed from users' expectations. Moreover, they found that many free apps that target or appeal to children are among the worst offenders with regard to appropriate collection and use of personal data. For example, a game may state in the fine print of its policy statement that phone status information (such as phone number or device ID) will be collected, but parents would likely not notice or anticipate how that information is used (e.g., consumer analysis and ads). While website and app producers may largely follow the letter of the law, many do not seem to follow the spirit of the law. Hong and his colleagues have created a free site that analyzes apps and reports grades for how well each app's data collection and use procedures match people's expectations (privacygrade.org).

Research shows that children circumvent privacy policies fairly easily, specifically, by lying about their birth date. A survey by Boyd et al. (2011) found that many parents help their children lie about their age to gain entry to various sites and services. Research by Consumer Reports indicated that as of 2012, approximately 5.6 million Facebook users were under the age of 13 years (Consumer Reports, 2012).

Exposure to marketing. Beyond regulating what and how information can be collected from children under age 13, the U.S. government does not regulate advertising to youth through the Internet or mobile apps. Several studies have found that the characteristics of advertisements in newer digital media (e.g., Internet ads; product placement in videogames) are "fundamentally different from those of other media, including elements such as interactivity, immersion, viral messaging, user-generated content, and location-based targeting" (Rideout, 2014, p. 15). Moreover, these new techniques may interact with developmental status such that youth are particularly vulnerable to new, digital marketing. In the words of Montgomery (2013):

> Because of adolescents' emotional volatility and their tendency to act impulsively, they are more vulnerable than adults to such techniques as real-time bidding, location targeting (especially when the user is near a point of purchase), and 'dynamic creative' ads tailored to their individual profile and behavioral patterns. (p. 771).

In light of these new, stealth marketing practices and the particular vulnerability of youth, Montgomery and others have urged greater attention to research and policy development in this area (Montgomery, Chester, Grier, & Dorfman, 2012).

Children's media products and programs can carry seductive marketing statements that also appeal to parents. This trend has been observed particularly with regard to educational claims. For example, many children's app developers claim or suggest that their apps teach a variety of knowledge and skills to children, such as reading, math, and science (Vaala et al., 2015). Yet there is little research evidence or even expert educational development (e.g., education experts involved in development; specific curriculum) to defend developers' claims or further inform parents. In addition, app developers designate the app store category where their apps will appear, rather than the app store itself or any objective entity. Thus, there are no observable repercussions for misleading parents about educational value of children's mobile media content and no pressure for developers to confirm or back up their claims.

Ostensibly, the FTC regulates deceptive and misleading marketing practices, including of children's apps and other mobile media products. There is some precedent for the FTC to act in such cases. Academic research indicates that infants and toddlers do not readily learn from content presented via video, particularly commercially available baby videos such as Baby Einstein (DeLoache et al., 2010). Yet, producers of baby media content commonly tout educational benefits for infants and toddlers to market their products (Fenstermacher et al., 2010). After complaints were made to them in 2011 about deceptive marketing claims on infant/toddler videos/DVDs, the FTC eventually issued an injunction against the producer of the *Your Baby Can Read* video series (FTC, 2014). The lack of more widespread penalization of media companies who use misleading or unverifiable marketing claims may be due in part to the fact that the FTC relies largely on complaints by consumers and consumer-advocated organizations to investigate and penalize companies for deceptive marketing practices.

DEVELOPMENT AND ADVOCACY POLICIES: BOOSTING THE POSITIVE POTENTIAL OF MOBILE MEDIA

Increasing access to Internet and educational media. Although public discourse disproportionately emphasizes concerns about possible negative repercussions of children's media use, policies are also underway that are designed to promote the positive potential of mobile media for children's learning and development. Youth cannot learn from media to which they do not have access; thus, numerous policies are aimed at putting high-quality mobile media into children's hands. For many youth, particularly those from lower income and racial/ethnic minority households, access to high-quality digital media is thwarted by the degree of access to broadband Internet more generally. Recently, the Joan Ganz Cooney Center conducted a nationally representative survey of nearly 1200 parents of school-age children (6–13 years) with household incomes below the national median level for families (Rideout & Katz, 2016). They found that 94% of lower income families had some access to the Internet, but many were "underconnected," as they did not have home broadband Internet (now defined as 25 megabits per second by the FCC, Singleton, 2015). A third of families below the poverty line had mobile-only Internet (i.e., through a smartphone or tablet plan), which for many, was not consistently active. This difference in the mode and quality of access to the Internet manifested in differences in whether and how children used the Internet. For example, those whose families had mobile-only access were less likely than peers with home Internet access to go online to look up information (35% vs. 52%). Access to and use of high-speed Internet reflects socio-economic privilege, while also incurring socio-economic benefits via enhanced access to enriching educational, employment, and entertainment opportunities. In the words of the US Council of Economic Advisors, "The digital divide is likely both a cause and a consequence of other demographic disparities, and sorting out the precise impact of closing the divide is more difficult than characterizing the current disparities" (2015, p. 9).

Numerous government and private organizations have sought to close the digital divide through a variety of national and local policies. The Connect2Compete initiative was introduced in 2011 with the goal of providing broadband Internet access to low-income families. Through a partnership between the US government and Internet service providers (ISPs), families who meet certain criteria can receive broadband Internet for $9.95 per month through the program (Everyoneon.org, 2016). To qualify for the Connect2Compete program, households must have at least one school-age child eligible for free or reduced lunch, have been without Internet service within the previous 90 days, and have no outstanding Internet service bills. However, research by Katz and colleagues has revealed that in practice the service is underutilized or does not fit the needs of many families who are eligible for the program (Katz & Gonzalez, 2016; Rideout & Katz, 2016). In interviews, Katz and colleagues found that many eligible families did not know about Connect2Compete. Others who did use the reduced cost service experienced slow Internet connections and found that it was only available for one device via an ethernet cord for a limited amount of data per month. Because local schools were the purveyors of information about the program and the technologies themselves, the distribution of information and technology varied by school district (Katz & Gonzalez, 2016). Consequently, some eligible families had greater access to information and technology than others.

Despite the observed limitations of the Connect2Compete program, increasing equity of access to high-quality Internet service is a worthy goal given the integral role of Internet media in our daily lives. The FCC has identified additional avenues for pushing telecommunication companies to provide reduced-cost Internet services to low-income households. For example, the FCC stipulated for a merger deal with DirectTV that AT&T must provide $5 per month Internet service to homes in which at least one person receives food stamps (Kelly, 2016). Such efforts combined with the recent Net Neutrality order (2015) suggest a shift toward considering Internet access as more of a public resource, much like broadcast radio and television networks, than a luxury subscription, like cable or satellite television. The Net Neutrality legislation mandates that ISPs must provide equal access to all online content, and may not block or limit access (i.e., through slower speeds or higher costs) to any legal content or application (FCC, 2015).

There is a history of administrations working to address the digital divide through public policy. For example, in the early days of his first term, President Bill Clinton announced a strategy to build a national information infrastructure. Vice President Al Gore chaired an advisory council that focused on funding community-based institutions serving the public, such as schools and libraries, to provide Internet services and access. They proposed a system of discounted education rates, or "E-Rates," for supporting the infrastructures needed in the schools and libraries, which was passed into law with the Telecommunications Act of 1996. This legislation mandated discounts for high-speed connectivity for schools, libraries, and rural health care centers (Hudson, 2004). By January 1998, the first round of E-Rate applications was being received (Barone & Lombardo, 2015). By many accounts, it appeared successful. In 1994, only 35% of public schools had access to the Internet. By the fall of 2000, almost all public schools in the US (98%) had access (Cattagni & Farris, 2001), indicating that awarding subsidies did succeed in significantly increasing Internet investment, particularly among urban schools and schools with large black and Hispanic student populations (Goolsbee & Guryan, 2006). But the E-Rate program was not without its critics. Some argued that wealthier districts were using the discounts to "gold plate" the media technologies they provided to their students, exacerbating the digital divide (Hudson, 2004). Others pointed out that the mandated filtering software that went along with accepting government funding meant that students were unable to access useful content given overprotective filters (Jaeger, McClure, & Bertot, 2005). In 2014, the Federal Communication Commission took the "next step" in modernizing the E-Rate program by, for example, expanding the budget, equalizing the costs of high-speed broadband between rural and urban areas, and providing an incentive for state support of "last-mile" broadband facilities through a match from E-rate of up to 10% of the cost of construction (FCC, 2014).

A similar example is President Obama's ConnectED initiative, which ensures that "99% of American students will have access to next-generation broadband by 2018" (WhiteHouse.gov, 2016). The initiative represents a public-private partnership between the FCC and telecommunications and computer hardware and software companies such as Apple, Microsoft, and Verizon aimed at providing Internet access to schools and libraries and connecting rural communities through updated infrastructure. The program also includes investment in technology-related curricula and teacher training around effective technology use in the classroom. As of Spring 2016, the Obama administration cited that more than $10 billion in private and public resources had been dedicated to the ConnectED initiative.

In addition to reduced rates of access to broadband Internet service, children from lower income families have disproportionately lower rates of access to media programs and products that have the highest potential to teach. In 2013 Common Sense Media conducted a national survey of over 1400 US parents regarding the home media environment of children between birth and age eight years. They found that only 35% of parents with an annual household income of less than $30,000 had ever downloaded an educational app for their children, compared to 75% of parents making more than $75,000 per year (Rideout, 2013). Common Sense Media have dubbed this disparity the "app gap," denoting a disparity in the nature of children's mobile media use based on socioeconomic characteristics, rather than the extent of access or use. Research by Vaala and colleagues indicate that the cost of high-quality apps may promote this gap (Vaala et al., 2015). They found that literacy-focused children's apps that had won awards from expert media review sites, such as Common Sense Media, tended to be more expensive than other popular literacy apps (i.e., those listed among the "Top 50 educational" in app stores).

Mirroring efforts to boost Internet connectivity among underserved families, various public and private sector efforts are currently focused on providing high-quality educational media to disadvantaged families. Recently, FirstBook, the Obama administration, the Digital Public Library of America, and the New York Public Library launched a program making ebooks and other educational apps available to low-income families and educators serving in-need students. The Open eBooks program allows low-income families to download up to 10 ebooks at a time through an app on their device. Books can be used for 56 days before they must be renewed again, much like a traditional library.

In 1994, the US Department of Education committed substantial resources to using public television programming to promote school readiness (i.e., Ready to Learn initiative). The Ready to Learn (RTL) initiative funded children's educational television programming, with a particular focus on literacy-focused programming, and research testing the programs' effectiveness (see PBSkids.org/readytolearn/). Today, more than a dozen years later, the investment has moved well beyond television and into innovative transmedia production. As Pasnik, Llorente, Hupert, and Moorthy (2016) write, "During the 2010-2015 grant period, change has been dramatic, if also intermittent and quixotic; touchscreens did not exist when the funding cycle began, much less had they found their way into many parents' pockets" (p. 229).

The experts behind the RTL initiative recognized the opportunities that media could present as another learning resource in children's lives. Just as the AAP has reexamined screen time in ways that acknowledged that not all screen media were created equal (Mendelson, 2016), they have also sought to develop consensus around what constituted the "developmental appropriateness" of a media experience. To this end, Pasnik et al. (2016) reviewed research conducted between 2010 and 2015 through the RTL initiative and conducted interviews with research staff to distill convergent lessons from the most recent RTL grant cycle. With regard to evaluating developmental appropriateness of media for children, the authors recommend a focus on the following four domains:

(a) the quality of the media content;

(b) the context in which the child's media experience unfolds;

(c) the opportunities it offers for rich social interactions; and,

(d) engaging and interactive features that enhance children's learning

As most would recognize, the challenge facing producers is finding the best ways to translate these principles into concrete experiences; that is, integrating them into the experiences children have with educational media, including mobile media. For example, some researchers have found that media experiences are enriched when shared by children and caregivers. Under coviewing conditions, children both learn more effectively and adults can become more engaged with young children's learning (Takeuchi & Stevens, 2011; Strouse, O'Doherty, & Troseth, 2013). Other scholars have shown that combined use of multiple media can produce greater learning than a single media component—the "transmedia" experience (Fisch, Damashek, & Alade, 2016). Designing children's media experiences to reflect these domains (i.e., quality, context) and to leverage these opportunities (i.e., parent–child engagement, transmedia experience) requires a large financial commitment and a broad base of expertise. Funding for RTL has come from the U.S. Department of Education and has contributed to research and development of broadcast and online content including PBS favorites such as "Odd Squad," "Peg+Cat," and "Sesame Street" (Mook, 2015).

Leveraging mobile media for child health and development. The ubiquity and appeal of mobile technologies have spawned outreach efforts and educational interventions in the m-health (mobile health) arena. In 2014, Sesame Workshop, Too Small to Fail, and Text4Baby partnered to launch a freely available service for parents of babies which sends research-based tips via text message to help parents encourage young children's language development (Too Small to Fail, 2014). This national effort was preceded by similar local text-to-parent initiatives that evidenced success. For example, a study of families in San Francisco found that parents who received text messages with specific tips for encouraging children's language development engaged in more literacy-focused activities with their preschool-age children and were more involved in their children's schools (Too Small to Fail, 2014; York & Loeb, 2014). In addition, their children had higher scores on literacy tests than peers whose parents did not receive the text messages.

In 2015, Guernsey and Levine identified and described the efforts of numerous "pioneers" applying technology in the service of children's literacy development. The pioneers varied in scale from a forthcoming app from Sesame Workshop that used artificial intelligence to understand and respond to preschoolers to the small Comienza en Casa (It Starts at Home) program in rural Maine. Comienza en Casa provides Maine's migrant parents with an iPad, educational apps and activities, and training to help children prepare for kindergarten (see Guernsey & Levine, 2015). Program staff visits families to get feedback from parents, provide support, and discuss children's learning goals (Mano en Mano, 2015).

Academic researchers also design and test youth-focused apps, websites, and other mobile tools (e.g., SMS) that address various behaviors and domains, from curbing children's anxiety (Berry & Lai, 2014; Pramana, Parmanto, Kendall, & Silk, 2014) to boosting medical regimen adherence among teenagers with type 1 diabetes (Vaala et al., 2016) and helping children with autism develop communication skills (Fletcher-Watson et al., 2015). While the research base is still nascent on the general success of m-health tools for youth health and development and in specifying what are particularly effective design or implementation strategies, early evidence suggests that mobile media technologies can promote healthy behavior (e.g., Turner, Spruijt-Metz, Wen, & Hingle, 2015; Vandelanotte et al., 2015). Unfortunately, due in part to funding constraints and the pace of academic research, the apps designed and tested by academic researchers are often not publicly available. Rather, the health-focused apps that are commercially available to youth are often not evidence-based or subjected to rigorous research testing (e.g., Eng & Lee, 2013; Scott, Gome, Richards, & Caldwell, 2015; Spigner, Hinson, Escobar-Viera, & Hart, 2015).

RESOURCES FOR FAMILIES, EDUCATORS, AND OTHER STAKEHOLDERS

The field of research on the effects of mobile media is nascent and evolving, and more research is needed, but resources do exist to aid caregivers, health care providers, and educators maximize the potential benefits of children's mobile media use.

Guidance to families. **The American Academy of Pediatrics** publishes guidelines for healthy media use. Pediatricians are also encouraged to ask families about children's media use and provide guideline-based recommendations during well-child visits (AAP, 2013), although research indicates that more effort is needed to ensure pediatricians are trained to provide comprehensive information regarding children's use of digital media (e.g., covering topics such as social media, Internet safety, and cyberbullying; Christakis, Frintner, Mulligan, Fuld, & Olson, 2013). Notably, parents who do list the AAP as a source of guidance are more likely to follow the AAP guidelines (e.g., keep TV sets out of children's bedrooms, limit screen time; Lapierre, Piotrowski, & Linebarger, 2014).

Common Sense Media, Children's Technology Review, and **Parent's Choice** independently review children's media products and provide reviews and awards in searchable websites for parents and educators, as noted elsewhere in this chapter. Other academic and non-academic institutions, including the **Technology in Early Childhood (TEC) Center** at Erickson Institute, **Joan Ganz Cooney Center** at Sesame Workshop, and the **Fred Rogers Center**, conduct, translate, and disseminate research for parents, educators, policymakers, producers, and other stakeholders interested in children's educational media.

Librarians are also stepping forward to guide families in healthy and educational use of media. The **Association for Library Service to Children (ALSC)** published a white paper in 2015 proposing that library staff nationwide become trained and serve as "media mentors" (Association for Library Service to Children, Campbell, Haines, Koester, & Stoltz, 2015; Guernsey, 2013). In their white paper, the ALSC urges "every library have librarians and other staff serving youth who embrace their role as media mentors for their community" (p. 7) and that formal training and professional development be offered to librarians to equip them for this role.

Engagement opportunities. **The National STEM Video Game Challenge** is held every year by E-Line Media, Entertainment Software Association, and the Joan Ganz Cooney Center and a host of partners. Middle and high school students submit video games that they have designed and created themselves, and winners are selected to receive cash awards and other prizes. Winners have also presented their work at the White House Science Fair (see stemchallenge.org). As youth produce or remix media content they become actively engaged with the underpinnings and culture of media (rather than merely media consumers), while also developing technical proficiencies as well as traditional, technical, and media literacies (Ito et al., 2009; Kafai & Peppler, 2011). The "affinity-driven" nature of creating media prompts children and adolescents to persist when they encounter obstacles and to apply academic skills, such as math, literacy, and critical thinking in an endeavor with real-life application and personal meaning.

The **Connected Educators** project is a collaboration of numerous partners including the American Institutes of Research and the US Department of Education. The initiative seeks to connect and inform educators regarding best practices for using technology in education. Various resources are freely available at **connectededucators.org**, including a blog, an online community for members, and various professional development opportunities. Each October is **Connected Educator Month**, during which additional thematic presentations, participation and discussion opportunities, and other resources are made available from industry, research, and advocacy partners.

CONCLUSION

In this chapter, we have outlined the challenges and opportunities of the new digital, mobile media context in several arenas, including policy, education, and health. We have shown that while the technology continues to rapidly develop, mobile media have become important in the lives of children and adolescents. Policymakers struggle to keep pace with the new ways in which children are gaining access to content, with older forms of regulation and self-regulation no longer particularly useful or adequate. Yet, we also observe that there is great potential for digital and mobile media to enrich children's learning and well-being, both through innovative development of media properties that span multiple platforms (transmedia) and through evidence-informed interventions aimed at parents and children. Numerous resources, of which we have outlined a few, have emerged to help families, educators, and other stakeholders encourage children's constructive uses of digital media while avoiding exposure and use that might be harmful. Yet, amidst the constantly evolving and proliferating media in children's lives, our collective efforts have merely scratched the surface of the knowledge we need to acquire, translate, and disseminate in order to spur and inform sufficient resources and policies within children's new digital environment.

REFERENCES

American Academy of Pediatrics. (2013). Policy statement: Children, adolescents, and the media. *Pediatrics, 132*(5), 958–961.

Apple.com. (2016). *iPad in Education.* Accessed July 26, 2016 from: http://www.apple.com/education/apps-books-and-more/.

Association for Library Service to Children, Campbell, C., Haines, C., Koester, A., & Stoltz, D. (2015). *Media mentorship in libraries serving youth.* Chicago, IL: American Library Association.

Barone, C., & Lombardo, M. (2015). *Elvis and the E-rate: How Bill Clinton ensured school access to the Internet.* Education Reform Now. https://edreformnow.org/bill-clinton-e-rate/#_ftn1.

Berry, R. R., & Lai, B. (2014). The emerging role of technology in cognitive-behavioral therapy for anxious youth: A review. *Journal of Rational-Emotive & Cognitive-Behavioral Therapy, 32*(1), 57–66.

Bleakley, A., Vaala, S. E., Jordan, A. B., & Romer, D. (2014). The Annenberg Media Environment Survey. Media and the well-being of children and adolescents. In A. B. Jordan & D. Romer (Eds.), *Media and the well-being of children and adolescents* (pp. 1–19). New York: Oxford University Press.

Boyd, D., Hargittai, E., Schultz, J., Palfrey, J., Hargittai, E., Schultz, J., et al. (2011). Why parents help their children lie to Facebook about age: Unintended consequences of the 'Children's Online Privacy Protection Act'. *First Monday, 16*(11) Accessed August 11, 2016 from: http://firstmonday.org/ojs/index.php/fm/article/view/3850.

Brown v. Entertainment Merchants Association, 564 U.S. 08-1448 (2011). Accessed August 11, 2016 from: https://www.supremecourt.gov/opinions/10pdf/08-1448.pdf.

Brown, A., Shifrin, D. L., & Hill, D. L. (2015). Beyond 'turn it off': How to advise families on media use. *AAP News, 36*(10), 54.

Buijzen, M. (2009). The effectiveness of parental communication in modifying the relation between food advertising and children's consumption behaviour. *British Journal of Developmental Psychology, 27,* 105–121.

Cattagni, A., & Farris, E. (2001). *Internet access in US public schools and classrooms: 1994-2000.* Washington, DC: US Department of Education, Office of Educational Research and Improvement.

Christakis, D. A., Frintner, M. P., Mulligan, D. A., Fuld, G. L., & Olson, L. M. (2013). Media education in pediatric residencies: A national survey. *Academic Pediatrics, 13*(1), 55–58.

Christakis, D. A., & Zimmerman, F. J. (2006). Media as a public health issue. *Archives of Pediatrics and Adolescent Medicine, 160,* 445–446.

Consumer Reports. (2012). Facebook & your privacy: Who sees the data you share on the biggest social network? *Consumer Reports Magazine.* Accessed August 11, 2016 from: http://www.consumerreports.org/cro/magazine/2012/06/facebook-your-privacy/index.htm.

DeLoache, J. S., Chiong, C., Sherman, K., Islam, N., Vanderborght, M., Troseth, G. L., et al. (2010). Do babies learn from baby media? *Psychological Science, 21*(11), 1570–1574.

Eng, D. S., & Lee, J. M. (2013). The promise and peril of mobile health applications for diabetes and endocrinology. *Pediatric Diabetes, 14*(4), 231–238.

Falloon, G. (2016). An analysis of young students' thinking when completing basic coding tasks using Scratch Jr. On the iPad. *Journal of Computer Assisted Learning 32*(6), 576–593.

Falloon, G., & Khoo, E. (2014). Exploring young children's talk in iPad-supported collaborative learning environments. *Computers & Education, 77,* 13–28.

Federal Communications Commission (2014). *Universal service program for schools and libraries (E-Rate).* Accessed August 11, 2016 from: https://www.fcc.gov/general/universal-service-program-schools-and-libraries-e-rate.

Federal Communications Commission (2015). *In the matter of protecting and promoting the open Internet, GN Docket No. 14-28.* (Adopted February 26, 2015). Accessed August 11, 2016 from: https://apps.fcc.gov/edocs_public/attachmatch/FCC-15-24A1.pdf.

Federal Trade Commission (2014). *Defendents settle FTC charges related to "Your Baby Can Read" program.* Press Release. Accessed August 11, 2016 from: https://www.ftc.gov/news-events/press-releases/2014/08/defendants-settle-ftc-charges-related-your-baby-can-read-program.

Fenstermacher, S. K., Barr, R., Salerno, K., Garcia, A., Shwery, C. E., Calvert, S. L., et al. (2010). Infant-directed media: An analysis of product information and claims. *Infant and Child Development, 19,* 557–576.

Fisch, S. M., Damashek, S., & Alade, F. (2016). Designing media for cross-platform learning: Developing models for production and instructional design. *Journal of Children and Media, 10*(2), 238–247.

Fletcher-Watson, S., Petrou, A., Scott-Barrett, J., Dicks, P., Graham, C., O'Hare, A., et al. (2015). A trial of an iPad intervention targeting social communication skills in children with autism. *Autism 20*(7), 771–782.

Gentile, D. A., Reimer, R. A., Nathanson, A. I., Walsh, D. A., & Eisenmann, J. C. (2014). Protective effects of parental monitoring of children's media use: A prospective study. *JAMA Pediatrics, 168*(5), 479–484.

Goolsbee, A., & Guryan, J. (2006). The impact of Internet subsidies in public schools. *The Review of Economics and Statistics, 88*(2), 336–347.

Greenberg, B. (2001). *The alphabet soup of television program ratings.* Cresskill, NJ: Hampton Press.

Guernsey, L. (2013). *How the iPad affect young children and what we can do about it. Presentation at the annual TEDxMidAtlantic conference, Washington, DC* Available from: http://tedxmidatlantic.com/2013-talks/.

Guernsey, L., & Levine, M. (2015). *Tap, click, read: Growing readers in a world of screens.* San Francisco, CA: Jossey-Bass.

Guernsey, L., Levine, M., Chiong, C., & Severns, M. (2012). *Pioneering literacy in the digital wild west: Empowering parents and educators.* New York: The Joan Ganz Cooney Center at Sesame Workshop. Available from: http://gradelevelreading.net/wp-content/uploads/2012/12/GLR_TechnologyGuide_final.pdf.

Hess, R. D., & Goldman, H. (1962). Parents' views of the effect of television on their children. *Child Development, 33*(2), 411–426.

Homer, B. D., Kinzer, C. K., Plass, J. L., Letourneau, S. M., Hoffman, D., Bromley, M., et al. (2014). Moved to learn: The effects of interactivity in a Kinect-based literacy game for beginning readers. *Computers & Education, 74,* 37–49.

Hudson, H. (2004). Universal access: What have we learned from the E-rate? *Telecommunications Policy, 28*(3–4), 309–321.

Ito, M., Baumer, S., Bittanti, M., Cody, R., Stephenson, B. H., Horst, H. A., et al. (2009). *Hanging out, messing around, and geeking out: Kids living and learning with new media.* Cambridge, MA: MIT Press.

Ito, M., Gutierrez, K., Livingstone, S., Penuel, B., Rhodes, J., Salen, K., et al. (2013). *Connected learning: An agenda for research and design.* Irvine, CA: Digital Media and Learning Research Hub.

Jaeger, P. T., McClure, C. R., & Bertot, J. C. (2005). The E-rate program and libraries and library consortia, 2000-2004: Trends and issues. *Information Technology and Libraries, 24*(2), 57–67.

Jordan, A. B. (2008). Children's media policy. *The Future of Children, 18*(1), 235–253.

Jordan, A. B. (2013). The impact of media policy on children's media exposure. In A. N. Valdivia (Ed.), *The international encyclopedia of media studies.* Hoboken, NJ: Wiley

Kabali, H. K., Irigogyen, M. M., Nunez-Davis, R., Budacki, J. G., Mohanty, S. H., Liester, K. P., et al. (2015). Exposure and use of mobile media devices by young children. *Pediatrics, 136*(6), 1044–1050.

Kafai, Y. B., & Peppler, K. A. (2011). Youth, technology, & DIY: Developing participatory competencies in creative media production. *Review of Research in Education, 35*(1), 89–119.

Katz, V. S., & Gonzalez, C. (2016). Community variations in low-income families' technology adoption and integration. *American Behavioral Scientist, 60*(1), 59–80.

Kelly, H. (2016). *AT&T offering $5 Internet to low-income families. CNNMoney.* Accessed August 11, 2016 from: http://money.cnn.com/2016/04/22/technology/access-from-att-digital-divide/.

Kunkel, D. L., Castonguay, J. S., & Filer, C. R. (2015). Evaluating industry self-regulation of food marketing to children. *American Journal of Preventive Medicine, 49*(2), 181–187.

Lapierre, M. A., Piotrowski, J. T., & Linebarger, D. L. (2014). Assessing the relationship between pediatric media guidance and media use in American families. *Clinical Pediatrics, 53*(12), 1166–1173.

Levesque, R. J. R. (2007). *Adolescents, media, and the law: What developmental science reveals and free speech requires.* Oxford, UK: Oxford University Press.

Lieberman, D. A., Bates, C. H., & So, J. (2009). Young children's learning with digital media. *Computers in the Schools, 26,* 271–283.

Magid, L. (2013). *FTC clarifies children's online privacy law (COPPA). Forbes Tech.* Accessed July 27, 2016, from: http://www.forbes.com/sites/larrymagid/2013/04/25/ftc-clarifies-childrens-online-privacy-law-coppa/#2d9a42587a0a.

Mano en Mano. (2015). *Comienza en Casa: "It Starts at Home"* Accessed July 28, 2016 from: http://www.manomaine.org/programs/mep/comienzaencasa.

Mendelson, R. A. (2016). Mastering the media: When advising families on media, remember all screens not created equal. *AAP News*,(2016) Accessed August 11, 2016 from: http://www.aappublications.org/news/2016/05/24/MasteringMedia052416.

Montgomery, K. C. (2013). Youth and surveillance in the Facebook era: Policy interventions and social implications. *Telecommunications Policy, 39*, 771–786.

Montgomery, K. C., Chester, J., Grier, S. A., & Dorfman, L. (2012). The new threat of digital marketing. *Pediatric Clinics of North America, 59*(3), 659–675.

Mook, B. (2015). *CPB, TPT receive ready to learn grants as budget fight looms.* (Current) Accessed August 11, 2016 from: http://current.org/2015/09/cpb-tpt-receive-ready-to-learn-grants-as-budget-fight-looms/.

Motion Picture Association of America. (2016). *Film ratings.* Accessed August 11, 2016 from: http://www.mpaa.org/film-ratings/.

Neuman, M. M., & Neuman, D. L. (2014). Touch screen tablets and emergent literacy. *Early Child Education Journal, 42*, 231–239.

Pasnik, S., Llorente, C., Hupert, N., & Moorthy, S. (2016). Dramatic change, persistent challenges: A five-year review of children's educational media as resources for equity. *Journal of Children and Media, 10*(2), 229–237.

Patel, N. V. (2014). *Which mobile apps are worst privacy offenders? IEEE Spectrum.* Tech Talk. Accessed July 27, 2016 from: http://spectrum.ieee.org/tech-talk/consumer-electronics/portable-devices/new-website-shows-lists-which-mobile-apps-are-worst-privacy-offenders.

Pramana, G., Parmanto, B., Kendall, P. C., & Silk, J. S. (2014). The SmartCAT: An m-health platform for ecological momentary intervention in child anxiety treatment. *Telemedicine Journal and e-Health, 20*(5), 419–427.

Reno v. American Civil Liberties Union, 521 U.S. 844, No. 96-511 (1997).

Rideout, V. (2013). Zero to eight: Children's media use in America 2013. In *A common sense media research study.* San Francisco, CA: Common Sense Media.

Rideout, V. (2014). *Advertising to children and teens: Current practices.* San Francisco, CA: Common Sense Media.

Rideout, V. (2015). *The common sense census: Media use by teens and tweens.* San Francisco, CA: Common Sense Media.

Rideout, V. J., Foehr, U. G., & Roberts, D. F. (2010). *Generation M2: Media in the lives of 8- to 18-year-olds.* Menlo Park, CA: Kaiser Family Foundation.

Rideout, V., & Katz, V. S. (2016). *Opportunity for all?: Technology and learning in lower-income families.* New York, NY: The Joan Ganz Cooney Center.

Scantlin, R. M., & Jordan, A. B. (2006). Families' experiences with the V-chip: An exploratory study. *Journal of Family Communication, 6*(2), 139–159.

Scott, K. M., Gome, G. A., Richards, D., & Caldwell, P. H. Y. (2015). How trustworthy are apps for maternal and child health? *Health and Technology, 4*(4), 329–336.

Singleton, M. (2015). *The FCC has changed the definition of broadband. TheVerge.com.* Accessed April 28, 2016 from: http://www.theverge.com/2015/1/29/7932653/fcc-changed-definition-broadband-25mbps.

Spigner, J., Hinson, W. P., Escobar-Viera, C., & Hart, M. (2015). Is there an (evidence-based app for that? A review of mental health management apps available for adolescents and young adults). *Paper presented at the 2015 convention of the American Public Health Association, Chicago, IL.*

Strouse, G., O'Doherty, K., & Troseth, G. (2013). Effective coviewing: Preschoolers' learning from video after a dialogic questioning intervention. *Developmental Psychology, 49*, 2368–2382.

Takeuchi, L., & Stevens, R. (2011). *The new co-viewing: Designing for learning through joint media engagement.* New York, NY: The Joan Ganz Cooney Center at Sesame Workshop and LIFE Center.

Too Small to Fail (2014). *Too Small to Fail, Text4Baby and Sesame Street launch first national text-to-parents program to support young children's early language development.* Press Release. Accessed July 28, 2016 from: http://toosmall.org/news/press-releases/too-small-to-fail-text4baby-and-sesame-street-launch-first-national-text-to-parents-program-to-support-young-childrens-early-language-development.

Turner, T., Spruijt-Metz, D., Wen, C. K. F., & Hingle, M. D. (2015). Prevention and treatment of pediatric obesity using mobile and wireless technologies: A systematic review. *Pediatric Obesity, 10*(6), 403–409.

Vaala, S. E., Bleakley, A., Jordan, A. B., & Castonguay, J. (2017). Parents' use of the V-chip and perceptions of television ratings: The role of family characteristics and the home media environment. *Journal of Broadcasting and Electronic Media,.*

Vaala, S. E., Carroll, R., Williams, L. K., Hood, K. K., Lybarger, C., Laffel, L., et al. (2016). A mobile app that facilitates diabetes problem solving through integration of blood glucose and psychosocial data. *Paper presented at the annual convention of the American Diabetes Association, New Orleans, LA.*

Vaala, S. E., Ly, A., & Levine, M. H. (2015). *Getting a read on the app stores: A market scan and analysis of children's literacy apps.* New York: The Joan Ganz Cooney Center at Sesame Workshop. Available from: http://www.joanganzcooneycenter.org/wp-content/uploads/2015/12/jgcc_gettingaread.pdf.

Vandelanotte, C., Muller, A. M., Short, C. E., Hingle, M., Nathan, N., Williams, S. L., et al. (2015). Past, present, and future of eHealth and mHealth research to improve physical activity and dietary behaviors. *Journal of Nutrition Education and Behavior, 48*(3), 219–228.

Villani, S. (2001). Impact of media on children and adolescents: A 10-year review of the research. *Adolescent Psychiatry, 40*(4), 392–401.

Wartella, E. A., & Jennings, N. (2000). Children and computers: New technology, old concerns. *The Future of Children, 10*(2), 31–43.

WhiteHouse.gov (2016). *ConnectED initiative.* Accessed August 11, 2016 from: https://www.whitehouse.gov/issues/education/k-12/connected.

York, B. N., & Loeb, S. (2014). *One step at a time: The effects of an early literacy text messaging program for parents of preschoolers, No. w20659.* Cambridge, MA: National Bureau of Economic Research.

CHAPTER 16

How Parents Mediate Children's Media Consumption

Yalda T. Uhls*,†, Michael B. Robb†

*UCLA, Los Angeles, CA, United States
†Common Sense Media, San Francisco, CA, United States

In 2016, one would expect to find a typical child in the United States spending many hours a day consuming a variety of media content through interactive technology, both in formal and informal learning environments (Common Sense Media & VJR Consulting, 2015). The rapid adoption of media by "digital natives" and the ubiquity of devices within family life seem to have exacerbated the anxieties of modern parenting (Uhls, 2015). In the early days of the Internet, parents worried about sexual predators and "stranger danger," while more recently, many express concerns over the addictive allure of devices (Felt & Robb, 2016; Livingstone & Blum-Ross, 2016). Traditionally, the introduction of a new medium (e.g., the romantic novel, the radio, the computer) has brought on a host of worries on the part of adults who look to understand its influence on healthy development; the current anxieties about digital media may be part of that oft-repeated pattern (Brooks-Gunn & Donahue, 2008). Adults who are unfamiliar with the technology often feel overwhelmed, and with media headlines highlighting all of the dangers, some envision the rare worst-case scenario (Uhls, 2015). This kind of fear can impact parents' ability to provide guidance in an important environment with the potential for positive and negative cognitive learning. Yet, one of the recurring themes in research on media effects is the importance of parents in children's media experience (Alexander, 2008).

Despite concerns about the negative influences of new media, parents also express confidence that the net impact of digital media is positive, in particular when associated with education, learning and career potential, and accordingly want to learn how to guide their families on best media practice and use (Lauricella, Cingel, Beaudoin-Ryan, Robb, & Wartella,

Cognitive Development in Digital Contexts
http://dx.doi.org/10.1016/B978-0-12-809481-5.00016-X

2016; Romer, Bagdasarov, & More, 2013). According to a recent Common Sense Census, 94% of parents believe that technology supports their children with schoolwork and education (Lauricella et al., 2016). In addition, an increasing body of social science research finds cognitive benefits associated with use of interactive technologies, such as playing video games, which include improved spatial learning, self-regulation, and information processing (Brown & Bobkowski, 2011; Powers, Brooks, Aldrich, Palladino, & Alfieri, 2013). Thus, it is crucial to help parents determine mediation strategies that minimize the risks and maximize the benefits of their children's engagement with media. Parental mediation is important to understand because mediation can impact what media a child is exposed to and how they use the technology (Gentile, Nathanson, Rasmussen, Reimer, & Walsh, 2012). Parental mediation often results in less screen time and selection of higher quality content, in line with recommendations made by trusted family resources, such as Common Sense Media and the American Academy of Pediatrics (2016). In addition, consistent exposure to high-quality content can promote learning (Cantlon & Li, 2013; Morrow, 2005).

Decades of research on parenting can inform the study of helping children to safely, productively, and proactively use media. Moreover, much of the literature on parenting practices that are correlated with optimal development also applies to the digital realm (Jago, Edwards, Urbanski, & Sebire, 2013). In the last few years, researchers have turned their attention to parenting practices with newer media and now know much more about how parents mediate their children's use of media.

This chapter examines the extant literature on parental mediation of their 0- to 18-year-old children's media use. Much of this literature is concerned about positive or negative effects on cognitive development and how parents may influence their children's cognitive development through active and restrictive mediation strategies. Our focus is on newer interactive technologies such as the Internet, social media, and videogames, as informed by the literature on television viewing and parenting practices, as this body of work often applies to newer media and family dynamics. Moreover, children still consume more television content than any other content (Common Sense Media & VJR Consulting, 2015), albeit on a variety of devices rather than a fixed television set in one room (Uhls, 2015). Thus, the literature on parental mediation of children's television use is relevant; for example, decades of research on the TV show *Sesame Street* found that when parents choose content to promote learning the effect was substantial (Cantlon & Li, 2013; Sammond, 2007).

PARENTAL MEDIATION STRATEGIES

Parents turn to a variety of mediation strategies when scaffolding their children's use of interactive technologies. Thus, parents may monitor their children by checking which websites they visit, checking their social media profiles, limiting their time using media, checking their text messages on phones, and using filtering software on home computers (Anderson, 2016; Jago et al., 2013). Some parents rely heavily on specific types of mediation strategies each with their own suite of cognitive outcomes (Brown, Halpern, & L'Engle, 2005; Collier et al., 2016; Samuel, 2015). However, parents who spend time getting involved with their children's media usage often use several different types of mediation strategies depending on the context and age of the child. We describe these below.

Restrictive Mediation

This method of parental mediation relies on restricting a child's access to media content and/or interactive technology. This can manifest itself through installing Internet filters, setting time limits, restricting access to mobile devices, and controlling content choices. This strategy has also been called cocooning, monitoring, and rule setting, and parents who use this strategy have been referred to as limiters (Livingstone & Blum-Ross, 2016; Samuel, 2015; Valcke, Bonte, De Wever, & Rots, 2010). Research finds that restrictive mediation tends to be used more when children are younger, usually before preadolescence when it may in fact be the most effective strategy (Davies & Gentile, 2012; Top, 2016). However, as children age, the strategy is not as effective given that adolescents begin to desire autonomy and become more interested in peers, thus wishing to make their own decisions concerning media and using it to connect with friends. Teens themselves report that this strategy is not useful and believe that trust is a better strategy in the family (Vaterlaus, Beckert, Tulane, & Bird, 2014).

Restrictive mediation can in fact backfire during adolescence leading to behavior that is not sanctioned by adults. For example, a recent study found that restrictive mediation of middle and older children's playing of video games was associated with higher levels of child delinquency (Martins, Mathews, & Ratan, 2015). A meta-analysis found this strategy to be associated with higher levels of child aggression (Collier et al., 2016). Interestingly enough, the same meta-analysis also found a relationship between restrictive mediation and sexual outcomes, such that children whose parents relied on this strategy engaged in less sexual activity and at later ages. By contrast, a longitudinal study found that restrictive mediation at time one was the only strategy related to more sexual experience at time two (Nikken & Graaf, 2012). This same study found that communicating about sex with friends or parents was a better predictor of sexual activity than parental mediation. As this research indicates, the effects of using restrictive mediation with teenagers may differ by individual and are likely to be context specific.

Context Versus Activity Constraints

Hiniker, Schoenebeck, and Kientz (2016) surveyed 249 parent–child (ages 10–17) dyads from 40 states to examine the types of rules within restrictive mediation, which they characterized as context versus activity constraints. The researchers asked an open-ended question to children that queried them on their home rules. This resulted in a list of 455 reported rules, which were then categorized into context and activity rules, with each representing nearly 50% of the total. Context rules restricted technology use as a whole, while activity rules banned certain kinds of content such as violent video games. The researchers found that both parents and children found context rules (e.g., no phones at the dinner table) more difficult to enforce than activity rules (e.g., no using Instagram). Children reported that they found it easier to follow rules about what to post and to watch than to not use their devices, highlighting the consuming nature of these interactive technologies. This finding lends support to parents getting involved in guiding their children's content choices, which in turn will affect their technology use for activities that promote cognitive learning (Ito et al., 2009).

PERMISSIVE MEDIATION

Much like the laissez-faire parenting strategy in the parenting styles literature, parents who use this mediation strategy do nothing to monitor their children's media use. This type of strategy has also been called nonintervention, and parents who adopt this strategy have been referred to as enablers (Samuel, 2015). One large study of North American families found that while a third of parents of young children adopted this approach, when their children reached adolescence, nearly half the sample of parents allowed them to set the family's technology agenda. This approach is frequently associated with children spending the most time consuming media (Samuel, 2015; Valcke et al., 2010). Researchers also have shown that when teens report on parental mediation, the majority of them report permissive mediation as the strategy their parents use most (Vaterlaus et al., 2014).

Active Mediation

Parents who rely on active mediation work to participate in their children's media experience through discussion and conversation, thus supporting cognitive learning, both academic and social. For example, parents who actively mediate their children's media consumption will engage in open communication and discuss the content; this kind of mediation can develop a child's critical thinking skills vis-à-vis the content (Davies & Gentile, 2012; Rasmussen et al., 2016). Other names for this form of mediation include "media mentor" and instructive mediation (Samuel, 2015). Teens report that active mediation means asking questions and letting them talk about their media use (Vaterlaus et al., 2014).

This kind of mediation is generally found to be most effective for teaching children to be responsible consumers of media (Top, 2016). In fact, Collier et al. (2016) found that when parents talked to their children about violent TV, they later developed negative attitudes toward these kinds of programs. Active mediation of media content has also been associated with lower hours of video gaming (Mendoza, 2009; Smith, Gradisar, & King, 2015) and lower levels of aggression and substance abuse. Additionally, as with restrictive mediation, active mediation predicted later and fewer sexual outcomes for children and teens (Collier et al., 2016). A variety of measures have been used to measure mediation, with few attempts to understand the reliability or validity of the measures being used. As Jago et al. (2013) point out, interpreting the associations between parenting media practices and screen-viewing time is difficult without this knowledge. Interventions could be better targeted with increased understanding of which practices are related to positive or negative outcomes (limiting time, limiting content, co-viewing), and how those practices can best be applied with children at different ages in multiple contexts. The rise of smartphones, tablets, and video games, for example, further compromises the application of these practices.

Subcategories of Active Mediation: Positive, Negative, and Neutral

Recently, researchers have begun to tease apart active mediation to better examine its efficacy (Collier et al., 2016; Martins et al., 2015). Three sub-categories have been identified: positive, negative, and neutral. Positive active mediation refers to messages that are complimentary about the media, negative refers to condemning the content, and neutral is neither positive nor negative with regard to evaluation of the content. Limited research has addressed these subcategories, but one recent study found an association between child delinquency and parents' use of negative mediation of video game play (Martins et al., 2015).

CHILD AND TEEN PERCEPTIONS OF PARENTAL MEDIATION

A robust finding is that parent and adolescent perception of parental mediation often varies, with teens' perceptions differing from parents, such that teens have reported fewer rules than adults (Gentile et al., 2012). Vaterlaus et al. (2014) interviewed 80 adolescents, aged 16–18 years, and their parents, to further examine this finding. As with other larger samples, they found that 76% of the teens reported that their parents did not mediate their Internet use; only 45% of parents reported as such. The authors examined how parents monitored their teens' cell phone and Internet use and found methods such as checking use summaries and content on the devices, as well as engaging in discussion about usage.

In other cultures, researchers found similar results. For example, in a study across eight cultural contexts, teens in Europe perceived that their parents paid no attention to what they did on the Internet (Martínez de Morentin, Cortés, Medrano, & Apodaca, 2014). Here, teens were asked what they considered was the most effective means of mediation. Surprisingly, the largest number (33%) advocated for monitoring content and usage. The next largest group (26%) suggested active participation and open communication. A further 18% suggested rule setting and 15% indicated that restrictions would be most effective. Similarly, other studies have reported differences in parent and teen perceptions. For example, Smith et al. (2015) examined parental influences on video game play and found that while 74% parents reported that they talked to their teens about cyber-safety, 64% of teens said their parents allowed gaming in the bedroom, and 75% of teens reported that their parents rarely or never limited the online content they accessed.

ROLE MODELING MEDIA BEHAVIOR

Role modeling is a critical component of parenting. A robust finding in the TV effects literature (Wisniewski, Jia, Xu, Rosson, & Carroll, 2015) is that a child's TV viewing is highly correlated with their parents' viewing (Bleakley, Jordan, & Hennessy, 2013). More research is needed to reveal whether this pattern is likely to hold with digital media and interactive technologies. Moreover, children, particularly younger ones, are sensitive to when parents spend time looking at their phones rather than giving them their attention (Highlights Magazine, 2014; Uhls, 2015). Thus, parents and adults who teach children would be wise to examine their own media behavior before deciding on rules for their children.

One salient example is that parents often want their children to exercise caution about posting photos online despite their own posting of photos of their children online. Hiniker et al. (2016) recently found that children were frustrated by this parental practice with 18% of children reporting that "oversharing" photos of children without asking was inappropriate behavior. Further, only 17% of the participants believed that parents should not be held to similar rules and expectations as they expected for their offspring.

AGE DIFFERENCES IN PARENTAL MEDIATION

Nearly every study that looks at age as a moderator finds that parental mediation varies by age. As a child develops socially, emotionally, and cognitively, it is natural that parental mediation will also develop. Specifically, parents of younger children tend to co-view and use restrictive mediation while parents of older teens either stop mediating all together (i.e., laissez-faire) or continue to use instructive mediation if that was a part of their strategy when their children were younger.

Parental Mediation of Children

How parents communicate with their young children around media can greatly influence what messages they internalize, what they learn, and what they retain. Even the American Academy of Pediatrics has pointed to the importance of parental involvement in their policy statement on media, recommending that parents monitor their children's media use and consider that use with their children as a way of talking about family values (American Academy of Pediatrics, 2016). Decades of research on children's television watching speak to one aspect of active mediation called co-viewing, the act of watching television and video content with children.

Co-viewing is not a monolithic act—there is substantial variation in when and how parents choose to co-view with their children, ranging from very high to very low levels of involvement. For example, some parents may be present with their children while watching a TV show, but not engaging or talking with them. Other parents may be highly involved, trying to be sensitive to children's developmental level and needs when talking about what their children are seeing or hearing. For example, they might choose to label on-screen objects (Krcmar, Grela, & Lin, 2007), encourage their children to imitate what they see (such as singing a song or dancing), or ask questions after a show is over. Even low levels of co-viewing can have positive benefits. For example, researchers have shown that cueing children to think of a media experience as educational, instead of merely entertainment, can lead to learning outcomes (Salomon, 1984). Not all co-viewing behaviors are equal, and parents can engage in different levels of co-viewing at different times.

The value of co-viewing has been demonstrated in several studies. Many of the earliest involved studies of *Sesame Street* found that children often understood program content more when watching with adults (for a review of research on the role of parents and caregivers in supporting learning from *Sesame Street*, see Sammond, 2007). For example, Rice, Huston, Truglio, & Wright (1990) found that children learned letters and numbers better when parents watched the program with them and asked the children to repeat them while viewing. While getting children to repeat content out loud can be effective for learning, just having a parent say the letters and numbers is not as effective (Reiser, Tessmer, & Phelps, 1984; Reiser, Williamson, & Suzuki, 1988).

Researchers have also demonstrated the effectiveness of active mediation on social and emotional outcomes. In Rasmussen et al.'s, 2016 study, 127 2- to 6-year-olds and their parents were randomly assigned to watch or not watch 10 episodes of the animated program *Daniel Tiger's Neighborhood,* a show designed to teach socio-emotional skills. Parents were randomly assigned to one of three treatment conditions or to a control group. In the first group, parents were instructed to watch each episode with their child and talk about the show as much as possible over the following 2 weeks (active mediation). In a second group, parents watched each episode with their child but did not discuss the episodes with their child. In the third group, children watched the show without parents present and parents were instructed not to talk about the show. Children in the control group watched a different show, and parents were not given instructions about interacting with their child. Findings showed that watching the program was associated with high levels of empathy but only when children received frequent active mediation.

Similarly, a study of 3-year-old children suggested that adapting dialogic reading techniques for television viewing could have positive effects on story comprehension and vocabulary (Strouse, O'Doherty, & Troseth, 2013). Pausing, asking questions, and encouraging children to tell parts of the story they were viewing were effective in producing learning gains, while pausing to comment but not asking questions to children was less effective. Interestingly, using an onscreen actress to engage in dialogic questioning was also effective (though less so than having a live parent do the questioning), indicating the potential impact of using nonlive characters in mediating content.

Mediating behaviors also can be effective in directing attention among infants. A study of 12- to 21-month-old children and their parents found that parents were able to guide their child's focus to a television by looking at the screen themselves and by talking to their children to direct their attention to the screen (Demers, Hanson, Kirkorian, Pempek, & Anderson, 2013). Parental looking behaviors also seemed to alert infants to content that would be relevant or comprehensible to them. Further findings show that scaffolding in the form of questions, labeling, or providing descriptions is an effective means of orienting infant attention and responsiveness to television (Barr, Zack, Garcia, & Muentener, 2008).

One interesting way of facilitating active co-viewing is using onscreen prompts to assist parents. A study of 59 parent-child dyads with children aged 3 to 5 years found that parents who viewed enhanced text prompts embedded within a children's show engaged in more educationally valuable interactions with their children as compared to parents viewing a show without on-screen text prompts (Fisch et al., 2008). Parents were more likely to talk about characters' emotions, encourage children to participate in the show, and connect onscreen events to children's lives. Thus, parents were the mechanism for learning, but only when prompts modeled specific comments or behaviors. A separate group of parents who saw prompts with general parenting advice and jokes did not interact with their children in ways that contributed to story comprehension or language development. Again, these findings suggest the potential of using nonlive characters to encourage or enable mediating behaviors (in this case, only text was necessary absent an actual character).

Beyond co-viewing, parents can influence their children's viewing experiences through their monitoring practices. Monitoring can take many forms, including co-use, setting time limits, setting rules around types of content, and active mediation. Parents and children do not always agree on the extent of monitoring that occurs within a household. For example, one study of parental monitoring of television and video games found that parents of third, fourth, and fifth grade children reported more monitoring (of all kinds) than their children, with the exception of playing video games, where parents reported significantly less co-play (Gentile et al., 2012). Further, girls were monitored more closely than boys, perhaps indicating parental gender stereotyping. Parental monitoring also declined with age, as parents may have believed that they had less control of their children's media experiences as they got older and scaled back their monitoring.

With respect to interactive products, joint media engagement expands the definition of co-viewing to describe the experiences of people using media together and includes co-viewing, playing, reading, creating, and other forms of interactions around media (Takeuchi & Stevens, 2011). However, new media present special challenges for parents trying to mediate technology and media experiences (Livingstone & Helsper, 2008). Televisions may be conducive to parents who want to be able to monitor their children's media from a distance because of their larger size and louder volume. A parent can more easily glance at a TV screen from within the same room, or keep tabs on it by monitoring the audio when out of the room, and decide if and when to actively mediate. However, smartphones, tablets, and other mobile devices prove more difficult because screens are smaller, and because they are more portable and can move to new environments. Thus, it is more difficult for a parent to monitor or mediate their child's game, video, or other media when that child is holding a five-inch screen or taking it into the backseat of the car. Parental mediation of Internet use is of special concern because of children's difficulty in understanding what can be accessed on it. In a study of Australian 5- to 8-year-olds, children were unable to employ Internet safety behaviors because they were unable to recognize potential dangers (Ey & Cupit, 2011).

Parental Mediation of Adolescents

As children reach later childhood and transition from their parents being the primary agents of socialization to their peers, media become more important and are sometimes called a super-peer (Brown et al., 2005). For many families, children's ability to own and control their own mobile devices has increased the stress placed on the parents. The myriad of choices of interactive technology and devices befuddles many adults, who did not grow up with these kinds of choices. Parents express the most confusion about how to best mediate this age group with frequent questions such as "When should I get them a phone?" and "When should I allow my child on social media?" and "How much time should I allow my child to play video games?" (Uhls, 2015). Parental mediation can be fraught with conflict between the child and the adult.

As children reach their teenage years and push for autonomy, parental mediation of media usually becomes less frequent (Collier et al., 2016). During these years, some theorists suggest that children self-socialize with their media content because they make their own choices about what to watch

(Arnett, 1995; Martins et al., 2015). Thus, active mediation in earlier years, which helps guide children to process and think critically about their content choices, becomes all the more important. Interactive technology connects teenagers with their peers, and mobile devices allow them to do so more easily without the oversight of parents. While some parents attempt to continue mediating media usage, many parents become less active in doing so as children reach adolescence. However, parents of younger teens aged 13–14 tend to use parental controls more often and check web history. In addition, parents of younger teens report having frequent conversations about acceptable online and media content. Roughly a third of parents know their children's password to a social media account. Many parents report talking to their children about their online behavior and about what they share digitally (Anderson, 2016).

Studies find that during adolescence, the choice of mediation strategy correlates with a variety of behaviors, including sexual activity, delinquency, and online sharing of content. For example, researchers found that the consumption of sexual media was positively related to sexual behavior (American Psychological Association, 2010; Brown et al., 2005). Counterintuitively, a longitudinal study that examined this relationship found that Dutch parents who were more restrictive with their daughters' media use at time one were more sexually experienced at time two. Further, no mediation strategy was related to a decrease in sexual experience and less permissive attitudes toward sex (Nikken & Graaf, 2012). The authors speculated that the idiosyncratic nature of the Dutch culture might have contributed to this finding. Martins et al. (2015) found that when parents were still using mediation during adolescence, they tended to use more negative mediation. Moreover, she and her colleagues found that when parents used negative mediation, their middle-aged and older children were more likely to rebel or engage in delinquency.

One important concern for adolescents, and for anyone who uses the Internet, is privacy behaviors. Researchers from Penn State found that direct parental intervention, similar to restrictive mediation, had no relationship to sensitive information disclosures but was positively associated with advice seeking (Wisniewski et al., 2015). In contrast, active meditation was associated with more sensitive online disclosures. Moreover, the teens whose parents actively mediated took more corrective measures on their own when they made a mistake, such as posting sensitive information online, while those whose parents intervened were not proactive in seeking solutions by themselves. The researchers concluded that teens whose parents intervened too frequently were losing valuable learning opportunities to practice autonomy and problem solving, key components of executive functioning (Wisniewski et al., 2015). Other researchers also find that heavy restriction on media use leads to fewer opportunities for learning and engagement (Livingstone & Blum-Ross, 2016).

OTHER MODERATORS OF PARENTAL MEDIATION
Gender Differences

The literature on how gender affects parental mediation strategies is mixed. For example, parents tend to mediate how girls use media more than boys, in particular when it comes to video game exposure (Nikken & Graaf, 2012; Nikken & Jansz, 2006). However, other studies have yielded no gender differences in parental mediation (Connell, Lauricella, & Wartella, 2015), or have shown, for video game play, that parents used more negative mediation with sons than daughters (Martins et al., 2015).

Ethnicity and Culture

One study measured ethnicity and parental monitoring to determine if different groups, such as White, African-American, Hispanic and Asian, exhibited varied strategies. The researchers found that Asian parents limited the time their children spent with TV and video games the most. In addition, Hispanic families limited their children the least (Connell et al., 2015).

Culture can deeply affect a variety of attitudes and behaviors (Greenfield, 2009), and researchers have begun to examine how parental mediation of digital media differs across cultures. A 2013 study queried 1238 adolescents between the ages of 14 to 19 and their parents in eight different cultural contexts (i.e., Spain—three cities, Ireland, Mexico, Dominican Republic, Bolivia, and Chile). The findings showed that parents reported three different parenting styles: co-viewing, instructive, and restrictive. Teens, however, reported an additional parenting style called inhibitive (which refers to not doing anything), which teens reported as the most frequent form of parental mediation (Martínez de Morentin et al., 2014). Few differences were found in parental report of mediation by country, with both teens and adults reporting that the restrictive style was the most frequent. Teens in Bolivia, however, reported that their parents used the instructive style most frequently. Parents in Ireland were most often reported to use inhibited mediation with nearly 63% of teens reporting this parental style. In Aragon, Spain, parents reported using the restrictive style more than other cities, and the Dominican Republic parents reported they used co-viewing the most. Interestingly enough, the researchers found that the greater the level of parental mediation, the more adolescents reported using the Internet to search for information. The researchers also examined how teens in these different contexts used the Internet. In six of the cities, teens used the Internet most to communicate and least to shop; in two countries, Bolivia and the Dominican Republic, the Internet was used mostly by adolescents for looking up information.

Gender of Parents

A nationally representative survey of over 2300 parents of children aged 0–8 years provides insight into demographic differences in joint media engagement behaviors (Connell et al., 2015). Mothers tended to spend more time co-using media with their children, likely because they spent more time with children overall than fathers. However, while mothers were more likely to read books with children, fathers were more likely to play video games with children, and co-use computers and smartphones. Parents' age and education level also influenced mediation behavior as younger parents and/or parents with a high school education or less were more likely to co-play video games. Co-use of media was higher in families with younger children and decreased as they got older, perhaps because older children were perceived as able to handle technology more independently.

PARENTAL MEDIATION OF MEDIA LITERACY

Media literacy skills are defined as the abilities to access, analyze, evaluate, create, and act using all forms of communication (National Association for Media Literacy Education, 2010). Traditionally, the teaching of these skills was relegated to the K–12 classroom, but more recently, some scholars have noted that parental involvement in their children's media consumption can greatly contribute to their developing media literacy skills (Duerager & Livingstone, 2012). As such, Mendoza (2009) reviewed the parental mediation literature as based in the television literature to determine how it might map onto the media literacy framework. She reported that co-viewing was the most common form of parental mediation but did not find that watching content with a child promoted media literacy, which may reflect that the majority of parents who co-view do not discuss the content with their children. Thus, the opportunity to learn critical thinking skills through analyzing content is minimized. Indeed, a parent's co-viewing of a show may act as a "silent" endorsement of the content, even if it is inappropriate for a child. Mendoza further reported that active mediation would be the most effective way for parents to get involved in teaching their children media literacy. Other researchers concur (Top, 2016). However, more research is needed to determine whether the forms in which parents traditionally actively mediate, through sharing values about the content versus inquiry based discussion, which is the kind of pedagogy recommended by scholars of media literacy, can effectively teach critical thinking skills.

PARENTAL MEDIATION BY TYPE OF MEDIA
Video Games

The literature on video games is robust with many studies finding a host of positive cognitive, social, and emotional effects (Blumberg & Fisch, 2013; Granic, Lobel, & Engels, 2014; Powers et al., 2013). Nevertheless, parents worry more about video games than any other media content. More so than with other media, gender differences emerge, with parents being more restrictive of girls' video game exposure (Nikken & Jansz, 2006). As with other kinds of media, parents rely on similar strategies: restrictive, active, and laissez-faire.

One study looked at which type of monitoring was related to the number of hours of video game play (Smith et al., 2015). The researchers measured parental discussion of cyber-safety, limiting online content, and physically monitoring video game play. The only parenting strategy that predicted the number of hours teens spent playing games was a discussion of cyber-safety; in other words, active mediation. Interestingly, the study also measured whether the ability to carry mobile devices that hosted video games would increase gaming hours, and this variable was not significant. The strongest predictor of game play was the number of devices owned by the adolescents.

Another study looked at different kinds of active mediation used with children during video game play and whether any of these were related to child delinquency (Martins et al., 2015). The researchers found that negative mediation of video game play was associated with higher levels of child delinquency. Thus, parents who had negative attitudes about video games were more likely to have delinquent children than those who felt less negatively. In addition, parents used negative mediation more with boys and older children. Restrictive mediation was also measured and this strategy was negatively related to delinquency. Consistent with findings from studies of parental attitudes toward different media (e.g., video games, TV, etc.), Martins and colleagues found very few parents used positive mediation when speaking to their children about these games.

Social Media

As children reach later preteen years, they increasingly join social media networks, even though COPPA forbids children younger than thirteen from joining the majority of social media (e.g., Instagram, Facebook, Snapchat, etc.). Among 8- to 18-year-olds who have a social media account, parents reported that they first joined one at 12.6 years (Lauricella et al., 2016). Pew Research Center found that parents of younger teens were more concerned about their online privacy than those of older teens and used more parental controls (Anderson, 2016). Not surprisingly, when parents directly intervened with their teen's use of social media, the amount of time their teens were on social networking sites was reduced. Some of the parental mediation measures that these parents used include reading website privacy policies, helping set up privacy settings, and using parental monitoring systems. The most risky online behavior, being contacted and connecting to strangers online who made them feel uncomfortable, was not associated with any parental mediation strategy (Wisniewski et al., 2015).

RECOMMENDATIONS AND BEST PRACTICES

Digital media are a tool that can be used for both positive and negative learning. Parental mediation of their children's consumption of interactive technologies and media can serve as a means to mitigate negative effects while promoting positive effects. As such, it is incumbent on anyone concerned with positive youth development to seek information to guide parents on best practices, grounded in well-designed research.

While each family and context is different, the literature does seem to suggest a few overall ways to mediate children's media use proactively to help them learn safe online behavior. We list these below.

1. Educators and policy makers should guide *parents to consider how they are role modeling their own media use to their children*. Children learn from watching their parents and learning media behavior is no different than other forms of activities (Bleakley et al., 2013; Uhls, 2015).

2. Educators and policy makers should guide parents to *provide clear and consistent rules*. Teens in one study suggested that parents are the authorities and they should provide consequences when misbehavior occurs. However, trust and communication were incredibly important, and

adolescents suggest that they prefer when their parents include them in the process of deciding the rules around technology. Interestingly enough the most common recommended rule was to put the phone away during family meals, both parents and children felt this was important (Hiniker et al., 2016).

3. *Those working with parents should suggest that they involve children in determining the family media plan.* Organizations such as Common Sense that provide guidance for parents have long advocated using family media agreements and device contracts to help develop and enforce rules. Data confirm that child buy-in of rules helps. In one study, giving children input into the process was strongly correlated with their ability to follow rules (Hiniker et al., 2016). The authors also suggest that other successful strategies include discussing the reasoning behind rules, making similar rules for parents and kids, and being consistent. Another study found similar thinking from their participants (Vaterlaus et al., 2014). Not surprisingly, children report that they follow parental mediation rules most when the rule is easy to follow and they believe it to be fair.

REFERENCES

Alexander, A. (2008). Media and the family. In S. Calvert & B. Wilson (Eds.), *The handbook of children, media, and development* (pp. 121–140). West Sussex, UK: Blackwell Publishing Ltd.

American Academy of Pediatrics (2016). Media and young minds. *Pediatrics, 138*(5), e20162591. https://doi.org/10.1542/peds.2016-2591.

American Psychological Association. (2010). *Report of the APA task force on the sexualization of girls.* Washington, DC: Author.

Anderson, M. (2016). *Parents, teens and digital monitoring.* Pew Research Center. Retrieved from http://www.pewinternet.org/2016/01/07/parents-teens-and-digital-monitoring/.

Arnett, J. J. (1995). Adolescent's uses of media for self-socialization. *Journal of Youth and Adolescence, 24,* 519–532.

Barr, R., Zack, E., Garcia, A., & Muentener, P. (2008). Infants' attention and responsiveness to television increases with prior exposure and parental interaction. *Infancy, 13*(1), 30–56. http://dx.doi.org/10.1080/15250000701779378.

Bleakley, A., Jordan, A. B., & Hennessy, M. (2013). The relationship between parents' and childrens' television viewing. *Pediatrics, 132,* 364–371.

Blumberg, F. C., & Fisch, S. M. (2013). Introduction: Digital games as a context for cognitive development, learning, and developmental research. *New Directions for Child and Adolescent Development, 2013*(139), 1–9. https://doi.org/10.1002/cad.20026.

Brooks-Gunn, J., & Donahue, E. H. (2008). Children and electronic media. *The Future of Children, 18*(1), 3–10.

Brown, J. D., & Bobkowski, P. S. (2011). Older and newer media: Patterns of use and effects on adolescents' health and well-being. *Journal of Research on Adolescence, 21,* 95–113.

Brown, J., Halpern, C., & L'Engle, K. (2005). Mass media as a sexual super peer for early maturing girls. *Journal of Adolescent Health, 36*(5), 420–427. http://dx.doi.org/10.1016/j.jadohealth.2004.06.003.

Cantlon, J. F., & Li, R. (2013). Neural activity during natural viewing of sesame street statistically predicts test scores in early childhood. *PLoS Biology, 11*(1), e1001462. http://dx.doi.org/10.1371/journal.pbio.1001462.

Collier, K. M., Coyne, S. M., Rasmussen, E. E., Hawkins, A. J., Padilla-Walker, L. M., Erickson, S. E., et al. (2016). Does parental mediation of media influence child outcomes? A meta-analysis on media time, aggression, substance use, and sexual behavior. *Developmental Psychology, 52*(5), 798–812. http://dx.doi.org/10.1037/dev0000108.

Common Sense Media, & VJR Consulting. (2015). The common sense census: Media use by tweens and teens.

Connell, S. L., Lauricella, A. R., & Wartella, E. (2015). Parental co-use of media technology with their young children in the USA. *Journal of Children and Media, 9*(1), 5–21. http://dx.doi.org/10.1080/17482798.2015.997440.

Davies, J. J., & Gentile, D. A. (2012). Responses to children's media use in families with and without siblings: A family development perspective. *Family Relations, 61*, 410–425.

Demers, L. B., Hanson, K. G., Kirkorian, H. L., Pempek, T. A., & Anderson, D. R. (2013). Infant gaze following during parent-infant coviewing of baby videos. *Child Development, 84*(2), 591–603. http://dx.doi.org/10.1111/j.1467-8624.2012.01868.x.

Duerager, A., & Livingstone, S. (2012). *How can parents support children's internet safety? EU Kids Online.* Retrieved from http://eprints.lse.ac.uk/42872/1/How%20can%20parents%20support%20children's%20internet%20safety(lsero).pdf.

Ey, L., & Cupit, C. (2011). Exploring young children's understanding of risks associated with Internet usage and their concepts of management strategies. *Journal of Early Childhood Research, 9*(1), 53–65.

Felt, L., & Robb, M. (2016). *Technology addiction: Concern, controversy, and finding balance.* San Francisco, CA: Common Sense Media Retrieved from https://www.commonsensemedia.org/research/technology-addiction-concern-controversy-and-finding-balance.

Fisch, S. M., Akerman, A., Morgenlander, M., McCann Brown, S. K., Fisch, S. R. D., Schwartz, B. B., et al. (2008). Coviewing preschool television in the US: Eliciting parent-child interaction via onscreen prompts. *Journal of Children and Media, 2*(2), 163–173. http://dx.doi.org/10.1080/17482790802078680.

Gentile, D. A., Nathanson, A. I., Rasmussen, E. E., Reimer, R. A., & Walsh, D. A. (2012). Do you see what I see? Parent and child reports of parental monitoring of media. *Family Relations, 61*(3), 470–487. http://dx.doi.org/10.1111/j.1741-3729.2012.00709.x.

Granic, I., Granic, I., Lobel, A., & Engels, R. C. (2014). The benefits of playing video games. *American Psychologist, 69*(1), 66–78.

Greenfield, P. M. (2009). Technology and informal education: What is taught, what is learned. *Science, 323*, 69–71.

Highlights Magazine (2014). *The state of the kid.* Retrieved from https://www2.highlights.com/state-of-the-kid-2014.

Hiniker, A., Schoenebeck, S. Y., & Kientz, J. A. (2016). Not at the dinner table. *Presented at the 19th ACM conference on computer-supported cooperative work and social computing, CSCW 2016,* Association for Computing Machinery. http://dx.doi.org/10.1145/2818048.2819940.

Ito, M., Baumer, S., Bittanti, M., Boyd, D., Cody, R., Herr-Stephenson, B., et al. (2009). Hanging out, messing around, and geeking out: Kids living and learning with new media. In (1st ed.). Cambridge, Mass: MIT Press.

Jago, R., Edwards, M., Urbanski, C., & Sebire, S. (2013). General and specific approaches to media parenting: A systematic review of current measures, associations with screen-viewing, and measurement implications. *Childhood Obesity, 9*(s1), S51–S72.

Krcmar, M., Grela, B., & Lin, K. (2007). Can toddlers learn vocabulary from television? An experimental approach. *Media Psychology*, *10*(1), 41–63. http://dx.doi.org/10.1080/15213260701300931.

Lauricella, A., Cingel, D., Beaudoin-Ryan, L., Robb, M., & Wartella, E. (2016). *The Common Sense census: Plugged-in parents of tweens and teens*. Common Sense. Retrieved from: https://www.commonsensemedia.org/research/the-common-sense-census-plugged-in-parents-of-tweens-and-teens-2016.

Livingstone, S., & Blum-Ross, A. (2016). *Families and screen time: Current advice and emerging research (No. 17)*. London, UK: The London School of Economics and Political Science Department of Media and Communications. Retrieved from http://eprints.lse.ac.uk/66927/1/Policy%20Brief%2017-%20Families%20%20Screen%20Time.pdf.

Livingstone, S., & Helsper, E. (2008). Parental mediation of children's internet use. *Journal of Broadcasting & Electronic Media*, *52*, 581–599.

Martínez de Morentin, J. I., Cortés, A., Medrano, C., & Apodaca, P. (2014). Internet use and parental mediation: A cross-cultural study. *Computers & Education*, *70*, 212–221. http://dx.doi.org/10.1016/j.compedu.2013.07.036.

Martins, N., Mathews, N., & Ratan, R. (2015). Playing by the rules parental mediation of video game play. *Journal of Family Issues*. http://dx.doi.org/10.1177/0192513x15613822.

Mendoza, K. (2009). Surveying parental mediation: Connections, challenges and questions for media literacy. *Journal of Media Literacy Education*, *1*, 28–41.

Morrow, R. W. (2005). *Sesame Street and the reform of children's television*. Baltimore, MD: Johns Hopkins University Press.

National Association for Media Literacy Education. (2010, April 6). *Media literacy defined*. Retrieved from https://namle.net/publications/media-literacy-definitions/.

Nikken, P., & Graaf, H. (2012). Reciprocal relationships between friends' and parental mediation of adolescents' media use and their sexual attitudes and behavior. *Journal of Youth Adolescence*, *42*(11), 1696–1707.

Nikken, P., & Jansz, J. (2006). Parental mediation of children's videogame playing: A comparison of the reports by parents and children. *Learning, Media and Technology*, *31*(2), 181–202. http://dx.doi.org/10.1080/17439880600756803.

Powers, K. L., Brooks, P. J., Aldrich, N. J., Palladino, M. A., & Alfieri, L. (2013). Effects of video-game play on information processing: A meta-analytic investigation. *Psychonomic Bulletin & Review*, *20*(6), 1055–1079. http://dx.doi.org/10.3758/s13423-013-0418-z.

Rasmussen, E. E., Shafer, A., Colwell, M. J., White, S., Punyanunt-Carter, N., Densley, R. L., et al. (2016). Relation between active mediation, exposure to Daniel Tiger's neighborhood, and US preschoolers' social and emotional development. *Journal of Children and Media*, *10*(4), 443–461. http://dx.doi.org/10.1080/17482798.2016.1203806.

Reiser, R. A., Tessmer, M. A., & Phelps, P. C. (1984). Adult-child interaction in children's learning from "Sesame Street" *ECTJ*, *32*(4), 217–223. http://dx.doi.org/10.1007/BF02768893.

Reiser, R. A., Williamson, N., & Suzuki, K. (1988). Using "Sesame Street" to facilitate children's recognition of letters and numbers. *ECTJ*, *36*(1), 15–21.

Rice, M. L., Huston, A. C., Truglio, R., & Wright, J. C. (1990). Words from "Sesame Street": Learning vocabulary while viewing. *Developmental Psychology*, *26*(3), 421–428.

Romer, D., Bagdasarov, Z., & More, E. (2013). Older versus newer media and the well-being of United States youth: Results from a national longitudinal panel. *The Journal of Adolescent Health: Official Publication of the Society for Adolescent Medicine*, *52*(5), 613–619. http://dx.doi.org/10.1016/j.jadohealth.2012.11.012.

Salomon, G. (1984). Television is "easy" and print is "tough": The differential investment of mental effort in learning as a function of perceptions and attributions. *Journal of Educational Psychology*, *76*(4), 647–658. http://dx.doi.org/10.1037/0022-0663.76.4.647.

Sammond, N. (2007). Robert W. Morrow. Sesame Street and the reform of children's television. *The American Historical Review, 112*(2), 549–550. http://dx.doi.org/10.1086/ahr.112.2.549a.

Samuel, A. (2015, November 4). Parents: Reject technology shame. *The Atlantic.* Retrieved from http://www.theatlantic.com/technology/archive/2015/11/why-parents-shouldnt-feel-technology-shame/414163/

Smith, L. J., Gradisar, M., & King, D. L. (2015). Parental influences on adolescent video game play: A study of accessibility, rules, limit setting, monitoring and cybersafety. *Cyberpsychology, Behavior and Social Networking, 18*(5), 273–279. http://dx.doi.org/10.1089/cyber.2014.0611.

Strouse, G. A., O'Doherty, K., & Troseth, G. L. (2013). Effective coviewing: Preschoolers' learning from video after a dialogic questioning intervention. *Developmental Psychology, 49*(12), 2368–2382. http://dx.doi.org/10.1037/a0032463.

Takeuchi, L., & Stevens, R. (2011). *The new coviewing: Designing for learning through joint media engagement.* New York, NY: The Joan Ganz Cooney Center at Sesame Workshop Retrieved from http://www.joanganzcooneycenter.org/publication/the-new-coviewing-designing-for-learning-through-joint-media-engagement/.

Top, N. (2016). Socio-demographic differences in parental monitoring of children in late childhood and adolescents' screen-based media use. *Journal of Broadcasting & Electronic Media, 60*(2), 195–212. http://dx.doi.org/10.1080/08838151.2016.1164168.

Uhls, Y. T. (2015). *Media moms & digital dads.* Brookline, MA: Bibliomotion.

Valcke, M., Bonte, S., De Wever, B., & Rots, I. (2010). Internet parenting styles and the impact on Internet use of primary school children. *Computers & Education, 55*(2), 454–464. http://dx.doi.org/10.1016/j.compedu.2010.02.009.

Vaterlaus, J. M., Beckert, T. E., Tulane, S., & Bird, C. V. (2014). "They always ask what I'm doing and who I'm talking to": Parental mediation of adolescent interactive technology use. *Marriage and Family Review, 50*, 691–713.

Wisniewski, P., Jia, H., Xu, H., Rosson, M. B., & Carroll, J. M. (2015). "Preventative" vs. "reactive": How parental mediation influences teens' social media privacy behaviors. In *Proceedings of the 18th ACM conference on computer supported cooperative work & social computing*, (pp. 302–316). New York, NY: ACM. http://dx.doi.org/10.1145/2675133.2675293.

INDEX

Note: Page numbers followed by *f* indicate figures, *t* indicate tables, and *np* indicate footnotes.